Business Law & Practice

Business Law & Practice

J. SCOTT SLORACH

JASON ELLIS

4th edition

OXFORD
UNIVERSITY PRESS

OXFORD
UNIVERSITY PRESS

Great Clarendon Street, Oxford, OX2 6DP,
United Kingdom

Oxford University Press is a department of the University of Oxford.
It furthers the University's objective of excellence in research, scholarship, and education by publishing worldwide. Oxford is a registered trade mark of Oxford University Press in the UK and in certain other countries

Third edition 2023
Second edition 2022
First edition 2021

Published in the United States of America by Oxford University Press
198 Madison Avenue, New York, NY 10016, United States of America

British Library Cataloguing in Publication Data
Data available

Library of Congress Control Number: 2024939140

ISBN 978–0–19–893273–4

Acknowledgements

Some content under Crown copyright regarding different court structures is reproduced by kind permission under the Open Government Licence (http://www.nationalarchives.gov.uk/doc/open-government-licence/).

Grateful acknowledgement is made to the Solicitors Regulation Authority for copyright material which appears in this book.

For the latest version of the SRA Standards and Regulations please visit their website (https://www.sra.org.uk/solicitors/standards-regulations/).

Every effort has been made to trace and contact copyright holders prior to going to press. If notified, the publisher will undertake to rectify any errors or omissions at the earliest opportunity.

Contents

Table of Cases

United Kingdom

National Courts

Australia

Table of Legislation

Table of Civil Procedure Rules, Practice Directions and Protocols

Table of Statutes

Table of Statutory Instruments

European Union

Directives

Table of Professional Conduct Rules

Exam Technique

A.1 Introduction

The functioning legal knowledge (FLK) assessments for SQE 1 comprise two assessments of 180 questions each.

The FLK assessments will cover the following subject areas:

1. Business Law and Practice; Dispute Resolution; Contract; Tort; Legal System of England and Wales; Constitutional and Administrative Law; and EU Law and Legal Services.
2. Property Practice; Wills and the Administration of Estates; Solicitors Accounts; Land Law; Trusts; Criminal Law and Practice.

The objective of the assessments, which is linked to the Statement of Solicitor Competence, is to assess the depth and breadth of your knowledge of the law of England and Wales. The assessments are not just about nuggets of knowledge but about demonstrating how well you can apply that knowledge to demonstrate the threshold competence required of a newly qualified solicitor on day one of practice.

In practice, the reality is that you will often look up information which you need to know either to confirm your thinking, to refresh your memory or, indeed, to find out about an issue with which you are unfamiliar. However, the FLK assessments are closed book. This means that, without reference to books and notes, you are answering the questions based upon your knowledge derived from your prior learning, including that provided and supported through these manuals, and through the practise questions.

Each question in the assessment contributes to the overall validity of the assessment; that is, it allows you the opportunity to demonstrate your knowledge and understanding about the application of the law. Therefore, it should be possible to infer that a successful candidate has demonstrated their competence to meet the threshold and is thus capable of being a solicitor.

The purpose of this chapter is to talk you through the assessment questions: how they are structured, what to look for and what to avoid. Be encouraged; the questions in the assessments and the questions in the question bank are written by human beings so bear in mind that the same thinking process which has been used to generate the question can be used by you to determine the correct answer. Questions are not written in a way purposefully to catch you out, as the point of a question is to assess what you *do* know, not what you *do not* know. If you have prepared thoroughly, you should be in a position to respond positively to the assessment.

A.2 Question structure

To begin, let us take a question from the SRA SQE 1 FLK sample questions published on 16 December 2019. These sample questions were published to give a guide as to what might be expected in the live assessment, and frequent reference will be made to them throughout this chapter.

The question is split into three parts, as illustrated in **Figure A.1**:

- the context;
- the stem; and
- the options.

In the course of a trial various arguments are put to the judge as to the exact meaning of a particular section of a relevant statute. When deciding the case, the judge first looks at the natural ordinary meaning of the words used. However, such an interpretation of those words results in an absurd meaning being given to the section. The judge, therefore, in coming to his decision, interprets the words in a different way which does not result in an absurd meaning. — **Context**

What method of statutory interpretation has the judge used? → **Stem**

A. The literal rule.
B. The mischief rule.
C. The extrinsic evidence rule.
D. The golden rule.
E. The intrinsic evidence rule.
— **Options**

FIGURE A.1 Example of question structure (SRA sample question 15)

A.2.1 The context

The context may be objective, for example, just a couple of generalised sentences before the stem, which puts the question to be answered and which aims to capture a particular piece of knowledge. SRA sample question number 6 demonstrates an objective context:

EXAMPLE

A decision is made by the Court of Appeal (Civil Division) in favour of the claimant. The defendant wishes to obtain permission to appeal.

Which of the following courts have the power to grant permission to appeal?

Or, as in question 15, the context may be subjective and contain more scene-setting for the question which follows, providing details about where, who and why something happened, as represented in **Figure A.2**.

You should read the context carefully because it will contain clues which have been laid by the question writer to help you answer the question.

FIGURE A.2 Subjective context

Here is the question 15 context again with highlighted relevant sections which give a good idea as to what is in the question writer's mind—the rules of statutory interpretation:

> **EXAMPLE**
>
> In the course of a trial various arguments are put to the judge as to the *exact meaning* of a particular section of a relevant statute. When deciding the case, the judge first looks at the *natural ordinary meaning of the words* used. However, such an interpretation of those words *results in an absurd meaning* being given to the section. The judge, therefore, in coming to his decision, *interprets the words* in a different way which *does not result in an absurd meaning.*
>
> What method of statutory interpretation has the judge used?

In this particular question, the stem itself also tells you that the question is about statutory interpretation but the stem might not always be quite so helpful. You may have to consider the facts carefully to establish which area of knowledge is being assessed; each assessment covers multiple subject areas, so you will not know what kind of question you are attempting until you read it. Having read the context carefully, you should be in the right mental zone as the context contains all of the relevant facts which are needed to give the correct answer to the stem which follows and which supports the answer.

A.2.2 The stem

Look at the stem very carefully—after all, it is the link to the correct answer. Given its importance, the stem should be absolutely clear, should be connected to the context and include as much information as possible to be precise about what is being asked. Stems, properly written, should pass what is known as the *cover test*. The cover test means that the correct answer should, without seeing any of the options, pop into your head as soon as you read the stem. This is a very useful step to take as it prompts your memory to offer up the right answer without being conflicted by any distracting options. If you think of what you believe to be the correct answer and then, to your surprise, you do not see it in the options, double-check that you have read the stem correctly!

> **TIP**
>
> When you use the practise question bank, get into the habit of using the *cover test* as a technique as it is good for revision and will improve your recollection. A good habit to have! Having read the stem thoroughly, take a moment to pause and think what answer you expect to see amongst the options. When you read through the options, if that answer appears, you know you might be on the right track but pause again before you enthusiastically tick the box and move on to the next question! Check what you believe to be the answer very carefully to make sure that it matches what you had expected to see, then look through the other options to be doubly sure that you are correct in your selection. This is especially important in relation to single best answer questions which are discussed more fully later in the chapter; bear in mind that the 'best' answer might be very close to the second best answer giving you all the more reason to look carefully at all options. Only when this process is complete should you make your selection.

A.2.2.1 Types of question

The SQE 1 FLK assessment contains what are described as single best answer questions. They are likely to be of two types. The stems for each are different although both lead to the selection of a single correct or a single best answer:

- a traditional multiple-choice question leading to a single correct answer; and
- a single best answer question leading to a single best answer.

A.2.2.2 Traditional multiple-choice questions (MCQ)

For this type of question, there must be *only one unambiguously correct answer*. The answer is supported by the stem which will be worded in such a way that it can only lead to that one correct answer and is a heavy hint that you are looking for that one correct answer. As there is just one correct answer, these questions are an ideal way to practise using the cover test (see **A.2.2**).

Stem examples:

- Which of the following . . .
- What must X do . . .
- By when . . .
- What is the next step which should be taken . . .
- What is the correct advice to give . . .
- What is the correct procedure to . . .
- What is the accurate description of . . .

In question 15, the stem is worded: 'What method of statutory interpretation has the judge used?' The language is very precise: 'What method . . .'. It is an MCQ as there can only be one unambiguously correct answer.

A.2.2.3 Single best answer questions (SBA)

A single best answer question may need a little more unravelling than a traditional MCQ. For an SBA, a range of responses might be possible or reasonable within the context of the question. However, only one will be the star option as it is the most preferable, reasonable and appropriate as the *SBA* in the circumstances as provided by the context.

The context, here, is particularly important and is likely to require evaluation in order to determine what course of action is for the best. As there is no immediate stand-out correct answer, as for a traditional MCQ, the possible solutions require an evaluative judgement as to what is best to do in the situation. Each judgement-based option may be represented visually; see **Figure A.3** which shows how the options may be ranged from least suitable or worst option to the best option. Note that there is only *ONE* best option. You should bear in mind that the least suitable option, here B, may simply be wrong which is explanation in itself as to why it is the least suitable option!

In **Figure A.3**, A is identified as the best option on a given set of facts; B and E are identified as the least suitable options on the same set of facts with C and D somewhere in between. D is clearly challenging A for the star option spot but there is no provision to choose both options and so there will be a particular reason on the facts why option A trumps the other options.

As you can see, more thought is needed to work through and determine the best option in an SBA. The options are likely to be carefully nuanced and these types of questions demonstrate a higher degree of application in a professional context. For example, you can envisage a circumstance in which a solicitor needs to advise a client in the client's best interests. All options might present possible and plausible advice which might be given, although one option might definitely not be in the client's interests while another is recognisably the *best* advice.

Stem examples:

- Which of the following is the most appropriate ground upon which . . .
- Which of the following represents the best advice which might be given . . .
- What is the best course of action to recommend in these circumstances?

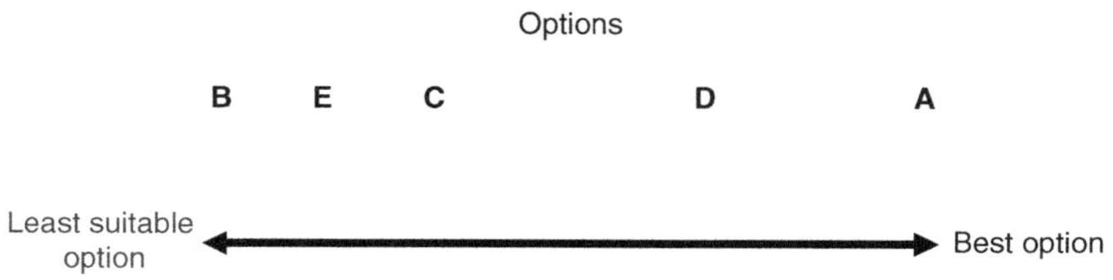

FIGURE A.3 Range of responses

- How is the court most likely to determine the claimant's application?
- What approach is the most sensible to adopt on these facts?

TIP

As you work through the practise questions in the question bank, familiarise yourself with the stem types and see how the options differ so that you are best prepared. Remember that identifying the type of question you are being asked naturally links to the type of answer which is expected. If the stem looks to be an MCQ, then the expected answer should be an unambiguously correct response; if the stem looks to be an SBA, then the expected answer will be what is best in the circumstances. The feedback which is provided to the practise questions will help you to understand why a particular best option has been identified on the facts of the question.

A.2.3 **The options**

After the stem come the five options lettered (A–E) from which you are to select your answer. Rest assured that the options will always include the right answer so there is some comfort in that! If the question has been carefully written, the answer should not stand out as being the correct answer, it should have been carefully embedded within the options which should all offer plausible alternatives to sway your choice. If you consider that the purpose of the question is to be able to infer competence, it is clear why it is unlikely that the right answer will stand out.

The remaining options are known as *distractors*, which is an apt description as they are there to distract you from the right answer. The distractors are likely to be plausibly based on common misconceptions or misunderstandings and be compatible with, and flow from, the stem. A distractor may look very similar to the right answer but will differ in a small but significant way, for example:

EXAMPLE

Which of the following is the correct explanation to provide about an unless order requiring filing and service of the defendant's list of documents by 4 pm on 21 May?

A. That unless by 4 pm on 21 May the defendant has filed and served its list of documents, the claim will be struck out.

B. That unless by 4 pm on 21 May the defendant has filed and served its list of documents, the defence will be struck out.

In this example there is a one-word difference between A and B. In the rush to answer and move on to the next question, the temptation may be to plump immediately for the first answer because it looks about right but, of course, it is wrong.

A distractor may also offer the wrong explanation for a definitive answer.

EXAMPLE

If the stem asks simply: 'Is the client entitled to take this course of action, and for what reason?', you know that the expected answer will be unambiguously correct because this is a traditional MCQ. The options might be presented as three 'Yes' options each followed by a different reason, one of which is correct, and two 'No' options each followed by a different reason.

A. Yes, because . . .

B. Yes, because . . .

C. Yes, because . . .

D. No, because . . .

E. No, because . . .

In some ways, these questions are quite helpfully structured because you might readily be able to eliminate the two 'no' options but you must still look carefully through the three remaining options to ensure that you home in on the correct reason for the 'yes' response.

> **TIP**
>
> If there are three positive options and two negative options, *do not immediately discount the negative options* and assume that one of the positive options is bound to be the right answer; the imbalance might be trying to lull you into a false sense of safety in numbers and prompt you to select a positive answer. Only eliminate options if you are sure that they are wrong.

The best distractors will also look similar to the answer in construction and length: they have symmetry. This is demonstrated in SRA sample question 15 where the options are given as:

A. The literal rule.
B. The mischief rule.
C. The extrinsic evidence rule.
D. The golden rule.
E. The intrinsic evidence rule.

A distractor must work hard to distract you from the correct answer. In the same way that a stand-out correct answer does little to assess competence, a stand-out wrong option is also unhelpful to assessors because it can be eliminated from the running and so increases the chances of a candidate getting the question right without actually knowing the answer! In the FLK assessments, there are five options and you have a 1 in 5 chance of getting the answer correct even if you guess (more on this in **A.4.1**). If two of the options are implausible, the probability of selecting the correct answer increases to 1 in 3.

In SRA sample question 6 about appeals, these are the options:

A. The Court of Appeal only.
B. The Supreme Court only.
C. The House of Lords only.
D. The Court of Appeal and the Supreme Court.
E. The Court of Appeal and the House of Lords.

There are two stand out options here, C and E, which can be eliminated as they are plainly wrong because they contain a reference to the House of Lords rather than the Supreme Court. The choice has now reduced to A, B and D.

Notice that A and B include the word 'only'. Be wary of such limiting phrasing and ask yourself whether this could possibly be correct in the context.

> **TIP**
>
> It is worth bearing in mind that options which include 'always' and 'never' are (almost) always wrong and never right. Do not discount them without some thought as such phrasing may be appropriate for the context, but bear in mind that such absolute phrasing often hints that the option is likely to be incorrect as it is inflexible and allows for no exceptions. This is often too rigid an approach in the field of law.

By this process of elimination, A and B include the word 'only' which is too absolute for the reality of those options. Therefore, only option D remains and that is the correct answer to the question.

The words 'must' and 'may' are frequently encountered in MCQs. Bearing in mind that the stem supports the answer and connects to the distractors, look carefully at whether either of those words appear in the options.

EXAMPLE

What is the likely costs order which the judge will make?

If any of the options contains the word 'must', for example:

A. The judge *must* make an order for the claimant to pay the defendant's costs in any event think carefully; costs are discretionary and, therefore, you would expect the correct answer to read:

A. The judge *may* make an order for the claimant to pay the defendant's costs in any event'.

TIP

Through use of the cover test technique, you will hopefully have in mind what you believe to be the answer and may mentally benchmark an option as soon as you see it. Do not bank that option too soon until you have reviewed the other options; use it as the measure against which the other options are considered as being correct/incorrect or better/worse. Then, eliminate options to narrow your choice further. Think logically, analyse the wording carefully and eliminate options based upon the *specific facts* you are given and not the general law, practice or procedure. The majority of questions will have a specific set of facts and the correct answer depends on those. If, after that analysis, you are still persuaded that your initial thought was correct, go ahead and bank the option!

A.3 Worked examples

Now that you understand how a question is constructed, you can see that there are four simple steps to take to approach each question:

Step 1. Read the context carefully, taking note of key words to identify which topic area the question is about.

Step 2. Read the stem and identify whether this is an MCQ or SBA.

Step 3. From the stem, conduct the cover test.

Step 4. Read the options and identify the distractors.

Using these steps, have a look through these worked examples and try to think one step ahead.

WORKED EXAMPLE: DISPUTE RESOLUTION

A claimant, in proceedings in which they had raised a claim and a defence to counterclaim, does not attend court on the first day of trial.

What order should the defendant ask the court to make?

A. To adjourn the trial.
B. To give judgment on the counterclaim.
C. To make a wasted costs order.
D. To strike out the claim.
E. To strike out the claim and the defence to counterclaim.

Step 1: Review the context.

A claimant, in proceedings in which *they had raised a claim and a defence to counterclaim, does not attend court* on the first day of *trial.*

Your first thoughts might be that this is a very short fact-pattern and so unlikely to be a tricky question but it packs in a considerable amount of detail. The key words have been highlighted: we know that the claimant pursues a claim but is also defending a counterclaim, and does not attend court for the trial. Of those key words, perhaps the most significant is the presence of a counterclaim, which is a claim in its own right pursued by the defendant against the claimant and which can alter the dynamic between the parties. Having got a grip on the facts, read the stem.

Step 2: Read the stem and identify whether this is an MCQ or SBA.

What order should *the defendant* ask the court to make?

Is this an MCQ or an SBA? You might be thinking that this looks like an MCQ as it begins 'What order . . .' as if only one precise and correct answer is possible. However, look again; this is an SBA. The use of the word 'should' is a hint here. It is more or less asking: what is the best thing to do in these circumstances if you were the defendant. Note that the use of the word 'should' might also appear in an MCQ to indicate what should be done correctly in the circumstances—close reading of the fact-pattern and the stem will help you to decide what you are being asked. There is also a shift of context here: the fact-pattern sets up the scenario from the claimant's perspective but the question itself is asked from the defendant's perspective.

Step 3: From the stem, conduct the cover test.

Before looking at the options, try the cover test: what pops into your head as to what order the defendant should be seeking? Anything? Do not worry if not as we can now take a look at the options.

Step 4: Read the options and identify the distractors.

Read through all of the options once. This may provide an immediate prompt as to which of the options might possibly be the answer.

A. To adjourn the trial.
B. To give judgment on the counterclaim.
C. To make a wasted costs order.
D. To strike out the claim.
E. To strike out the claim and the defence to counterclaim.

Now go back and begin the process of elimination taking each option in turn and thinking from the defendant's perspective:

A cannot be right as, although a defendant can, of course, ask the court to adjourn the trial, there is no reason for a defendant to ask the court to adjourn the trial as the court may proceed with the trial in the absence of the claimant. Why would a defendant give up the opportunity to succeed against the claimant in their absence? B looks like a possibility, but this would not dispose of the claimant's claim, only the counterclaim; but something is beginning to emerge here as to what might be best for the defendant. C seems like a good idea to make the claimant pay but this is going down the wrong track because costs orders are consequential upon an event. Some event must occur first on which to hang the costs order. Also, there is something here that is not quite right as a wasted costs order is made against the legal representatives and there is nothing on the facts to suggest that the claimant's legal representatives are at fault. Let us look at D. This does not look right as it would leave the counterclaim live so let us look closely at E: asking for an order to strike out the claim and the defence to counterclaim looks to be a good answer on these facts as although the court may proceed with the trial in the absence of a party, if the claimant does not attend the trial, the court may strike out the claim and any defence to counterclaim. Got to the best answer, E, in the end!

WORKED EXAMPLE: PROPERTY LAW

A solicitor is acting for the buyer of a house which has a registered title. The house was first registered in 2004 following a sale. The house was the subject of a further sale which was registered in 2012. The house is built on land which is near the church within a Church of England parish. There is no entry in the register as to chancel repair liability.

Which one of the following correctly describes whether the buyer's solicitor needs to carry out a chancel repair liability search?

A. No, because the title was registered under the Land Registration Act 2002.

B. Yes, because chancel repair liability takes effect as an overriding interest.

C. No, because there has been a registered transfer on sale subsequent to first registration of title.

D. No, because no entry has been made in the register in respect of any chancel repair liability.

E. Yes, because there has been no registered transfer on sale after 12 October 2013.

Step 1: Review the fact pattern.

A solicitor is acting for the buyer of a house which has a *registered* title. The house was first registered in *2004* following a sale. The house was the subject of a *further sale* which was registered in *2012*. The house is built on land which is near the church within a *Church of England* parish. There is no entry in the register as to *chancel repair liability.*

This fact-pattern sets the context for the question, which relates to a purchase of a house with registered title which is near a church. The key words and dates have been highlighted and these identify the issue—which is whether the house could be subject to chancel repair liability—and provide the important details which will be relevant to this issue. Those details include both dates and facts, so this should flag up to you that you will need to consider not just what events have taken place, but how the timing of those events could affect the outcome. With this in mind, you can now look at the stem.

Step 2: Read the stem and identify whether this is an MCQ or SBA.

Which one of the following correctly describes whether the buyer's solicitor needs to carry out a chancel repair liability search?

Is this an MCQ or an SBA? The key words here are 'correctly' and 'needs', which indicate that this is an MCQ rather than an SBA. Although the focus of the question is on whether a search is considered necessary, the determining factor is objective; that is, it is based on the underlying law rather than subjective judgement as to which of several courses of action might be 'best' in the circumstances.

Step 3: From the stem, conduct the cover test.

Before looking at the options, try the cover test: what pops into your head as to whether a search might be necessary? Anything? If so, apply this when considering your answer, but do not pre-empt your conclusion until you have read the options. Do not worry if nothing occurs to you at this stage, as we can now take a look at the options.

Step 4: Read the options and identify the distractors.

Read through all of the options once. This may provide an immediate prompt as to which of the options might possibly be the correct answer.

A. No, because the title was registered under the Land Registration Act 2002.

B. Yes, because chancel repair liability takes effect as an overriding interest.

C. No, because there has been a registered transfer on sale subsequent to first registration of title.

D. No, because no entry has been made in the register in respect of any chancel repair liability.

E. Yes, because there has been no registered transfer on sale after 12 October 2013.

Now go back and begin the process of elimination taking each option in turn and thinking from the solicitor's perspective:

A can be discounted because although the title was first registered in 2004, after the 2002 Act came into force, at that time chancel repair liability continued to be an overriding interest in the same way as it had previously.

B superficially looks as though it might be correct—chancel repair liability *was* originally within the list of overriding interests. But the key word here is 'was'—it ceased to be within the list after 12 October 2013. So, again, this option can be discounted.

C is a technical point where timing comes into play. Consider this option in conjunction with option B: when did chancel repair liability cease to be an overriding interest? In 2013—so if this transfer took place in 2009, the liability will have been binding on the transferee because it was an overriding interest at that time.

D looks, on the face of it, as though it could be a correct option: if chancel repair liability is no longer an overriding interest and there is no entry in the register as to any liability, will the buyer not take free of it? But again, remember the importance of timing here—the buyer has not yet completed their purchase, so is there still a risk? Bear in mind that just because chancel repair liability ceased to be an overriding interest in 2013, this did not mean the liability automatically ceased to exist.

E raises a technical point where again timing comes into play. Although there is currently no entry in the register and chancel repair liability no longer takes effect as an overriding interest after that date, the property remains subject to any existing liability until the next transfer on sale is registered. Consider whether there is a risk, at this stage of the transaction, that an application could still be made to register any such liability and the buyer would then be bound by it if they proceeded with their purchase.

Having evaluated the options, go back to the stem and check exactly what the question is asking. With this in mind, confirm the results of your evaluation and select the option you consider to be correct. In this instance, the correct option is E.

WORKED EXAMPLE: BUSINESS LAW

A woman has been appointed to the board of directors of a private limited company (with unamended model articles). It is her first directorship and she wants to understand the legal requirements relating to decisions taken by the board of directors.

Which one of the following correctly describes the requirements of the company's articles and/or the Companies Act 2006 in respect of decisions taken by the board of directors of the company?

A. Only the directors can attend board meetings.
B. If the director cannot attend a board meeting, she can appoint a proxy.
C. The directors may take decisions by way of written resolution.
D. The directors can vote at board meetings on either a show of hands or by a poll vote.
E. Minutes of the board meetings must be filed with the Registrar of Companies.

Step 1: Review the context.

A woman has been appointed to the board of directors of *a private limited company* (with unamended model articles) and seeks your advice. It is her first directorship and she wants to understand the legal requirements relating to *decisions taken by the board of directors*.

When you look at the context, you will see that this is one of those generalised style questions which seeks to test your understanding of a particular topic. The key words have been highlighted for you: we are told that the woman is seeking advice about the requirements relating to decisions taken by the board of directors of a private limited company. It is important to recognise that the question focuses entirely on board decisions. This question is not asking about shareholder decisions so you should already be thinking about the difference in formalities and procedure of the two. It is also significant that we are told about this company's constitution: it has unamended model articles. Now that you have understood the context, you must read the stem.

Step 2: Read the stem and identify whether this is an MCQ or SBA.

Which one of the following correctly describes the requirements of the company's articles and/or the Companies Act 2006 in respect of decisions taken by the board of directors of the company?

Is this an MCQ or an SBA? The clue here is the use of the words 'Which one of the following' and 'correctly'. It is an MCQ as there can only be one correct answer. This stem does not ask you to advise the woman which is the best course of action when taking a decision as a director, but rather to confirm which one of the statements is a correct option.

Step 3: From the stem, conduct the cover test.

Before looking at the options, try the cover test: what pops into your head about the requirements for the decisions of the board of directors of private limited companies? What rules governing the taking of board decisions do you expect to see amongst the options? Now, move on to look at the options.

Step 4: Read the options and identify the distractors.

Carefully read through all of the options once. This may provide an immediate prompt as to which of the options might possibly be the answer.

A. Only the directors can attend board meetings.
B. If the director cannot attend a board meeting, she can appoint a proxy.
C. The directors may take decisions by way of written resolution.
D. The directors can vote at board meetings on either a show of hands or by a poll vote.
E. Minutes of the board meetings must be filed with the Registrar of Companies.

Now go back and begin the process of elimination, taking each option in turn.

A cannot be correct as others—for example, a company secretary, the company's lawyers or accountants—may also attend board meetings. Whilst they do not have a right to vote, they may attend. This option needs to be eliminated. This option also includes the word 'only'. Be alert to the use of this word as it is creating an exclusive category. It may be appropriate for a context but here it is clearly not appropriate as others may attend the meetings.

At first glance B might look like a correct answer; however, this is where a solid understanding of the differences between board decisions and shareholder decisions is important. If the director cannot attend a board meeting, she could, if the articles of association allow (and the model articles do not), appoint an alternate director to attend in her place. A proxy is the term used for someone who attends a shareholders' meeting on behalf of the shareholder, so this is not a correct option and this option needs to be ruled out. Furthermore, this option uses the word 'can'. Again, be alert to this. 'Can' means the same as to be able to do something but bear in mind that just because you can do something does not mean that you should or that it is the correct thing to do. Here, although the option is worded that the director 'can appoint a proxy' and, literally, she can do that, it would be the wrong thing to do in her position to meet requirements.

How about C? The model articles do allow the directors to take decisions either at a board meeting or in writing. This looks like it is a correct option. If you think that C is the correct answer, pause before you select the option and move on to the next question. Look through the final two options to be doubly sure that you are correct in your selection. The word 'may' is used in this option which is an expression of possibility and means that a choice may be exercised to do something or not to do something; there is no obligation to do a specific thing. Here, the directors have a choice as they may take decisions either at a board meeting *or* in writing and so C looks like a good contender for the correct answer as the option provides that the directors may take decisions by way of written resolution.

D is incorrect as directors can only vote for or against the resolution by a show of hands. A poll vote is an alternative way of voting at a general meeting of shareholders. Again, this is where a good understanding of the differences between board decisions and shareholder decisions is important. Here, again, we meet use of the word 'can'. In this context, just because the directors are physically able to vote by a show of hands does not mean that they should or that it is the correct thing to do to meet requirements.

Finally, E is incorrect as the minutes are a private record of the decisions taken by the board and there is no requirement under either the articles or the Companies Act 2006 for them to be filed with the Registrar of Companies. The use of the word 'must' creates an obligation, a necessity or requirement to do something. It may be appropriate to a given context but be alert to it being a categorical answer; there is no doubt or any choice but to do something.

Having carefully considered each of the options, go back to the stem and check exactly what the question is asking. Apply the results of your evaluation and select the option you considered to be correct. In this instance, the correct option is C.

A.4 Time management

Each FLK assessment is likely to allow five hours to answer 180 questions; just 1.6 minutes per question. So, it is clearly important to practise your time management. You can use the practise questions however you wish but to get the most from them you might:

- use the questions to support your learning as you work through the manuals. You might read a section or a chapter of the manual and then try your hand at answering some of the questions to reinforce your learning;
- come to the questions fresh and try your hand at a random selection of questions to keep you on your toes and to embed learning over a period of time and to highlight where you may need to look again at a topic to deepen your understanding. The feedback on each question and cross-referencing with the manual will be helpful here;
- practise the questions against the clock to replicate the assessment time constraint and to be sure that you can complete the assessment within the allocated time.

A.4.1 Blind guessing against making an educated choice

This chapter would be incomplete without facing down the old chestnut that you can guess your way through a multiple-choice assessment. Statistically speaking, it has a basis in truth. Simply, there are five options and, by making a selection, you have a 1 in 5 chance of getting the answer correct. But blind guessing is a risky strategy to deploy throughout an assessment. Think of it this way: for every question answered by guessing, you have 4 chances in 5 of getting it wrong! Statistically, that would be 144 out of 180 questions wrongly answered on an FLK assessment. You may also have heard that selecting option C consistently is bound to improve your chances. This is not true. Options are often randomised so option C is no more likely to be correct than A, B, D or E.

It is far better to make an educated guess which may be necessary where you are struggling either against time, in the closing minutes of the assessment, or against a mental blank which is blocking progress. Making an educated guess involves narrowing down the options by the process of elimination leaving perhaps a choice between two or three options. You now have, respectively, a 1 in 2 or 1 in 3 chance of selecting the right answer, which has significantly improved the odds. But let us be realistic. Under time pressure, you may temporarily be at a loss even to make an educated guess. Your memory has not been prompted by reading the stem and nothing stands out when you read through the options. What should you do? Be positive and hold your nerve; recognise that this is a temporary block and there are other questions which need your attention which you will be able to answer—so get a move on to the next question. You may even find that, in working through the other questions, your memory suddenly gives up the answer which had eluded you before. Near the end of the assessment, go back to any missed questions and make an educated guess; there is no negative marking in the assessment, that is losing a mark for an incorrect answer, but, as a certainty, skipping a question loses you the chance to gain a mark.

A.5 Summary

You will now appreciate that there is a method to the process of answering questions; just as there is a method to writing them. A methodical approach brings calm to the process; knowing that there is a structured approach to the creation of a question helps you to know that the question can also be deconstructed. An understanding of how that can be done, and the step-by-step process which has been outlined, will be a guide on your shoulder when you are either working your way through the question bank or working your way through the exam paper.

Of course, 'knowing your stuff' will provide the required bedrock of functioning legal knowledge, which is at the heart of the SQE assessments. The manuals, the question banks and your own preparation and practise will help put you into the best possible position to respond to the questions in the assessments.

TIP

This tip applies throughout the entire preparation process building up to sitting the FLK assessments. From studying the manual materials, going over a tricky area of law or procedure which you do not grasp at first, practising the questions until you know (and understand) why the answer is as given, to sitting the assessment: preparation and perseverance are key. *Remember, giving up assures a fail but the difference between failing and succeeding is trying one more time!*

Good luck!

Ethics, Professional Conduct and Client Care

FUNCTIONING LEGAL KNOWLEDGE

Candidates are required to demonstrate their ability to act honestly and with integrity, and in accordance with the SRA Standards and Regulations as follows:

- the purpose, scope and content of the SRA Principles
- the purpose, scope and content of the:
  - SRA Code of Conduct for Solicitors, Registered European Lawyers and Registered Foreign Lawyers
  - SRA Code of Conduct for Firms in relation to:
    - managers in authorised firms
    - complian e officers

AUTHORITIES UNDERPINNING PRACTICE

The key authorities that underpin this area of practice are listed below. Note that for legislation you are linked to legislation.gov.uk.

Although much of the legislation on this government website is available in its amended form, the incorporation of new amendments into the text of legislation can be delayed. You should refer to legal databases to ensure you are referencing the most up-to-date legislation.

- SRA Code of Conduct 2019 for Solicitors, REL's and RFL's
  https://www.sra.org.uk/solicitors/standards-regulations/code-conduct-solicitors/
- Solicitors Regulation Authority Standards and Regulations
  https://www.sra.org.uk/solicitors/standards-regulations
- Criminal Finances Act 2017
  http://www.legislation.gov.uk/ukpga/2017/22/contents
- Data Protection Act 2018
  http://www.legislation.gov.uk/ukpga/2018/12/contents/enacted
- Legal Services Act 2007
  http://www.legislation.gov.uk/ukpga/2007/29/contents
- Money Laundering, Terrorist, Financing and Transfer of Funds (Information on the Payer) Regulations 2017 (SI 2017/692)
  http://www.legislation.gov.uk/uksi/2017/692/contents/made
- Proceeds of Crime Act 2002
  https://www.legislation.gov.uk/ukpga/2002/29/contents
- Terrorism Act 2000
  https://www.legislation.gov.uk/ukpga/2000/11/contents

B.1 Introduction

This chapter introduces ethics, professional conduct and client care in relation to solicitors and law firms. A practical understanding of ethics and professional conduct are fundamental to being a good solicitor; indeed, it is paramount that solicitors act with integrity and honesty while recognising the need to be guided by certain moral principles. Client care is covered within this chapter because it is important for all businesses, even more so for law firms. As a solicitor, you have an obligation to take care of your clients, though these are not always thought of as ethical concerns. Clients are usually facing challenging life circumstances when they contact a solicitor and they need to have trust and confidence in them to be able to deal with their matter well, whether it is part of their ethical obligations or in addition to them.

B.2 Introduction to ethics and professional conduct

Ethical principles have been recognised by the solicitors' profession for centuries. Many have argued the need to ensure a neutral partisanship: this holds that a solicitor must pursue a legal end for any client by any legal means. It is difficult, however, to balance the ethical conflicts between professional and personal morality. Ethics which arise by virtue of a solicitor's professional status are identified as professional or legal ethics. These ethics may at times be incompatible with what is morally required of non-professionals.

The Law Society was founded in 1825. At the Law Society's inception, the organisation was both the representative body and regulatory body for solicitors in England and Wales. It was only in 1960, however, that an actual text incorporating principles was published. It was called *A Guide to the Professional Conduct and Etiquette of Solicitors* and was written by the Law Society. The Solicitors' Practice Rules were then established in 1990 and were adhered to by solicitors until 1 July 2007, when the Code of Conduct 2007 was implemented.

The Solicitors Regulation Authority (SRA) is now the independent regulatory body overseeing the regulation of solicitors on behalf of the Law Society in England and Wales. It was created in January 2007, in anticipation of the Legal Services Act 2007 but also due to conflict within the profession and in an attempt to restore public trust in solicitors, which was an issue around that time. The SRA supports solicitors who are faced with moral dilemmas that arise in practice by setting out the principles and code of conduct which all solicitors and law firms in England and Wales must regulate and uphold. In the event of a conflict, the principles which safeguard the wider public interest take precedence over those relating to an individual client's interests. Solicitors should, where relevant, inform their client of the circumstances in which their duty to the court and other professional obligations will outweigh their duty to them. At the present time, the Code of Conduct 2019 is guided by trust, confidence and the protection of the public interest. It is as much about ethical values as moral principles.

B.2.1 Changes to the Code of Conduct

Since the first Code of Conduct was implemented in 2007 there have been two updates, one in October 2011 and the second, most recently, in November 2019. These are discussed in more detail later.

B.2.2 Code of Conduct 2007

The Code of Conduct 2007 was a lengthy and prescriptive code, supported by guidance. Along with the Code, there were also the Solicitors' Account Rules 1998, the SRA Recognised Bodies Regulations and the Client Financial Protection Requirements, which formed the regulatory authority to which solicitors had to adhere. Clearly, this was a lot of information placed in a number of different sources, and so it was time-consuming for solicitors to be able to understand and consult these when faced with an ethical dilemma.

B.2.3 **Code of Conduct 2011 and SRA Handbook**

The Code of Conduct 2011 was contained in the SRA Handbook which came into force for all firms on 6 October 2011. The purpose of the Handbook was to provide an accompanying set of rules and regulations which supported the standards and requirements which all law firms, in-house legal departments and alternative business structures were expected to uphold. There were ten Principles. They were all-pervasive and underpinned all of the Handbook requirements. The Code of Conduct chapters showed how the Principles would apply in certain contexts and focused on the quality of the service a solicitor was delivering to a client, using outcomes and indicative behaviours to generate what is known as 'outcomes focused regulation'. The 2011 Code was shorter and less prescriptive. The SRA hoped that this would offer greater flexibility as solicitors would need to use greater professional judgement to ensure compliance with the SRA. It was more detailed in some areas than others, which created uncertainty and led to some criticism. However, it did reflect the overall aim of the SRA which was to focus on the quality of what a solicitor was delivering to a client rather than prescribing how the solicitor had reached that stage.

B.2.4 **Code of Conduct 2019**

The SRA Standards and Regulations came into effect on 25 November 2019 and replaced the SRA Handbook. They can be found on the SRA website and, as they are published online only, they can be updated and amended regularly, so it is important to keep up to date with the website as there may have been changes since this manual was published. As well as making it easier to update, publishing the Standards and Regulations online was intended to make access to a solicitor or barrister easier for members of the public.

There was a change in this Code from a focus on indicative behaviour to one on ethical conduct, and there are now seven Principles rather than ten. There are also two types of Code of Conduct in the 2019 set of SRA Standards and Regulations.

Code of Conduct for Solicitors, Registered European Lawyers (RELs) and Registered Foreign Lawyers (RFLs) applies to those individuals who are authorised by the SRA to provide legal services.

Code of Conduct for Firms which applies to all bodies authorised by the SRA to provide legal services.

One of the reasons for creating a code for individual solicitors and another for firms is that the onus is now on a firm's management team to establish processes, structures and controls to ensure uniformity across the firm.

In light of the UK's withdrawal from the European Union (Brexit), the SRA's guidance on RFLs, initially published on 23 July 2019, was updated on 24 March 2021. See SRA Guidance: Registered Foreign Lawyers.

B.2.4.1 The Principles

The Principles, alongside the Code of Conduct, are the basis of ethical behaviour which the SRA expects individual solicitors as well as law firms, managers and employees, to uphold. The Principles were established by the SRA Enforcement Strategy which underpins all the requirements set out in the Principles, Codes, and rules and regulations. It provides a detailed explanation of the approach to taking regulatory action in the public interest. If the Principles come into conflict, those which safeguard the wider public interest and public confidence in solicitors take precedence over an individual client's interest. It is important to explain this potential situation to a client.

EXAMPLE

To demonstrate how the Principles can come into conflict, suppose a solicitor is asked to allow a witness to give evidence in support of their client, in the knowledge that the evidence is untrue. The solicitor would have to refuse to do this as the wider public interest and public confidence take precedence over the client.

The Principles are mandatory, and so a breach of these Principles may constitute professional misconduct which could result in a warning, a financial penalty, a referral to the Solicitors Disciplinary Tribunal or some level of control or disqualification from acting in certain roles. When faced with an ethical dilemma in practice, the Principles are where a solicitor should look initially for guidance.

The seven current Principles are as follows.

1. To act in a way that upholds the constitutional principle of the rule of law, and the proper administration of justice.
2. To act in a way that upholds public trust and confidence in the solicitors' profession and in legal services provided by authorised persons.
3. To act with independence.
4. To act with honesty.
5. To act with integrity.
6. To act in a way that encourages equality, diversity and inclusion.
7. To act in the best interests of each client.

EXAMPLE

In a corporate firm, a solicitor may be approached by a firm of brokers to refer all clients to them. They may be offered a large financial incentive to do this. This, however, would compromise their independence and so would not comply with the Principles above, apart from where certain conditions are met (Code of Conduct paras 5.1–5.3)). In particular to act with independence and to act in the best interests of each client. The solicitor would usually need to decline to act and suggest that the brokers provide a list of corporate firms in the area or link to the Law Society Find a Solicitor webpage, to allow the client to decide who they wished to instruct. This would avoid any risk of compromising the solicitor's independence and would allow them to continue to act in the best interests of each client who instructed them.

B.2.4.2 SRA Regulation

In line with the SRA Enforcement Strategy, the SRA seeks to:

- ensure a strong, competitive, and highly effective legal market
- ensure a focus on quality and client care
- promote a culture in which ethical values and behaviours are embedded

The SRA have a number of regulatory tools which are used in order to support compliance from law firms. The SRA Enforcement Strategy lists these as including:

- conducting thematic reviews of areas of risk
- publishing a risk outlook highlighting our priority risks
- providing advice and support through our Professional Ethics helpline and a range of toolkits and guidance
- SRA Innovate, a service which helps legal services providers to develop their business in new ways

In addition to the regulatory requirements set by the SRA Codes, Principles, rules and regulations, the SRA monitor and enforce the requirements relating to referral fees set out in s56 of the Legal Aid, Sentencing and Punishment of Offenders Act 2012. They also look at provisions relating to anti-money laundering which is mentioned at **B.3**.

B.2.5 **Compliance officers**

There are two different types of compliance officers. Compliance officers for legal practice (COLPs) and compliance officers for finance and administration (COFAs). All practices authorised by the SRA must appoint a COLP and a COFA. They are both a fundamental part of a law firm's compliance and governance arrangements as well as the culture of compliance within the firm. They have a broad number of responsibilities and may be liable for regulatory action if they fail to meet them. The Law Society Practice Note on Compliance Officers sets out a full list of the compliance officer roles, and best practice as to how breaches should be recorded and monitored.

COLPs and COFAs have a duty to report a serious breach of compliance to the SRA. This may go against the wishes of the managers of the practice. They have a duty to keep records of all breaches in order to recognise when one may be a serious breach. Managers are, however, responsible for their firm's compliance with the Code of Conduct. This responsibility is joint and several, if they share management responsibility with other managers of the firm.

EXAMPLE

A potential new solicitor applies to a firm for a job and in his additional paperwork he gives details of a physical disability which will require various reasonable adjustments to be made by his employer. The day after he submits this paperwork, the firm withdraws the job offer, giving only a brief explanation as to the reasons behind this decision. The solicitor makes a formal complaint to the firm, alleging disability discrimination.

The firm's COLP has a duty to investigate the complaint and write a report with their conclusion. If the COLP is satisfied that there is no regulation issue, then they would not need to report this.

If the COLP is, however, concerned about being misled by any staff involved in the decision then this must be reported, as a regulatory concern has arisen regarding potentially being given misleading information relating to the job offer being withdrawn.

B.2.6 Complaints and the Legal Ombudsman

If a client believes that their solicitor has not treated them fairly or professionally, they are entitled to complain. The main issues they may complain about are the way the case was handled or the costs for the services. If a client does complain then they will have been provided with details of how to complain by the law firm. The first step is usually to contact the solicitor to explain what the issue is and how it may be resolved. In most situations where a client complains, the matter will be resolved internally, and the complaint and file could be closed.

If the complaint has not been dealt with to the client's satisfaction or within eight weeks, then the client is entitled to complain to the Legal Ombudsman. The Legal Ombudsman deals with complaints across the entire legal profession, not just solicitors. There is a £400 fee potentially payable by the law firm which is being complained about. The aim of the Ombudsman is to use speed and informality to try and come to an agreement between the parties. If an agreement cannot be reached, then a decision is made by an officer of the Ombudsman. There are several remedies which may be available if the Ombudsman finds in favour of the complainant. There are also time limits (revised on 1 April 2023) which need to be adhered to by the client and the Ombudsman. Further details on remedies, limitations and the Legal Ombudsman can be found on the Law Society's website.

EXAMPLE

A client believes that his solicitor has not been honest with him about his chances for success and has not acted in his best interests. He feels that the solicitor encouraged him to take a matter to litigation and pay a large amount in legal fees; he subsequently lost the case and was told by the judge that he did not have a strong case in the first place. The client can lodge a complaint to the law firm but, if not satisfied with their response, then he could take it to the Legal Ombudsman.

If the client believes that a solicitor has breached the SRA Code of Conduct then they may contact the SRA direct in order to report it. Examples of breaches which a client may be concerned about include discrimination, fraud and dishonesty.

EXAMPLE

If a solicitor refused to continue acting for a client due to their religious belief, this would be a form of discrimination and thus a breach of the SRA Code of Conduct. The client could make a complaint to the law firm but, again, if not satisfied with their response then they could take it to the Legal Ombudsman and/or to the SRA.

B.2.7 **Conflicts of interest**

A solicitor has a duty to act in the best interests of their client and to make sure that these interests do not conflict with each other. This is a key area within ethics and professional conduct as it is important for public protection and for acting in relation to the client's best interests. There will be occasions when you find that your firm already acts for a client whose interests conflict with a potential new client. When this happens, then it is almost impossible to be able to act for both in their best interests. The Code of Conduct 2019 (paras 6.1–6.2) prevents a solicitor acting where a conflict of interest exists, apart from in very limited circumstances.

As the SRA Guidance on Conflicts explains (SRA Case Studies: Conflict of Interest) there are two types of conflict of interest situations. The first is a conflict between two or more clients, known as a 'conflict of interest'. The second is a conflict between the client's interests and the solicitor's interests, known as an 'own interest conflict'.

A solicitor can never act in an 'own interest conflict'; however, in certain circumstances they can act in a 'conflict of interest' situation. The best interests of the clients continuously need to be considered. There is also another conflict to consider which relates to Principle 1, to uphold the law, as solicitors are also officers of the court. There could be occasions where there is a conflict between acting in the best interests of your client (Principle 7) and your duty as an officer of the court. This is more common when conducting litigation. In this situation, a person's duty to the court would outweigh their duty to the client. An example of this is calling a witness to give evidence when the solicitor knows they are lying.

Paragraph 6.2 of the Code of Conduct 2019 outlines the circumstances where a solicitor may be able to act in a 'conflict of interest' situation:

> You do not act in relation to a matter or particular aspect of it if you have a conflict of interest or a significant risk of such a conflict in relation to that matter or aspect of it, unless:
>
> - the clients have a substantially common interest in relation to the matter or the aspect of it, as appropriate; or
> - the clients are competing for the same objective,
> - and the conditions below are met, namely that:
> - all the clients have given informed consent, given or evidenced in writing, to you acting;
> - where appropriate, you put in place effective safeguards to protect your clients' confidential information; and
> - you are satisfied it is reasonable for you to act for all the clients.

In practice, it is important to carry out a conflict check as soon as possible. Ideally, this information should be obtained from the client before the interview:

- name, address and telephone number;
- area of law on which advice is needed (eg crime, property, contract);
- name and address of any potential opponent or other involved (if applicable).

If this information is not obtained in advance of the interview, a conflict check should be done when the client arrives at the office and then the interview may progress if there is no conflict of interest. On occasions a client may not understand who the other parties are in their case and so once you recognise who they are then a conflict check must be carried out as soon as practicable. Money laundering regulations (discussed in more detail at **B3.3**), also demand information being taken into account, which supports the notion of conflict checks.

The SRA provides a helpful case study—see SRA Case Studies: Conflicts of Interest: Solicitors Regulation Authority.

EXAMPLE

There are many ways in which a conflict can arise in practice and some areas of law have more likelihood of a conflict than others. In a family law situation, a person may come to a law firm for advice when they are thinking about leaving a relationship, despite the other person being unaware of it. The advice provided could simply be a one-off appointment. A conflict would arise if at a later date the other person in the relationship came to the law firm for advice. In criminal law, a conflict could be where the criminal department of a firm represents someone accused of assaulting their wife and the wife attends the family department for advice on separation. In both instances, a solicitor would have to decline the instructions and provide details of other solicitors in their area who could assist in that area of law and/or provide them with the Law Society Find a Solicitor webpage.

B.2.8 Confidentiality

Confidentiality between a solicitor and client is one of the most important parts of their relationship. It is significant in the area of ethics and professional conduct as it is an area in which it is important that the solicitor receives all of the information from the client in order to provide the best advice, and that the client is confident that their solicitor will not release this to the public. The duty of confidentiality remains when the client retainer is terminated and even on the death of the client. Paragraphs 6.3–6.5 of the Code of Conduct 2019 state that a solicitor must keep the affairs of clients and former clients confidential apart from in limited situations. The main situations are if the client consents to the disclosure or if permitted by law.

Paragraph 6.2 the Code of Conduct 2019 outlines the situation when a solicitor may limit the information provided to a client:

> Where you are acting for a client on a matter, you make the client aware of all information material to the matter of which you have knowledge, except when:
>
> - the disclosure of the information is prohibited by legal restrictions imposed in the interests of national security or the prevention of crime;
> - your client gives informed consent, given or evidenced in writing, to the information not being disclosed to them;
> - you have reason to believe that serious physical or mental injury will be caused to your client or another if the information is disclosed; or
> - the information is contained in a privileged document that you have knowledge of only because it has been mistakenly disclosed.

Paragraph 6.5 of the Code of Conduct 2019 explains the limited circumstances when you can act for a client who has an adverse interest and where you hold confidential information:

> You do not act for a client in a matter where that client has an interest adverse to the interest of another current or former client of you or your business or employer, for whom you or your business or employer holds confidential information which is material to that matter, unless:
>
> - effective measures have been taken which result in there being no real risk of disclosure of the confidential information; or
> - the current or former client whose information you or your business or employer holds has given informed consent, given or evidenced in writing, to you acting, including to any measures taken to protect their information.

EXAMPLE

There are many ways in which an issue around confidentiality can arise in practice. In a criminal law firm, a person may come to a law firm for advice and you may overhear them on the telephone planning to sell drugs. In this case, in order to prevent a crime you would have to disclose this information to the police and would therefore be breaching confidentiality.

In a private client firm, a solicitor may have drafted a will for a lady who has now died. If her son contacts the solicitor after she has passed to ask if he has been left anything, then because of the duty of confidentiality the solicitor would be unable to tell him without the consent of the personal representatives of the will.

B.2.9 **Undertakings**

An undertaking made by a solicitor is a commitment to do or not do something that someone places reliance upon. An undertaking is binding and does not necessarily have to be made by a solicitor or use the word 'undertake'. It is often made to clients or third parties in a matter. Once the undertaking has been relied upon, then it cannot be withdrawn without the agreement of both parties.

Many areas of practice, such as conveyancing and litigation, rely on the giving and receiving of undertakings to progress matters. The solicitor giving the undertaking needs to be careful and is not obliged to give undertakings. If an undertaking is breached, then the solicitor could be sued personally for the money which was promised within the undertaking. The solicitor would have also breached the Code of Conduct and disciplinary proceedings would likely follow.

The SRA's Guidance on Undertakings, given by, or on behalf of, incorporated practice explains your obligations when undertakings are provided, by or on behalf of incorporated practices. This is because the Supreme Court decision in *Harcus Sinclair v Your Lawyers* [2021] UKSC 32 confirmed that the courts have no jurisdiction to enforce undertakings against incorporated practices. However, an incorporated practice could still face regulatory proceedings as there might have been a breach of our rules.

EXAMPLE

A solicitor is acting for a client in relation to debt matters and one large debt of £80,000 is owed by him to Jones Construction, who have written to ask for payment of the full amount within ten days. The client is in the process of selling a flat at auction, which has been valued at £100,000. The auction is in seven days and the solicitor provides an undertaking to Jones Construction to pay the £80,000 from the proceeds of sale from the flat.

The flat is only sold for £70,000 and Jones Construction has demanded the £80,000 from the solicitor. The solicitor must perform the undertaking and pay the full amount of £80,000. Failure to do so could be considered a breach of professional conduct.

In hindsight, what the solicitor should have done was to draft the undertaking but state that the payment would be limited to the amount received from the auction sale, or make it clear that they were not accepting responsibility for any personal liability.

B.2.10 **Alternate Business Structures (ABSs)**

It is worth noting that all of these regulations also bind ABSs. ABSs were introduced by the Legal Services Act 2007 and the SRA began accepting applications from prospective ABSs in January 2012. This allowed non-lawyers to own or invest in a law firm, when previously only lawyers could seek to create and operate a law firm. At the time, this was seen to be a huge change in the way law firms could function. They are still overseen by the SRA and the SRA decides whether a firm or business can become an ABS.

There are two key distinct ABS roles, those which entail the appointment of a recognised lawyer and those which do not require a qualified lawyer. There was a great deal of scepticism by many in the legal profession when the ABS was introduced. It was feared that big businesses would reduce the quality of legal work provided and that 'Tesco Law'-type businesses would emerge.

B.3 Money laundering

Money laundering is an illegal practice in which money generated from criminal activities is disguised and made to appear to have come from a legitimate source, in order to make it easier to spend the money and avoid suspicion. There are a wide variety of activities in which money may be attempted to be laundered. Examples of these are fraud, prostitution, robbery and the trafficking of drugs or people.

The purpose of anti-money laundering legislation is because solicitors' firms are often targeted in order to assist with money laundering. They can legitimise a transaction, have access to financial markets and often advise on property and business deals. It is therefore important for solicitors to understand the legislation, remain vigilant and to have the right training and processes in place in order to avoid the risk of facilitating this crime.

The Legal Sector Affinity Group (LSAG)'s Anti-Money Laundering Guidance for the legal profession, published in 2021, provides detailed guidance in this area.

Ensuring that solicitors do not facilitate money laundering is, of course, as much an ethical issue as a financial one. For more detail on money laundering regulations, see the financial services chapter in *Public Law, Legal Services & the Legal System*.

B.4 Client care

Client care is a fundamental part of the role of a solicitor. A client is required to be given information in a way that they understand and allows them to make decisions about the services they need, how their case will be handled and the options which are available to them (para 8.6 of the 2019 Code). They are also required to be provided with information about costs both at the time of engagement and as the matter progresses (para 8.7 of the 2019 Code). Most complaints from clients are either regarding not being updated about how the matter is progressing or with issues about costs.

B.4.1 General Data Protection Regulation

The UK General Data Protection Regulation (GDPR) sets out key principles, rights and obligations when processing personal data. It sits alongside the Data Protection Act 2018 and incorporates the EU GDPR, but, following Brexit, it allows the UK government the flexibility to review and amends its provisions. Personal data is essentially data that allows a living person to be directly or indirectly identified from information that is available. All solicitors hold personal data relating to both clients and employees. It is therefore crucial to be able to comply with the regulations. Knowing what personal data you have is the first step in compliance.

Further detailed guidance on the GDPR for solicitors can be found on the Law Society website.

B.4.2 The first interview

Some practical considerations are necessary in relation to client care and when meeting the client for the first time, it is important to be fully prepared. Clients may have a range of emotions depending on the areas of law you are advising on. It is important that the client is reassured, offered an appointment promptly and also that the solicitor is fully prepared for the first interview.

Before the interview, the Law Society, in its client information requirements practice note, advises that when the client attends the interview the following information must be explained to them and confirmed in writing:

- name and status of the solicitor or other person conducting the interview;
- information on the costs for the interview;
- details of who to contact if they have a complaint including the right to complain to the Legal Ombudsman, the time frame and the contact details.

This information can be prepared in a pro forma document in advance. It is important to keep a copy on file.

In the first interview, you must remember to cover all of the professional conduct issues, money laundering regulations, the GDPR and legal issues as well as to obtain the basic details from the client.

B.4.3 Client care letter

This letter is used by most law firms to set out the necessary client care information to a client. It is usually the first piece of correspondence you will send to your client and it is therefore an extremely important document. It must have certain regulatory information in it in order to comply with the Code of Conduct. It is usually also the retainer or contract between you and your client and is the beginning of the solicitor/client relationship. The Consumer Contracts (Information, Cancellation and Additional Charges) Regulations 2013 (SI 2013/3134) apply when you enter into a retainer with a consumer client who you have not met. This is often known as a distance contract.

B.4.4 Fees and costs

In most circumstances, you will have a direct retainer with the client and the client will be responsible for paying your costs. In certain areas of law, this may be different such as criminal law, family law and personal injury. In those areas, a client may be eligible for Legal Aid or there may be a 'no win, no fee' arrangement. Legal aid is the provision of assistance to people who are unable to afford legal representation and/or access to the court system. Firms must have a legal aid contract in order to be able to offer this service to clients and legal aid is only available in certain areas of law (usually family law and criminal law) and for clients who, in most cases, have a low income. More information regarding legal aid and how it is assessed can be found on the Gov.uk website.

'No win, no fee', often called a conditional fee agreement, is a legal fee arrangement whereby the client agrees to pay only if they win their case and is generally used in personal injury law. A damages-based agreement is another legal fee arrangement under which the client agrees to pay the solicitor a set percentage of the compensation they receive if they win the case.

In the situation where a client is paying your costs, there are several options available regarding how to charge a client for work. The main two ways of charging a client are by hourly rates or a fixed fee arrangement. Whichever way you do charge, it is essential to communicate this to the client and to provide the client with a likely overall cost of the matter. If the likely overall cost changes then it is important to advise the client of this as soon as possible in order to avoid any issues which may give rise to a complaint or a potential breach of the Code of Conduct.

B.4.5 Advertising

A solicitor cannot make an unsolicited approach to members of the public regarding the advertising of its legal services, but this does not apply to current or former clients. Any potential client referred to the firm by a current or former client will be seen as a member of the public (para 8.9 Code of Conduct for Solicitors, RELs and RFLs).

KEY POINT SUMMARY

- Ethics and professional conduct are fundamental to being a good solicitor.
- The Code of Conduct 2019 and the Principles provide the most up-to-date set of standards and requirements expected of solicitors, RELs and RFLs, and you should refer to them frequently.
- Breach of the Code of Conduct may constitute professional misconduct and could result in being fined, lead to criminal proceedings and/or being struck off from the roll of solicitors.
- It is crucial that solicitors have knowledge and understanding of the GDPR, money laundering and client care.

PART A
Basic Fundamentals

CHAPTER 1
Available Business Structures in the UK

FUNCTIONING LEGAL KNOWLEDGE

This chapter considers the following functioning legal knowledge included in the SRA's SQE 1 assessment specification:

1 Starting a new business through the vehicle of a company, partnership, LLP or as a sole trader.

2 The interests, rights, obligations and powers of stakeholders in a business.

To fulfil these learning objectives, a practitioner must have a functioning understanding of the following substantive legal knowledge:

Business and organisational characteristics (sole trader/partnership/LLP/private and unlisted public companies)

Legal personality and limited liability

Finance:

- funding options: debt and equity
- distribution of profits and gains
- financial records, information and accounting requirements.

Corporate governance and compliance:

- documentary, record-keeping, statutory filing and disclosure requirements

Income tax:

- chargeable persons/entities (employees, sole traders, partners, **shareholder**, lenders and **debenture** holders)

1.1 Introduction

After consulting this chapter, you will have been introduced to:

(a) the main types of business structure available in the UK;

(b) the features of each; and

(c) the important distinctions between them.

A business needs to be operated through a recognised legal structure (or medium). Most businesses are operated through the following legal structures:

1 A limited company.

2 A limited liability partnership (LLP).

3 A partnership.

4 A sole trader.

It should be recognised at the outset that the structure adopted is not a neutral one. The structure chosen can have major legal and taxation implications. (Relevant taxation matters are considered in **Chapters 30–4**). As such, of fundamental concern to any business lawyer is the nature of the relevant business entity which they are required to advise about.

This chapter is a brief introduction. More specific detail on individual business structures can be found in relevant chapters throughout the text.

To keep up with significant changes in the law, there is an Updates resource within the Additional Materials section of the Business Law & Practice module on the *SQE Prep & Practise* platform. Should key changes to practices and procedures come into force between editions of this manual, we will endeavour to provide updated guidance there.

1.2 Number of proprietors

Only one person is required to set up a private limited company and, as the name suggests, only one person will operate as a sole trader. As such, if the business is to be operated by a single proprietor, a choice must be made between these two media.

Two or more proprietors excludes the possibility of a sole trader, but allows for the possibility of a partnership or LLP, as well as a company.

1.3 Formalities of creation

There are no formalities for a sole trader. The proprietor is the business and vice versa.

Similarly, there are no formalities to create a partnership. Two or more persons in business with a view of profit means that a partnership exists. As such, there are no registration or disclosure requirements on the creation of either a partnership or sole trader. (However, there may be value in the creation of a formal partnership agreement–see **Chapters 5** and **27** for further detail.)

Each of a company and an LLP can only be brought into existence through a formal registration process at **Companies House**. (See **Chapters 3** and **6** respectively for further detail.) Effectively, they can both be considered as *corporate* entities.

In simple terms, partnerships are the product of agreement; companies and LLPs are creatures of statute.

1.4 Separate legal personality

As already mentioned, regarding sole traders there is no legal difference between the business proprietor and the business they undertake. A contract with the 'business' is effectively a contract with the sole trader.

Partnerships are similar, in that, again, there is no distinction between the business being undertaken and the partners. A contract with the 'firm' is a contract with all the partners.

Both companies and LLPs, by contrast, have a legal status which is independent of the persons who set them up. As such, contractual dealings with either a company or LLP will be dealings with that corporate entity, rather than the persons who own and manage them. Similarly, an unlawful or illegal act of a company or LLP will usually only have consequences for the company or LLP. Conversely, unlawful or illegal acts committed by either a sole trader or partnership will be seen as acts of the proprietors themselves.

1.5 Management and ownership

Those persons who run a business are often referred to as its proprietors. The legal status of such proprietors needs to be understood at the outset.

1. A sole trader is just that. They have total, unilateral control and responsibility for the business.
2. Those persons involved in a partnership are, not unnaturally, known as partners; between them they exercise management rights and ownership rights over the partnership business and assets.

3 Those persons involved in an LLP are legally defined as **members**. They control and manage the LLP; however, unlike partners in a partnership, they do not have a direct legal entitlement to the assets and business of the LLP. Instead, they will each have a defined stake in the business which the LLP undertakes.

4 Companies are more complex, in that they are legally required to have both **directors** and **shareholders**. The former are regarded as the senior management of the company, acting through authority delegated down to them by the company; the latter are investors and owners, having a stake in the company which is defined by the percentage size of their shareholding. However, neither directors nor shareholders have any proprietorship rights over or in the assets which the company owns. It may be the case that directors and shareholders of a company are one and the same people. Therefore, care should always be taken to identify the capacity in which they are acting.

1.6 Limited liability

One considerable advantage of a company over a partnership is that a company can be formed with limited liability. This means that the shareholders must contribute the amount unpaid on their **shares**, but no more, if the company becomes insolvent.

In the majority of cases, shares will have been fully paid for, so that no contribution towards the company's debts has to be made. However, shareholders stand to lose the value of their shares if a company fails, so that, realistically, the limit to their financial exposure is what they have invested in the company.

The creation of an LLP will also afford the proprietors of the business limited liability, but through a different mechanism. In this case, the members agree contractually the amount they will contribute on the insolvency of the LLP, which theoretically could be nothing. (Of course, if the LLP is insolvent, then the value of each member's stake will presumably be worthless.)

If a partnership becomes insolvent, each of the partners is jointly and severally liable for all the debts of the partnership. This means that they stand to lose not only what they have invested in the business but also any other property which they own. The liability of partners is, therefore, unlimited in amount. The partnership agreement may make provision as to how losses are to be shared between the partners, but this does not prevent external creditors claiming in full from a wealthy partner whose other partners are unable to pay their share of the loss.

Limited liability would seem to be an enormous advantage to the proprietors of a business. However, limited liability can sometimes be made illusory by the directors (and/or shareholders) of a company (or members of an LLP) having to give guarantees. Many businesses rely on borrowed money. A bank lending to a company (or LLP) without any real track record of trading or with a low capital base will often require personal guarantees from the directors or shareholders, so that, if the company (or LLP) cannot repay the loan, the bank has further **security**. Guarantees may also be required by the landlord of any premises which a company (or LLP) may lease. These will usually be in respect of obligations to pay rent but may also cover performance obligations, such as those requiring a tenant to keep the property in good repair.

1.7 Documentation and expense

Certain expenses will be incurred when a company or LLP is formed. These include the fee payable to Companies House as part of the process of incorporation and the cost of preparing the application for registration.

Companies are required to have a constitution (**articles of association**). There may be cost involved in the creation of these, but usually their content involves standard precedent wording. An LLP, by contrast, is not required to have an internal constitution; however, it would be unwise to create an LLP in which the relationship between the members (and the LLP) was not formalised in some way. As such, there may be some cost in the preparation of this agreement.

If a partnership is formed, no expenses need be incurred since there are no registration requirements. However, in many cases the partners will want a properly drawn up partnership agreement, thus incurring professional costs in its creation.

After formation, the major administrative costs of a business will again depend on the complexity of the business. However, in respect of accounts, companies and LLPs are at a disadvantage when compared with partnerships. All types of business will wish to keep financial records, and prepare final accounts annually. Nearly all businesses will wish to pay a qualified accountant to draw up these accounts (if only to make sure that advantage is taken of tax reliefs and exemptions). Companies and LLPs, however, must draw up the accounts in a particular way and may have to have them audited. This will usually involve extra cost.

1.8 Publicity

A company is required to make a considerable amount of information, including annual accounts, available to the public. (Limited liability partnerships have approximately the same disclosure obligations as companies.) A partnership is not required to make such information available. A desire to keep the affairs of a business secret may influence some people to prefer a partnership to a company or LLP.

1.9 Taxation

What follows is a brief summary of a complex topic. You will find further information in **Chapters 30–34**.

A company has a choice as to how to use the money it makes to reward those persons involved with it:

(a) dividends may be paid out to shareholders;

(b) directors can be paid a salary and bonuses.

A company also has the option to retain a certain amount of profit to maintain ongoing funds for its operations. Each of these possibilities has different tax consequences.

Generally speaking, in a small, **private company**, where the directors and shareholders are one and the same persons, this 'duality' of status will allow for flexibility in a reward structure. In turn, this will allow such owner-managers of companies to take out a combination of salary and dividends calculated to produce the most favourable overall income tax result.

Linked to this is the fact that a company will incur its own corporation tax liability on the profits which it generates. Many payments which a company makes are regarded as tax-deductible, which will reduce the amount of profit which is taxed.

Some factors which are likely to be influential are:

(a) Salaries are tax-deductible, so can be used to reduce a company's taxable profits. However, they are taxable for income tax purposes in the hands of the recipient (usually at 20 or 40%) and the company is obliged to deduct such tax at source. Salaries also usually attract both employers' and employees' **National Insurance**, which would be a tax burden for the company.

(b) Dividends will be paid out of profits available after corporation tax has been paid, and so, are non-deductible for the paying company. However, such payments do not incur any National Insurance liability for either the company or a director and they also benefit from a Dividend Allowance of £500, which allows up to £500 of dividends to be received income tax free. Further, the basic rate of income tax on dividends is 8.75%.

A decision to pay dividends may, of course, be taken for non-tax reasons, since it is the only way to provide a shareholder, who is not also a director, with a return on their investment. Similarly, a director who is not also a shareholder can only receive a salary.

It should be noted, in any event, that dividends can only be paid out of available profits, as determined by the rule in s830 of the Companies Act 2006 (CA 2006), so a company does not have total discretion to pay dividends.

Arguably, a partnership offers less scope for tax planning in relation to income profits than a company. (The same is true of LLPs which are taxed in a similar way to partnerships. All references to partners which follow should, therefore, be read as applying to members of LLPs also.)

All the income profits are taxed as income of the individual partners whether they are actually paid to them or are retained in the business. (There is no such thing as a partnership or LLP tax liability.) Each partner will be liable for income tax on a proportion of the partnership profits based on their agreed share of the latter.

1.10 National Insurance

The National Insurance treatment of directors and partners is somewhat different. Contributions (in the form of National Insurance) must be made by both the employer and employee in respect of an employed person; in the context of this discussion, a director. No employers' contributions are payable in respect of a self-employed person, such as a partner.

1.11 Raising finance

1.11.1 Introduction

This topic is dealt with specifically in respect of companies in **Chapters** 7 and **12**. As regards partnerships, it is dealt with in **Chapter 23**.

All businesses will look to two main sources of finance:

(a) Investment by the persons promoting and running the business.

(b) Borrowings (usually from a bank but also from the promoters of the business).

The medium through which the business is run can have an impact upon the way in which finance is raised and structured. However, a significant practical issue will be the personal funds which those setting up a company have or wish to risk in the venture. For this reason, borrowing from a third party may be the main source of funding.

1.11.2 Partnerships

It is usual for partners to make a contribution in the form of capital. Usually this amount will not be returned to a partner until they leave the partnership or it is dissolved.

A lender to a partnership will, in effect, be lending to the partners, so all partners will, in turn, be personally liable to the lender.

As regards future investment, the only feasible source of this would be a new partner who would make a further capital contribution.

1.11.3 Companies

An investment in a company will take the form of shares. Effectively the promoter of the business will buy shares from the company. In this way, the funds go to the company. As with partnerships, this investment is unlikely to be returned to the shareholder during the continuance of the company. (However, a shareholder may have the option to sell on their investment at a later date.)

A lender to a company will do just that; as such, the obligation lies with the company to repay the money borrowed. For this reason, a lender may choose to take security over any assets the company owes and may also require personal guarantees from the promoters of the company. A lender could be a third party or it could be one of the promoters themselves.

As regards future investment, companies have an advantage over partnerships, in that shares can be used as an 'arm's length' investment mechanism to allow third parties to take a stake in the company without necessarily acquiring any management responsibilities or personal liability.

1.11.4 Limited liability partnerships

As LLPs are effectively an amalgam of facets of a company and a partnership, any financing of an LLP reflects this. Although an LLP is a legal person in its own right, it is not possible for an LLP to issue shares. As such, the members, as with partners, will have to make a capital contribution to the LLP. Alternatively or additionally, they could lend money to the LLP.

Should the LLP borrow money from an external source, the LLP, not the members, will be obliged to repay the indebtedness. As with companies, a lender in such circumstances is likely to want security over any assets owned by the LLP itself and personal guarantees from the members.

As regards future investment, this is likely to come from newly appointed members of the LLP who make a capital contribution. (It is suggested that it is highly unlikely that a third party would want to be an arm's length investor in an LLP without membership status; further, to arrange such an investment in a way which was satisfactory to that third party would be problematic.)

1.12 Professional conduct and ethical issues

1.12.1 Introduction

A general explanation of this topic area is given in Part B. You are advised to consult that first. Also, throughout the text specific examples of conduct and ethical issues are provided. This section is designed to introduce you to some of the main issues which should be considered by a solicitor advising business clients. Those issues are:

(a) conflicts of interest;

(b) client confidentiality;

(c) financial services regulation; and

(d) money laundering.

1.12.2 Conflicts of interest

The recognition and avoidance of conflicts of interest between clients is of general relevance to all solicitors. The relevant rules are to be found in regs 6.1 and 6.2 of the SRA Standards and Regulations.

Business lawyers need to be particularly aware of the fact that business transactions can involve multiple parties. It is not possible to advise 'a transaction'; one can only advise parties to the transaction. In turn, it is likely that each party to the transaction will have their own specific interests and needs. As such, a solicitor must recognise where their instructions originate from and they must only meet the needs and advise that client.

Further, as has been seen earlier in the chapter, business organisations often involve more than one person. Again, a solicitor must recognise with whom their retainer lies.

EXAMPLE

Wonderland Wholesale Ltd is a company owned and managed by Dieter and Kumar. They are each the only directors in this company and each have 50% shareholdings.

Their solicitor has advised the company for several years on general matters of contract and company law.

Kumar and Dieter have fallen out and are in major disagreement about the future of the company. As such, the company is in a position of deadlock, with each party refusing to comply with or consent to the wishes of the other.

Their solicitor cannot act to resolve the dispute. First, their client is the company. If the company is in a state of paralysis, it cannot effectively provide instructions. Secondly, because the company is the solicitor's client, the solicitor cannot separately represent either Kumar or Dieter. As such, they need to be advised to seek separate representation in order to resolve their difficulties.

1.12.3 Client confidentiality

As with conflicts of interest, client confidentiality is of fundamental concern to all lawyers throughout their professional lives. Lawyers can receive instructions from all types of persons in a variety of contexts, so it is necessary to remember the obligation of confidentiality, especially in respect of former clients.

EXAMPLE

Three years ago Charles, a solicitor, acted for Amy, who was a director threatened with removal from her company due to various allegations of misconduct on Amy's part. In the end, a severance package was agreed between Amy and her company.

Charles has acted for ExampleCo Ltd for several years and is instructed by the company to draw up a **service contract** for a director who is soon to be appointed to the company. That person is Amy.

Charles is now in a difficult position. The duty of confidentiality to Amy is still 'live': however, there is also a duty to reveal to a client any information in the solicitor's possession which is relevant to the client's matter. Arguably, Amy's previous dispute in her capacity as a director with another company is material to ExampleCo's interests. The only safe course of action for Charles is to decline to act on this particular matter without revealing the reason why, as this would breach the duty owed to Amy. Alternatively, Amy may be asked to consent to disclosure to ExampleCo of details of her previous dispute with another company.

1.12.4 Financial services regulation

In the commercial sphere, lawyers are likely to encounter many situations where the Financial Services and Markets Act 2000 (FSMA 2000) (and concomitant regulation) is relevant. For the purposes of this discussion, it should be noted that the status of shares as defined investments may mean that advising on transactions which involve shares in a company is classed as a regulated activity pursuant to s22 FSMA 2000. The two most likely regulated activities (as defined by the Financial Services and Markets Act 2000 (Regulated Activities) Order 2001) are:

(a) arranging deals in investments; or

(b) advising on investments.

The contexts where these are matters for consideration are:

(a) Buying and selling shares in a company.

(b) Subscribing for shares in a company.

See discussion at **7.12**, **9.4.10** and **10.7** for further consideration of these issues.

1.12.5 Money laundering

Because of the relevant criminal sanctions, money laundering is something which many providers of professional and financial services need to be aware of. Business lawyers need, in particular, to consider the fact that companies can be used to assist money laundering. The fact that a company is a legally recognised person means that it can operate its own banking facilities and spend and receive money in its own name. However, the ultimate beneficiaries of this activity can be directors or shareholders of the company. Further, interests in companies need not be direct. For example, Company X may be a shareholder in Company Y, and the entire issued share capital of Company X may be held in a trust for the benefit of Z. As such, Z has a controlling interest in Company X (as the sole beneficiary under the trust), so, in turn, has an indirect interest in its shareholding in Company Y.

Because of the ingenuity of criminals and because money laundering can be 'absorbed' into or screened behind an apparently legitimate business transaction, lawyers need to be constantly vigilant as to its existence.

It is to be hoped that law firms and their lawyers do not knowingly choose to assist or engage with money laundering. (Direct money laundering offences under the Proceeds of Crime Act 2002 require knowledge or suspicion that criminal property (as defined by s340(3) of that Act) is being laundered.) It is more likely that lawyers will fall foul of the requirement to disclose a suspicion of money laundering.

Two issues need to be noted:

1 Disclosure is usually a defence to a charge of money laundering; a so-called authorised disclosure.
2 Failure to disclose is likely to be an offence in itself.

Lawyers and law firms must also comply with their obligations under the Money Laundering, Terrorist Financing and Transfer of Funds (Information on the Payer) Regulations 2017. Two particular regulations must be noted:

1 Regulation 27–the obligation to apply customer due diligence measures whenever a business relationship is established with a client or when an 'occasional transaction' (as defined) is to be undertaken for a client.
2 Regulation 28–which defines the extent of required customer due diligence.

EXAMPLE

Claire receives instructions from a new client, Mr Jay. Mr Jay explains that he is looking to buy shares in a company from an existing shareholder in that company. As such, he wants legal advice to make sure that the purchase is valid and binding. The only communication with Mr Jay is on the telephone.

To begin with, it will be essential to confirm and verify Mr Jay's identity. As he is not being dealt with face to face, enhanced measures may have to be employed.

Claire also asks for details of the potential seller of shares and the company in question. Mr Jay is rather evasive at this point and explains that the seller would rather remain confidential at this stage. Claire should be uneasy at this point, but decides to wait for confirmation of Mr Jay's identity, which is confirmed effectively.

Mr Jay then telephones Claire to explain that the money to buy the shares is being lent to him by 'a cousin'. Mr Jay also explains that the cousin has said that he does not want Mr Jay to hold the money in the meantime, but would like Claire's firm to hold the money on Mr Jay's behalf until it is needed to buy the shares.

Claire provides Mr Jay with the firm's bank account details. Twenty-four hours later, £45,000 is deposited in the firm's bank account by Mr Jay.

A week later, Claire receives a phone call from Mr Jay explaining that the share deal has fallen through and his cousin wants his money back. Mr Jay asks that the £45,000 be transferred to a company called Cashwash Ltd, which he explains is owned by his cousin. Claire duly arranges this.

Claire is likely to be in serious trouble. If it transpires that the £45,000 is criminal property, the firm has unwittingly assisted money laundering. The use of law firm's bank accounts is a recognised method of doing so. Further, at some stage in the process, Claire needed to report a suspicion of money laundering to the firm's Money Laundering Reporting Officer (MLRO) to avoid an offence of failure to report. The warning signs were:

(a) The evasive/vague nature of the client's instructions.

(b) The unusual circumstances in which the purchase money was to be provided.

(c) The request from the client to use the firm's bank account to hold money.

(d) The supposed 'collapse' of the deal and the request to return the money to a person other than the client.

KEY POINT SUMMARY

- The main business media in the UK are sole trader, company, partnership and limited liability partnership.
- The creation of an LLP or a company requires a specific registration process to be fulfilled with Companies House.
- The creation of an LLP or a company creates a legally recognised person separate from the person(s) who set the entity up.
- No formalities are required to create a sole tradership or a partnership.
- The taxation treatment of an LLP and partnership are very similar, with the partners or members being subject to income tax on their individual share of the partnership's profits.
- Companies must pay corporation tax on their own profits and directors will pay income tax on payments they receive, as will shareholders on any dividends.
- Investment in a partnership or LLP will take the form of a capital contribution, usually coupled with partnership or membership.
- Investment in a company will take the form of the purchase of shares in the same.
- All forms of business media may rely upon borrowing as a further source of capital.
- Matters of professional conduct and ethical behaviour need to be in the forefront of a business lawyer's mind at all times.

PART B

Business Organisations, Rules and Procedures

CHAPTER 2
Companies: An Introduction

FUNCTIONING LEGAL KNOWLEDGE

This chapter considers the following functioning legal knowledge included in the SRA's SQE 1 assessment specification:

Legal personality and limited liability

Procedures and documentation required to incorporate a company/form a partnership/ LLP and other steps required under companies and partnerships legislation to enable the entity to commence operating:

- constitutional documents
- Companies House filing requirements.

Corporate governance and compliance:

- documentary, record-keeping, statutory filing and disclosure requirements

AUTHORITIES UNDERPINNING PRACTICE

The key authorities that underpin this area of practice are listed below. Note that for legislation you are linked to legislation.gov.uk.

Although much of the legislation on this government website is available in its amended form, the incorporation of new amendments into the text of legislation can be delayed. You should refer to legal databases to ensure you are referencing the most up-to-date legislation.

- Companies Act 2006
  https://www.legislation.gov.uk/ukpga/2006/46/contents
- Insolvency Act 1986
  https://www.legislation.gov.uk/ukpga/1986/45

2.1 Introduction

After consulting this chapter, you will have been introduced to:

(a) the legal status of limited companies;

(b) the types of companies available; and

(c) the distinction between private and public companies.

Many businesses are run by limited companies. These range from international conglomerates to companies owned by one person running a small business. Detailed legal rules about types of companies are discussed in **Chapters 3** and **4**; this introduction will demonstrate how they fit into the complex pattern of institutions which the law has created.

2.2 Companies Act 2006

A 'company' is in law a corporation; that is, an artificial legal 'person' with rights and obligations distinct from those of its **members**. Arguably the concept of the company as a medium for any business came into being with the introduction of the Companies Act 1862. Thereafter, numerous Companies Acts were introduced during the nineteenth and twentieth centuries, culminating in the current regime provided by the Companies Act 2006 (CA 2006). The 2006 Act is now the primary legislation governing companies. The 2006 Act applies throughout the UK, although a number of provisions apply only to Scotland or only to England and Wales and Northern Ireland.

It is important, therefore, at the outset to recognise that the rules governing companies are primarily statutory.

2.3 Tax legislation

Companies are often profit-generating entities. As such, profits and gains which many companies make are taxable. The taxation of companies is largely dealt with in the Corporation Tax Acts 2009 and 2010. Companies' capital gains are largely dealt with in accordance with the Taxation of Chargeable Gains Act 1992, as amended. The taxation of companies is examined in detail in **Chapter 33**.

2.4 The general law

Much general law that applies to individuals applies equally to companies, on the basis that a company is a legal person it its own right. The general law of contract, for example, applies to companies with very few modifications, as does the law of tort, competition and so on.

2.5 The company's constitution: articles of association

To provide for its own internal administration, each company must have a set of regulations known as *articles of association*. These may be specially prepared for the company; alternatively, it is possible to adopt standard articles stipulated by regulation.

Previously this form of standard articles was known as Table A. A new set of standard articles known as the Model Articles has since superseded Table A. In practice, lawyers are most likely to come across companies whose articles are heavily influenced by either Table A or the Model Articles.

A more detailed discussion of articles of association can be found in **Chapter 13**.

2.6 Registration

Companies are formed (or incorporated) by a process called *registration*. The conditions for registration are determined by the CA 2006.

Registration involves sending a number of documents and a fee to the Registrar of Companies (often referred to as 'Companies House'), the official responsible for registering companies. A company comes into existence on the issue of a *certificate of incorporation* by the Registrar.

The Registrar is also responsible for maintaining records relating to registered companies. These records contain information which companies are required by law to disclose in relation to a wide range of matters. Records are kept at Companies House, which for companies incorporated in England and Wales is in Cardiff. For companies registered in Scotland, a separate Companies House is based in Edinburgh. For those registered in Northern Ireland, the relevant office is based in Belfast. You will find the Companies House website a useful reference source.

The process of registration is examined in more detail in **Chapter 3**.

2.7 Types of registered company

2.7.1 Companies limited by shares

Most registered companies are 'limited by shares'. This expression refers to the *liability* of the members (or shareholders–the terms are almost interchangeable, but see the discussion about companies limited by guarantee which follows) of the company for that company's debts on a **liquidation**. The effect of a company being limited by shares is that, on a liquidation, the liability of a member is limited to the amount, if any, which remains unpaid on their shares.

When a company issues shares, the person taking the shares must agree to pay the company for them. Usually payment will be made immediately but occasionally shares will be issued 'unpaid' (sometimes expressed as 'nil-paid') or 'partly paid', in which case payment must be made later. If the company goes into liquidation and is insolvent, any member who has not fully paid for their shares is liable to pay the amount outstanding to the liquidator (s74 Insolvency Act 1986). That is the extent of that member's liability for the company's debts. As such, in the case of a member who has paid in full for their shares, they will have no liability (in normal circumstances) for the company's debts.

EXAMPLE

Charlotte subscribes for 500 £1 shares in Regency Furnishings Ltd ('Regency').

If Charlotte pays £500 for the shares, her shares are said to be fully paid, so no further liability for Regency's debts can fall on Charlotte.

Instead, if Charlotte pays 50p per share, her shares are said to be partly paid. In effect, £250 remains as an outstanding obligation to Regency. Regency's constitution may contain rules about how and when it can demand the outstanding balance but, in any event, on any liquidation of Regency, Charlotte will be obliged to contribute the remaining £250.

2.7.2 Companies limited by guarantee

A small number of companies in existence are limited by guarantee rather than by shares. This means that each member undertakes to pay a specified amount if the company is wound up (ie the guarantee) while they are a member or within a year after they cease to be a member. As such, this is an example of a company which has members who are not simultaneously shareholders.

Most companies limited by guarantee are charities or other non-trading companies where the likelihood of exposure to trading risks is negligible.

2.7.3 Unlimited companies

An unlimited company is one which is registered under the 2006 Act but without any limit on the liability of the members. An unlimited company may or may not choose to issue shares, but, if it does so, they will not relate to the liability of the members, as with a company limited by shares.

If an unlimited company goes into liquidation the members are liable to contribute the whole of their private wealth (if so much is needed) to the payment of the company's debts. The creditors cannot sue the members direct but must claim in the liquidation. The liquidator then calls for contributions from the members. For this reason, unlimited companies are uncommon.

2.7.4 **Public and private companies**

Nearly all company law rules apply equally to all companies. There are, however, a number of rules which distinguish between 'public' companies and 'private' companies. The important issue to note is that public and private companies are creatures of statute and the differences between them are determined by the 2006 Act. Any company will be private unless it is specifically incorporated as a public one.

Bringing a **public company** into being is effectively an administrative task. The only substantive matter is that the company's share capital must satisfy certain minimum requirements, namely:

(a) the aggregate **nominal value** of all shares in issue must be at least £50,000; and

(b) each share must be at least one-quarter paid up.

In other words, the company must have received at least £12,500 from its shareholders for those shares.

The vast majority of companies in existence are private. Public companies, being more heavily regulated, are less attractive. The principal reason for wanting a public company is that only public companies can issue shares or debt securities to the public (hence the description 'public company'); a private company is prohibited from so doing. Private companies which want to circumvent this prohibition will have to convert to public status first. (These issues are discussed in more detail in **Chapter 4**.)

2.7.5 **Other definitions**

All companies are public or private but there are other categories of company to which special rules apply.

2.7.5.1 Listed company

A company is in this category if its shares are listed with the UK Listing Authority and traded on a stock exchange. Because of UK Listing Authority and London Stock Exchange rules, only public companies can obtain a listing. Listed companies are subject to a more stringent regulatory regime. Listed companies may also be referred to as 'quoted' companies and in general parlance the two terms are synonymous. However, the CA 2006 includes within it the use of the defined term 'quoted company', so care should be taken in the use of this term.

2.7.5.2 Close company

This category is relevant only for tax purposes; special tax rules apply to close companies. The primary purpose of these rules is to stop the exploitation of the corporate form to gain a tax advantage, often by attempting to 'disguise' payments to shareholders as something other than income. Virtually all private companies are close.

2.7.5.3 Small and medium-sized companies

These are companies which, because of their relatively small size (in financial terms), are exempt from providing certain information in their accounts. In addition, certain categories of small companies are now exempt from the requirement to have an audit of their accounts. Further discussion of this topic can be found in **Chapter 22**.

2.8 **Separate legal personality**

A company is a 'body corporate'; that is, it is a legal person distinct from its members and officers (ie its directors and secretary, if one is appointed). Even if a company is 100% owned and controlled by a single shareholder, that company has a completely separate legal personality from that of the shareholder. This is clearly illustrated in the leading case of *Salomon v A Salomon and Co Ltd* [1897] AC 22.

A number of consequences flow from this separate legal personality, so that a company:

(a) is able to own property;
(b) is liable for its own debts;
(c) can sue its debtors;
(d) can be a party to a contract; and
(e) has 'perpetual succession'–this means that the company does not cease to exist just because a member dies or otherwise ceases to be a member.

2.9 'Lifting the veil of incorporation'

2.9.1 Introduction

There is the possibility for a court to ignore the fact that a company is a separate legal person. Legislation also sometimes ignores the distinction between a company and its members (or directors). These circumstances are metaphorically described as 'lifting the veil of incorporation' or 'piercing the veil' because the law looks behind the legal 'veil' which separates the company from its members and officers to enable the claimant to seek redress directly against those persons.

The occasions when the veil of incorporation will actually be lifted/pierced are hard to classify and very limited. The case of *Prest v Petrodel Resources Ltd* [2013] UKSC 34 suggests considerable judicial reluctance to lift/pierce the veil. The circumstances where the principle might be applied are often far removed from general day-to-day business operations and are confined to situations where the proprietor of a company appears to be gaining an unlawful advantage from the separate legal personality of the company they control or is avoiding a legal obligation by the use of a company as a bulwark against that obligation.

The preferred approach endorsed by *Prest* seems to be to look to other legal concepts, for example agency or tortious liability (if such can be established), as a way of providing a solution to the problem at hand.

2.9.2 Attempts to avoid legal obligations

The courts have occasionally lifted the veil of incorporation by making orders against companies where the proprietors have used a company as a means of avoiding a personal legal obligation. For example, in *Jones v Lipman* [1962] 1 WLR 832 the defendant had contracted to sell land to the plaintiff and later conveyed it to a company in an attempt to avoid the possibility of an order of specific performance (an order of specific performance cannot normally be made once a third party has acquired rights in the subject matter of the contract). The company was owned and controlled by the defendant, and so an order of specific performance was made against both the defendant and the company.

2.9.3 Agency and trusts

In a few cases, the court has held that a company is either an agent for its shareholders or their trustee. The exact scope of these decisions, however, is rather unclear and these cases ought to be regarded as providing exceptions rather than general rules. A company will *not* generally be regarded as either an agent for, or trustee of, its members.

2.9.4 Legislation

The CA 2006 and the Insolvency Act 1986 (IA 1986) contain a number of rules which depart from the general principle of separate legal personality as shown in the following sections.

2.9.4.1 Fraudulent trading

Sections 213 and 246ZA IA 1986 provide that any person who is or was knowingly a party to fraudulent trading by a company whose business is being carried on with intent to defraud creditors or other persons, may be liable to pay the debts of the company. This liability arises only if the company is being wound up or is in administration (although criminal penalties may be imposed for fraudulent trading under s993 CA 2006 even if the company is not being wound up).

2.9.4.2 Wrongful trading

Sections 214 and 246ZB IA 1986 provide that directors of the company may be personally liable in cases of wrongful trading. This arises where a company becomes insolvent and the directors then fail to take steps to protect creditors. This type of liability only arises if the company is being wound up or is in administration.

Section 214 is discussed further in **Chapter 28**.

2.9.4.3 Group accounts

Where companies are members of a group, group accounts must be produced to reflect the fact that the financial transactions of the **subsidiaries** are in reality activities of the holding company (s399 CA 2006).

2.10 Disclosure obligations of companies

2.10.1 Introduction

One of the core concepts of company law is that information about a company, its constitution and its financial status should be made available to the public. (This is one of the 'trade-offs' for limited liability.) The purpose of this policy is to enable anyone interested in the affairs of a company (eg current or prospective shareholders or its creditors) to have access to the information they need to make an informed judgement on the company's financial affairs and the abilities of the company's management.

When entering into any relationship or arrangement with a company, it is prudent to carry out relevant searches to obtain necessary information.

Information is made available by the company:

(a) keeping at its **registered office** records and registers available for inspection by its members and the public;

(b) disclosing financial information to its members through the annual directors' report and annual accounts;

(c) delivering to the Registrar of Companies documents which the Registrar in turn makes available to the public for inspection; and

(d) publishing certain information about the company in **The Gazette**.

We will now look in more detail at the type of company information which is publicly available.

2.10.2 Company searches

While information about a company can be obtained by inspecting the records and registers maintained by the company itself, the initial method of acquiring information on a company is by making a search at the Companies' Registry. The Registrar of Companies keeps copies of the information supplied by the company and this is available for public inspection. The best starting point is to consult the Companies House website to see what information is directly available through the site.

2.10.3 **Information available for inspection**

The information available for inspection at the Companies' Registry includes the following:

(a) a company's articles of association;

(b) particulars of past and current directors and secretary;

(c) particulars of the issue of shares;

(d) particulars of security and charges given in respect of borrowing;

(e) particulars of all **special resolutions** of the shareholders;

(f) notice of the accounting reference date;

(g) notice of any decrease/reduction of capital;

(h) particulars of resolutions granting directors authority to allot shares;

(i) particulars of the address of the registered office;

(j) an annual confirmation statement; and

(k) the accounts.

Of this list, the last two items merit further consideration. Further information on accounting obligations is contained in **Chapter 22**. Submission of an annual confirmation statement is required under s853A CA 2006. (Previously companies were required to submit an annual return.)

The confirmation statement regime requires a company to deliver to Companies House an annual statement (on form CS01) confirming that all information required to be delivered by the company to Companies House in the period to which the statement relates either:

(a) has been delivered; or

(b) is being delivered at the same time as the confirmation statement.

Companies that have had no registrable events in a 12-month period, or that have complied with disclosure and information requirements during that period, simply need to submit a statement to that effect.

Alternatively, when a confirmation statement is submitted, a company is also required to provide:

- a statement of capital;
- details of its principal business activities;
- details of shareholders;

if there have occurred any relevant changes to the above aspects of the company during the period covered by the confirmation statement.

Note that s60 Economic Crime and Corporate Transparency Act 2023 has introduced a new requirement into the CA 2006 that companies must also confirm in their confirmation statement that the future intended activities of the company will be lawful.

2.10.4 **Failure to file annual information**

Both accounts and a confirmation statement are disclosures which Companies House expects a company to make every year. As such, policing default is very easy. For example, failure to submit a confirmation statement in the due time period–14 days from the end of each 12-month review period–is a criminal offence and both the company and all officers thereof who are in default are liable to a fine (s853L CA 2006). (There are similar sanctions in respect of a failure to file accounts–see **22.5**.)

Additionally, persistent failure to comply with filing obligations can be grounds for a **disqualification** order being made against a director (s3 Company Directors Disqualification Act 1986).

KEY POINT SUMMARY

- The primary source of regulation governing companies is the Companies Act 2006.
- There are several types of company available, but by far the most common type is the company limited by shares.
- Companies can be private or public–both are creatures of statute. Most companies are, in fact, private.
- Companies are legally recognised persons in their own right and their existence cannot be conflated with that of shareholders or directors.
- Limited liability for the shareholders of a company is by far the biggest advantage which the corporate form affords; however, the 'trade-off' is that companies and their directors are subject to public disclosure obligations.

CHAPTER 3
Formation of a Limited Company

FUNCTIONING LEGAL KNOWLEDGE

This chapter considers the following functioning legal knowledge included in the SRA's SQE 1 assessment specification:

Business and organisational characteristics (sole trader/partnership/LLP/private and unlisted public companies)

Legal personality and limited liability

Procedures and documentation required to incorporate a company/form a partnership/LLP and other steps required under companies and partnerships legislation to enable the entity to commence operating:

- constitutional documents
- Companies House filing requirements.

Corporate governance and compliance:

- documentary, record-keeping, statutory filing and disclosure requirements

AUTHORITIES UNDERPINNING PRACTICE

The key authorities that underpin this area of practice are listed below. Note that for legislation you are linked to legislation.gov.uk.

Although much of the legislation on this government website is available in its amended form, the incorporation of new amendments into the text of legislation can be delayed. You should refer to legal databases to ensure you are referencing the most up-to-date legislation.

- Companies Act 2006
  https://www.legislation.gov.uk/ukpga/2006/46/contents
- Company, Limited Liability Partnership and Business (Names and Trading Disclosures) Regulations 2015 (SI 2015/17)
  https://www.legislation.gov.uk/uksi/2015/17
- Company, Limited Liability Partnership and Business Names (Sensitive Words and Expressions) Regulations 2014 (SI 2014/3140)
  https://www.legislation.gov.uk/uksi/2014/3140
- Companies (Model Articles) Regulations 2008
  https://www.legislation.gov.uk/uksi/2008/3229

3.1 Introduction

Note that provisions of the Economic Crime and Corporate Transparency Act 2023 (ECCTA 2023) will affect certain elements of this chapter. However, at the time of writing, many provisions of ECCTA 2023 were yet to come into force. Readers should, therefore, confirm the status and content of those provisions at the time of consulting this chapter. Provisions in force at the time of writing will be explained accordingly; a summary of expected changes is given at 3.16.

After consulting this chapter, you will have been introduced to the process by which a *private* limited company is formed and issues which may need to be addressed prior to and immediately following its formation. (For the formation of public companies, refer to **Chapter 4**.)

The usual reason to incorporate a company is to provide an appropriate structure through which a new (or existing) business can be operated. However, it would be a mistake to assume that this is the only reason to create a company. It is, for example, possible to operate a charity under the guise of a company (usually limited by guarantee, rather than shares). A company may, instead, be created to carry out a specific project or to provide particular services.

Further, companies do not have to exist in isolation from each other. An existing company can set up other companies to operate as its subsidiaries; in this way the operations of a large and sophisticated business can be allocated across a group of interconnected companies.

Companies may also be set up to facilitate commercial transactions. For example, a company may be set up to fulfil a specific function within a transaction, or trading assets may be transferred into a newly formed company and that company sold on, rather than the assets themselves being sold.

3.2 Promoters

Those who wish to form a company are usually known as the 'promoters' of the company. There is no legal definition of a promoter; we will use the term 'promoters' to mean any person or persons wishing to set up a company which will be used as a vehicle for their business.

3.3 Pre-incorporation contracts

It is important to advise promoters of their potential liability for any contracts which they might enter into on behalf of the proposed company prior to its incorporation. They may wish to make contracts to rent premises, buy machinery, and so on, prior to the company becoming incorporated. This may be due to a desire to have things 'up and running', so that trading can commence immediately the company is incorporated. This creates a problem, as the company cannot enter into contracts until it has been incorporated. (Until such time, it is not a legal person.) Moreover, the promoters cannot act as its agents since the principal does not exist.

Should the promoters purport to enter into a contract *on behalf of* the unformed company, s51 of the Companies Act 2006 (CA 2006) will apply. This provides that:

> A contract that purports to be made by or on behalf of a company at a time when the company has not been formed has effect, subject to any agreement to the contrary, as one made with the person purporting to act for the company or as agent for it, and he is personally liable on the contract accordingly.

The threat of personal liability means that the safest course is to enter into contracts only after incorporation when they can be entered into by the company.

3.4 Bringing a company into existence

There are two main methods by which a promoter client can be provided with a company. The solicitor may form a new company *from scratch*. This ensures that the company meets the client's particular requirements in every way; that is, the company is effectively 'tailor-made' and brought into existence for the client.

Alternatively, for reasons usually of cost or expediency, the client may use the services of a company-formation agent. Often this can be done relatively simply through the agent's website. Irrespective of the method used, the same requirements have to be met. We will now consider those steps.

3.5 Steps leading to incorporation

All new companies are set up under the provisions of the Companies Act 2006 (the 2006 Act or CA 2006). The main relevant provisions are to be found in Pts 2 and 3 CA 2006. Any promoter of a new company must subscribe their name to a memorandum of association and comply with the requirements for registration (s7 CA 2006). (See **3.6.2** for further discussion of the memorandum of association.) For this reason, promoters are more properly referred to as **subscribers**.

Perhaps the most significant document in the process is the application for registration (s9 CA 2006) known as form IN01. The application for registration must state:

(a) the proposed name of the company (see discussion at **3.6.3**);
(b) the proposed situation of the company's registered office, for example England, Wales, Scotland or Northern Ireland (this will determine the relevant branch of Companies House to which the application must be submitted);
(c) whether or not the liability of the members is to be limited (either by shares or by guarantee), which will normally be the case;
(d) whether or not the company is to be public or private.

Additionally, the application must also contain:

(a) a statement of share capital and initial shareholdings (see **3.9**);
(b) a statement setting out details of any persons who may be registrable persons with significant control (PSCs) or registrable Relevant Legal Entities (RLEs) on incorporation. In very simple terms these will be any initial shareholder with more than 25% of the shares in the company. (Fuller discussion of this topic can be found at **20.3**.);
(c) a statement of the company's proposed officers. Usually this will mean details of those persons who are to be the initial directors of the company. (It is assumed that a company secretary, although another type of officer, is unlikely to be appointed in a private company and will, therefore, not be specifically considered.) A private company need only have one director (s154(1) CA 2006);
(d) a statement of the intended address of the company's registered office (see discussion at **3.6.4**);
(e) an email address (see discussion at **3.6.5**).

Section 13 CA 2006 requires a statement of compliance to be submitted with the application, which is confirmation by all the relevant subscribers that all requirements as to registration have been complied with. This statement is included within form IN01.

A new requirement introduced by s2 ECCTA 2023 is that the subscribers must also confirm in the application for registration that the company is being incorporated for a lawful purpose. (Such a statement will also have to be repeated during each year of a company's life when it submits its annual confirmation statement to Companies House. See **2.10.3** for discussion generally of the confirmation statement.)

If particular articles of association are required (see **3.10** and **Chapter 13**), they should be submitted with the application for registration (s9(5)(b)). If this is not done, the relevant Model Articles will be deemed to be the articles of the company by default (s20 CA 2006).

All these documents must be sent to the Registrar of Companies together with the relevant fee. The size of the fee will be determined by the nature of the application. A 'standard' application is in paper form and will take approximately five days from receipt to process.

Web-based incorporation is possible as an alternative. The fee is less for this type of service and the application is usually processed within 24 hours. However, it is not possible to incorporate every type of company in this way. (Companies House website should be consulted for the most current methods of incorporation available.)

Details of relevant fees are as follows:

Fees for incorporation (as on 1 May 2024)

Digital Incorporation	£50
Software Incorporation	£50
Software Incorporation (same day)	£78
Paper Incorporation	£71

These fees may change, so reference should be made to the Companies House website for the up-to-date position.

As a postscript to the above discussion, it is important to note that a sizeable percentage of companies currently in existence will have been registered under the Companies Act 1985. Companies formed under the 1985 Act will display some differences in their make-up, mostly with regard to their memoranda of association, which can have specific consequences for that type of company. (See **3.6.2** for further discussion of the memorandum of association.)

3.6 Issues to be considered on registration

3.6.1 Introduction

We shall now consider the specific issues which the process of registration raises. There are several features of a company which need to be confirmed to ensure that the proposed company meets specific statutory requirements.

3.6.2 Memorandum of association

Every company must have a memorandum. Historically its principal function was to set out the *raison d'être* of the company and to regulate its dealings with outsiders. Together with the articles, the memorandum formed the constitution of a company.

The position now under the 2006 Act is very different; the memorandum is only relevant to the application for registration (s9(1)). Once a company has been registered, the memorandum is of historical interest only and is not part of the company's constitution. The memorandum needs to contain only two clauses (s8 CA 2006):

(a) a statement of intent of the subscribers (promoters) to form a company;

(b) a statement by the subscribers (promoters) that they agree to become members of the company and to take at least one share each. (In the case of a single member company, there will obviously only be one subscriber.)

An example of a memorandum of association follows.

SPECIMEN COMPANIES ACT 2006 MEMORANDUM

Companies Act 2006

COMPANY HAVING A SHARE CAPITAL

Memorandum of Association of OXP (222) Limited

Each subscriber to this memorandum of association wishes to form a company under the Companies Act 2006 and agrees to become a member of the company and to take at least one share.

Name of each subscriber	***Authentication by each subscriber***
[ ]	*[ ]*

[DETAILS OF SUBSCRIBERS NOT SUPPLIED]
Dated:

Prior to the advent of the CA 2006, the memorandum of a company was a more detailed and more extensive document. The CA 2006 has not, however, downgraded the significance of the memoranda of older companies. Instead, those elements which are no longer required for inclusion in a valid memorandum are deemed to be included within the articles (s28 CA 2006), most notably, the objects clause and the authorised share capital clause. In this way, they still have constitutional effect. For this reason, it is not possible to ignore the contents of the memorandum of a 1985 Act company.

3.6.3 The name of a company

3.6.3.1 Choice of name

Generally, the promoters have freedom of choice as far as the company's name is concerned. The main purpose of a company's name is to indicate a company's status and to differentiate it from all other registered companies. The CA 2006 therefore prohibits the Registrar from registering a company with a name which:

(a) does not end with the word 'limited' (or its Welsh equivalent 'cyfyngedig' if appropriate) if the company is a private limited company (s59 CA 2006);

(b) is the same as that of an existing registered company (s66(1) CA 2006); or

(c) in the opinion of the Secretary of State constitutes a criminal offence, or is offensive (s53 CA 2006).

In addition, the approval of the Secretary of State is necessary for the registration of a company under a name which suggests a connection with the government or a local or public authority (s54 CA 2006 and Sch 4 Company, Limited Liability Partnership and Business (Names and Trading Disclosures) Regulations 2015 (SI 2015/17)).

Furthermore, the inclusion in a company's name of particular words specified in regulations made under s55 CA 2006 (so-called 'sensitive' words) will also require the approval of the Secretary of State. (Details of sensitive words are contained in the Company, Limited Liability Partnership and Business Names (Sensitive Words and Expressions) Regulations 2014 (SI 2014/3140).)

Consultation with the relevant government department or institution specified in the Regulations is usually required before the Registrar gives its approval. (The appropriate departments are listed in the relevant Regulations mentioned earlier.)

If a name is rejected by the Registrar, a certain amount of expense and delay is bound to occur as the application for registration will be rejected. Therefore, to minimise the risk of this happening, the promoters or solicitor should consult the index of company names kept by the Registrar of Companies shortly before the application for registration. If the name is already in use, a new name should be chosen. Further, careful consideration should be given to any name chosen which may either fall within a prohibition or require permission of another.

3.6.3.2 Impact of ECCTA 2023 on choice of name

Control over the choice of company names has been extended by changes made by ECCTA 2023 to the CA 2006. In addition to the restrictions already mentioned, it is now not possible to register a name which either:

(a) contains computer code;

(b) gives the false impression that the company is connected with either a foreign government or an international organisation; or

(c) is intended to facilitate the commission of an offence involving either dishonesty or deception (essentially fraud), or to facilitate the carrying out of conduct that would amount to such an offence in the UK.

To reinforce these extra prohibitions on company names, the Secretary of State now has increased powers to order a change to an existing company's name. (See also discussion which follows regarding compulsory change of name.)

3.6.3.3 Power of Secretary of State to order change of name

The Secretary of State has the power to direct a company to change its name in the following circumstances:

(a) within 12 months of registration, if the name is the same as or, in the opinion of the Secretary of State, too like a name appearing in the index of names at the time of registration (ss67 and 68 CA 2006);

(b) within five years of registration, if misleading information was given at the time of registration for the purposes of a company's registration by a particular name (s75 CA 2006); and

(c) at any time, if the name gives so misleading an indication of the nature of the company's activities as to pose a risk of harm to the public either in the UK or elsewhere (s76 CA 2006).

New provisions introduced by ECCTA 2023 extend the circumstances in which the Secretary of State may direct a company to change its registered name, namely:

(a) where the name was incorrectly registered in contravention of any requirement regarding registered names;

(b) where the name has been used, or is intended to be used, by the company to facilitate the commission of an offence involving either dishonesty or deception, or to facilitate the carrying out of conduct that would amount to such an offence in the UK; and

(c) where the name contains computer code.

ECCTA 2023 has also introduced further provisions to strengthen the above provisions, namely:

(a) No company which has been ordered to change its name can subsequently be registered with that name or one similar to it.

(b) No company can adopt the name of a company which has been ordered to change its name or a name similar to that name where there is a person with a 'relevant relationship' to both companies. Relevant relationship mainly includes a person who is either a shareholder or director. It is presumed that this provision is designed to avoid a situation where an existing company or a newly created company is used to circumvent an existing prohibition on the use of a registered name.

More generally, if a company fails to comply with a direction to change its name, the registrar of companies now has the power to determine a new name for that company.

3.6.3.4 Passing-off

Registration of a company with a particular name does not give the company any protection against a passing-off action if an existing business trades under a similar name and its business is likely to be affected by the similarity.

Additionally, third parties are able to object to a company's registered name on the basis that they already have goodwill in the same or a similar name (s69 CA 2006). Such an objection will have to be made to a company names adjudicator who may or may not uphold the objection (s70 CA 2006).

3.6.3.5 Trade marks

If a company registered a name which included a registered **trade mark** of another business, it would be open to an action for infringement of such trade mark. It may therefore be prudent for the promoters or their solicitor to inspect the trade marks register before applying for registration, should there be any concern in this regard.

3.6.4 Registered office

A company's registered office determines the jurisdiction under which it is formed. For a company to be registered under the CA 2006, its registered office must be situated and remain in the UK. This requirement is satisfied by the need to state both the intended situation of the company's registered office and its actual address in the application for registration (s9(2)(b) and (5)(a) CA 2006).

New provisions introduced into the CA 2006 by ECCTA 2023 now require that a registered office must at all times meet the new definition of an 'appropriate address'. As such, both on an application for registration of a company and on any subsequent change to a registered office, this requirement must be met.

According to the statutory definition, an address will be an appropriate address if:

(a) a document addressed to the company, and delivered there by hand or by post, would be expected to come to the attention of a person acting on behalf of the company, and

(b) the delivery of documents there is capable of being recorded by the obtaining of an acknowledgement of delivery.

It is clear, therefore, that the intention is that the registered office of a company will be more than a 'letterbox'.

Failure to comply with this requirement will be an offence committed by both the relevant company and any directors (and secretary) of that company who are in default of this provision.

3.6.5 Registered email address

Section 29 ECCTA 2023 has introduced a new requirement into CA 2006 for companies to provide details of a registered email address as part of an application for registration. Such an address only qualifies as an appropriate address if, in the ordinary course of events, emails sent to it by Companies House would come to the attention of somebody acting on the company's behalf.

Existing companies will also be required to put such an email address on record at Companies House. Details of this address will have to be provided in the first confirmation statement which the company is required to provide after 4 March 2024.

These requirements are reinforced by an ongoing duty to maintain an appropriate email address. Failure to comply with this requirement will be an offence committed by both the relevant company and any directors (and secretary) of that company who are in default of this provision.

3.7 A company's objects and the *ultra vires* doctrine

3.7.1 Historical background

Because a company is an artificial person, there exists the concept of a company's objects and the powers it is to have. Due to the historical development of this concept, the wording and location of a company's objects can differ from company to company. It is, therefore, important to analyse it chronologically.

Until the introduction of the CA 2006, the objects had to be stated in the memorandum of association. Originally any contracts made, or acts done, by a company not within its stated objects, or reasonably incidental thereto, used to be void on the basis that they were *ultra vires*. Because of this rule, objects clauses were traditionally drafted very widely.

3.7.2 Section 35 CA 1985 (now s39 CA 2006)

The introduction of s35 CA 1985 all but abolished the effect of the *ultra vires* rule in relation to transactions between *a company and an outsider*. (This provision was carried over into s39 CA 2006.) Despite this, many companies still submitted a long form of objects clause when they registered.

An alternative, short-form objects clause was possible under s3A CA 1985, the intention being to allow companies to replace their extensive objects clauses with a single sentence. However, due to uncertainty about the ambit of the clause, many companies adopted a conservative approach and had both the s3A clause and a traditional long-form objects clause following it.

3.7.3 The current position

The position has now been reversed under the CA 2006; the objects of any company now registered will be completely unrestricted, unless a specific provision to the contrary is included in a company's articles (s31 CA 2006). For this reason, the current form of memorandum no longer has to contain an objects clause.

For companies set up otherwise than under the 2006 Act, the importation of the pre-existing objects clause from the memorandum into the articles (s28 CA 2006) has the effect of continuing to impose limits on the company's objects. Therefore, such companies may wish to alter their articles (by special resolution of the shareholders) to remove any such restriction and take advantage of s31 CA 2006.

Overall, the significance of a company's objects is now minimal, especially for those companies registered under the 2006 Act with unrestricted objects. However, directors are under a duty to observe a company's constitution (s171 CA 2006); so, in relevant circumstances, lawyers must continue to determine whether or not a company's constitution restricts its activities in any way.

3.8 **Limited liability**

There exists the possibility of both limited and unlimited companies (see **2.7.1–2.7.3**). As such, the status of a company's members should be indicated in the application for registration (s9(2)(c) -CA 2006). For the purposes of this discussion, members will want the benefit of limited liability.

3.9 **Initial shareholders and share capital**

Most companies will be created with a share capital. In turn, this means that those companies must have shareholders, although it is possible to set up a company with only one shareholder (s7(1) CA 2006). A company's initial shareholders will be the subscribers to the memorandum, who must agree to take a minimum of one share each (s8(1)(b) CA 2006).

Specific details of the subscribers' shareholdings must be set out in the statement of capital and initial shareholdings, which forms part of form IN01. This statement will provide details of:

(a) the total number of shares taken on formation by the subscribers;

(b) the aggregate nominal value of those shares;

(c) the rights attaching to those shares;

(d) the number, nominal value and class of shares taken by each subscriber and the amount paid up on each share.

Specific discussion of a company's share capital is contained in **Chapter 7**. For these purposes, it is sufficient to recognise that all shares must have a nominal financial value attributed to them, normally denominated in pounds sterling. In turn, the relevant shareholder will normally agree to pay the company an amount at least equivalent to the nominal value of the shares subscribed for.

EXAMPLE

Charles and William set up a company by subscribing to the memorandum. They each agree to take 50 shares fully paid with a nominal value each of £1. As a consequence:

(a) The total nominal value of shares taken by Charles and William is £100.

(b) Each of Charles and William will have a shareholding with a nominal value of £50 and will, accordingly, each have to pay to the company £50.

It should be noted, in addition, that both Charles and William will qualify as persons with initial significant control, as they both own more than 25% of the share capital in the company. (See 20.3 for discussion of this topic.)

Often ordinary shares will be sufficient for the promoters of a company, but shares with specifically enhanced or restricted rights may also be thought necessary. (Again, see **Chapter 7** for discussion of share rights.)

3.10 The articles of association

This important topic has already been considered briefly at **2.5** and a fuller discussion can be found in **Chapter 13**. This section, therefore, simply acts as an introduction.

The articles are the main constitutional document of a company (s17 CA 2006). They regulate the company's internal affairs and contain provisions dealing with such matters as directors' powers, proceedings at shareholders' meetings and conduct of board meetings.

By statutory implication, a company and all its members are bound into the provisions of the articles (s33(1) CA 2006). When preparing to incorporate a company, one of the most important matters to discuss with the promoters is the contents of the articles and their effect.

A company is able to choose the type of articles it thinks appropriate, but standard-form articles have been provided by statutory instrument for many years to assist with the process. The latest versions of these are referred to as the Model Articles and are set out in the Companies (Model Articles) Regulations 2008.

Effectively, a company has four choices:

(a) It can have prepared specially drafted articles from scratch. (This is likely to be a rare occurrence and will be expensive.)

(b) It can adopt standard articles supplied by its legal advisors (or formation agents) with or without amendment.

(c) It can adopt the Model Articles wholesale with no amendments.

(d) It can adopt the Model Articles but with bespoke amendments.

With the exception of choice (c), a company must register a copy of its chosen articles as part of its application for registration. A failure to do so will mean that the Model Articles will apply to the company by default (s20 CA 2006).

3.11 The certificate of incorporation

Upon a successful application for registration of a company, Companies House will generate a certificate of incorporation stating that the company is incorporated on a particular date and that it is limited (if appropriate). The Registrar of Companies specifies the company's unique registered number on the certificate and this must be quoted on all official documents and business letters.

From the date of incorporation the company becomes a legal entity (s16(3) CA 2006). At the same time as the Registrar issues the certificate, they must (under s1064 CA 2006) officially notify the fact of issue by placing a notice to that effect in the government's official 'newspaper' (in England and Wales, *The Gazette*).

3.12 Steps necessary after incorporation

Once the certificate of incorporation has been issued, the company's existence begins. One of the first things which is likely to happen is for the board of directors to conduct its first meeting. The agenda for this will include such matters as:

(a) The approval and execution of any service contracts for directors. (See **15.2.5** for further discussion.)

(b) The allotment of any shares over and above those allocated to the subscribers to the memorandum.

(c) The appointment of **auditors** to the company (if thought necessary).

(d) The appointment of bankers to the company.

(e) Instructions to make the necessary entries in relevant registers of the company, most notably the register of members. (See **Chapter 20** for further discussion of record-keeping by companies.)

(f) Alteration of the company's automatically designated accounting reference date (if thought necessary). (See **21.3** for further discussion.)

In turn, items (a) and (b) may require reference to the shareholders. This would also require the calling of a **general meeting** of the shareholders or the circulation to them of a **written resolution** to seek their approval. (See **Chapter 18** for further discussion of shareholder decision-making.)

3.13 Publication of a company's name

3.13.1 Statutory requirements

There are several statutory provisions concerning publication of a company's name. Note, however, that whilst the 2006 Act imposes the obligation to make disclosures, the detailed provisions are contained within the Company, Limited Liability Partnership and Business (Names and Trading Disclosures) Regulations 2015.

3.13.2 Disclosure of registered name

A company is required to:

(a) display its registered name at its registered office, any other place of business in which its business is carried on and at any location where there is available for inspection company records, other than the registered office (a so-called 'inspection place');

(b) ensure that its registered name appears on business letters, correspondence and documentation, notices, official publications, cheques, orders for money or goods, invoices and websites.

3.13.3 Additional disclosures

A company's business letters, order forms and website should also contain the following information:

(a) the place (ie country) of registration of the company;

(b) its registered number;

(c) the address of its registered office.

There is no need to include the names of directors on a company's stationery, but if the name of *any* director appears on a business letter (other than in the text or as a signatory) on which the company's name appears, then the names of *all* the directors who are individuals and the corporate names of all the corporate directors must appear in legible characters.

3.13.4 Penalties for default

Failure to comply with any of these disclosure requirements without reasonable excuse makes the company and every officer authorising the issue of a letter etc, liable to a fine.

3.14 Striking off

In theory, once a company is created, it enjoys perpetual succession, that is, its existence is independent of the persons involved with it. However, it may be that the existence of a company is brought to an end involuntarily by intervention of the registrar of companies–so-called striking off. Under s1000 CA 2006 the registrar may take such action where it has reasonable cause to believe that a company is not carrying on business or is not in operation. If the company is subsequently struck off, it will be treated as dissolved and will cease to be recognised as a corporate entity.

More relevant to this discussion, however, is the fact that s70 ECCTA 2023 will introduce a new provision into the CA 2006 which will allow the registrar of companies to strike off a company where the registrar has reasonable cause to believe that information supplied to it as part of the application for registration of the company was either misleading, false or deceptive. (At the time of writing, this section was not yet in force. The reader should, therefore, check the status of this provision for the up-to-date position.)

3.15 Conduct/ethical matters

If a solicitor is approached by two or more persons and instructed to create a company for those persons, the issue of a conflict of interest should be considered. If all those persons are to have equal status within the company, for example they are all to be directors and to invest equivalent sums for equivalent shareholdings, there is unlikely to be an issue. However, if each person has varying perspectives on their involvement and the size and format of investment they are likely to make, the solicitor needs to recognise that such a difference may result in a conflict of interest between those clients.

Even if there is a possibility of conflict, the exception regarding substantial common interest may allow the solicitor to act for all clients to achieve their goal. To a large extent, this will depend on the variances between the clients' perspectives and compliance with the required conditions to take advantage of the exception. In any event, compliance with Principle 7, to act in the best interest of a client, should be an overriding factor.

Alternatively, if the scope of the clients' instruction is simply to provide a registered company, there is unlikely to be an issue; however, if the solicitor's involvement subsequently extends beyond this to involvement in funding arrangements between prospective shareholders, the solicitor must not act for all those shareholders.

The fact that a company is a legal person in its own right also raises an important consideration regarding with whom the retainer rests. A lawyer cannot represent the individual interests of shareholders or directors and also advise the company itself. For example, if the retainer is with the company and a new director is to be appointed, operating under a service contract, the solicitor cannot advise that new director on the legal implications of their proposed relationship with the company, even though the proposal has originated with the company. The proposed director must seek independent legal advice.

The incorporation of companies is also recognised as an area where money laundering may be facilitated. For example, proceeds of crime could be used to capitalise a company (by buying shares in it) and the company could spend that money in its own name, for example by leasing cars for its directors. A solicitor should be sensitive to any instructions in this regard which appear abnormal.

EXAMPLE

Mary receives instructions from her client to incorporate a company for that client, as its sole director and shareholder. After discussions with the client regarding the proposed purpose of the company, to which the answers from the client are somewhat vague and evasive, the client indicates that they would like to subscribe for £50,000 worth of shares in the company. The client indicates that they would rather not borrow money at the outset to generate working capital for the company.

The solicitor at this point should be, at the very least, uneasy about these instructions, not least because there is no clear indication of a defined business purpose for the company and because the initial funding seems disproportionate. (It should be remembered that an offence will be committed under s330 of the Proceeds of Crime Act 2002, if the solicitor fails to make an appropriate disclosure when they know or suspect or have reasonable grounds for knowing or suspecting that money laundering is occurring.)

Two months later, the same client contacts the solicitor asking for a subsidiary of the original company to be created. The proposal is that the original company will take £25,000 worth of shares in the new subsidiary. Again, the client is not very forthcoming in explaining why a subsidiary company is necessary. Also, when asked about how the original company will pay for the shares in the subsidiary, the client explains that they are going to lend the original company the money.

There are clear indicators that should lead to a suspicion that money laundering is taking place and the solicitor should make a disclosure to the firm's Money Laundering Reporting Officer who, in turn, may make a disclosure to the National Crime Agency. Additionally, the solicitor should not continue to process the client's instructions until the outcome of this process has been confirmed. Should the client, in the meantime, insist on a speedy resolution to this matter, the solicitor should avoid using their suspicion of money laundering as a way of justifying the delay–this will likely amount to 'tipping off' the client, which is an offence under s333A of the Proceeds of Crime Act 2002.

If instructions come from a new client, it will be essential to comply with the due diligence requirements of the Money Laundering Regulations 2017 before establishing a business relationship with the client. Again, the client may be an individual, for example seeking advice in their capacity as a shareholder, or it may be a company which is seeking advice, for example in respect of a purchase of its own shares.

In simple terms, if the new client is an individual, the lawyer must:

1. Identify the customer.
2. Verify the identity of the customer.
3. Inquire as to the purpose or nature of the business relationship.

In simple terms, if the new client is a company, the lawyer must obtain and verify:

1. The name of the company.
2. The registered number of the company.
3. The registered office of the company.
4. Details of the control structure of the company, including any beneficial ownership.
5. The governing law under which the company operates.
6. Details of the directors/senior management of the company.

In turn, items 4 and 6 may require verification of the persons identified.

Much of the above can be found by conducting a company search against the company at Companies House, although it may not be sufficient to rely solely upon the results of such a search, especially in respect of beneficial ownership of shares. In any event, if the company is incorporated in another jurisdiction, the approach taken may have to vary.

3.16 Impact of the Economic Crime and Corporate Transparency Act 2023

3.16.1 Introduction

This section sets out the changes to be brought into effect by the above (in addition to those which have already been introduced and discussed). These changes are expected to result in alterations to processes at Companies House which deal with incorporation of companies. *As such, the reader should both confirm the status of the law and the impact on Companies House's procedures at the time of reading.*

3.16.2 Additional requirements for incorporation

Further information is expected to be necessary on future applications for registration, namely, a statement that none of the subscribers is disqualified from acting as a director under the directors' disqualification legislation (see **14.8**).

Another important stipulation will be that any proposed director of a new company must at the time of application for registration neither be:

(a) disqualified under the directors disqualification legislation; nor

(b) otherwise ineligible to be appointed as a director by virtue of any other legislation.

A statement to this effect will have to be made by the subscribers to the memorandum of association as part of the application for registration. (Note, however, that s40 ECCTA 2023 has already introduced a specific prohibition into the CA 2006 that no person may be appointed a director if already disqualified.)

A further stipulation will be that any person likely to have significant control at the outset must not be at that time disqualified as acting as a director under the directors disqualification legislation. A statement to this effect will have to be included as part of the application for registration.

In respect of any proposed director, it will be necessary to have their identity verified in advance by Companies House. A statement confirming this fact must be included in the application for registration.

In respect of any proposed PSC or RLE of the proposed new company, it will not be necessary to confirm verification of their identities at the time of application for registration, although it will be optional to do so. If such verification does not accompany the application, the registrar of companies will subsequently require such persons to provide a statement regarding verification of their identities. PSCs, as natural persons, will be able to do this personally. RLEs, as corporate entities, will, instead, be required to notify the identity of its relevant officer and their verified status. A relevant officer will usually be a natural person who is either a director of the RLE, where such is a company, or a member of the RLE, where such is a limited liability partnership. In turn, that relevant officer will have to confirm their status as such a person. (See **20.3** for discussion generally of PSCs and RLEs.)

KEY POINT SUMMARY

The registration of a company raises several important considerations, in particular:

- Who are to be the first directors?
- Who will be the subscribers and how many shares will they each take?
- Will the company's share capital comprise entirely of ordinary shares or will alternative types of shares also be necessary?
- What name will be given to the company?
- Can the company operate with a 'generic' constitution or will something more bespoke be necessary?
- Where will the company's registered office be located?

CHAPTER 4
Public Companies

FUNCTIONING LEGAL KNOWLEDGE

This chapter considers the following functioning legal knowledge included in the SRA's SQE 1 assessment specification:

Business and organisational characteristics (sole trader/partnership/LLP/private and unlisted public companies)

Legal personality and limited liability

Procedures and documentation required to incorporate a company/form a partnership/LLP and other steps required under companies and partnerships legislation to enable the entity to commence operating:

- constitutional documents
- Companies House filing requirements

Corporate governance and compliance:

- company decision-making and meetings: procedural, disclosure and approval requirements
- documentary, record-keeping, statutory filing and disclosure requirements

AUTHORITIES UNDERPINNING PRACTICE

The key authorities that underpin this area of practice are listed below. Note that for legislation you are linked to legislation.gov.uk.

Although much of the legislation on this government website is available in its amended form, the incorporation of new amendments into the text of legislation can be delayed. You should refer to legal databases to ensure you are referencing the most up-to-date legislation.

- Companies Act 2006
  https://www.legislation.gov.uk/ukpga/2006/46

4.1 Introduction

After consulting this chapter, you will have been introduced to the distinguishing features of a public company. You are advised to have read **Chapters 1** and **2** first, before considering this chapter.

It is possible to create three different types of company:

(a) a company limited by shares;

(b) a company limited by guarantee; and

(c) an unlimited company.

It is possible to incorporate all three types of company as a private company but only companies limited by shares can be public companies.

The differences between public and private companies are important and we will consider them briefly in this chapter. In addition, we will look at the rules for re-registering a private company as a public company and vice versa.

Although the most well-known companies in the country will (with a few exceptions) be public companies, they represent a tiny minority of the total number of companies registered at the Companies' Registry.

Also, being a public company does not automatically mean the company is listed. This is a common misconception. Only a public company which has been successful in gaining a listing of its shares and whose shares have been admitted to trading is referred to in practice as a 'listed company'.

4.2 Definition of a public company

A public company is defined by s4(2) of the Companies Act 2006 (CA 2006) as a company whose certificate of incorporation states that it is public.

4.3 Differences between public and private companies

The following is a non-exhaustive list of some of the differences between public and private companies.

4.3.1 Name

The name of a public company must end with the words 'Public Limited Company' or its equivalent. Equivalent for this purpose includes 'PLC' (although there is no requirement that these letters be capitalised) and, for Welsh companies, Cwmni Cyfyngedig Cyhoeddus (or CCC).

4.3.2 The company's memorandum of association

As the memorandum is simply a registration document, expressing the wish of those setting up the company to be formed as one (s8 CA 2006), there is no difference between the memorandum of a public and private company. Instead, the registration document (form IN01) will have to include a statement that the company should be public. If registration is successful, the fact that the certificate of incorporation states that the company is public will be sufficient evidence of the fact (s4(2) CA 2006).

4.3.3 Amount of share capital

The nominal value of the public company's issued share capital must not be less than the 'authorised minimum' which is currently £50,000 (s763(1) CA 2006). When a public company allots shares, it is under an obligation to ensure that at least 25% of the nominal value of each of the shares issued (plus the whole amount of any premium on the shares) is paid on allotment (s586 CA 2006).

4.3.4 Number of members and officers

The 2006 Act permits single-member public companies (s7(1) CA 2006). However, in contrast to private companies, public companies must appoint at least two directors (s154(2) CA 2006). Also, public companies must have a suitably qualified secretary appointed (ss271 and 273 CA 2006).

4.3.5 The issue of shares or debentures

The principal advantage which a public company has over a private company is its ability to raise capital by offering shares or debentures to the public for cash or other consideration; private companies are prohibited from doing so (s755 CA 2006).

(Note that offers of shares to the public are governed by Pt VI of the Financial Services and Markets Act 2000. These require the publication of a prospectus approved by the Financial Conduct Authority (FCA) in any case where shares are to be 'offered to the public' within the terms of the legislation.)

4.3.6 Trading certificate

Before the public company can do business or borrow money, the company must obtain from the Registrar a trading certificate which will only be issued if the Registrar is satisfied that the company's share capital is adequate (s761 CA 2006). The procedure which the company must go through to get this trading certificate involves a director or the company secretary filing a statement of compliance with the Registrar. The declaration will state that the nominal value of the company's allotted share capital is at least equal to the authorised minimum (of £50,000). The company must also supply details of:

(a) the amount paid up on the allotted share capital;
(b) the amount of the preliminary expenses and details of who will meet them; and
(c) any amount or benefit paid to the company's promoters.

A company which does not obtain a trading certificate before it commences business can face some severe consequences (s767 CA 2006). If the company fails to meet its obligations in connection with a transaction entered into at a time when it does not have a trading certificate, the directors will be jointly and severally liable to indemnify the other parties to the transaction for any loss. Furthermore, both the company and its officers will be liable to a fine and, if the company fails to obtain this certificate within one year of its registration, the court can wind the company up (s122 Insolvency Act 1986).

4.4 Special rules applicable to public companies

A public company can raise capital by offering shares to the public. This can give the company a much wider source of potential investors than is the case with a private company. The price of this is that to protect the public, public companies are subject to a number of restrictions which do not apply to private companies.

4.4.1 Payment for share capital

(a) The original subscribers to a public company's memorandum are required to pay cash for their shares (s584 CA 2006).
(b) At least 25% of the nominal value and the whole of any premium on shares in a public company must be paid on allotment (s586(1) CA 2006).
(c) A public company cannot accept an undertaking to do work or perform services as consideration for the allotment of shares (s585(1) CA 2006). (In any event, it is unusual for a private company to seek such consideration for any allotment it may make.)
(d) A public company can allot shares for non-cash consideration, but the company must take steps to satisfy itself that the value of the assets to be transferred to the company is appropriate by obtaining an expert's valuation and report (ss593(1) and 596 CA 2006).

4.4.2 Pre-emption rights on the allotment of shares

A public company, unlike a private company, cannot make a general exclusion of the statutory pre-emption rights set out in s561 CA 2006 by a provision in its articles. However, in respect of specified allotments where the directors are authorised to make those allotments, a public company (like a private company) can exclude these pre-emption rights by passing a special resolution or through a provision in its articles (ss570 and 571 CA 2006).

4.4.3 Serious loss of capital

The directors of a public company are under an obligation to convene a general meeting if the company's **net assets** are 50% or less of its **called-up share capital**. The purpose of the meeting is for the problem to be considered, but the governing provision (s656 CA 2006) does not require the directors to take any definite steps to remedy the position.

4.4.4 Purchase by a public company of its own shares

Public companies, like private companies, can buy back their own shares and issue **redeemable shares**. However, only private companies can use capital to purchase or redeem shares (s709 CA 2006).

4.4.5 Financial assistance for the acquisition of shares and loans to directors

The rules prohibiting companies from providing financial assistance for the purchase of their own shares now only apply to public companies (s678 CA 2006). (See **Chapter 11** for further discussion of this topic.) If this situation could impede a proposed transaction, the answer may be to re-register the company as private to avoid the prohibition (see **4.5**).

4.4.6 Loans to directors

Whilst loans to directors by all types of company will require shareholders' approval by **ordinary resolution** (subject to a number of exceptions), only quasi-loans to, and credit transactions with, directors of public companies or of private companies associated with public companies need similar shareholders' approval (ss197–214 CA 2006). (For the meaning of 'associated' in this context, see s256 CA 2006.)

4.4.7 Distribution of profits

In addition to the general rules restricting the funds from which companies can make distributions, s831 CA 2006 imposes extra conditions on a public company before it can make a distribution, as follows:

(a) Its net assets must not be less than the aggregate of its called-up share capital and undistributable reserves.

(b) The distribution itself must not reduce the net assets to less than the above aggregate.

The undistributable reserves are:

(a) Its share premium account (which will reflect any premium paid to the company by shareholders for their shares).

(b) Its capital redemption reserve (which will have been created if any buy-back of shares has occurred).

(c) The amount by which its accumulated, unrealised profits exceed its accumulated, unrealised losses (on the basis that only realised sums are relevant in the context of distributions).

(d) Any other reserve it is prevented from distributing, either by statute or its articles.

If this prohibition applies and the company wishes to continue to make a distribution, the usual approach is to reduce the share capital, such that the aggregate is then less than the net assets.

4.4.8 Accounting requirements

The provisions which permit 'small' and 'medium-sized' companies to prepare and file less detailed accounts with the Registrar of Companies do not apply to public companies. (See **Chapter 22** for further discussion.)

4.4.9 Written resolutions

The ability of the members of private companies to take decisions by written resolutions rather than passing resolutions at general meetings does not extend to public companies (s 288 CA 2006).

4.4.10 Annual general meetings

In contrast to private companies, the CA 2006 requires public companies to hold **annual general meetings** (s336 CA 2006) and public companies are likely to continue to use these as an opportunity to fulfil their statutory obligations to lay audited accounts before a general meeting (s437 CA 2006) and to re-appoint auditors annually (s489 CA 2006).

4.5 Re-registration of a private company to a public company and vice versa

4.5.1 Introduction

Given the various special rules to which public companies are subject, promoters of a company are unlikely to want to incorporate their company as a public company unless they intend to issue securities in the company to the public within the foreseeable future. However, many companies start life as private companies and are then converted into public companies, usually so that they can be listed and have their shares traded on the Stock Exchange.

Equally, although perhaps less frequently, the shareholders and/or directors of a public company may decide to convert the company into a private company. They may do so for a variety of reasons, for example:

(a) to avoid the prohibition on financial assistance by public companies;
(b) where the board has decided that the company's securities should no longer be in public hands (normally because of the wish to assume a greater control over the company without reference to external investors–this is often referred to as a 'public to private' deal);
(c) after a successful **takeover**, where the purchaser of the shares in the takeover target wants the target to continue to operate as a wholly owned private subsidiary.

4.5.2 Re-registration of a private company as a public company

The relevant procedure is set out in ss90–96 CA 2006. A private company cannot be re-registered unless it satisfies the various requirements in relation to share capital to which public companies are subject (as explained earlier).

Provided the requirements with regard to share capital are satisfied, the company must pass a special resolution which:

(a) states that the company should be re-registered as a public company; and
(b) alters the company's articles to meet the company's new circumstances (by, eg, removing restrictions on transferability).

Once the resolution has been passed, an application for re-registration has to be submitted to the Registrar of Companies (on form RR01) with:

(a) a printed copy of the company's articles in their altered form;
(b) a copy of the special resolution;
(c) a copy of a statement in writing by the company's auditors confirming that the company's net assets are not less than the combined total of its called-up share capital and distributable reserves;

(d) a copy of the balance sheet on which the auditors based their written statement referred to in (c) above together with an unqualified report on the balance sheet by the company's auditors;
(e) certain reports and statutory declarations where shares have been allotted for non-cash consideration since the date of the balance sheet;
(f) confirmation of the details of the proposed secretary where the company does not have a secretary at the time (s94(1)(b) CA 2006); and
(g) a fee of £71.

Once the Registrar of Companies is satisfied with these papers, a certificate will be issued confirming that the company has been re-registered as a public limited company (s96 CA 2006). The changes to the company's articles and name also take effect as a result.

4.5.3 **Re-registration of a public company as a private company**

It is easier for a public company to be re-registered as a private company for the reason that there are no specific criteria for private companies to fulfil (with the exception of having at least one director and one shareholder). Section 97 CA 2006 stipulates that a company must pass a special resolution by which it:

(a) resolves to re-register as a private company;
(b) removes the words 'public limited company' (or their equivalent) from its name and replaces them with 'limited'; and
(c) makes any other alterations to the articles of the company to suit its new circumstances.

An application to re-register pursuant to s100 CA 2006 must be delivered to the Registrar (on form RR02), together with the special resolution, a printed copy of the altered articles and the relevant fee of £71.

Once the Registrar of Companies is satisfied with these papers, a certificate will be issued confirming that the company has been re-registered as a private limited company (s101 CA 2006). The change to the company's articles and name also take effect as a result.

One consequence of a public company re-registering as a private company is that its securities may be less easily transferred. Therefore, pursuant to s98 minority shareholders have the right to apply to the court within 28 days of the special resolution being passed to have the resolution cancelled. Such an application for cancellation can only be made by:

(a) shareholders holding not less than 5% of the nominal value of the company's issued share capital (or for any class of the share capital, if there is more than one); or
(b) not less than 50 of the company's members.

The application for cancellation can only be made by a person who has not consented to or voted in favour of the resolution and the court can make an order either cancelling or confirming the resolution on such terms and conditions as it thinks fit (which could, eg, include ordering that the company should buy the shares of the dissentient member or members).

KEY POINT SUMMARY

- Public companies are creatures of statute and much of the law which governs them can be found in the Companies Act 2006.
- Public companies are subject to more stringent requirements and restrictions than private companies.
- The method of creation of public companies is no different to that for private companies.

- There are specific requirements which need to be fulfilled if a company is to be public, namely:
  - a public company must have a minimum of two directors;
  - a public company must appoint a suitably qualified secretary;
  - a public company must fulfil minimum share capital requirements;
  - a public company must apply for a trading certificate from Companies House before it can undertake business operations or borrow money.
- It should also be noted that the status of a company is not fixed and can be converted from private to public and vice versa.

CHAPTER 5
Fundamentals of Partnerships

FUNCTIONING LEGAL KNOWLEDGE

This chapter considers the following functioning legal knowledge included in the SRA's SQE 1 assessment specification:

Business and organisational characteristics (sole trader/partnership/LLP/private and unlisted public companies)

Legal personality and limited liability

Procedures and documentation required to incorporate a company/form a partnership/LLP and other steps required under companies and partnerships legislation to enable the entity to commence operating:

- constitutional documents

Finance:

- financial records, information and accounting requirements

Partnership decision-making and authority of partners:

- procedures and authority under the Partnership Act 1890

AUTHORITIES UNDERPINNING PRACTICE

The key authorities that underpin this area of practice are listed below. Note that for legislation you are linked to legislation.gov.uk.

Although much of the legislation on this government website is available in its amended form, the incorporation of new amendments into the text of legislation can be delayed. You should refer to legal databases to ensure you are referencing the most up-to-date legislation.

- Partnership Act 1890
  https://www.legislation.gov.uk/ukpga/Vict/53-54/39
- Companies Act 2006
  https://www.legislation.gov.uk/ukpga/2006/46
- Company, Limited Liability Partnership and Business (Names and Trading Disclosures) Regulations 2015 (SI 2015/17)
  https://www.legislation.gov.uk/uksi/2015/17
- Company, Limited Liability Partnership and Business Names (Sensitive Words and Expressions) Regulations 2014 (SI 2014/3140)
  https://www.legislation.gov.uk/uksi/2014/3140

5.1 Introduction

After consulting this chapter, you will have been introduced to the rules for determining whether a partnership has come into existence and the essential features of a partnership, more particularly:

(a) the definition of partnership;

(b) the nature and effect of partnership;

(c) number of partners;

(d) the duration of partnership;

(e) the partnership name and publicity of information.

The traditional business structures in the UK are sole traders, partnerships and companies. Since 2001, the business medium of the limited liability partnership (LLP) has also been in existence and has grown in significance. This is discussed in **Chapter 6**.

Sole traders tend to be relatively small concerns, as do partnerships, although a number of professional partnerships did overturn this assumption for many years, prior to the introduction of LLPs. Companies cover the full spectrum of business sizes.

To put this into perspective, statistical information released by the Department for Business, Energy and Industrial Strategy in 2020 showed the breakdown of *actively trading* businesses in the UK was as follows:

(a) 3.5 million sole traders;

(b) 2 million companies (this figure includes both companies and LLPs. Note that the number of companies actually in existence is far higher);

(c) 414,000 partnerships.

As such, whilst most trading activities are carried out by sole traders and companies, partnerships are still relatively numerous.

Chapters 23–27 of this manual cover partnerships in more detail; this chapter operates as an introduction.

This manual will not consider the rules relating to limited partnerships created under the Limited Partnership Act 1907 nor will sole traders be considered.

5.2 Relevant law

Much of the law relating to partnerships is to be found in the Partnership Act 1890 (PA 1890). The PA 1890 was mainly declaratory of the law of partnership as it had developed up to 1890 and does not provide a complete code of partnership law, and indeed s46 specifically provides that:

> The rules of equity and of common law applicable to partnership shall continue in force except so far as they are inconsistent with the express provisions of this Act.

5.3 Definition of partnership

The definition of a partnership is to be found in s1(1) PA 1890, which states:

> Partnership is the relation which subsists between persons carrying on a business in common with a view of profit

(Note that the relationship between members in a company is specifically excluded as a partnership relationship by s1(2) PA 1890.)

To satisfy the definition, two or more persons must be carrying on a business with the intention of making a profit. It follows from this that an agreement to run a business in the future does not constitute an immediate partnership, nor does the taking of preliminary steps to enable a business to be run. 'Business' is defined by s45 PA 1890 as including 'every trade, occupation or profession'.

Section 2 PA 1890 lays down certain 'rules for determining the existence of a partnership'. These provide that:

(a) Joint or common ownership of property 'does not of itself create a partnership' even where profits from the property are shared (s2(1));

(b) The sharing of *gross* returns does not of itself create a partnership (s2(2)). A person is not, therefore, a partner in a business merely because they receive commission on sales which they have introduced.

(c) The receipt of a share of *profits* is prima facie evidence of partnership (s2(3)). This topic is dealt with in **23.6**.

It should be noted that a written partnership agreement is *not* a prerequisite for the existence of a partnership. The existence of a partnership is *always* a question of fact. It can be the case, therefore, that without any formal acknowledgement of the creation of a partnership, people can find themselves in a partnership relationship. In turn, any subsequent dispute between those parties would have to be determined by the rules of partnership and any attempt to bring the relationship to an end will similarly be governed by special rules.

EXAMPLE

Andy and Fatima are both made redundant. As a way of earning a living, Andy and Fatima start buying old furniture to renovate, the intention being that such items can be sold on at a profit. Andy has a small workshop in which they do this. The cost of any items bought and renovated is shared 50:50 between Andy and Fatima and any profit generated is split 50:50.

After six months of this activity, each of Andy and Fatima has made £1,500. There is every chance that Andy and Fatima have formed a partnership.

5.4 Nature and effect of partnership

A partnership is, in law, a very different type of institution from a company. The most significant difference is that partners have unlimited liability for the debts of the partnership business, whereas the liability of shareholders for a company's debts is (usually) limited. (The liability of partners to creditors is considered specifically in **Chapter 24**.)

Partnerships, unlike companies, are not required to go through any registration process when they are formed and, again unlike companies, they are under no obligation to make their accounts public.

A partnership is not a separate legal entity from its partners (in contrast to companies, which are legally distinct from their shareholders). As such, a partnership could be regarded as a matrix of legal (and equitable) relationships and obligations between the partners.

This also has implications for third parties who deal with a partnership–effectively they will be contracting with each and every partner. Third parties who deal with companies are contracting solely with that entity (unless they make specific provision to contract with directors or shareholders).

As a means of recognising the differences which exist between a partnership and a company, the former is commonly referred to as a *firm*.

5.5 Number of partners

Historically, the maximum number of partners allowed to form a partnership was 20, although numerous exemptions to this limit existed. This rule was abolished in 2002, so that no limits now apply in any circumstances.

5.6 Capacity to create a partnership

Generally speaking, any person is legally capable of forming a partnership with any other person. Additionally, companies can enter into a partnership with other companies or with individuals. (This is a consequence of a company being a legally recognised person. The same is also true of limited liability partnerships–see **Chapter 6**.)

EXAMPLE

Three individuals, Martin, Berta and Carole, enter into a partnership with each other. Alternatively, it would also be possible for each of those persons to set up a private limited company, of which they were the sole director and shareholder. In turn, those three companies could agree to form a partnership.

5.7 Duration of partnership

Many partnerships are partnerships 'at will'. This means that no particular period is agreed upon for the duration of the partnership. A partnership at will can be dissolved (ie brought to an end) by notice by any partner unless there is an agreement to the contrary (see ss26(1) and 32(c) PA 1890).

A partnership for a fixed term or for a term defined by reference to some event (eg the completion of some particular job) is also possible. Such a partnership cannot generally be dissolved by notice.

There may sometimes be difficulty in deciding when a partnership begins. Because of the way a partnership is defined, this is essentially a question of fact. The terms of a partnership agreement (should one exist) as to commencement may be evidence (though not conclusive) of when a partnership began. (We have already seen that partnerships can begin inadvertently through the actions of partners. There may be instances, therefore, where partners formally enter into a partnership agreement, but the partnership has already come into existence.)

Because a partnership is a 'bundle' of legal relationships, a partnership is made up the actual partners. A change in the identity of the partners will, therefore, be legally significant.

EXAMPLE

Assume Noah and Robbie are in partnership. If Martina is admitted as a new partner to the firm and the business continues, technically speaking, this will bring to an end the partnership between Noah and Robbie and create a new one, which comprises Noah, Robbie and Martina.

Assume, instead, that Daniel, Ronan and Roman are in partnership and Roman dies. Again, the original partnership no longer exists. Significantly, unless the contrary is agreed, the partnership will have been dissolved by Roman's death, which will trigger the rules regarding distribution of partnership assets between creditors and partners.

The lifespan of a partnership can be seen as rather unpredictable. This is a compelling reason for the partners to enter into a formal agreement, so proper provision can be made in anticipation of events which can affect the duration of a partnership.

5.8 Partnership name and publicity of information

A partnership is entitled (subject to what is said later) to choose any name which it wishes. There is nothing in partnership law corresponding with the requirement that a company should have a corporate name which is registered with the Registrar of Companies.

The law relating to partnership names is contained in Pt 41 of the Companies Act 2006 (CA 2006). The Act permits the free use of certain names and requires approval for others. In addition, it contains rules requiring publicity as to the membership of partnerships in certain circumstances.

5.8.1 Automatically permitted names

If the business of a partnership is carried on under a name which consists of the surnames of all the partners, no restrictions apply (s1192 CA 2006). This is also the case where the name consists of the partners' surnames together with 'permitted additions' and nothing else. The permitted additions are:

(a) the forenames or initials of the partners;

(b) the addition of an 's' to a surname to signify that there is more than one partner with that name; and/or

(c) a statement that the business is being carried on in succession to the business of a former owner.

Where the name of the partnership does not consist solely of the surnames of the partners, or of the surnames of the partners together with permitted additions, then the disclosure requirements of s1200 CA 2006 will apply and in some cases approval of the name may be required under either s1193 or s1194.

5.8.2 Disclosure requirements of s1200 CA 2006

Any partnership which uses a business name (other than one comprising only the surnames of the partners, as explained earlier) is required to state the name of each partner (together with an address for service in the UK) on every:

(a) business letter;

(b) order for goods or services;

(c) invoice;

(d) receipt; and

(e) written demand for payment of a debt (s1202(1) CA 2006).

The same information must also be given by a notice in a prominent position at each place of business of the partnership (s1204(1) CA 2006). The same information must also be given (in writing) to anyone with whom the partnership has had business dealings and who asks for the information (s1202(2) CA 2006).

The requirement of including names and addresses in letters etc, does not apply to a partnership with more than 20 members (s1203(1) CA 2006) provided that, instead of the partners' names, the letter states the address of the principal place of business and that the names and addresses of the partners can be inspected there (s1203(2) CA 2006).

5.8.3 Approval under ss1193 and 1194 CA 2006

Section 1193 CA 2006 makes it an offence to carry on business (without the approval of the Secretary of State) under a name which suggests a connection with the government or a local or public authority. If such a name is used, it may be necessary first to consult the specified public authority before seeking the Secretary of State's approval. Details of such bodies are contained in Sch 4 to the Company, Limited Liability Partnership and Business (Names and Trading Disclosures) Regulations 2015.

Furthermore, s1194 CA 2006 also makes it an offence to include in a business name a word specified in regulations made under that section, namely the Company, Limited Liability Partnership and Business Names (Sensitive Words and Expressions) Regulations 2014 (SI 2014/3140). The list of 'sensitive' words contained in the regulations is extensive and should be consulted for the complete picture. However, by way of a general understanding of the sort of words regarded as 'sensitive', the following are a few examples:

(a) adjudicator;

(b) banking;

(c) charitable;

(d) dental;

(e) institute;

(f) police;

(g) royal;

(h) tribunal; and

(i) trust.

Partners who are starting a business (or their advisors) should consult the Sensitive Words Regulations. If they find that their name includes a word covered by those regulations, they should first write to the government department or other body (as specified in the regulations) which is to be consulted in relation to that word, asking whether it objects. They should then apply to the

Secretary of State for approval stating that they have made such a request and enclosing a copy of any reply that they have received from the government department or other body that they have consulted.

CONDUCT POINT

If a solicitor is approached by two or more persons and instructed to assist with the creation of a partnership for those persons, the issue of a conflict of interest should be considered. If all those persons are to have equal status within the partnership, for example equal management responsibility and equivalent capital funding, there is unlikely to be an issue. However, if each person has varying perspectives on their involvement and the size and format of their financial contribution they are likely to make, the solicitor needs to recognise the possibility of conflict.

Even if there is a possibility of conflict, the exception regarding substantial common interest may allow the solicitor to act for all clients to achieve their goal. To a large extent, this will depend on the variances between the clients' perspectives and compliance with the required conditions of the exception. In any event, compliance with Principle 7, to act in the best interest of a client, should be an overriding factor.

EXAMPLE

Phoebe is approached by Grace, Ollie and Kayla regarding the creation of a partnership. Grace and Ollie are expecting to contribute £5,000 each to capitalise the partnership and they will each work full time in the business. Kayla is expected to contribute £25,000, but will take no active part in management. Shares of any profit will be Grace 40%, Ollie 40%, Kayla 20%. All this is to be confirmed in a partnership agreement.

Arguably, Grace and Ollie have a substantially common interest so could be advised simultaneously, albeit that discussion of the complete contents of any proposed partnership agreement may throw up differing viewpoints between them. In any event, Kayla must clearly be asked to seek independent legal advice.

KEY POINT SUMMARY

Some basic considerations regarding partnerships are:

- The creation of a partnership is a question of fact.
- In the main, partnerships are governed by the Partnership Act 1890.
- Partnership is a legal and equitable relationship which exists between partners.
- No formal written agreement is necessary for a partnership to function in law (but it is advisable).
- A partnership has no discrete identity from the partners.
- Because partnerships operate businesses, they are subject to rules which govern businesses, for example those which regulate the use of business names.

CHAPTER 6
Limited Liability Partnerships

FUNCTIONING LEGAL KNOWLEDGE

This chapter considers the following functioning legal knowledge included in the SRA's SQE 1 assessment specification:

Business and organisational characteristics (sole trader/partnership/LLP/private and unlisted public companies)

Legal personality and limited liability

Procedures and documentation required to incorporate a company/form a partnership/ LLP and other steps required under companies and partnerships legislation to enable the entity to commence operating:

- constitutional documents

Finance:

- funding options: debt and equity
- distribution of profits and gains
- financial records, information and accounting requirements

Corporate governance and compliance:

- documentary, record-keeping, statutory filing and disclosure requirements

Income tax:

- chargeable persons/entities (employees, sole traders, partners, shareholder, lenders and debenture holders)

AUTHORITIES UNDERPINNING PRACTICE

The key authorities that underpin this area of practice are listed below. Note that for legislation you are linked to legislation.gov.uk.

Although much of the legislation on this government website is available in its amended form, the incorporation of new amendments into the text of legislation can be delayed. You should refer to legal databases to ensure you are referencing the most up-to-date legislation.

- Limited Liability Partnerships Act 2000
  https://www.legislation.gov.uk/ukpga/2000/12
- Limited Liability Partnerships (Register of People with Significant Control) Regulations 2016
  https://www.legislation.gov.uk/uksi/2016/340
- Limited Liability Partnerships Regulations 2001
  https://www.legislation.gov.uk/uksi/2001/1090
- Limited Liability Partnerships (Application of the Companies Act 2006) Regulations 2009
  https://www.legislation.gov.uk/uksi/2009/1804
- Companies Act 2006
  https://www.legislation.gov.uk/ukpga/2006/46

- Company, Limited Liability Partnership and Business (Names and Trading Disclosures) Regulations 2015 (SI 2015/17)
  https://www.legislation.gov.uk/uksi/2015/17
- Company, Limited Liability Partnership and Business Names (Sensitive Words and Expressions) Regulations 2014 (SI 2014/3140)
  https://www.legislation.gov.uk/uksi/2014/3140

6.1 Introduction

It is recommended that the concepts governing both partnerships and companies have been studied and understood before reading this chapter. In particular, as most of the regulation which governs companies also governs limited liability partnerships (LLPs), it is recommended that the reader has acquired a working knowledge of the regime which covers companies before considering LLPs.

Related to this is the fact that many of the changes to company law to be introduced by the Economic Crime and Corporate Transparency Act 2023 (ECCTA 2023) will result in parallel changes to the regulation of LLPs through enabling regulations. Because such changes are to be introduced in tranches, an indication of the position as understood at the time of writing will be provided, where relevant, within this chapter. However, the reader is advised to confirm the up-to-date position at the time of reading.

After consulting this chapter, you will have been introduced to:

(a) the nature of an LLP;
(b) its formation;
(c) the status of members of an LLP;
(d) the relationship between members of an LLP and between members and an LLP itself;
(e) the taxation treatment of members (in outline);
(f) various legislative controls or obligations on either LLPs or members thereof.

Brief consideration will also be given to comparing LLPs with other business structures.

The major disincentive to operating a business through a partnership structure is the potentially unlimited exposure which each partner faces for liabilities of the partnership. Historically, this was a source of considerable concern to large professional partnerships–the threat of a massive (and potentially ruinous) claim by clients was ever present.

Against this background, the concept of LLPs was introduced by the Limited Liability Partnerships Act (LLPA) 2000. This Act is, in turn, supplemented by further regulations, designed both to enhance the rules specific to LLPs and to ensure that much of the legislation which governs companies is also applicable to LLPs. The key regulations in existence are:

(a) Limited Liability Partnerships Regulations 2001 (LLP Regulations 2001; as amended) and
(b) Limited Liability Partnerships (Application of the Companies Act 2006) Regulations 2009 (as amended).

In addition, there are regulations which impose the companies accounts regime onto LLPs.

It should be noted at the outset that LLPs are available to any type of business and not limited to professional partnerships. One restriction on their use, however, is the fact that the persons involved must be carrying on business with a view to profit (s2(1)(a) LLPA 2000). Non-profit-making entities, therefore, cannot operate as LLPs.

The key rationale for the creation of LLPs was to allow entrepreneurs and professionals the protection of limited liability while preserving the flexibility of the partnership structure. As such, LLPs can best be described as a hybrid of both companies and partnerships. However, as will be demonstrated in this chapter, they owe much more to the former than the latter. (This is reinforced by the fact that s1(5) LLPA 2000 states that the law of partnerships does not apply to LLPs.)

A word on terminology. Those who own and manage an LLP are called 'members'. This term will feature throughout the chapter.

6.2 Key elements of LLPs

6.2.1 Creation

An LLP will have to be registered with the Registrar of Companies and a certificate of incorporation will be issued as proof of this fact (ss2 and 3 LLPA 2000). An LLP can be registered in England and Wales, Scotland or Northern Ireland.

To achieve incorporation, details of the LLP must be entered on form LL IN01 and submitted to the relevant Registrar of Companies with a fee. (Further details regarding fees are provided in **Table 6.1** later in the chapter.)

The basic contents of the form are:

(a) the name of the LLP (which must end with the words 'Limited Liability Partnership' or 'LLP');
(b) a statement about the intended location of the registered office and the actual address of the same;
(c) the names and addresses of those persons who are to be members of the LLP. The LLP must have a minimum of two members. (As with directors, both a service address and a residential address must be supplied, of which only the former will appear on the public record.)
(d) details of any members/persons who will be persons with significant control on the registration of the LLP (see **6.4** for further discussion).

This process shares similarities with the procedure for registration of a company. However, one major difference is that there is no specimen constitution which an LLP can adopt (as the Model Articles for companies), nor must the LLP register its constitution (effectively any agreement between the members) with Companies House as a matter of public record.

The enactment of ECCTA 2023 has been significant, in that many provisions which impact upon registration of companies will, in parallel, apply to LLPs. A brief explanation of these provisions follows. (Some of these provisions were in force at the time of writing (see the Limited Liability Partnerships (Application of Company Law) Regulations 2024) and some were not, so the reader is advised to confirm the up-to-date situation when consulting this chapter.)

Those provisions in force as from 4th March 2024 are:

(a) The registered office of the LLP will have to satisfy the definition of an 'appropriate address'. There will also be an ongoing obligation to ensure that the registered office remains an appropriate address.
(b) The LLP will have to confirm in its application for registration a registered email address. There will also be an ongoing obligation to ensure that the email address remains an appropriate email address. (Existing LLPs will be required to confirm such an address on the submission of their first confirmation statement submitted after 4 March 2024.)
(c) No disqualified person under the directors' disqualification legislation can become a member of an LLP.
(d) The chosen name of the LLP will be subject to the increased restrictions which apply to company names (see **3.6.3** for discussion of this area).

Further changes which are expected to be introduced at a later date are:

(a) The application for registration will have to contain a statement that the future activities of the LLP will be for a lawful purpose;
(b) The identity of members and PSCs within the LLP will have to be verified.

6.2.2 Limited liability

Third parties who deal with LLPs will contract with the LLP as a distinct legal entity (s 1(2) LLPA 2000). This means that any recourse the third party has will be against the LLP itself and its assets rather than the members of the LLP themselves.

Section 74 of the Insolvency Act 1986 (as it applies to LLPs) states that members of an LLP shall contribute to the assets of the LLP in the event of it being wound up as is provided for in the LLP agreement. Therefore, it is feasible that members' liability could be limited to as little as £1 or could be excluded altogether.

However, it is perhaps an oversimplification to imagine that members of an LLP will never incur any form of personal liability. Although the issue is not clear-cut, the view is that liability for negligent misstatement will still attach to the errors of a member (assuming that a duty of care can be established). This is particularly germane in the instance of a professional LLP, such as a law or accountancy firm. As such, whilst the members as a whole may not bear the liability for negligent advice, the individual who gave that advice may be liable. One way to address this is by way of an indemnity for such a member from the LLP. Regulation 7(2) of the LLP Regulations 2001 implies an indemnity in respect of payments made and liabilities incurred by a member in the ordinary and proper conduct of the business of the LLP. However, it is arguable that such an indemnity does not cover negligence. It may be preferable, therefore, to include a comprehensively drafted indemnity in an LLP agreement.

Furthermore, members of an LLP are subject to the provisions within the Insolvency Act 1986 (IA 1986) which govern directors' liability for wrongful and fraudulent trading. In addition, s214A IA 1986 applies specifically to LLPs. Any member who made withdrawals of any amounts in the two-year period prior to the insolvency of the LLP may find that those amounts are clawed back by the liquidator if it can be shown that the member in question knew or ought to have concluded that there was no reasonable prospect of the LLP avoiding insolvent liquidation.

Finally, creditors of an LLP, particularly those providing lending or credit facilities, may require personal guarantees from the members, as may any landlord of the LLP.

6.2.3 **Unlimited capacity**

Section 1(3) LLPA 2000 states that an LLP has unlimited capacity in the same way that companies formed under the Companies Act 2006 (CA 2006) have unrestricted objects.

6.2.4 **Members**

The initial members of the LLP are those who signed the incorporation document. Further members can join the LLP with the consent of the then current members. Members will usually be natural persons, but it is also possible for companies (and other LLPs) to act as members.

A properly drafted LLP agreement should make specific provision for the appointment (and removal) of members during the life of the LLP. In the absence of such provision, reg 7(5) LLP Regulations 2001 will imply a prohibition on the admission of a new member unless agreed to by all members. Regulation 8, on the other hand, excludes any right of expulsion of a member by a majority of members, unless that right has been specifically reserved by agreement of the members.

In the same way that companies are obliged to maintain registers in respect of directors, so must an LLP maintain similar registers in respect of its members (ss162 and 165 CA 2006 as modified to apply to LLPs in Pt 5, **Chapter 1** of the LLPs (Application of Companies Act 2006) Regulations 2009).

An LLP must have a minimum of two members. Should the number fall to one and remain so for at least six months, the benefit of limited liability will cease and the remaining member will be liable, together with the LLP, for all debts and liabilities incurred during that period (s4A LLPA 2000). This requirement, therefore, excludes the availability of LLPs for sole traders. It also puts LLPs at a disadvantage as compared to private limited companies which can allow their membership to fall to one should the situation ever arise.

A new duty upon members of an LLP has been introduced by the Limited Liability Partnerships (Application of Company Law) Regulations 2024 as from 4th March 2024. Upon any member becoming a disqualified person, all other members of the LLP are under a duty to ensure that that person ceases to be a member of the LLP. Failure to do so will be a criminal offence.

6.2.5 **Designated members**

There is a special class of members known as 'designated members', as specified by s8 LLPA 2000. The incorporation document will have to contain details of such members, although different persons can assume this role during the life of the LLP. There must always be a minimum of two designated members.

The LLPA 2000 imposes specific responsibilities on designated members, namely:

(a) to appoint an auditor, if it is necessary to do so;
(b) to sign off an LLP's accounts and file them with the Registrar of Companies;
(c) to ensure that a confirmation statement for an LLP is filed with the Registrar of Companies annually;
(d) to ensure that an LLP complies with all statutory filing requirements.

6.3 Disclosure requirements

As with companies, the quid pro quo for limited liability is public disclosure. The key filing responsibilities of an LLP are:

(a) the filing of annual accounts;
(b) the filing of an annual confirmation statement, together with the appropriate fee (see **Table 6.1** later in the chapter for details);
(c) the notification of appointments to the membership (on form LL AP01);
(d) the notification of termination of membership (on form LL TM01);
(e) the notification of changes in members or designated members (on form LL CH01);
(f) the notification of a change to its registered office (on form LL AD01); and
(g) the notification of a change to its registered name (on form LL NM01), together with the appropriate fee (see **Table 6.1** later in the chapter for details).

The Limited Liability Partnerships (Application of Company Law) Regulations 2024 have introduced from 4th March 2024 two further considerations in this area (which echo those in respect of companies), namely:

(a) A confirmation statement must now include a statement that the intended future activities of the LLP are to remain lawful; and
(b) The need for LLPs to formally register any change to their registered email address (after its initial registration).

6.4 Members as PSCs

Part 21A of the CA 2006, which imposes an obligation upon companies to maintain a register of persons exercising significant control (PSCs), also applies to LLPs through the effect of the Limited Liability Partnerships (Register of People with Significant Control) Regulations 2016.

Obviously, ownership and management structures between the two entities are different, so alternative definitions of a PSC are necessary. Within the context of an LLP, a PSC will normally be an individual who falls into one or more of the following categories:

(a) directly or indirectly holds rights over more than 25% of the surplus assets on a winding up;
(b) directly or indirectly holds more than 25% of the voting rights of members as a whole;
(c) directly or indirectly holds the right to appoint or remove the majority of those involved in management;
(d) otherwise has the right to exercise, or actually does exercise, significant influence or control.

(A further fifth category also exists, but the context within which that is relevant is beyond the scope of this manual.)

Identifying a PSC, therefore, will usually be a matter of analysis of the contractual relationship between the members (assuming that no outside third party has the ability to influence or control the actions of the LLP). However, as for companies with small numbers of directors and shareholders, this analysis should not be too difficult in the context of an LLP with a small number of members. (It should be noted that, as with members of a company, a member of an LLP may become a PSC either on the registration of the LLP or at a later date.)

EXAMPLE

Bright Skies LLP has three members. Each member has:

- an equal say in management matters;
- an equal entitlement to a share of both income and capital profits;
- made an equal capital contribution of £20,000 into the LLP.

It is understood that on a winding up of the LLP, each member will receive their capital contribution back and any remaining assets thereafter will be shared equally amongst them.

All members fall into categories (a) and (b) above, so all constitute PSCs.

By contrast, if Bright Skies had six members whose relationship was identical to the one described, none of the members would be PSCs.

A change in membership, as with a change in shareholders, may result in a reclassification of PSCs within an LLP.

As with companies, LLPs are obliged to make relevant changes to their PSC registers within 14 days of confirmation of the change. They are also obliged to notify Companies House of any changes within 14 days of those changes being made to the register. The most likely forms to be used in this context are:

- LL PSC01–Notice of a Person becoming a PSC.
- LL PSC04–Change of details of a PSC.
- LL PSC07–Notice of Person ceasing to be a PSC.

6.5 Borrowing and security

Unlike partnerships, LLPs are capable of granting a floating charge, which may mean that there are greater financing opportunities than for a traditional partnership. In any event, the assets used as security will be owned by the LLP not the members themselves. (Most charges created by an LLP will be registrable at Companies House in the same way as for security granted by a company.)

For further discussion of funding issues relating to business structures, see **1.11**.

6.6 Relationship of members with the LLP

Section 5 LLPA 2000 stipulates that the mutual rights and duties of the members of an LLP and the mutual rights and duties of an LLP and its members are governed by any LLP agreement in existence. In the absence of such an agreement, the LLP Regulations 2001 are determinative. This led the court in *F & C Alternative Investments v Barthelemy* [2012] Ch 613 to regard a highly detailed and comprehensive LLP agreement as being primarily indicative of the relationship between the members and the LLP. As such, context would appear to be highly significant in terms of duties owed to an LLP.

In the absence of an LLP agreement, however, it would appear that whilst the statutory duties which directors owe to their companies are not imposed on members of an LLP (the rationale being that within an LLP there is no distinction between the owners of an LLP and its management), the legal and equitable principles upon which those duties are based may be equally applicable to members. Thus, in *Re CJ & RA Eade LLP* [2019] EWHC 1673 (Ch), ICC Judge Jones was prepared to treat the two members of the relevant LLP as akin to directors and, hence, subject to the same duties.

(As this is an area where some uncertainty exists, it is recommended that you consult a recognised text on the area for further explanation.)

Every member is an agent of the LLP (s6(1) LLPA 2000). As such, the common law fiduciary duties that an agent owes to a principal would appear to apply to members of an LLP, in any event (subject to the effect of any LLP agreement). It is beyond the scope of this manual to consider the relationship between an agent and its principal, but the basic parameters will be that the member:

(a) must act in good faith towards the LLP;
(b) must not put themselves in a position of conflict with the LLP;
(c) must not profit personally from their position;
(d) must make full disclosure of information which is of legitimate interest to the LLP.

These implications would appear to be reinforced to an extent by certain provisions of the LLP Regulations 2001, namely:

(a) a duty to account to the LLP for any profits derived from a similar business which competes with the business of the LLP (reg 7(9));
(b) a duty to account for any personal benefit derived from a transaction with the LLP or from the use of LLP property (reg 7(10)).

This agency relationship presumably also means that members acting with either actual or apparent authority have the power to bind the firm. An exception to this basic rule is found in s6(2) LLPA 2000, which is akin to the 'unless' exception in s5 of the Partnership Act 1890. Thus, if any member is acting without authority and the person they are dealing with either knows that they have no authority or does not know or believe them to be a member, the LLP will not be bound by the acts of the member.

Persons ceasing to be members of LLPs can still operate as their agents until either the third party is notified of the fact or notice is sent to the Registrar of Companies (s6(3)).

LLPs are also liable for the wrongful acts or omissions of individual members when acting in the course of the LLP's business (s6(4)) to the same extent as the member. The LLPA 2000 is silent on the meaning of 'wrongful acts or omissions'. This will likely include tortious acts, and it may also include criminal acts.

A problematic issue is that of ownership by the members of a stake in the LLP. Shareholders in a company can point to an asset which represents their holding in the company. Similarly, partners in a 'traditional' partnership have a direct proprietorial stake in the assets used by the partnership or at least a claim in their proceeds of sale (see *Popat v Schonchhatra* [1997] 3 All ER 800). However, with LLPs the separation between the legal entity and its owners exists without any legal mechanism being in place to record ownership. Therefore, if an LLP uses its funds to buy an asset, that asset is owned by the LLP not by the members. Furthermore, profits made by the LLP will be profits generated by the business owned by the LLP but belong directly to the members.

Regulation 7, para (1) of the LLP Regulations 2001 provides that members are entitled to share equally in the capital and profits of the LLP and borrows heavily from s24(1) of the Partnership Act 1890. Section 24(1) operates to allocate the entitlements of partners and does not act as a basis for determining ownership. There is no reason to assume that reg 7, para (1) should be treated differently. As such, it is arguable that in neither the LLPA 2000 nor the LLP Regulations 2001 is there an absolute statement about the rights of ownership which members enjoy in an LLP.

Therefore, to ensure certainty, members will have to enter into arrangements with their LLPs to provide for these issues; namely, how a member's share in the LLP is determined, what a member may or may not do with that share and any specific entitlement of a member when they leave the LLP or die.

A further peculiarity is that s4(4) provides that a member of an LLP has no employment relationship with the LLP unless, on the assumption that all the members of the LLP were actually partners in a partnership, that member would, instead, be considered an employee of the hypothetical partnership. On the basis that partners are not normally employees, the assumption must be that members are in a similar situation. (This issue is mainly relevant in the context of the expulsion or departure of a member, where that member wishes to assert actual dismissal as an employee and, in turn, their concomitant rights.)

6.7 Relationship of members with each other

Members of LLPs are free to organise their internal affairs as they wish through agreement. Should such an agreement not be in place, the default provisions in the LLP Regulations 2001 can be relied upon. Whilst no absolute conclusion can currently be reached, it does appear, therefore, that members do not (in contrast to partners) owe each other certain legal duties, for example those of good faith, unless context provides or the LLP agreement itself sets out specific obligations.

(As this is an area where some uncertainty exists, it is recommended that you consult a recognised text on the area for further explanation.)

Many of the default provisions in the 2001 Regulations will not be satisfactory for all but the simplest of LLP arrangements. For example, despite the duty to account for profits arising from a competing business implied by reg 7(9), a well-drafted LLP agreement should probably contain a specific non-competition clause applicable both during and after cessation of membership.

Furthermore, the specifics of an agreed decision-making process should also be set out, including, if thought necessary, the identification of any decisions which need to be passed either by a 'super majority', for example three-quarters of the members, or unanimously. The default position under reg 7(6) would be that 'ordinary matters' connected with the business of the LLP should be decided by simple majority but that no change could be made to the nature of the business without unanimous consent.

6.8 Relationship between members and third parties

Essentially there is no automatic relationship between members of LLPs and third parties. Therefore, unlike in a partnership, issues of liabilities of a business following a member after retirement do not usually arise.

However, as has already been mentioned, contractual or tortious liability may sometimes fall upon an individual member.

6.9 Unfair prejudice

As with shareholders in a company, members of an LLP can bring a claim for unfair prejudice under s994 CA 2006. (Effectively a member or members in a minority position would be complaining about the behaviour of the remaining members.) However, this may be more of a theoretical possibility than real, if an LLP agreement exists, for two reasons:

(a) The members can agree to exclude the possibility of such a claim in the LLP agreement.

(b) The agreement may be comprehensive enough to provide mechanisms to deal with all internal disputes, excluding the need to assert unfair prejudice.

(Unfair prejudice in a company context is considered in **Chapter 19**.)

6.10 Taxation

The principle of separate legal personality is not maintained as far as taxation is concerned, so an LLP is not a taxable person. Instead, as with partners, it is the members who are taxed on their profit shares. Accordingly, the profits which an LLP makes must be allocated amongst the members and the members themselves pay income tax on those profit shares. As a consequence, the LLP will make a return to HMRC explaining profit allocation and each individual member will include their profit share in their tax return. (Taxation of partners is dealt with in **Chapter 30**.)

Certain advantages arise from this presumption, mainly the fact that a member's receipts from the business (in whatever form) are not taxed at source and a more favourable National Insurance regime applies to both the member and the LLP. As such, it can suit persons to claim member status even if they are on the fringes of what it means to be a member of an LLP.

To counter abuse of this possibility, the government introduced legislation in April 2014 to ensure that 'members' who are, in reality, employees are taxed as such in respect of their income tax and National Insurance liabilities. These rules are primarily aimed at members who:

(a) take out a fixed entitlement from the LLP in return for performing services for the LLP;
(b) have little or no management influence; and
(c) who contribute relatively low amounts of capital to the LLP.

6.11 Execution of documents

LLPs execute documents in the same way as companies.

Any authorised member may execute a contract *on behalf* of an LLP. If, however, the document is to be executed *by the LLP* itself, the signatures of two members are required or a single member must sign in the presence of a witness (ss43–46 CA 2006 as modified to apply to LLPs in Pt 2 of the LLPs (Application of Companies Act 2006) Regulations 2009).

Note that it is also possible for an LLP to have a seal for the purpose of executing documents but, as for companies, it is not compulsory.

6.12 Impact of other Acts

Sections 14–16 LLPA 2000 allow for the Secretary of State to make provision for company and insolvency law to apply to LLPs. This has been done primarily through the regulations already mentioned. As such, large tracts of the CA 2006, the Company Directors Disqualification Act 1986 and the IA 1986 apply to LLPs. As a general rule, it is safe to assume that much of the legislation which applies to companies and their directors applies equally to LLPs and their members, for example:

(a) The choice of an LLP's registered name is subject to the same controls and restrictions as a company's registered name. Furthermore, LLPs are subject to the same disclosure requirements about registered names as companies.
(b) LLPs' accounts may have to be audited in accordance with the CA 2006 to give a true and fair view of the business. In any event, LLPs are subject to the same filing responsibilities in respect of their accounts as companies are.
(c) Charges granted by LLPs over their assets have to be registered at Companies House, together with the appropriate fee (see **Table 6.1**).
(d) Members of LLPs can face disqualification orders, such that they can be neither members of other LLPs nor company directors.
(e) Insolvent LLPs are subject to the same insolvency regime as companies, on the basis that they are both separate legal entities. As such, it is possible for an LLP to be wound up (both voluntarily and compulsorily) or put into administration. Further, members will find themselves subject to the same scrutiny as directors of insolvent companies, for example they could commit wrongful trading.
(f) In the same way that company law recognises the concept and influence of a **shadow director**, so there exists the possibility of a 'shadow member'. In turn, shadow members can be both subject to disqualification proceedings and found liable for wrongful trading.
(g) As for directors who are undischarged **bankrupts**, it is also an offence for a member to be involved with the promotion or management of an LLP when bankrupt.

One material exception to this general principle is that LLPs are not subject to any capital maintenance obligations in the way that companies are.

As has already been indicated elsewhere, both the CA 2006 and the Company Directors Disqualification Act 1986 have been and will be amended by ECCTA 2023. Many of those changes will be equally applicable to LLPs and their members. At the time of writing the only enabling regulations in force were the Limited Liability Partnerships (Application of Company Law) Regulations 2024, which amend in part both the Limited Liability Partnerships Act 2000 and the Limited Liability Partnerships (Application of the Companies Act 2006) Regulations 2009. Further regulations are anticipated, as and when further changes to the Company Law regime are introduced.

6.13 Factors influencing choice of business entity

One easy decision can be made at the outset; if only one person is to be involved in the venture, an LLP is not possible (nor is a partnership). Thereafter the basic choice is between a corporate entity (company or LLP) or a partnership. In turn, this means a choice between:

(a) limited liability, public disclosure, substantial regulations and compliance (corporate entity); and

(b) unlimited liability, greater privacy and very limited compliance (partnership).

This distinction is, however, blurred when taxation is considered because LLPs share the taxation regime of partnerships rather than companies. In addition, the internal management of an LLP is more akin to that of a partnership.

If a decision is made in favour of a corporate entity, then some of the distinctions to be drawn between the two possibilities are as follows:

(a) The decision-making regime within an LLP can be as simple or as complex as the members wish. There is no such choice with companies. However, the two-tier decision-making process within companies (ie directors and shareholders) may allow for greater flexibility in power-sharing.

(b) Raising capital is still likely to be easier through a company because of the flexibility inherent in shares as an investment mechanism. If, however, the business is likely to remain close-knit and to rely primarily upon its initial members for finance, this may not be a disincentive to choosing an LLP.

(c) An LLP has the ability to grant a floating charge over its assets and can be made subject to the same insolvency procedures as may be available in a company context. As such, the ability of an LLP to secure bank borrowing should, in theory, be no different to that of a company. (Bear in mind that members, as with directors, may be required to give guarantees in respect of borrowing by their respective entities.)

(d) Within the framework of a company, there is more flexibility in dealing with profits. They can be maintained in the company, paid out as directors' bonuses or as dividends to shareholders. Within an LLP, profits earned are taxed in the hands of the members, irrespective of whether or not they are drawn out.

(e) It is relatively inexpensive to set up a company and considerable precedents exist for many permutations of articles, including the Model Articles, as set out in statutory instrument (see **3.10**). Whilst an LLP members' agreement is not a requirement of law, clients would be ill-advised not to have one. The length and complexity of such documents may result in an initial cost burden.

(f) The claw-back provisions of s214A IA 1986 are substantial, so it is arguable that members of an LLP face greater exposure to contribute to an insolvent LLP than directors in respect of their companies. (See, for example, *Re CJ & RA Eade LLP* [2019] EWHC 1673 (Ch), where the liquidator of an LLP successfully enforced s214A against the members of an LLP.)

CONDUCT POINT

If a solicitor is approached by two or more persons and instructed to create an LLP for those persons, the issue of a conflict of interest should be considered. If all those persons are to have equal status within the LLP, for example they are all to be members and to invest equivalent capital sums, there is unlikely to be an issue. However, if each person has varying perspectives on their involvement and the size and format of capital contribution they are likely to make, the solicitor needs to recognise that a conflict may result from such differing perspectives.

Even if there is a possibility of conflict, the exception regarding substantial common interest may allow the solicitor to act for all clients to achieve their goal. To a large extent, this will depend on the variances between the clients' perspectives and compliance with the required conditions for the exception to apply. In any event, compliance with Principle 7, to act in the best interest of a client, should be an overriding factor.

Alternatively, if the scope of the clients' instruction is simply to provide a registered LLP, there is unlikely to be an issue; however, if the solicitor's involvement subsequently extends beyond this to the generation of an agreement between the members to regulate their relationship, the solicitor must not act for all those members.

The fact that an LLP is a legal person its own right also raises an important consideration regarding with whom the retainer rests. A lawyer cannot represent the individual interests of members and also advise the LLP itself. For example, if the retainer is with the LLP and a new member is to be introduced, the solicitor cannot advise that new member on the legal implications of their proposed new status, even though the proposal has originated with the LLP. The proposed new member must seek independent legal advice.

Table 6.1 sets out some of the more common fees which an LLP may have to pay in its lifetime. (They are, in fact, identical to the fees payable by companies.) At the time of writing there was a proposal to increase certain fees on 1 May 2024. The following table reflects that change. However, fees can change, so reference should be made to the Companies House website for the up-to-date position.

TABLE 6.1 Companies House fees: limited liability partnerships (as on 1 May 2024)

Digital Incorporation	£50.00
Digital Incorporation (same day)	£78.00
Paper Incorporation	£71.00
Digital change of name	£20.00
Digital change of name (same day)	£83.00
Paper change of name	£30.00
Digital Confirmation Statement	£34.00
Paper Confirmation Statement	£62.00
Digital registration of charge	£15.00
Paper registration of charge	£24.00

KEY POINT SUMMARY

The following are some of the main features of an LLP:

- They are creatures of statute and must be registered with Companies House. This creates a recognised legal entity.
- They require a minimum of two members, who are both the owners and managers of the LLP.
- No formal constitution or agreement is required to govern the workings of the LLP; however, there are many reasons why such an agreement is advisable.
- Many of the compliance provisions of the Companies Act 2006 apply equally to LLPs.
- Third parties will deal with an LLP. As such, there is usually no contractual nexus between members of an LLP and customers, suppliers etc. of the LLP's business.
- The liability of members for an LLP's obligation can effectively be zero.
- An LLP is not subject to any tax liabilities; instead, the members are liable to income tax on their profit shares.

PART C
Company Finance

CHAPTER 7
Equity Finance: Share Capital and Allotment of Shares

FUNCTIONING LEGAL KNOWLEDGE

This chapter considers the following functioning legal knowledge included in the SRA's SQE 1 assessment specification:

Finance:

- funding options: debt and equity

AUTHORITIES UNDERPINNING PRACTICE

The key authorities that underpin this area of practice are listed below. Note that for legislation you are linked to legislation.gov.uk.

Although much of the legislation on this government website is available in its amended form, the incorporation of new amendments into the text of legislation can be delayed. You should refer to legal databases to ensure you are referencing the most up-to-date legislation.

- Companies Act 2006
  https://www.legislation.gov.uk/ukpga/2006/46/contents
- Financial Services and Markets Act 2000
  https://www.legislation.gov.uk/ukpga/2000/8/contents

7.1 Introduction

Once a company is formed it will need to spend money to get its business going. It will likely need to buy stock, buy or rent premises, pay wages, advertise and pay the general expenses involved in running a business. The money that the company needs to start and grow its business is often called working capital.

A company can raise money either in the form of an investment by shareholders ('equity finance') or in the form of borrowing ('debt finance'). Once the business is established, profits may be retained in the business, thus producing a third source of finance.

After consulting this chapter, you will have been introduced to how companies raise money through equity finance, in particular:

(a) the concept of shares;

(b) the concept of a company's share capital; and

(c) the process by which shares are allotted by companies.

(Debt finance is considered in **Chapter 12**).

7.2 The balance sheet

It should be noted at the outset that an important source of information as to how a company is capitalised is the balance sheet, which will provide details of both debt and share funding. (It is recommended that **Chapter 22**, which looks at the balance sheet in more detail, is read in conjunction with this chapter.)

EXAMPLE

A Ltd is funded in the following manner:

Share capital	£1,000
Retained profits	£25,000
Borrowings	£10,000

A total, therefore, of £36,000 has gone into funding the company, but there is also a corresponding liability to pay back the borrowings. In very simple terms, the assets would be represented as follows in A Ltd's balance sheet:

ASSETS	
Cash	£36,000
Liabilities	£10,000
Net assets	**£26,000**
CAPITAL	
Share capital	£1,000
Retained profit	£25,000
Total	**£26,000**

Note how the assets -match the capital, hence the fact that the figures 'balance'.

It should also be noted from the above example that borrowings exceed shareholder investment by 10:1. The relationship between a company's debt and equity finance is usually called 'gearing'. In very simple terms, if a company is capitalised with a substantial amount of debt in comparison to the money raised from its shareholders, it is said to be highly geared.

7.3 The nature of shares

7.3.1 Legal nature of shares

A share in a company is a chose in action. Its value to a shareholder depends on the particular rights which the share carries.

Shares are normally acquired by three methods:

1 an allotment by the company itself;

2 transfer from a shareholder; or

3 transmission by operation of law from a shareholder.

This section is concerned with the allotment of shares by a company; transfer and transmission of shares are dealt with in **Chapter 10**.

7.3.2 Rights attaching to shares

The rights attached to shares vary from company to company and a company may issue different classes of shares with different rights attached to them. It is, therefore, difficult to generalise about the exact nature of a share, but the following points may be of assistance:

(a) Nearly all shares give the shareholder a *right to a dividend* (ie a share in profits), but a dividend is only payable if the company has available profits and it is decided to pay a dividend. (See **Chapter 8** where dividends are looked at in more detail.)

(b) Most, but not all, shares give the shareholder a *right to vote* at general meetings of the company.

(c) If the company is wound up (liquidated) the shareholder will have a *right to repayment* of their investment (assuming that the company is then solvent) and, in most cases, a *right to participate* in any surplus capital.

(d) The Stock Transfer Act 1963 lays down a method for the transfer of shares but does not guarantee the shareholder a *right to transfer*–this will be determined by the company's articles.

(e) Shareholders are given certain rights *as a matter of law* by the Companies Act 2006 (CA 2006). Many of these rights are, however, only given to shareholders who have a right to vote at company meetings (eg the rights to remove directors discussed in **Chapter 15**).

In the case of a private company, voting rights will often be as important as financial rights. This is especially so in the case of a shareholding which gives voting control, since it effectively carries with it the right to control many major decisions of the company.

7.3.3 **Differing classes of shares**

Different types of shares are possible. The main driver for these rights will be that shares can be considered as both:

(a) a mechanism for control and influence (because of the possible voting rights they may carry); and

(b) an investment (either because of dividends which are paid out by the company or the fact that they increase in value as the company increases in value).

Some shareholders will be more concerned with the latter than the former, and vice versa. Therefore, more than one type of share may be necessary to satisfy this demand. Shares are then said to belong to different classes. For example, a company may issue preference shares; that is, shares which have a better right to receive a dividend than ordinary shares. It is also possible to give some shareholders a greater measure of control over the affairs of the company either by creating voting and non-voting shares or by providing that all shares are to carry a right to vote but that some will have more votes than others.

It is not intended to provide an exhaustive explanation of all possible share rights. However, it is important to distinguish between the two most common types of share in issue–ordinary and preference shares.

7.3.3.1 Ordinary shares

The most common type of share in issue is the ordinary share. Ordinary shares entitle the holder to dividends, should such be payable. They also entitle the holder to voting rights.

7.3.3.2 Preference shares

Preference shares are a more sophisticated investment mechanism than ordinary shares. They may be 'preferred' in two particular ways:

(a) They may carry the automatic right to a fixed, annual dividend, normally calculated as a percentage of the nominal value of the shares. This right may, in addition, be cumulative, which means that should funds not be available to satisfy a dividend payment in a particular year, the preferred shareholder's entitlement is carried forward until funds are available.

(b) On a winding up, they may stand ahead of other shareholders in having their capital contribution to the company repaid to them.

Each of these rights is independent of the other, so some preference shares may carry one or both entitlements.

Thus, preference shares appear to have clear advantages over ordinary shares. However, they tend not to carry voting rights, and the preferred rights themselves are normally restricted to a fixed amount. This can mean, for example, that in certain situations ordinary shareholders may receive better dividends than preferred shareholders.

As a way of redressing the balance, preference shares may also carry with them rights of participation, which effectively means that as well as enjoying preferred rights, they may also enjoy the rights which ordinary shares carry in respect of dividends.

Rights of participation are not compulsory and must be negotiated between the company and the potential shareholder, along with all other preferential rights.

EXAMPLE

Dividend

Tony has 50 ordinary shares of £1 each and Demisha has 100 5% preference shares of £1 each in Lineout Ltd. Should Lineout have £5 with which it can pay out a dividend, Demisha will be paid first, which will use up the full amount, so none will go to Tony. However, should Lineout have £50 with which it can pay out a dividend, Demisha will be paid first, but will still only receive £5, allowing Tony to receive £45.

If, however, all Demisha's shares were also participating, the balance of £45 would have to be divided between Demisha and Tony, resulting in Demisha receiving two-thirds of this amount and Tony one-third.

Winding up

If Demisha's shares also carry preferential rights on a winding up and the amount left for distribution to shareholders is £100, Demisha will have her capital contribution returned first, resulting in nothing being available for Tony. However, should the amount left be £1,000, Demisha will still receive £100 first, but Tony will receive both his capital contribution plus the remainder; that is, the full £900.

Instead, if Demisha also had rights of participation on a winding up, the order of pay-out would be:

(a) Demisha £100;

(b) Tony £50;

(c) balance of £850, split one-third Tony; two-thirds Demisha.

7.3.3.3 Rights of redemption

Strictly speaking, redeemable shares are not a class of shares separate from ordinary or preference shares; instead, rights of redemption can be attached to either of these types of shares.

Shares that are redeemable can be bought back by the company or sold back to the company in certain pre-determined situations. It is usual for the terms of redemption to be set out in the company's articles of association.

7.3.3.4 Rights of conversion

It may be that an investor in a company is happy to take shares with specific or restricted rights, but these shares can be vulnerable to problems or changes which may arise at a later date. As such, it may be appropriate that those shares carry a right to convert to another type of share (usually ordinary) in certain defined situations. Again, as with redeemable shares, convertible shares are not a discrete class.

7.3.4 Recording share rights

If only ordinary shares are in issue, then there is no need specifically to identify the rights which they carry. However, if more than one class of share will be in issue, it then becomes more important to have an explicit record of the rights which each class of shares enjoys. Usually a company's articles will provide for the ability to create different classes of shares and for their respective rights to be set out in an ordinary resolution. (See, for example, art 22(1) of the Model Articles for Private Companies.) However, it is often preferable to set out those rights in the articles of association–this has the practical advantage that they are contained within the company's main constitutional document, rather than a single resolution, and the legal certainty that those rights are fully binding on every subsequent owner of those shares, because of the effect of s33(1) CA 2006.

7.3.5 The value of shares

The value of shares clearly depends to some extent on the rights attached to them but it also depends on other factors–particularly the profitability of the company and its asset worth.

In accordance with s542(1) CA 2006, all shares must have a 'nominal value' (also called 'par value'). For many UK registered companies, the nominal value chosen is often £1. This figure says little about the true value of the shares since shares can be issued for more (but not less) than nominal value and, once issued, their true value will fluctuate either upwards or downwards, depending on the financial condition of the company.

EXAMPLE

Control Systems Ltd has 1,000 ordinary shares in issue. Each of these shares has a *nominal* value of £1. However, if Control Systems, as a business entity, is worth £2 million, to buy all the shares in this company and, thus, assume total control over it, would cost this amount. Therefore, each share has an *actual* worth of £2,000.

7.4 Procedure for the allotment of shares

7.4.1 Introduction

When new shares are created by a company they are said to be 'issued' or 'allotted' by the company to the people who have contracted to buy them. Any proposed issue of shares is likely to raise a number of complex legal matters. These will now be considered.

7.4.2 Effect on share capital

The relevant share capital of a company (its issued or allotted share capital–s546 CA 2006) will be increased automatically every time an allotment of shares is made by the size of the fresh allotment (s617(2)(a) CA 2006).

The 'default position', therefore, is that companies are free to make allotments of any size at any time. However, it is always possible for a company to impose a restriction on its issued share capital in its articles; for example, a ceiling limit on the number of shares which can be allotted over a designated time span.

7.4.3 Directors' authorisation

At the outset of this discussion, it should be noted that the power to allot shares rests with the directors; however, this power may be qualified or restricted in several ways.

For private companies with only one class of share in issue, directors are free to allot further shares of the same class without prior reference to the shareholders, subject to any restriction imposed upon them in the articles (s550 CA 2006). However, the advance consent of shareholders by ordinary resolution or authority from the articles will be required (s551 CA 2006) for an allotment where either:

(a) the company is public; or

(b) more than one class of shares is already in issue; or

(c) the proposed allotment will result in the creation of more than one class of shares.

EXAMPLE

Proposed allotment	Applicability of s550 CA 2006	Applicability of s551 CA 2006
A Ltd has 150 ordinary shares of £1 each in issue. The board of directors wishes to allot a further 50 ordinary shares of £1 each. There are no restrictions in its articles on the size of future allotments.	The section applies. There will only be ordinary shares in issue both prior to and after the proposed allotment. The board may make the allotment without any prior authorisation from the shareholders.	N/A
A Ltd has 150 ordinary shares of £1 each in issue. The board of directors wishes to allot 50 preference shares of £5 each. There are no restrictions in its articles on the size of future allotments.	N/A	The section applies. There will be both ordinary shares and preference shares in issue after the proposed allotment. The board may only make the allotment with the prior authorisation of the shareholders, either in the form of an ordinary resolution or from authority contained in the articles.
B Ltd has 100 ordinary shares of £1 each and 100 preference shares of £10 each in issue. The board of directors wishes to allot a further 50 ordinary shares of £1 each. There are no restrictions in its articles on the size of future allotments.	N/A	The section applies. There are both ordinary shares and preference shares in issue prior to the proposed allotment. The board may only make the allotment with the prior authorisation of the shareholders, either in the form of an ordinary resolution or from authority contained in the articles.

7.4.4 Scope of directors' authorisation

Any necessary shareholder authorisation may be:

(a) either for a particular exercise of the directors' power or generally;

(b) unconditional or subject to conditions.

Whether the authorisation is given by ordinary resolution of the members in general meeting or by the articles, it must state:

(a) the maximum amount of shares which the directors may issue; and

(b) the date when the authority will expire.

The authority cannot be given for more than five years from formation of the company or the passing of the resolution (as the case may be) and can be revoked or varied by the company in general meeting at any time. Once given, the authority can be extended by up to five years by a further resolution of the company.

If the directors issue shares without authority they commit an offence (s549(4)) (and possibly would be liable to the company for breach of duty) but the issue of shares remains valid (s549(5)).

7.4.5 Rights of pre-emption

Under s561 CA 2006, any proposed issue of shares may first have to be offered to the existing shareholders, in proportion to their existing holdings, on terms at least as favourable as those proposed for the issue to the intended allottee.

Section 562 stipulates the manner in which offers under s561 must be made; in particular, the members must be given at least 14 days to accept the offer or reject it (s562(4) and (5)).

However, s561 will only apply if the shares to be allotted are 'equity securities', as defined by s560(1). What constitutes an equity security depends upon the rights which the share does or does not enjoy and, therefore, understanding the concept first requires a sound knowledge of such potential rights. Put simply, shares which enjoy only fixed entitlements in respect of *both* dividends *and* a return of capital are not equity shares and do not trigger s561.

EXAMPLE

Thunderstruck (222) Ltd is proposing to allot:

(a) 10,000 ordinary shares of £1 each.

(b) 5,000 4% preference shares of £5 each, which carry a fixed entitlement to a dividend but which, on a return of capital, entitle the holder to a return of the nominal value of the shares, together with an entitlement to share in any surplus available for the shareholders as a whole.

The ordinary shares constitute equity securities because, by their very nature, they carry unrestricted rights both to a dividend and surplus capital.

The preference shares, whilst restricted as to dividends, are not restricted as to surplus capital so are also equity securities.

Both these proposed allotments would, therefore, trigger s561.

Section 561 gives shareholders a useful degree of protection in cases where the effect of issuing shares would be to dilute their influence and/or their entitlements. For this reason, pre-emption rights are only afforded to existing holders of equity securities (s561(1)).

EXAMPLE

AllotCo 123 Ltd has two shareholders, owning shares as follows:

Michael: 50 £1 ordinary shares.

Serena: 50 £1 ordinary shares.

There is a proposal to allot 50 £1 ordinary shares to Caroline.

Matters of note are:

(a) The proposal triggers pre-emption rights, as an allotment of equity securities.

(b) Michael and Serena each hold equity securities, so would benefit from these rights.

(c) In fulfilment of pre-emption rights, the company should offer each of Michael and Serena 25 of the proposed new shares on the same terms as they would be offered to Caroline.

(d) If Michael and Serena each accept the offer, their status as 50% shareholders in the company will be maintained.

(e) If Michael and Serena decline the offer and the shares are allotted to Caroline, each of Michael, Serena and Caroline will become one-third shareholders in the company.

One major exception is that rights of pre-emption do not apply if the relevant shares are to be issued wholly or partly for non-cash consideration (s565).

A failure to comply with either s561 or 562 will result in any director who knowingly authorised or permitted such failure being liable to compensate any shareholder to whom an offer should have been made for any loss, damage, costs or expenses (s563).

Section 561 is only concerned with the *issue* of shares. It should not be confused with any provision in a company's articles which provides for pre-emption rights where an existing shareholder wants to *transfer* their shares (see **Chapter 10**).

7.4.6 Excluding rights of pre-emption

Section 567 allows *private* companies the possibility of excluding the effect of ss561 and 562, either wholly or partially, through a provision in the articles. Additionally, companies can disapply the effect of s561 in respect of specific allotments, either through a special resolution or through a provision in the articles, although it is important to distinguish between allotments where the directors do and do not require shareholders' authority to make the allotment, and the extent and nature of the authority granted to them (contrast ss569, 570 and 571).

For example, in a s550 context where the directors do not need authorisation from the shareholders, any special resolution to disapply the effect of s561 will be made pursuant to s569(1).

By contrast, where directors are generally authorised by s551 to make an allotment of shares, any such special resolution will be made pursuant to s570(1).

Disapplication means that the company can ignore pre-emption rights of existing shareholders on the basis that a special majority of them have voted for it.

7.4.7 Directors' fiduciary duties

The directors may not issue shares in breach of their fiduciary duty; that is, they must exercise their powers for the purposes for which they are granted pursuant to s171 CA 2006. As such, if the motive behind the issue is anything other than the raising of further investment in the company, for example to thwart a takeover bid or to dilute the status of an existing shareholder, it is likely that the allotment will constitute a breach of duty by the directors.

7.5 Payment for shares

A contract for the issue of shares may provide for payment in cash or for some other consideration. If the full *nominal* amount is paid at the time of the allotment, the shares are said to be 'fully paid up'. If not, they are 'partly paid'. In this case, the outstanding amount can be asked for by the company making a 'call'. (The details of such a device will normally be specific to the company's articles.)

Additionally, if the company goes into liquidation, any shareholder owning **partly paid shares** is obliged to contribute the outstanding sum to the company. (See **28.7.1** for further discussion of this area.)

Payment in full on issue of shares is usually required (see, eg, art 21(1) of the Model Articles for Private Companies), so partly paid shares are rare.

Companies may not issue shares at a *discount* to their nominal value. This is prohibited by s580 CA 2006, which makes the allottee liable to the company for the shortfall (plus interest on the outstanding amount). As such, it is unlawful to pay less than the nominal value of a share and for that share to be treated as fully paid up by the company.

EXAMPLE

Sage Pharmacies Ltd purports to allot to Constance 2,000 £1 ordinary shares as *fully paid*. Constance only pays 60p per share. This is a breach of s580.

As such, Constance still owes 40p per share.

The correct approach for Sage Pharmacies was to treat all the shares as *partly paid*, thereby acknowledging Constance's obligation to meet the shortfall at a later date.

7.6 Share premium

Shares can be issued at a premium, that is, for more than their nominal value. (For the accounting consequences of this, see **Chapter 22**.)

EXAMPLE

Sage Pharmacies Ltd allots to Cedric 200 £1 ordinary shares at a premium of £4 per share. Cedric, therefore, will pay a total of £1,000 for these shares; that is, £5 for each share.

7.7 Registration of allotments

7.7.1 Filings with Companies House

Section 555(2) CA 2006 requires a return of allotment to be made to the Registrar of Companies within one month of the issue of shares. This return provides details of the allotment which has taken place. The return must also be accompanied by a statement of capital, giving details of the company's share capital at that time (s555(4)). This registration obligation is achieved by the completion and submission of form SH01.

Copies of several shareholder resolutions may need to be submitted to the Registrar within 15 days of the allotment, depending upon whether or not they were necessary to effect the allotment. The most common are likely to be:

(a) any special resolution passed to disapply pre-emption rights;

(b) any ordinary resolution passed pursuant to s551 to grant directors authority to make the allotment;

(c) any special resolution required to alter the articles to enable the insertion of rights attaching to a new class of shares (in which case, a copy of the amended articles will also have to be submitted).

7.7.2 Internal matters

Section 554 CA 2006 imposes on companies an obligation to register any allotment in the *internal* register of members within two months of its occurrence.

Section 769 CA 2006 requires a company within the same time period to have share certificates ready for delivery to the relevant shareholders.

An allotment of shares may have an impact on the status of people with significant control because either:

a) an existing shareholder's status is diluted by the allotment; and/or

b) a new person exercising significant control (PSC) is created by it.

In such circumstances, the PSC register must be altered to reflect the new situation and one or more of forms PSC 01, 04 and 07 will need to be submitted to Companies House. (See **20.3** for more information on the PSC register and the likely removal of the need to maintain such a register in the future.)

7.8 Issue of shares to the public

Section 755 CA 2006 prohibits a private company from offering shares to the public or from issuing them with a view to an offer for sale to the public. Any action in contravention of this prohibition can result in a court ordering that the company in question re-register as a public company (ss757 and 758). (An application to the court in this instance can be made by either a member or creditor of the company or the Secretary of State.)

7.9 Allotment of shares: summary

The following is a non-exhaustive summary of the main issues already discussed in respect of a proposed allotment of shares by a *private* company.

Usually there are three main questions to consider:

1 Do the articles contain a numerical restriction on issued shares? If so, will this restriction need to be amended to permit the increase in share capital?

2 Do the directors need shareholders' authorisation by ordinary resolution to effect the allotment?

3 Do pre-emption rights apply to the allotment, in which case must they be disapplied?

Looking at these issues in turn:

1 Do the articles contain any restriction on the number of shares which the company may issue? If yes, would the proposed allotment go beyond this restriction? A special resolution would be required to alter the articles to increase or remove this restriction. (The Model Articles, for example, do not contain such a restriction.)

2 What types of share are currently in issue and what type of share is proposed to be issued? If only one type exists both before and after, s550 CA 2006 applies: permission to allot is automatic. If more than one type exists either before or after, s551 CA 2006 applies: permission is required by ordinary resolution, unless the company's articles already contain a permission to the directors to make the allotment in question. (If the Model Articles are relevant, no such permission is included.)

3 Do the shares to be allotted fall within the definition of 'equity securities' in s560 CA 2006? If yes, s561 pre-emption rights apply and may have to be disapplied by special resolution, unless:

   (a) they are excluded already by the company's articles (the Model Articles contain no such exclusion);

   (b) they are substituted by alternative pre-emption rights in the company's articles (the Model Articles do not include such rights); or

   (c) consideration for the allotment is wholly or partly non-cash (s565 CA 2006).

7.10 Share capital

7.10.1 Quantification of share capital

Once shares have been issued, they are said to form part of the 'capital' of the company. Issued capital is measured by reference to the nominal value of the shares in question.

EXAMPLE

Scenario One

If 500 shares with a nominal value of £1 each have been issued, the issued capital is £500. If those shares have been issued at nominal (or par) value, the issued share capital will be matched by £500 cash received for the shares and this fact will be represented in the balance sheet.

The basic accounting treatment would be as follows:

ASSETS	
Current assets	£500
CAPITAL	
Share capital	£500

Scenario Two

If, in fact, those shares were issued for more than their nominal value, for example shareholders paid £10 each for their shares (ie at a premium of £9 per share), the issued share capital will remain the same at £500. However, the company will have received a total of £5,000 for the shares.

To ensure that there is a matching correlation between the company's assets and shareholders' contributions, the total amount of the premium (ie £4,500) will have to be recorded in the balance sheet of the company as a separate item. The issued share capital figure plus the share premium will then represent the £5,000 received.

Again, by way of simple example, the accounting treatment would be as follows:

ASSETS	
Current assets	£5,000
CAPITAL	
Share capital	£500
Share premium	£4,500
Total	£5,000

(See **Chapter 22** for further discussion of the share premium account.)

7.10.2 Alteration to share capital

Most instances of an alteration to a company's share capital under s617 CA 2006 will be brought about by an allotment of shares. However, it is also possible under that section to alter share capital in the following ways:

(a) by consolidation;

(b) by subdivision;

(c) by reduction.

Shares are consolidated if they are consolidated into a smaller number of shares of a larger nominal amount (eg 1,000 £1 shares become 100 £10 shares); subdivision is the opposite (1,000 £1 shares become 10,000 10p shares).

Any consolidation or subdivision of share capital can be achieved by ordinary resolution of the shareholders, unless the company's articles prohibit or restrict such alteration.

Since the change brought about by any consolidation or subdivision is really only a nominal one, there will seldom be any advantage in making it, unless the value of each share is either extremely large or extremely small, in which case subdivision or consolidation may be of some value.

Under ss641–653 CA 2006, companies may reduce their share capital. The reasons for wanting to do this vary and are often quite technical. For example, public companies are only permitted to pay dividends if their net assets exceed their share capital (s831 CA 2006). If this is not the case, one solution is to reduce the share capital. (For public companies listed on the Stock Exchange, a failure to pay out a dividend can be prejudicial to the share price of the company.)

It is beyond the scope of this manual to deal with this issue in any detail. In order to have a basic understanding, the following important issues should be borne in mind:

(a) shareholders must approve the reduction by special resolution;

(b) any reduction must be sanctioned by the court;

(c) in a number of circumstances, creditors have a right to object to the proposed reduction;

(d) should the reduction affect separate classes of shareholders differently, there may be a class rights issue under s630 CA 2006, in which case consent of each class affected should be sought, by way of special resolution.

Reduction of share capital in this way can be undertaken by any company (s641(1)(b)). However, an alternative process is also available for private companies which involves, instead, a special resolution to authorise the reduction, together with statements of solvency about the company from each relevant director (s641(1)(a)). This is a simpler and cheaper process for private companies to reduce their share capital, removing the need for an application to the court.

Reduction of share capital should not be confused with a buy-back of a company's shares– discussed in **Chapter 9**.

7.11 Maintenance of capital

For the protection of people dealing with the company, namely its creditors, share capital has to be 'maintained' by the company. This does not mean that the money invested has to be deposited or set aside as a discrete fund; the money is available to be used by the company as 'working' capital, to pay for the expenses of its business. What maintaining capital means is that it must not, normally, be returned to the members in any way while the company is a going concern.

Three major consequences of this rule are that:

1 dividends may only be paid out of available profits;

2 capital invested cannot be returned to the members except:

(a) on a winding up of the company (see **Chapter 28**);

(b) by a properly approved reduction in capital; or

(c) where the company redeems or purchases its own shares (see **Chapter 9**);

3 a company should not provide funding for the acquisition of shares in itself (see **Chapter 11**).

As has already been explained, it is common for shares to be issued for more than their nominal value. The excess is not strictly speaking share capital, but is required by s610(1) CA 2006 to be credited to a 'share premium account'. The share premium account has to be maintained in the same way as share capital; thus assets representing it cannot be returned to members.

7.12 Conduct/ethical matters

7.12.1 Introduction

Any instructions involving arrangements with shares in a company should trigger consideration of the Financial Services and Markets Act 2000 (FSMA).

Reasons for this are:

1 Regulated activities (as defined in Sch 2, Pt I FSMA) include (a) arranging deals in investments and (b) investment advice.

2 Shares constitute relevant investments, as defined in Sch 2, Pt II FSMA.

A fundamental question then arises which is whether or not the general prohibition under s19 FSMA is triggered, in which case is appropriate authorisation necessary before the work can be undertaken by a solicitor?

It should be remembered that FSMA must be read in conjunction with the FSMA 2000 (Regulated Activities) Order 2001 (RAO).

Two matters of general application in this context are:

1 Is the activity excluded generally or specifically under the RAO?

2 If not, is specific Financial Conduct Authority (FCA) authorisation unnecessary due to the Designated Professional Bodies exemption and compliance with the SRA Financial Services (Scope) Rules and the Conduct of Business Rules?

7.12.2 Arranging deals in investments

Article 25 of the RAO defines the above as either:

(a) 'Making arrangements for another person . . . to buy, sell, subscribe for or underwrite a particular investment . . .'; or

(b) 'Making arrangements with a view to another person who participates in the arrangements buying, selling, subscribing for or underwriting investments . . .'

In this context, 'investment' includes company shares.

Arguably, therefore, assisting either a company with the allotment of shares or a third party with a subscription for shares could be classed as 'arranging'.

Having said that, art 34 RAO contains an exclusion regarding arrangements for the purpose of the issue of shares by a company. This would appear to cover much of the work which a solicitor may carry out for a company client in advising on statutory and constitutional compliance (albeit that pure advice would not be arranging at all).

Further, art 67 RAO excludes any activity which is carried on in the course of carrying on a profession which does not otherwise consist of carrying on regulated activities and may be reasonably regarded as a necessary part of other professional services. (This exclusion is removed if the solicitor receives discrete remuneration for the activity in question.) As such, so long as the solicitor is engaged to assist with compliance with legal formalities, for example meeting Companies Act requirements and ensuring correct transfer of title, art 67 is likely to apply.

7.12.3 **Investment advice**

Article 53 RAO defines investment advice as advising a *potential investor* on the merits of (inter alia) buying, selling or subscribing for shares.

As such, the main focus of discussion will be on acting for the purchaser of shares, rather than the company itself.

Several factors come into play which will usually assist a solicitor in avoiding falling foul of s19 FSMA, namely:

1 Only generic advice may be required by the client, for example an explanation of the difference between different types of shares or an explanation of particular share rights, as stipulated in the relevant company's articles.
2 The exclusion within art 67 RAO may apply, although justifying advice on the merits of a particular investment as a necessary part of wider activities may be difficult, especially if the client has expressly asked for this.
3 Investment advice may be provided on the basis that the firm for which the solicitor works is regulated by a Designated Professional Body and there is complete compliance with the SRA's Scope Rules and Conduct of Business Rules. Two important elements need to be considered:
   (a) Was the investment advice (as a regulated activity) complementary to professional services being provided to the client?
   (b) Was the activity incidental to the professional services which the firm provides?

No hard-and-fast answers can be given to these matters; much will depend upon the scope of the retainer from the client seeking to buy shares.

EXAMPLE

Bridget is approached by Anna for advice. Anna explains that they have £25,000 to invest in a business proposition, which is a company being operated by Anna's sister. Anna has been presented with a draft shareholders' agreement and the articles of association of the relevant company. Anna wants to know 'where they will stand' as a shareholder in this company.

Arguably this is not investment advice at all–it is simply legal advice on the contractual effect of the documents in question should the client become a shareholder. Further, any explanation of shares as an investment mechanism which feature as part of the solicitor's advice is likely either to be generic or a necessary part of the wider legal advice provided.

Alternatively, Anna asks Bridget if she thinks that this will be a good investment or whether or not 'there are better ways of investing my money'. To respond to this would clearly be stand-alone investment advice; there is nothing about it which would appear to be either generic, necessary, complementary or incidental. As such, without authorisation from the FCA, this would constitute the carrying on of a regulated activity by an unauthorised person in contravention of the general prohibition in s19 FSMA. As such, an offence would be committed under s23 FSMA.

KEY POINT SUMMARY

From reading this chapter, it will be seen that:

- Shares allow for investment in a company. As such, they are a useful capital raising device for companies.
- Shares may carry with them voting rights, which also means they can be used to allocate power within a company. Logically, the larger the investment, the greater the influence a shareholder may have.
- Shares may carry varying rights which determine such matters as the amount of dividends a shareholder may receive and entitlement to a return of investment on the winding up of a company.
- Allotment of shares is primarily a matter for the directors. However, the exercise of this power may be regulated, for example the imposition by the Companies Act 2006 of pre-emption rights for existing shareholders.
- Changes can be made to a company's share capital, for example by a further allotment of shares or, conversely, by a reduction in capital.
- The return of funds to shareholders, except on a winding up, is usually prohibited due to the maintenance of capital doctrine. However, there are well-defined statutory exceptions to this rule.

CHAPTER 8
Dividends

FUNCTIONING LEGAL KNOWLEDGE

This chapter considers the following functioning legal knowledge included in the SRA's SQE 1 assessment specification:

Finance:

- distribution of profits and gains

Corporate governance and compliance:

- rights, duties and powers of directors and shareholders of companies

AUTHORITIES UNDERPINNING PRACTICE

The key authorities that underpin this area of practice are listed below. Note that for legislation you are linked to legislation.gov.uk.

Although much of the legislation on this government website is available in its amended form, the incorporation of new amendments into the text of legislation can be delayed. You should refer to legal databases to ensure you are referencing the most up-to-date legislation.

- Companies Act 2006
  https://www.legislation.gov.uk/ukpga/2006/46
- Companies (Model Articles) Regulations 2008
  https://www.legislation.gov.uk/uksi/2008/3229

8.1 Introduction

After consulting this chapter, you will have been introduced to the concept of returning profits to shareholders by way of dividends.

As will be seen, the payment of a dividend is a highly regulated process, both in terms of the profits which can be paid out and the way in which the payment is approved. This chapter will finish by considering the relatively serious consequences of an unlawful dividend.

8.2 Use of company earnings

There are four main ways in which a company can deal with its earnings:

(a) retain them in the business;

(b) use them to pay interest on debentures and other borrowings;

(c) pay directors' fees (and bonuses);

(d) pay them as dividends to the shareholders.

If earnings are retained in the business, the shareholders ought to benefit in the long run, since the capital value of the company (and thus of the shares in it) will increase.

A payment of interest on borrowings will often be a payment to an outsider, which reduces profits available to the shareholders.

Directors' fees are expenses of the business which effectively reduce the sums available to shareholders (by reducing profit), but in the case of many **closely held**, private companies, the directors and shareholders are the same people. Thus, in a financial sense, payment of directors' fees can be regarded as equivalent to a payment of a dividend to shareholders–they are both methods of reward for involvement in the company. However, the tax consequences are quite different, which can be a factor in which type of payment is chosen.

A company may be, in any event, not entirely free to choose between different uses of earnings for the following reasons:

(a) It will often be contractually bound to make payments of interest and directors' fees.

(b) There are company law rules which prevent the company from paying dividends except to the extent of 'profits available for the purpose'.

(c) It will often be commercially unwise for the company to pay out all its profits, since some will be required to provide for future contingencies or for the expansion of the business.

8.3 Declaration and payment of dividends

8.3.1 Introduction

A dividend is a payment to the shareholders of the company which provides them with a return on their investment. It is not a payment of interest on the money invested, since the shareholder does not have an automatic right to the dividend–as we shall see, it becomes payable only if 'declared' by the company (or otherwise authorised under the articles) and only if the Companies Act 2006 (CA 2006) permits payment in the circumstances.

The method of payment of a dividend is essentially an internal matter for a company determined by its articles. By way of example, we shall focus on the method set out in art 30 of the Model Articles for Private Companies, which contains a relatively common approach to dividends. However, in all circumstances the articles of the relevant company should be referred to.

8.3.2 Final or year-end dividends

The payment of a dividend must be made out of profits available for this purpose (s830 CA 2006), discussed later. In turn, any such payment must be made by reference to relevant accounts (s836 CA 2006). It is usual, therefore, for dividends to be paid by reference to the year-end accounts of a company.

A dividend can be paid once it has been *declared* by ordinary resolution (art 30(1)). However, no declaration can take place unless a dividend has first been *recommended* by the board (art 30(2)). The process, therefore, would be:

(a) After the accounts have been prepared, the directors will consider what dividend, if any, ought to be declared, and will make a recommendation of that amount.

(b) A meeting of the shareholders will be held at which the question of declaring a dividend will be considered. (Alternatively, a written resolution could be used.) The members may reject the directors' recommendation or declare a dividend smaller than that recommended, but art 30(2) prevents them exceeding the amount recommended by the directors.

Once the dividend has been declared, the members will be paid the dividend by the company. The amount of dividend paid to each member depends on the nominal value of the shares held, no account being taken of any premium paid on the shares.

The reason why the members cannot declare a dividend in excess of the directors' recommendation is that the directors are the managers of the company's business, and so are in a better position than the members to assess the economic ability of the company to pay dividends; it is therefore probably a sensible provision to include in the articles. If members with a majority of the votes object to the dividend policy of the directors, they can exercise their right to remove the directors from office under s168 CA 2006.

Traditionally, the declaration of a dividend was a standing item on the agenda of the annual general meeting of every company (AGM). The demise of the AGM for private companies has altered practice in this area and may result in a greater opportunity or need for the board to declare dividends independently of the members, normally as interim dividends, considered next.

8.3.3 Interim dividends

During the course of an accounting period (ie a 12-month period in respect of which the company's accounts are prepared), the directors may decide to pay an interim dividend (art 30(1)). It is not necessary for such dividends to be formally declared by ordinary resolution of the shareholders. However, the same legal safeguards apply to interim dividends as final ones.

8.4 Differing classes of share

If there are different classes of share they may have different rights to dividends. Thus, if there are preference shares, the ordinary shareholders will usually not be entitled to any dividend until the preference shareholders have received their dividend (which will be expressed as a fixed amount per share or a fixed percentage).

EXAMPLE

A company has 2,000 £1 shares of which 1,000 are ordinary shares and 1,000 are 10% preference shares; the company declares a dividend of £150. The preference shareholders are entitled to £100 (ie 10% of the nominal value of their shares) and the ordinary shareholders get the balance (ie £50 or 5p per share).

Further, if preferred shareholders also benefit from cumulation of their entitlement, this right must also be recognised.

EXAMPLE

A company, Caboa, has 2,000 £1 shares of which 1,000 are ordinary shares and 1,000 are 10% *cumulative* preference shares.

Caboa has available a total of £300 to pay out as a dividend. The company has been in existence for three years and this is the first dividend to be paid.

The preference shareholders are entitled to an annual dividend of £100 (ie 10% of the nominal value of their shares); however, this right has accumulated over three years, meaning that all profits will be paid to them.

The ordinary shareholders, therefore, will receive nothing on this occasion.

The payment of an *interim* dividend can potentially eat into profits which should be first used for the payment of preferential dividends. As such, if any preferred dividends are in arrears, it is usually the case that no interim dividend can be paid in respect of other shares (see, eg, art 30(5) of the Model Articles for Private Companies).

8.5 Legal entitlement to dividend

Once declared by the members in general meeting, a dividend is a debt due to the members from the company. Any member is, therefore, entitled to sue the company if the dividend is not paid. An interim dividend is not, however, a debt due from the company, so that the members have no right to it until it is actually paid.

8.6 Restrictions on sources of dividends

8.6.1 The basic rule

To ensure that money invested by shareholders is not returned to them before the company is wound up, there have always been rules based on judicial decisions preventing the payment of dividends other than out of profits. Statute now lays down clear rules as to what funds are available for the payment of dividends. These rules, which were first introduced in 1980, were designed to implement the European Communities' Second Directive on Company Law and differ somewhat from the rules previously established by the courts–the statutory rules (now contained in the CA 2006) are generally more restrictive.

Section 830(1) CA 2006 provides that: 'A company shall not make a distribution except out of profits available for the purpose.'

The term 'distribution' is defined by s829 and includes all distributions of company assets to members *except*:

(a) the issue of bonus shares;

(b) the redemption or purchase of its own shares by the company (see **Chapter 9**;

(c) reduction of capital; or

(d) a distribution on winding up.

Most dividends are paid in cash and are included in the definition of 'distributions', since cash is just as much an asset as other types of property.

8.6.2 'Profits available'

'Profits available for the purpose' of paying dividends are defined by s830(2) as:

> accumulated, realised profits, so far as not previously utilised by distribution ... less ... accumulated, realised losses ...

This means that each year it is necessary to calculate the company's trading profit and any capital profits that have been made on the disposal of fixed assets. These are the 'realised profits' from which must be deducted any realised losses; that is, any trading loss or loss made on the disposal of a fixed asset. However, a dividend can only be payable if there are *accumulated* realised profits in excess of *accumulated* realised losses. This means that the balance of realised profits can be carried forward from year to year.

It is not, therefore, necessary to make a profit every year in order to pay a dividend–all that is required is that there should be a balance of profits taking this year and previous years together.

EXAMPLE

	Realised profit/(loss)	Dividend	Balance to carry forward
Year 1	4,000	1,000	3,000
Year 2	2,000	1,000	4,000
Year 3	(3,000)	1,000	nil

The dividend in year 3 is lawful because:

(a) In year 1, the realised profits were £4,000 and the dividend paid only £1,000, so that £3,000 worth of profits could be carried forward.

(b) In year 2, the accumulated realised profits were £5,000 (£3,000 + £2,000) and the dividend £1,000, so that a £4,000 could be carried forward.

(c) In year 3, there was a realised loss of £3,000, but accumulated profits of £4,000, thus leaving a balance of £1,000 for payment of a dividend.

Just as realised profits not used may be carried forward to later years, so realised losses which are not balanced by realised profits accumulated from previous years must be carried forward to later years and set off against realised profits before a dividend can be paid. Therefore, continuing with this example:

	Realised profit/(loss)	Dividend	Balance to carry forward
Year 4	(2,000)	nil	(2,000)
Year 5	1,000	nil	(1,000)
Year 6	2,000	1,000	nil

The dividend in year 3 is lawful because:

(a) In year 4, there was a loss, and since no accumulated profits remained from years 1 to 3, no dividend could be paid.

(b) In year 5, a profit of £1,000 was made but no dividend could be paid since the accumulated realised loss (£2,000 from year 4) was more than the realised profit.

(c) In year 6, the £1,000 dividend was the maximum which could be paid because £1,000 of the loss carried over from year 4 had to be set off against the profit.

8.6.3 **Unrealised losses**

It should be noted that although realised losses must be made good out of realised profits before a dividend can be paid, there is no requirement that *unrealised* losses must be made good. For example, if a company owns land which it knows to be declining in value, it can still go on paying dividends out of realised profits, since the loss on the land is only realised when the land is sold. Similarly, an unrealised profit cannot be used to justify payment of a dividend. A company which is making small realised losses cannot, therefore, pay a dividend even if its land is increasing in value by more than the losses.

8.6.4 **Calculation of profits and losses**

Section 830 does not lay down particular rules as to how profits and losses are to be calculated; normal accountancy practice must be applied in deciding whether a profit or loss has been realised.

8.6.5 **Justification of distribution by reference to the 'relevant accounts'**

8.6.5.1 The 'relevant accounts'

Whether a company has any profits available for distribution can only be judged by reference to properly drawn-up accounts. Section 836 CA 2006 lays down rules as to which accounts are to be used at any particular time for deciding whether there are profits available. Usually the company must rely on the last set of accounts prepared in accordance with the duty imposed on the company under Ch 4, Pt 15 CA 2006 and circulated to members pursuant to s423 CA 2006.

In *Bairstow v Queen's Moat Houses plc* [2001] 2 BCLC 531, the Court of Appeal emphasised the fact that failure to comply with this requirement would render any distribution unlawful, even if there existed available profits in reality.

8.6.5.2 Interim and initial accounts

If a company wants to pay a dividend which is not justified by its last accounts, it can prepare 'interim' accounts specially for the purpose of showing that profits are available for distribution (s836(2)(a)). This might be done, for example, if the company had made a loss and so could not pay a dividend but has now started to make profits again and does not want to wait until the next full set of accounts are produced. Similarly, if a company wishes to pay a dividend before it has prepared *any* accounts (ie broadly speaking during its first year after incorporation) it can prepare 'initial' accounts to justify the dividend payment (s836(2)(b)).

Interim and initial accounts must be prepared in much the same way as the normal final accounts of the company. Also, these accounts must enable a reasonable judgement to be made as to the amount of profits, losses, assets and liabilities of the company at the time (ss838(1) and 839(1) CA 2006). Because of the expense involved in preparing such accounts, it will usually be better to wait until accounts are produced in the normal way before paying the dividend.

8.7 Consequences of unlawful distributions

8.7.1 Shareholders

Section 847(2) CA 2006 requires any member to repay a distribution which he or she 'knows or has reasonable grounds for believing' to be unlawful. (See *It's a Wrap (UK) Ltd v Gula* [2006] 2 BCLC 634 for judicial interpretation of this phrase.)

Further, knowing receipt of an unlawful dividend may render a shareholder a constructive trustee of the sum in question on the company's behalf.

8.7.2 Directors

If a dividend is paid unlawfully, the directors will normally be personally liable to repay the amount of the dividend to the company, since they will have recommended and paid (or permitted payment of) the dividend in breach of their duty as trustees of the company's assets. (See, for example, *Bairstow v Queen's Moat Houses plc* [2001] 2 BCLC 531.)

KEY POINT SUMMARY

- Dividends can be seen as a method of profit allocation within a company.
- The type of shares a shareholder owns will determine their entitlement to a dividend and also any greater or lesser entitlement than other shareholders to such a payment.
- The main distinction should be drawn between ordinary shares which carry a general entitlement to dividends and preference shares which carry a preferred, but usually fixed, entitlement.
- The source of funds for a dividend is regulated by the Companies Act 2006, as is the method by which the amount of those funds is determined. As such, payment of dividends is not automatic.
- It is essential for directors to make payments of dividends entirely in accordance with the statutory rules, not least because of the personal liability which they may incur in contravening those rules.
- The method and process for declaring and paying dividends will be set out in a company's articles.

CHAPTER 9
Purchase by a Company of its Own Shares

FUNCTIONING LEGAL KNOWLEDGE

This chapter considers the following functioning legal knowledge included in the SRA's SQE 1 assessment specification:

Finance:

- financial records, information and accounting requirements

Corporate governance and compliance:

- rights, duties and powers of directors and shareholders of companies
- company decision-making and meetings: procedural, disclosure and approval requirements
- documentary, record-keeping, statutory filing and disclosure requirements

AUTHORITIES UNDERPINNING PRACTICE

The key authorities that underpin this area of practice are listed below. Note that for legislation you are linked to legislation.gov.uk.

Although much of the legislation on this government website is available in its amended form, the incorporation of new amendments into the text of legislation can be delayed. You should refer to legal databases to ensure you are referencing the most up-to-date legislation.

- Companies Act 2006
  https://www.legislation.gov.uk/ukpga/2006/46/contents
- Companies (Model Articles) Regulations 2008
  https://www.legislation.gov.uk/uksi/2008/3229

9.1 Introduction

The purchase by a company of its own shares (often referred to as a 'buy-back' of shares) is a highly regulated transaction which may be undertaken from time to time by a company.

After consulting this chapter, you will have been introduced to:

(a) The practical reasons for a buy-back.
(b) The regulations applicable to a buy-back.
(c) The reasons for the existence of such regulations.

9.2 The company as its own shareholder

As a basic rule, a company may not acquire its own shares (s658 Companies Act 2006 (CA 2006)). The traditional position was that it was illegal for a company to buy its own shares (*Trevor v Whitworth* (1887) 12 App Cas 409). This is because purchase of its own shares by a company is, in effect, a return to the shareholder of their investment and so is a reduction of capital. Statute has since intervened to modify this restriction, by the recognition of both redeemable shares and buy-back of shares in defined circumstances.

9.3 Redeemable shares

9.3.1 Authority to create redeemable shares

Redeemable shares can be described as shares with a limited 'shelf life' because at their creation they will constitute shares which can be either:

(a) bought back by the company at the option of the company; or

(b) sold back to the company at the option of the shareholder.

Section 684 CA 2006 gives companies power to issue redeemable shares.

In the case of a private company, its articles may exclude or restrict this possibility; a public company, by contrast, must be authorised by its articles to issue redeemable shares.

The terms of redemption must be set out in the articles (s685(4)); however, the directors can be left to determine those terms instead if such permission is granted either by the articles or by prior ordinary resolution (s685(1)). No share can be subsequently redeemed unless it is fully paid (s686(1)).

9.3.2 Notification of redemption

Any redemption has to be notified to the Registrar of Companies on form SH02 within 28 days of its happening (s689). This form also includes a statement of capital, setting out details of the company's share capital after the redemption.

9.4 Purchase of own shares by a company ('buy-back')

9.4.1 Introduction

It is thought to be desirable for companies, particularly small, closely held companies, to have the power to purchase their own shares, as this provides an 'exit route' for a shareholder wishing to divest themselves of their shares. (It should be remembered that the ready market for shares in this type of company is often very limited.) Section 690 CA 2006, therefore, gives companies power to purchase their own shares, unless this is displaced or restricted by a provision in their articles.

In fact, all companies have the possibility of buying back some of their shares. To reflect the diversity of companies which may effect buy-backs, the legislation distinguishes between 'off-market' and 'market' purchases (s693).

The specifics of this distinction are beyond the scope of this manual. Only a small number of companies whose shares are traded on an investment exchange, for example the London Stock Exchange, will have the option of undertaking a market purchase. (Also, it is worth noting that the commercial drivers for a buy-back by a publicly listed company will often vary considerably from those influencing a buy-back in a closely held, private company.)

What follows is an explanation of the mechanics of an off-market purchase.

Certain controls on buy-backs were eased in April 2013, primarily to meet the government's aspirations for greater ease of employee investment and ownership in private companies. This was achieved by the introduction of a less onerous regime for buy-backs which facilitate **employees' share schemes**.

The explanation that follows only covers the general regime not that relating to employees' share schemes.

9.4.2 Initial considerations on buy-back

A fundamental prohibition exists which may prevent a company purchasing its shares; namely, that a buy-back cannot be effected if the result is either that the share capital that remains after the buy-back comprises only:

(a) redeemable shares; or

(b) shares held in treasury, that is, shares that were previously bought back and subsequently held 'in treasury' by the company (s690(2)). (See **9.4.4** for further discussion of treasury shares.)

This rule effectively prevents a company either from ending up with share capital which is temporary in nature (because it is made up solely of redeemable shares) or from having no shareholders other than the company itself.

The relevant company's articles should also be consulted at the outset to confirm that they contain no prohibition on a buy-back (s690(1)). (The Model Articles, for example, contain no such prohibition.)

As with redeemable shares, no share can be bought back unless it is fully paid (s691(1)). Subject to an exemption in the context of an employees' share scheme (beyond the scope of this manual), a company must pay for the shares it is taking back at the time of purchase (s691(2)).

9.4.3 The contract to purchase

The contract for purchase (between the company and the relevant shareholder) must be approved by ordinary resolution before the company enters into it (s694(1)).

The resolution to approve the contract will be invalid unless:

(a) where a **general meeting** has been called for the purpose of passing the ordinary resolution, a copy of the contract (or a memorandum of its terms) is made available for inspection by the **members** at the company's **registered office** for a period of at least 15 days ending with the date of the meeting and also at the meeting itself (s696(2)(b));

(b) where a **written resolution** is being used instead, a copy of the contract (or a memorandum of its terms) is sent to every eligible member at the same time as the written resolution (s696(2)(a)).

The votes attaching to the shares of the member whose shares are to be purchased must not be influential. More specifically:

(a) if the vote is taken at a general meeting, the resolution will not be effective if any votes cast by the relevant member were necessary to reach the required majority; or

(b) if approval is by way of written resolution, the relevant member cannot be regarded as an eligible member so cannot consent to the resolution.

9.4.4 The consequences of buy-back on share capital

Once the shares have been purchased by the company, they are usually treated as cancelled and the company's issued share capital is reduced accordingly (s706(b)).

EXAMPLE

Buy Back (Example) Ltd has an issued share capital of £300 divided amongst three shareholders as follows:

Jim: 100 ordinary shares of £1 each

Arun: 100 ordinary shares of £1 each

Sascha: 100 ordinary shares of £1 each

If all Sascha's shares were bought back and cancelled, the issued share capital would be reduced to £200 divided between Jim and Arun.

However, the option exists for all companies to hold shares they have repurchased 'in treasury', so long as the prescribed method of finance has been used (s724); that is, shares bought with distributable reserves. (See **9.4.7** for further discussion of financing buy-backs.)

Effectively, this allows such treasury shares to be sold on by the company at a future date without the need for prior shareholder approval (s727), as might be the case with a new allotment of shares (see **7.4**).

As such, there may be three consequences of a buy-back for a company's share capital:

(a) If the shares bought back do not qualify for treasury status, they must be cancelled.

(b) If the shares bought back qualify for treasury status but the company does not wish to avail itself of this possibility, they can be cancelled immediately following the buy-back pursuant to s729.

(c) If the shares bought back qualify for treasury status and the company wishes to maintain them as such, it can do so and those shares are not cancelled at that stage. In turn, the company must deal with those shares in accordance with Ch 6 Pt 18 CA 2006 and be entered in the register of members as the holder of such shares, although it cannot vote on those shares or receive any dividends in respect of them.

9.4.5 **Filing and registration obligations**

A buy-back will trigger several filing/registration requirements, namely:

(a) Within 28 days from the date the shares have been purchased, a return must be made to the Registrar of Companies (on form SH03) giving details of the buy-back (s707). This return will have to bear stamp duty at the rate of 0.5% of the consideration paid, unless it is £1,000 or less in which case it is exempt. As such it will be necessary to submit the form to the Stamp Office, together with relevant stamp duty. In turn, the Stamp Office will confirm in writing that stamp duty has been paid. This confirmation must be sent to the Registrar together with form SH03.

(b) Section 708 requires separate notification to **Companies House** of cancellation of any shares, together with a statement of capital, which sets out details of the company's share capital after the cancellation. This information is provided on form SH06.

(c) The contract which effected the buy-back will have to be maintained at the company's registered office for ten years from completion of the buy-back (s702 CA 2006).

(d) The company's register of members will have to be amended to detail the fact that the shareholder whose shares have been purchased is no longer a member. That shareholder will also have to surrender their share certificate to the company as part of the buy-back.

There may also be consequential changes to the status of people with significant control in the company. For example, if the shareholder whose shares are bought back (and cancelled) was a person exercising significant control (PSC), they will cease to be a PSC; in turn, the existing shareholders will each have a higher percentage shareholding, which may either turn them into PSCs or alter their existing status as a PSC. (See **Chapter 20** for more information on this topic.)

EXAMPLE

ExampleCo Ltd has four shareholders:

Melissa: 20 shares

Beth: 20 shares

Nial: 20 shares

Charlotte: 40 shares

Only Charlotte is a PSC, as only Charlotte owns in excess of 25% of the issued shares.

If Charlotte's shares are bought back and cancelled:

(a) Charlotte ceases to be a PSC;

(b) each of Melissa, Beth and Nial become PSCs (20/60 = 33.3% shareholding).

9.4.6 Buy-back summary

The following example summarises a number of the important issues which must be considered whenever a buy-back is proposed. (Note that it does not consider any of the rules governing permitted finance of the share purchase, which will be considered in the next section.)

EXAMPLE

OXP 5050 Ltd has an issued share capital of £10,000, comprising 10,000 shares of £1 each, and is proposing to buy back 500 shares from Shareholder X for £20,000.

The company's advisors must consider the following:

(a) Will the effect of the buy-back be that only treasury shares or redeemable shares will exist in the company after it has taken place? The answer to this is in the negative, so the transaction is not prevented in this way.

(b) Do the company's articles prevent or restrict this buy-back in any way? If they do, will it be possible to pass the required **special resolution** to alter them?

(c) All the shares to be bought must be fully paid. Any that are not cannot be bought back.

(d) Does the company have the funds to buy all the shares at the moment of purchase?

(e) Assuming the transaction is not prevented under issues (b), (c) or (d), the contract governing the buy-back must be approved in advance by ordinary resolution. Can this resolution be achieved without Shareholder X voting in its favour?

(f) By what method will the necessary shareholders' resolution under (e) be obtained–general meeting or written resolution? In turn, the method chosen will govern the mechanism by which the contract must be made available to the shareholders.

(g) Assuming the buy-back goes ahead, the company must notify the Registrar of Companies within 28 days on form SH03 together with confirmation that stamp duty of £100 (0.5% × £20,000) has been paid.

(h) The shares bought back must be cancelled from the company's share capital, unless the option exists to hold them in treasury. In any event, will any such treasury shares be cancelled immediately? If any shares are cancelled, form SH06 must also be submitted to the Registrar of Companies within 28 days.

(i) A copy of the relevant contract must be kept available for inspection (usually at the company's registered office) for ten years from the date of purchase.

9.4.7 Financing buy-back or redemption

When shares are redeemed or purchased by the company, the money used to pay for them (including any payment representing a premium over the **nominal value**) must generally come out of distributable profits or the proceeds of a fresh issue of shares (s692(2) and (3)).

The ability also exists for *private* companies to use an annual amount not exceeding the lower of £15,000 or the cash equivalent of 5% of the nominal value of its issued share capital to fund a buy-back of shares (the *de minimis* amount) without reference to distributable reserves, so long as this is authorised by the articles (s692(1ZA)). As such, this method of payment should not be considered automatic. If no such permission already exists, a change to the articles will first be necessary. (Note that the Model Articles do not contain such a permission.) However, companies with issued share capital of a low value are likely to find the sum at their disposal to be relatively insignificant.

EXAMPLE

Flamingo 222 Ltd has an issued share capital of £1,000, fully paid.

Should it be able to take advantage of s692(1ZA), the amount available would be £50 (5% of £1,000 being lower than £15,000).

9.4.8 Use of distributable profits only: accounting treatment

Where shares are purchased or redeemed with assets representing profits, the legislation requires the capital of the company to be 'maintained'. Thus, s733 CA 2006 requires the company to open a 'capital redemption reserve' equal to the reduction in the share capital (assuming shares are not held in treasury). This reserve is treated in the same way as share capital or the share premium account; that is, it is shown in the balance sheet as shareholder funds which has to be maintained until the company goes into **liquidation**.

EXAMPLE: BUY-BACK USING DISTRIBUTABLE PROFITS ONLY

Balance sheet of JCT Ltd *prior* to buy-back

Fixed Assets	220,000
Current Assets	140,000
Current Liabilities	40,000
Net Current Assets	100,000
TOTAL NET ASSETS	320,000
CAPITAL AND RESERVES	
Share capital	250,000
Share premium	10,000
Profit and loss	60,000
TOTAL	320,000

Assume the following:

- JCT buys back 10,000 ordinary shares of £1 each at a price of £20,000.
- The purchase is made wholly out of available profits (using available cash).
- The shares bought are cancelled.

The amendments to the balance sheet will be:

- reduce current assets by £20,000 (ie what has been physically spent);
- reduce share capital by £10,000 (ie the nominal value of the shares bought);
- reduce profit and loss by £20,000 (to reflect the use of profits to buy back the shares);
- create capital redemption reserve of £10,000 (equivalent to the reduction in capital).

Balance sheet of JCT Ltd *following* buy-back

Fixed Assets	220,000
Current Assets	120,000
Current Liabilities	40,000
Net Current Assets	80,000
TOTAL NET ASSETS	300,000
CAPITAL AND RESERVES	
Share capital	240,000
Share premium	10,000
Capital redemption reserve	10,000
Profit and loss	40,000
	300,000

9.4.9 **Financing buy-back (or redemption) out of capital**

In the case of a *private* company, payment out of assets representing capital is permitted both in respect of a buy-back and a redemption (s709). The use of capital in this way (the 'permissible capital payment') is only possible once distributable profits and the proceeds of any fresh issue of shares made for the purpose have been used up (s710).

EXAMPLE

OXP 5050 Ltd has an issued share capital of £10,000, comprising 10,000 shares of £1 each, and is proposing to buy back 500 shares from Shareholder X for £20,000.

The company has distributable profits of £8,000. The permissible capital payment will, therefore, be £12,000.

In order to protect the interests of members and creditors, the following detailed procedural requirements must be satisfied (note that use of the *de minimis* amount under s692(1ZA) is not subject to these requirements):

(a) The articles must not expressly restrict or prohibit the use of capital assets for this purpose (s709).

(b) The directors must make a statement that the company will remain solvent and will, in their view, be able to carry on business as a going concern for at least a year (s714). The directors' certificate must be supported by an **auditors'** report, in which the auditors certify that they are not aware of anything which would indicate that the directors' view of the situation is unreasonable. The directors will commit a criminal offence if they have no reasonable grounds for the opinion expressed in their statement (s715). They also face personal liability pursuant to s76 of the Insolvency Act 1986 if the company is actually wound up due to insolvency within 12 months of the payment out of capital. In such circumstances, the directors (as well as the shareholder whose shares were bought using capital) will be required to contribute to the company an amount the maximum of which is equivalent to the capital used.

(c) Not later than one week after the date of the directors' statement, a special resolution approving the use of capital must be passed. The members whose shares are to be purchased may not use the votes on those shares on this resolution.

(d) Both a copy of the directors' statement and the auditors' report must be made available at any general meeting held for the purpose or must be sent out with any written resolution (s718).

(e) Within a week of the above resolution, the company must have published details of the proposed buy-back in **The *Gazette***. It should also notify its creditors directly or through a notice in a national newspaper (s719). This is to put all interested creditors on notice, as they have the right to object to the use of capital by applying to court for an order cancelling the resolution (s721). (Dissenting members also have this right.)

(f) The payment for the shares must be made by the company not less than five or more than seven weeks after the date on which the resolution is passed (s723). This period is laid down so that members or creditors who object to the purchase have time to challenge the purchase in court.

9.4.10 **The use of capital: accounting treatment**

Where a payment is made using capital, the company's accounts must reflect this.

Under s734 CA 2006:

(a) where the permissible capital payment is *less than* the nominal value of the shares redeemed, the amount of the difference must be transferred to a capital redemption reserve;

(b) where the permissible capital payment is *greater than* the nominal value of the shares redeemed, the company may then reduce the amount of any share premium account, fully paid share capital or unrealised profits of the company standing in any reserve by a sum not exceeding the amount by which the permissible capital payment exceeds the nominal amount of the shares.

EXAMPLES: BUY-BACK USING DISTRIBUTABLE PROFITS AND CAPITAL

Balance sheet of BHW Ltd *prior* to buy-back

Fixed Assets	120,000
Current Assets	140,000
Current Liabilities	40,000
Net Current Assets	100,000
TOTAL NET ASSETS	220,000
CAPITAL AND RESERVES	
Share capital	150,000
Share premium	50,000
Profit and loss	20,000
TOTAL	220,000

Buy-back version 1

BHW buys back 20,000 ordinary shares of £1 each at a price of £30,000. The purchase is made from a combination of:

1. available profits (£20,000); and
2. a permissible capital payment of £10,000.

Assume that the shares purchased are cancelled.
The amendments to the balance sheet will be:

- reduce current assets by £30,000 (to reflect the actual amount spent);
- reduce share capital by £20,000 (ie the nominal value of the shares purchased);
- reduce profit and loss by £20,000 (to reflect the use of profits to buy back the shares);
- create a capital redemption reserve of £10,000 (equivalent to the amount by which the permissible capital payment is *less* than the *nominal* value of shares redeemed).

Balance sheet of BHW Ltd *following* buy-back version 1

Fixed Assets	120,000
Current Assets	90,000
Current Liabilities	40,000
Net Current Assets	50,000
TOTAL NET ASSETS	170,000
CAPITAL AND RESERVES	
Share capital	130,000
Share premium	40,000
Profit and loss	(Nil)
TOTAL	170,000

Buy-back version 2

If BHW had bought the 20,000 ordinary shares of £1 each at a price of £50,000, then the accounting treatment would be different. In this case, the purchase would be made from a combination of:

1. available profits (£20,000); and
2. a permissible capital payment of £30,000.

Assume that the shares purchased are cancelled.
The amendments to the balance sheet will be:

- reduce current assets by £50,000 (to reflect the actual amount spent);
- reduce share capital by £20,000 (ie the nominal value of the shares);
- reduce profit and loss by £20,000 (to reflect the use of profits to buy back the shares);
- reduce share premium account by £10,000 (equivalent to the amount by which the permissible capital payment *exceeds* the nominal value of shares redeemed).

Balance sheet of BHW Ltd *following* buy-back version 2

Fixed Assets	120,000
Current Assets	110,000
Current Liabilities	40,000
Net Current Assets	70,000
TOTAL NET ASSETS	190,000
CAPITAL AND RESERVES	
Share capital	130,000
Share premium	50,000
Capital redemption reserve	10,000
Profit and loss	(Nil)
TOTAL	190,000

CONDUCT POINT

Conflict of interest

A solicitor cannot act 'for a buy-back'. This is a bipartite arrangement involving the company and the selling shareholder. If your retainer is with the company, you must represent the company alone. To act for the selling shareholder as well would be to overlook the possibility of a conflict of interest.

CARRYING ON A FSMA-REGULATED ACTIVITY

Advising either the company or the selling shareholder on a buy-back of shares should trigger consideration of the Financial Services and Markets Act 2000. See the discussion in **7.12.1**.

It is likely that any assistance provided by the solicitor to the company to facilitate the buy-back, either by advising on Companies Act requirements or generating the relevant documentation, will not constitute arranging a deal in investments because of the effect of art 67 of the FSMA 2000 (Regulated Activities) Order 2001 (RAO).

Further, it is submitted that if the company cannot be regarded as buying the shares in the capacity of an investor, no issue of investment advice can arise.

Similarly, if acting for the selling shareholder, anything which may be regarded as arranging, may be excluded by art 67 RAO, although the role that the solicitor takes could be crucial in answering this question. Arguably, the solicitor may also carry out investment advice, although again either art 67 RAO or fulfilment of the SRA's Scope Rules will assist. However, care should be taken if the selling shareholder raises alternative proposals, upon which they seek a value judgement, or asks for advice about using the proceeds of sale as an investment.

KEY POINT SUMMARY

Important matters pertaining to a buy-back of shares are:

- The purchase by a company of its own shares offends against the maintenance of capital doctrine. For this reason, it is controlled by statute.
- The primary source of funds for a buy-back is distributable profits. Again, this reflects the influence of the maintenance of capital doctrine. An exception is made for private companies, in that they can also use capital (subject to stringent requirements).
- The consequence of a buy-back is that the relevant shares are usually cancelled, which will reduce the share capital of the company. However, if the shares bought back constitute treasury shares, the company has the option to hold those shares 'in treasury'; that is, the company becomes the registered shareholder although with no discernible rights.
- Depending upon the consideration paid for the shares, a buy-back may result in a stamp duty liability for the company.
- A buy-back of shares will have to be reflected in a company's balance sheet, again, according to statutory requirements.
- A buy-back will trigger requirements to alter certain of a company's internal registers and the need to notify Companies House of the impact of the transaction on the company's share capital.

CHAPTER 10
Transfer and Transmission of Shares

FUNCTIONING LEGAL KNOWLEDGE

This chapter considers the following functioning legal knowledge included in the SRA's SQE 1 assessment specification:

Corporate governance and compliance:

- rights, duties and powers of directors and shareholders of companies
- company decision-making and meetings: procedural, disclosure and approval requirements
- documentary, record-keeping, statutory filing and disclosure requirements

AUTHORITIES UNDERPINNING PRACTICE

The key authorities that underpin this area of practice are listed below. Note that for legislation you are linked to legislation.gov.uk.

Although much of the legislation on this government website is available in its amended form, the incorporation of new amendments into the text of legislation can be delayed. You should refer to legal databases to ensure you are referencing the most up-to-date legislation.

- Companies Act 2006
  https://www.legislation.gov.uk/ukpga/2006/46/contents
- Companies (Model Articles) Regulations 2008
  https://www.legislation.gov.uk/uksi/2008/3229
- Stock Transfer Act 1963
  http://www.legislation.gov.uk/ukpga/1963/18

10.1 Introduction

After consulting this chapter, you will have been introduced to the various ways in which a shareholder in a company may dispose of their equity interest in a company either during their lifetime or on death.

A disposal of shares will either amount to:

(a) a transfer; that is, it is done willingly *inter vivos*; or

(b) a transmission, due to the effect of the company's articles or the effect of law, for example transmission to a **trustee in bankruptcy** on the personal insolvency of the shareholder.

A disposal of shares may have several consequences both for the company and the existing shareholders. These issues will be looked at in this section.

On a disposal of shares, tax will often become payable by the shareholder who is disposing of their shares; this topic is dealt with in **Chapter 31**. However, tax may also be payable by the buyer of shares, in the form of stamp duty. This consequence will be considered here.

10.2 Transfer of shares

10.2.1 Introduction

A transfer of shares may be made by means of a sale or a gift *inter vivos*. The motivations behind a transfer can be varied; however, the reasons are often:

(a) to realise the value in the company, as represented by its shares;

(b) to introduce an outsider (or family member) into the company as a shareholder (although this can also be achieved by an allotment of shares to them);

(c) tax or estate-planning reasons.

By contrast, the death or bankruptcy of a shareholder gives rise to an automatic transmission of shares (which will usually be followed by a transfer) and the special rules for transmission are dealt with later in the chapter.

A transfer of shares is likely to involve consideration of each of the Companies Act 2006 (CA 2006), the Stock Transfer Act 1963 and the relevant company's articles of association.

10.2.2 Acquiring legal title to shares

A shareholder who wishes to sell their shares may make a contract in any form that they wish. The contract for sale is sufficient to give the purchaser an equitable interest in the shares, with the vendor holding the legal title as trustee. However, *membership of the company* and, accordingly, legal ownership does not begin until the purchaser is registered as a member in the register of members which the company is required to keep (ss112(2) and 113 CA 2006).

An entry cannot be made in the register of members until the company has received a 'proper instrument of transfer' (s770(1) CA 2006): this will usually take the form of a stock transfer form. It is usually for the board of directors to decide to register any proposed transfer in accordance with the relevant provisions of the company's articles.

A transfer of shares may result in the transferor ceasing to be and the transferee becoming a person with significant control (PSC), so a concomitant change to the PSC register may also be necessary, as well as notification of the same to Companies House. (See **Chapter 20** for further discussion of the PSC register.) Note, however, that the enactment of the Economic Crime and Corporate Transparency Bill is likely to remove the need for a company to maintain a PSC register. The reader should check the status of this legislation at the time of reading to confirm the up-to-date position.

EXAMPLE

Anya is proposing to transfer her entire shareholding to Robert. Anya is currently a PSC, owning a 30% shareholding.

After the transfer, assuming it is registered by the company:

- Anya will cease to be both a member and a PSC of the company;
- Robert will become both a member and a PSC of the company.

As such, both the register of members and the PSC register of the company will have to be amended to take into account these changes.

10.2.3 Procedure for transfer

Section 1 of the Stock Transfer Act 1963 provides that a transfer of *fully paid* shares may be made on a stock transfer form signed by the transferor and specifying:

(a) particulars of the consideration;

(b) description of the number or amount of the shares;

(c) particulars of the person by whom the transfer is made; and

(d) the full name and address of the transferee.

The format of a stock transfer form is provided in Sch 1 to the Stock Transfer Act 1963. An example is provided in Figure 10.1 later in the chapter. Reference should be made to this as appropriate.

Once the sale of the shares has been agreed, the vendor/transferor should execute a stock transfer form and send it together with the share certificate to the purchaser, who pays the stamp duty. The purchaser will apply to the company for registration by sending the stamped transfer and share certificate to the company.

On receipt of such application:

(a) the transfer must be registered in the register of members within two months of the application (s771(1) CA 2006) (unless refused–see later); and

(b) the company must send the purchaser a share certificate within the same period (s776(1) CA 2006).

This procedure applies equally to a gift of shares as well as on a sale.

The process of registration is effectively controlled by the board and the way in which it can and should respond to any proposed transfer will be determined by the articles (considered in more detail later). However, any potential transferee should recognise that registration may not always be an automatic right and may in some circumstances be refused.

Section 771(1)(b) CA 2006 requires that any notice of refusal to register must be sent to the transferee within two months of their application, accompanied by reasons for the same. Section 771(2) also permits the transferee to request information on the reasons for refusal in addition to that supplied by the company in the first instance.

(It should be noted that shares of publicly quoted companies may be transferred electronically under the CREST system. Such shares are said to exist in uncertificated form. The details of this system are beyond the scope of this manual. Useful information on CREST can be found on its website.)

10.3 **Stamp duty on transfer of shares**

Stamp duty on a transfer of shares is charged at a rate of 0.5% of the consideration payable ('ad valorem') with the resulting figure being rounded up to the nearest £5.

In any circumstances where the consideration is £1,000 or less, no actual duty is payable. It is, however, necessary for the transferor to sign the certificate on the reverse of the stock transfer form to this effect. This certificate extends to the transfer being part of a larger transaction or series of transactions where the total consideration exceeds £1,000. As such, it is not possible to avoid stamp duty by dividing up a share transfer into 'sub units' of £1,000 or less.

Certain transfers of shares are, however, exempt from stamp duty. One of the most common types is a gift of shares; that is, a transfer for no consideration in money or money's worth.

The purchaser of the shares usually pays the relevant stamp duty. This must be done within 30 days of the execution of the stock transfer form.

EXAMPLE

Consideration payable	Stamp duty charged
£Nil	£Nil*
£830	£Nil**
£1,000	£Nil**
£1,620	£10***
£45,763	£230

*No certificate would be necessary here; simply the entry of the word 'Nil' in the consideration box.

**In each instance, the consideration does not exceed £1,000, so no duty is payable. However, a certificate on the reverse of the stock transfer form should be completed to this effect.

***0.5% of this consideration is actually £8.10; however, it must be rounded up to the nearest £5.

10.4 Restrictions on right to transfer

Unless the articles provide to the contrary, every shareholder has a *right* to transfer their shares. However, the articles of the company can impose a restriction on the right to transfer shares.

In the case of private companies, such a restriction is quite common. At one time, a company could not be a private company unless there was a restriction in its articles on the right to transfer shares. Whilst the historical premise for such a restriction has disappeared, a restriction may still be thought to be desirable, since it enables the company (usually through the directors) to control the identity of future shareholders.

Where there are restrictions on the right to transfer shares, the company must decide within two months of application for registration whether or not to permit the transfer. If within that time the company has not given notice of refusal of registration to the transferee together with its reasons, the company and its officers who are in default are liable to a fine (s771(3) and (4) CA 2006) and the transferee becomes *entitled* to be registered.

It is not possible to consider all the possible types of restriction on the right to register but some possible restrictions will now be considered.

10.4.1 'The directors may in their absolute discretion decline to register any transfer of any share, whether or not it is a fully paid share'

As with most restrictions on transfer, it is the directors who have power to refuse registration. The power is a negative one; that is, the directors have power to *refuse* registration. This means that a positive resolution of the directors is required to refuse registration, and since a resolution requires a majority in favour, an equality of votes will not be sufficient (unless, of course, the chairman has a casting vote and is against registration).

Any power of the directors to refuse registration must be exercised in good faith in the company's interests. (For an example of the effect of such a rule, see *Re Smith and Fawcett Ltd* [1942] 1 Ch 304.)

It should be noted that this restriction is a restriction on the right to *transfer* shares, it is not a restriction on the right to *sell* them. If shares are sold but the purchaser is not registered, the vendor will hold the shares on trust for the purchaser.

10.4.2 'The directors may refuse to register the transfer of a share, and if they do so, the instrument of transfer must be returned to the transferee with notice of refusal unless they suspect that the proposed transfer may be fraudulent'

This wording is found in art 26(5) of the Model Articles for Private Companies. It is not dissimilar to the previous one. Note that it expressly recognises the obligation under s 771(1) CA 2006 to provide the transferee with a notice of refusal to register.

10.4.3 'The directors may decline to register a transfer of any share in favour of a person of whom they disapprove or of a share over which the company has a lien'

This restriction gives the directors two grounds for refusing registration. One is clearly subjective, whilst the other is objective. A company may wish to restrict the transfer of a share over which it has a lien as a way of protecting its security over the asset. On the basis that partly paid shares in private companies are quite rare, this may be more of a theoretical restriction than a real one. In terms of an 'undesirable' shareholder, the provisions of s771 CA 2006, which require the company to give reasons for any refusal, will be particularly relevant. Moreover, the transferee is entitled to ask for further reasonable information about the reasons for the refusal (s771(2)). This could be fertile ground for dispute.

10.4.4 'The directors may decline to register a transfer of any share except a transfer to [an existing member of the company or to a member of the family of the transferor]'

This type of restriction may be appropriate to restrict a shareholder in their right to bring in outsiders against the wishes of other members of the company; it leaves them free to transfer to insiders (ie the existing members of the company) or their own family. The words in square brackets could be adapted to include various other groups of permitted transferees, for example named persons or employees of the company. The term 'member of the family' must, of course, be defined by the articles.

10.5 Pre-emption rights

The object of restrictions on the right to transfer shares is to keep ownership of a company within a relatively narrow group of potential shareholders. However, the restrictions referred to earlier are not entirely sufficient for that purpose since they are merely restrictions on transfer to any number of potential transferees. If it is decided that the shareholder body should be kept as much as possible to the existing shareholders only, the articles should include pre-emption rights. The basic effect of such a provision is that a member who wishes to transfer shares must first offer them to the existing members of the company.

When drafting an article providing for pre-emption rights, the following are some issues which may be significant.

(a) Should the transferring member be free to transfer to *any* existing member of the company of their choosing or should they always be obliged to offer their shares to *all* the existing members in proportion to their present holdings?

(b) What should happen if only a percentage of existing shareholders take up their pre-emption rights? Should the transferring member be obliged to transfer part of their holding to the accepting members? What should happen to the remaining shares? Alternatively, does the offer lapse unless all shareholders take up their entitlements? If the offer does lapse, is the transferring member then free to transfer to any person of their choosing?

(c) Should any exceptions be made to the pre-emption rights? For example, the articles may provide that the pre-emption rights do not apply to a transfer to a family member of the transferor.

(d) How is the price payable under the pre-emption offer to be fixed? It is quite common for the price to be fixed by agreement or by the auditors, if no price can be agreed between vendor and purchaser.

(e) How long are the offeree members to be given to make up their minds? A timescale for acceptance and a method of acceptance should be specified.

(f) How is the transferring member to give notice of their intention to sell? It is quite common to require notice to be given to the company. The directors will then initiate the procedure by making relevant offers of available shares to the other shareholders.

It is always important to preserve the distinction between pre-emption rights on transfer and those on allotment (see **Chapter 7** for discussion of allotment of shares). The former are not compulsory and can only be imposed by inclusion in the articles; the latter may be and are imposed by statute.

10.6 Transmission by operation of law

10.6.1 Death of a shareholder

When a member of a company dies, their shares vest automatically in their **personal representative**, who is usually entitled to any dividend paid by the company but may not vote at general meetings. The personal representative does not, however, automatically become a member of the company, since membership begins only with an entry in the register of members.

A personal representative will have to prove title to the shares by production of the grant of representation. Having done so, the courses of action open to them will usually be stipulated by the company's articles. In general terms:

(a) The articles of the company will usually contain a provision (such as art 27 of the Model Articles) permitting the personal representative to elect to be registered as a member. If they are registered as a member, the personal representative will be entitled to vote as a member of the company. Any subsequent transfer to a beneficiary or other person will be effected like any other proposed transfer.

(b) Alternatively, if the personal representative wishes to vest the shares directly in a beneficiary of the deceased shareholder, they can do so without first being registered themselves, by means of a stock transfer form. According to s773 CA 2006, such a transfer would be as effective as if the personal representative were a member at the time.

A restriction on the right to transfer shares does not apply to a transmission on death unless the articles specifically so provide. Further, a subsequent transfer by the personal representative will normally be subject to any restriction on transfer stipulated in the articles. As such, careful analysis of a company's articles will be required to establish exactly what the status of any personal representatives is and the options available to them. By way of a basic summary, the wishes of the deceased shareholder will not override the effect of the articles.

10.6.2 Bankruptcy of a shareholder

As a footnote to this discussion, parallel issues can arise on the bankruptcy of a shareholder and the options available to their trustee in bankruptcy as regards the relevant shareholding. Again, this will require careful analysis of the company's articles and the statutory powers afforded to the trustee.

CONDUCT POINT

It will be noted that a transfer of shares involves three parties: the transferor, the transferee and the company. A solicitor cannot act for all three persons. The buyer and the seller have alternative perspectives on the transaction and each may, in any event, require specific advice regarding their taxation position or their status after the sale. If your client is the company, it will want advice on how it must respond to any proposed transfer, in particular, the effect of the articles.

10.7 Carrying on a FSMA-regulated activity

This is of particular concern if the solicitor acts for either the buyer or seller of shares. One may be arranging a deal in investments or providing investment advice or both. See the discussion in **7.12.1**.

EXAMPLE

Nicolas, a solicitor, is approached by Olivia for advice. Olivia explains that she has agreed to sell all her shares in ExampleCo 123 Ltd to Camila for £120,000. Olivia wants to understand the process for doing so and would like the solicitor to draw up draft documentation.

It is possible to argue that the solicitor's actions amount to arranging a deal in investments. However, art 67 of the FSMA 2000 (Regulated Activities) Order 2001 (RAO) is likely to render it an excluded activity. Further, if the SRA's Scope Rules are satisfied (and there is compliance with the SRA's Conduct of Business Rules), the exemption in s327 of the Financial Services and Markets Act 2000 (FSMA) can be relied upon.

Alternatively, Olivia seeks advice from the solicitor on the best way of raising some cash. Olivia discusses her personal circumstances with the solicitor and the solicitor advises that the best asset to sell would be Olivia's shareholding in ExampleCo 123 Ltd. Nicolas's advice is based upon practical, legal and taxation factors.

The solicitor has carried out investment advice. Nicolas has advised the client to realise a particular investment for a specific reason. Also, neither art 67 RAO applies (the 'necessary' test), nor is the solicitor acting within the SRA Scope Rules (the advice cannot be classed as either complementary to a wider professional service or incidental to the services the firm provides).

As such, without authorisation from the Financial Conduct Authority, this would constitute the carrying on of a regulated activity by an unauthorised person in contravention of the general prohibition in s19 FSMA. As such, an offence would be committed under s23 FSMA.

FIGURE 10.1 Stock transfer form

<table>
<tr><td colspan="3">STOCK TRANSFER FORM</td></tr>
<tr><td>Consideration Money: £</td><td colspan="2">Certificate lodged with the Registrar

(For completion by the Registrar/Stock Exchange)</td></tr>
<tr><td>Name of Undertaking</td><td colspan="2"></td></tr>
<tr><td>Description of Security</td><td colspan="2"></td></tr>
<tr><td>Number or amount of Shares, Stock or other security and, in figures column only, number and denomination of units, if any.</td><td>Words</td><td>Figures

(units of)</td></tr>
<tr><td>Name(s) of registered holder(s) should be given in full: the address should be given where there is only one holder.

If the transfer is not made by the registered holder(s) insert also the name(s) and capacity (e.g., Executor(s)) of the person(s) making the transfer.</td><td colspan="2">In the name(s) of</td></tr>
</table>

FIGURE 10.1 Continued

(Delete words in italics except for stock exchange transactions) I/We hereby transfer the above security out of the name(s) aforesaid to the person(s) named below *or to the several persons named in Parts 2 of Brokers Transfer Forms relating to the above security:* Signature(s) of transferor(s): 1 2 3 4 A body corporate should execute this transfer under its common seal or otherwise in accordance with applicable statutory requirements.	**Stamp of Selling Broker**(s) **or, for transactions which are not stock exchange transactions, of Agent**(s)**, if any, acting for the Transferor**(s)**.** *Date*
Full name(s) and full postal address(es) (including County or, if applicable, Postal District number) of the person(s) to whom the security is transferred. Please state title, if any, or whether Mr., Mrs. or Miss. Please complete in type or in Block Capitals.	
I/We request that such entries be made in the register as are necessary to give effect to this transfer.	
Stamp of Buying Broker(s) (if any).	Stamp or name and address of person lodging this form (if other than the Buying Broker(s)).

Notes on stock transfer form:

The format and wording of a stock transfer form are set out in Sch 1 to the Stock Transfer Act 1963. What is set out above is not a pure facsimile of that Schedule but a re-versioning of the same for the purposes of illustration.

The form is designed to include the following relevant information:

1 The price being paid for the shares, if any. (It is possible to gift shares, instead.)
2 The company ('undertaking') in which the shares are issued.

3 The type of shares ('security') being transferred.
4 The number (both in words and figures) of shares being transferred.
5 The details of the transferor.
6 The details of the transferee.

So long as fully paid shares are being transferred, it is only necessary for the transferor to execute the form; the transferee need not sign. (In the case of partly paid or nil-paid shares, it is also necessary for the transferee to execute the form. Such shares are very uncommon, so this is rarely necessary.)

The box entitled 'Certificate lodged with the Registrar' refers to any registrar used by the company in question. It does not refer to the *Registrar of Companies*. Company registrars usually maintain the registers of companies with large and diverse numbers of shareholders, often listed public companies. Private limited companies do not, therefore, need the services of such a registrar. Instead, the form can be lodged directly with the company itself. There is no need to send the form to Companies House.

The form will attract stamp duty, unless a relevant exemption applies. (The reverse of the form, which contains certificates in respect of stamp duty exemptions (and explanations thereon), is not produced here.) If stamp duty is paid, the Stamp Office will confirm in writing that this has been done. This confirmation should be sent to the company along with the form.

KEY POINT SUMMARY

- Transfer and transmission of shares involves existing shareholders.
- Transfer is usually undertaken voluntarily; transmission operates through law in the context of the death or bankruptcy of the shareholder.
- Transfer of shares is effected by means of a stock transfer form. However, to acquire full legal title, a transferee must be registered as a member by the relevant company.
- The role of a company's constitution is significant in this area for the following two reasons:
  - the articles may contain restrictions on transfer of shares or may afford existing shareholders pre-emption rights; and
  - the articles may afford the directors extensive (or limited) discretion to refuse to register a proposed transfer.
- A transfer of shares will trigger consideration of stamp duty and its impact. In simple terms, if the amount paid for the shares is in excess of £1,000, the transferee will be liable to pay stamp duty of 0.5% of the consideration.

CHAPTER 11
Financial Assistance for the Purchase of Shares

FUNCTIONING LEGAL KNOWLEDGE

This chapter considers the following functioning legal knowledge included in the SRA's SQE 1 assessment specification:

Corporate governance and compliance:

- rights, duties and powers of directors and shareholders of companies
- company decision-making and meetings: procedural, disclosure and approval requirements

AUTHORITIES UNDERPINNING PRACTICE

The key authorities that underpin this area of practice are listed below. Note that for legislation you are linked to legislation.gov.uk.

Although much of the legislation on this government website is available in its amended form, the incorporation of new amendments into the text of legislation can be delayed. You should refer to legal databases to ensure you are referencing the most up-to-date legislation.

- Companies Act 2006
  https://www.legislation.gov.uk/ukpga/2006/46

11.1 Introduction

After consulting this chapter, you will have been introduced to the concept of financial assistance and its regulation.

A fundamental principle of company law is the concept of maintenance of capital. That is, the capital of a company, as represented by its assets, should be maintained for the benefit of the company, and its creditors. Companies should not generally return capital invested by shareholders, save on a winding up. Any derogation from this principle should be regulated to prevent abuse. This principle lies at the core of the regulation of financial assistance for the purchase of shares.

The general prohibition on financial assistance is designed, therefore, to maintain the capital of a company. In practical terms, it aims to prevent individuals acquiring a company's shares where that company's assets are used or put at risk by helping to finance the acquisition.

You should note at the outset, therefore, that financial assistance will be relevant in the context of a proposed acquisition of shares in a company, where that company, in some way, provides assistance of a financial nature to enable the acquisition to take place.

Until quite recently, the statutory prohibition on financial assistance was extensive. As such, there was great sensitivity in practice about its application. This led to a belief that the provisions on financial assistance resulted in greater inconvenience than the harm they were designed to prevent. As such, the Companies Act 2006 (CA 2006) introduced a substantially narrower regime, which is only of relevance to public companies. (However, a brief discussion of the position regarding private companies is given at the end of this chapter.)

11.2 General prohibitions on financial assistance

Unlawful financial assistance can occur in four defined situations.

1. Where a *public* company gives financial assistance directly or indirectly to any person for the purchase of its shares or any subsidiary thereof (either public or private) does the same (s678(1) CA 2006).
2. Where a public company subsidiary gives financial assistance directly or indirectly to any person for the purchase of shares in its private **parent company** (s679(1) CA 2006).
3. Where a public company (or any subsidiary thereof) gives financial assistance directly or indirectly for the purpose of reducing or discharging any liability incurred by a person in buying shares in that public company (s678(3) CA 2006).
4. Where a public company subsidiary gives financial assistance directly or indirectly for the purpose of reducing or discharging any liability incurred by a person in buying shares in that company's private parent company (s679(3) CA 2006).

Hence, assistance can be given before, at the same time as or following the time of the acquisition of the shares in question and may be given directly or indirectly, so, for example, assistance may be provided to a possible buyer through a circuitous route and still amount to financial assistance.

11.3 Types of financial assistance

These are defined in s677 CA 2006 and examples are provided in the sections that follow. The examples are by no means exhaustive and lawyers need to consider the full financial ramifications of the acts of relevant companies before, during and after acquisitions of shares in such companies or any of their parent companies. It should always be remembered that the assistance must emanate from the company in which the shares are being bought.

11.3.1 Financial assistance by way of gift

A simple example would be the provision by a company of funds to an individual to buy shares in that company or any parent company. Another example would be a sale by a company to an individual of an asset at an undervalue, which the individual then sold at full value in order to apply the realised funds in buying shares in the company.

11.3.2 Financial assistance given by way of guarantee, security or indemnity

These are forms of financial assistance which are provided indirectly. An example of each form follows.

11.3.2.1 Guarantee

A Ltd gives a guarantee to a bank in respect of the obligations of C, who has borrowed from the bank in order to buy shares in B plc, the parent company of A Ltd.

11.3.2.2 Security

E Ltd is acquiring F plc, a subsidiary of G Ltd. To finance the purchase, E Ltd is borrowing from a bank. The bank requires security for the loan in the form of charges over the assets of both E Ltd and F plc. The latter is therefore providing financial assistance by way of security for the purchase of its shares by E Ltd.

11.3.2.3 Indemnity

H plc offers its shares as consideration to buy the shares in T plc which H plc wishes to take over. It offers to the shareholders of T plc, in return for their agreement to sell their shares to H plc, an indemnity against any losses suffered as a result of their receipt of shares in H plc (due to, eg, fluctuations in their market value). Here, H plc is providing financial assistance by way of indemnity for the purchase of its shares by the shareholders of T plc.

11.3.3 Financial assistance given by way of loan

A public company providing a loan to one of its directors to allow them to buy shares in that company or its parent company is a simple example of this form of financial assistance. (Note also that the provisions of ss197 CA 2006 et seq would also have to be considered.)

However, s677(c)(i) also refers to assistance:

> by way of any . . . agreement under which any obligations of the person giving the assistance are to be fulfilled at a time when in accordance with the agreement any obligation of another party to the agreement remains unfulfilled.

This part of the section exists to extend its ambit beyond loans to other types of credit or deferred payment transactions. An example of this would be where K plc sells assets to M Ltd and allows deferred payment for those assets, in the knowledge that M Ltd is about to buy shares in K plc. By deferring payment, K plc has provided assistance to M Ltd for the purchase of shares in K plc.

11.3.4 Financial assistance reducing to a material extent a company's net assets

This provision covers any form of financial assistance, other than those described earlier, where the effect of providing the assistance is to reduce to a material extent a company's net assets. The latter are taken as being the aggregate of the company's assets less the aggregate of its liabilities, using the actual market value of the assets (as opposed to the book value) at the time of the provision of the assistance. There is no definition in the 2006 Act of what is a material reduction: it is a matter to be assessed by reference to the individual circumstances of each case.

An example of this form of financial assistance is where a private company subsidiary pays the professional fees of those involved in the purchase of shares in its public parent company, provided that the purpose of this was to assist the acquisition of the company's shares and the amount involved reduced the subsidiary company's net assets to a material extent.

11.4 Consequences of providing unlawful financial assistance

A company which provides unlawful financial assistance is liable to a fine and its directors may be liable to imprisonment or a fine, or both.

Any contract to provide financial assistance is illegal and therefore the obligations of the providing company usually cannot be enforced.

If the company providing financial assistance subsequently goes into insolvent liquidation, any directors who authorised the financial assistance may be subject to a declaration of unfitness under s6 of the Company Directors Disqualification Act 1986 and disqualified.

11.5 General exceptions

11.5.1 Principal and larger purpose exceptions

A number of exceptions exist to the general prohibitions described earlier, viz:

(a) if the company's principal purpose in giving the assistance is not to give it for the purpose of any such acquisition or the giving of assistance for that purpose is but an incidental part of some larger purpose of the company and in either instance the assistance is given in good faith in the interests of the company (ss678(2) and 679(2) CA 2006);

(b) if the company's principal purpose in giving the assistance is not to reduce or discharge any liability incurred by a person for the purpose of the acquisition of shares in the company or its holding company or the reduction or discharge of any such liability is but an incidental part of some larger purpose of the company and in either instance the assistance is given in good faith in the interests of the company (ss678(4) and 679(4) CA 2006).

Whether or not the principal or larger purpose exceptions can be relied upon will depend on the facts of each case. The burden of proof is on the company providing the assistance to convince the court that an exception applies.

The leading case on this matter is *Brady v Brady* [1989] AC 755, which considered s153 CA 1985, the forerunner to the above provisions. The financial assistance given in this case was part of a scheme to assist some shareholders in buying out others to resolve a management deadlock. The court drew a distinction between the purpose of providing financial assistance and the reason for so doing. The former was held as being to allow shareholders to acquire shares in the company, whilst the latter was held as being the resolution of the deadlock. The court found, on the facts, that there was no evidence of any principal purpose to which the assistance was subsidiary or any larger purpose.

The result of *Brady v Brady* is that 'purpose' has a narrow interpretation. For a company to rely on the exceptions in s153, there had to be clear evidence of either:

(a) a principal purpose other than the acquisition of shares for which financial assistance is given to an individual; or

(b) a larger purpose for the company (as opposed to individual shareholders, directors or prospective purchasers of shares) in providing financial assistance to an individual other than the acquisition of shares.

In addition, the company had to satisfy the court that it acted in good faith in the interests of the company. Given the narrow interpretation that was given to the exceptions in s153, and the requirement of good faith, it is difficult to be confident as to the circumstances in which the equivalent exceptions in the 2006 Act can be relied on.

11.5.2 Other exceptions

Section 681 explicitly provides that certain events will not amount to financial assistance. These include:

(a) a distribution by way of dividend or in the course of a company's winding up;

(b) an allotment of bonus shares;

(c) a reduction of capital;

(d) a redemption or buy-back of shares; and

(e) anything done under an order sanctioning a compromise or arrangement with members or creditors of the company.

Given that the exceptions described above are specific events, these may be relied on with more confidence than the exceptions in **11.5.1**.

Finally, there are some very specialised exceptions in s682 which relate mainly to issues concerning the provision of assistance to employees to partake in employee share schemes. The details of these are beyond the scope of this manual.

11.6 Private companies and financial assistance

It will be seen from the previous discussion that the provision of financial assistance by a private company to assist the purchase of shares in:

(a) itself; or

(b) its private subsidiary; or

(c) its private holding company

is not prohibited.

However, it is suggested that even where the prohibitions in ss678 and 679 are irrelevant, an instance of financial assistance may still need careful legal analysis, particularly from the perspective of directors' duties. An ill-conceived or irresponsible method of financial assistance which results in subsequent financial harm to the company providing it, could leave directors exposed to claims of breach of duty in that they neither promoted the success of the company nor acted with reasonable care and diligence.

There may be some wisdom, therefore, in seeking prior approval of shareholders in such circumstances, and directors may be well served to obtain appropriate accountancy advice about the financial repercussions of any proposed financial assistance, in any event.

KEY POINT SUMMARY

It has been shown in this chapter that the main aspects of financial assistance are:

- A company must be providing assistance to a prospective purchaser of shares.
- That purchase must either be of shares in the company itself or of shares in that company's subsidiary or holding company.
- The company providing the assistance must be public or must be the subsidiary or holding company of a public company.
- The assistance can be provided either directly to the prospective purchaser or indirectly. The result is that 'assistance' can take a wide variety of forms.
- The consequences of unlawful financial assistance are considerable, not least criminal sanctions for the company and the directors involved.

CHAPTER 12
Debt Finance for Companies

FUNCTIONING LEGAL KNOWLEDGE

This chapter considers the following functioning legal knowledge included in the SRA's SQE 1 assessment specification:

Finance:

- funding options: debt and equity
- types of security
- financial records, information and accounting requirements

Corporate governance and compliance:

- company decision-making and meetings: procedural, disclosure and approval requirements
- documentary, record-keeping, statutory filing and disclosure requirements

AUTHORITIES UNDERPINNING PRACTICE

The key authorities that underpin this area of practice are listed below. Note that for legislation you are linked to legislation.gov.uk.

Although much of the legislation on this government website is available in its amended form, the incorporation of new amendments into the text of legislation can be delayed. You should refer to legal databases to ensure you are referencing the most up-to-date legislation.

- Companies Act 2006
  https://www.legislation.gov.uk/ukpga/2006/46
- Enterprise Act 2002
  https://www.legislation.gov.uk/ukpga/2002/40/contents
- Insolvency Act 1986
  https://www.legislation.gov.uk/ukpga/1986/45/contents

12.1 Introduction

Once a company is formed it will need to spend money to operate its business. It may need to buy stock, rent premises, pay wages, advertise and pay the general expenses involved in running a business. The money that the company needs to start and grow its business is often called capital.

A company can raise capital either in the form of an investment by shareholders ('equity finance') or in the form of borrowing ('debt finance'). Once the business is established, profits may be retained in the business, thus producing a third source of finance.

After consulting this chapter, you will have been introduced to how companies raise money through debt finance. The corresponding requirement to provide security to a lender will also be looked at. (Equity finance is dealt with in **Chapter 7**.)

12.2 Relevance of the balance sheet

It should be noted at the outset that an important source of information as to how a company is capitalised is the balance sheet, which will provide details of both debt and share funding. (It is recommended that **Chapter 22**, which looks at the balance sheet in more detail, is read in conjunction with this chapter.)

EXAMPLE

A Ltd is financed in the following manner:

Share capital	£1,000
Retained profits	£25,000
Borrowings	£10,000

A total, therefore, of £36,000 has gone into funding the company, but there is also a corresponding liability to pay back the borrowings. In very simple terms, the assets would be represented as follows in A Ltd's balance sheet:

ASSETS	
Cash	£36,000
Liabilities	£10,000
Net assets	**£26,000**
CAPITAL	
Share capital	£1,000
Retained profit	£25,000
Total	**£26,000**

Note how the net assets match the capital, hence the fact that the figures 'balance'.

It should also be noted from the above example that borrowings exceed shareholder investment by 10:1. The relationship between a company's debt and equity finance is usually called 'gearing'. In very simple terms, if a company is capitalised with a substantial amount of debt in comparison to the money raised from its shareholders, it is said to be highly geared.

12.3 Types of debt finance

For many small and medium-sized companies, bank finance will be the standard source of debt finance.

Normally this will take two forms, either:

(a) an overdraft facility; or

(b) a term loan.

The detail of banking arrangements is beyond the scope of this manual. However, in simple terms:

(a) An overdraft is a source of finance which a company can draw upon, as it sees fit, normally subject to an overall limit. This is a relatively convenient form of finance (usually to meet cash-flow requirements) but also expensive, as a bank is likely to charge daily interest on the amount outstanding and a proportionately high fee for setting up and maintaining such a facility.

(b) A term loan is a fixed amount, normally provided in one go, which must be repaid according to the terms of the loan agreement (usually, but not always, by instalments of equal amounts). Interest will be charged on the amount outstanding and an arrangement fee will normally be charged at the outset. A term loan will often be taken out to meet a specific purpose.

Companies may simply rely upon one method of debt finance or a combination, depending on their needs for working and investment capital.

12.4 Power to borrow

Companies normally have the power to borrow money and grant security in respect thereof because:

(a) they were formed since the introduction of the Companies Act 2006 (CA 2006), so can take advantage of s31(1) CA 2006; or

(b) they were formed before this time, but their memorandum of association contained an express power to do so.

However, it is still important to check the constitution of any company to confirm this fact and, more importantly, to confirm that there are no restrictions on these powers, for example a ceiling limit on borrowing beyond which shareholder consent is required.

12.5 *Ultra vires* borrowing

As explained earlier, most companies are likely to have the ability to borrow. However, in the unlikely event that a company has limitations on its powers to borrow, s39 CA 2006 provides that:

> the validity of an act done by a company shall not be called into question on the ground of lack of capacity by reason of anything in the company's constitution.

As far as the outside world is concerned, companies cannot plead *ultra vires* in an attempt to deny the validity of a contract. At face value, therefore, a prospective lender need not concern itself with any limitations on a company's activities.

12.6 Exercise of borrowing powers

Borrowing will be conducted through the actions of the directors. This raises the ancillary issue of the duty of directors to act in accordance with the company's constitution and to exercise the power to borrow for the purposes for which it was conferred (s171 CA 2006).

From a lender's perspective, any failure on the directors' part to do so is partly ameliorated by s40 CA 2006 which renders such restrictions in the constitution generally irrelevant as far as third parties are concerned. However, a lender is likely to investigate this issue prior to lending to remove any doubt, not least because any actual or constructive knowledge on the bank's part that the directors are acting in breach of their duty may result in the transaction being subsequently voidable.

12.7 Execution of borrowing documentation

Any borrowing and supporting security will be recorded in formal documentation. As such, this will have to be properly executed by the debtor company, normally as a deed, in accordance with the requirements of ss44 and 46 CA 2006. In particular, this will require the signatures of two authorised signatories or the signature of a director, which is witnessed. (There is an implication that directors and company secretaries are authorised signatories to sign on the company's behalf (s44(3)(a)).)

12.8 Secured loans

12.8.1 Purpose of security

A prudent lender will usually require security for a loan made to a company. Any assets of the company may be charged by way of security. Usually security will be in the form of a:

(a) mortgage;

(b) fixed charge;

(c) floating charge; or
(d) combination of all three.

The essential benefit of such security is that it allows the lender the possibility of selling the assets of the borrower should the borrower default on repayments of the loan. The proceeds of sale can then be used by the lender to recoup some or all of the outstanding loan. Therefore, two key issues for any lender taking security are:

1 Does the company in question actually own the assets which will be charged?
2 Are other charges already attaching to such assets? If so, those charges may take priority over later ones taken by the lender.

In addition to such security, a lender may frequently require personal guarantees from the directors to support the company's obligation to repay the borrowing. Where the borrowing company is a subsidiary, a guarantee may also be sought from the parent company to the same effect.

To be enforceable, the Statute of Frauds 1677 requires guarantees to be in writing.

12.8.2 Some terminology explained

When companies borrow money, they will more often than not enter into a 'debenture' with the lender. Unfortunately, the term 'debenture' covers a variety of loan instruments and has no one specific usage. In its simplest form, it means a document issued by a company acknowledging a debt of that company. This will clearly cover unsecured loan agreements. However, in commercial circles the term very often implies that the debt is backed up by some form of security. (In fact, such documentation may be called a 'mortgage debenture'.)

It is quite common to find a debenture document providing a lender with a variety of different security rights and interests, backing up a loan made to a company. The loan itself will usually be the subject of a separate legal document, in which will be set out the terms of lending and repayment.

To complicate matters further, companies may issue 'loan stock' or 'debenture stock' which consists of transferable *securities* in a company, carrying with them a contractual right to interest and repayment of the sum paid for them. These can also be classed as debentures (s738 CA 2006) and are an alternative method of raising debt finance. Therefore, care should always be exercised in both the use and interpretation of the term and the actual documentation in question should be inspected to establish the nature of a company's indebtedness.

Some types of debenture stock are issued to people who have lent money to the company on a long-term basis and who may, therefore, be regarded as 'investors' in the business. The nature of their investment is, however, quite different from the investment made by shareholders. There are a number of important differences between the two types of investment, which may be summarised as follows:

(a) Debenture holders usually do not have the right to vote at shareholder meetings.
(b) Debenture interest is payable out of capital if the company fails to make profits, so that interest will always be paid, unlike a dividend.
(c) Debenture holders are creditors on a winding up and may have a charge over some or all of the company's assets, which means they stand some chance of receiving some of their debt back. By contrast, shareholders are unlikely to be repaid their investment unless the company is solvent.
(d) Debenture holders may be repaid while the company is a going concern (usually at a fixed date or at the option of the company). Shareholders may only be repaid where capital is reduced or where the company redeems or purchases its own shares.

It is equally important to distinguish between the terms 'security' and 'securities'. The former is a generic term for charges over property; the latter covers all forms of transferable instruments in a company, most commonly shares and loan stock.

Finally, note the following important distinctions:

(a) Chargor/mortgagor–the person who grants the security over their asset.
(b) Chargee/mortgagee–the person who receives the benefit of the security over the asset.

In the discussion which follows, a chargor/mortgagor means the borrower company and the chargee/mortgagee means the lender.

12.8.3 Mortgages and fixed charges

A lender may take security over an asset in the form of a mortgage or a fixed charge. The essential difference between the two is that a mortgage requires the formal transfer of title in the asset to the mortgagee (ie the lender), subject to an automatic right for title to be transferred back to the mortgagor once the debt is repaid–the so-called 'equity of redemption'. (Note, however, the major exception for real property discussed later.)

There are no such formalities required to create a fixed charge, merely an intention by the parties that the asset in question can be appropriated by the charge-holder and sold by it. However, in most security documentation it will be clear from the wording that a fixed charge is intended.

Both types of security must attach to specific, identifiable assets. Note that it is usually only possible to mortgage assets owned by the borrower at the time of the creation of the security. However, in certain circumstances equity will allow a charge to be taken over assets to be acquired in the future. (It is beyond the scope of this manual to consider these rules in any detail.)

In the case of a mortgage, the mortgagee actually owns title to the asset (again, subject to the exception in respect of land) and can, thus, sell it without reference to the mortgagor, provided that the mortgagor is in default under the loan. In the case of a fixed charge, title remains with the chargor but the chargor is not entitled to sell the asset without the consent of the chargee.

Mortgages can be either equitable or legal. Legal mortgages require specific formalities to be fulfilled, in particular the transfer of title in the property according to the law. An equitable mortgage is created where there is evidence of a desire to create a legal mortgage without fulfilling all such formalities.

By way of a major exception to these general rules, mortgages of freehold and leasehold property are different and are governed, inter alia, by Pt III Law of Property Act 1925 (LPA 1925). In particular, the creation of a mortgage over land is not possible by the transfer of the legal estate (s85 LPA 1925). Instead, it must be created by way of a charge by deed expressed to be by way of legal mortgage. In other words, there is no formal transfer of title to the mortgagee.

An equitable mortgage is weaker than a legal one, in that a bona fide purchaser for value without notice of the equitable mortgage takes the property free from it. However, there are in place specific registration requirements which make it more difficult for such a purchaser to claim ignorance of such a fact, particularly in relation to land.

All fixed charges are equitable. Confusingly, they may sometimes be referred to as equitable mortgages. In fact, commentators and judges often use the terminology loosely. The main distinction mentioned earlier should be borne in mind; that is, a mortgage either grants or purports to grant a proprietary interest in property, whereas a fixed charge grants an immediate right over property which can be exercised in certain situations.

A further important distinction is that between fixed and floating charges, discussed next.

12.8.4 Floating charges

A floating charge is an equitable charge over assets of a particular 'genus' owned by the company from time to time. A floating charge is usually given over assets which are repeatedly dealt with by the company. Perhaps stock-in-trade is the clearest example.

Due to some very technical issues arising out of the Bills of Sale Act, individuals and partnerships are effectively prevented from creating floating charges. By contrast, limited liability partnerships can grant these charges, on the basis that they are a legal personality akin to a company. (Any reference to a company which follows can apply equally to a limited liability partnership.)

It would be impractical for a company to give a fixed charge over its stock, since to do so would prevent it from selling that stock without first obtaining the consent of the mortgagee. This would obviously hinder the ability of the company to carry on its business. However, if it gives a floating charge over the stock, the charge will 'float' over whatever stock the company owns from time to time–it can therefore sell the stock free from the charge and buy new stock to which the charge will automatically attach.

However, a floating charge can also be taken in conjunction with mortgages and fixed charges to 'sweep up' all assets of the borrowing company not covered by these other types of security.

The nature of a floating charge was defined by Romer LJ in *Re Yorkshire Woolcombers' Association Ltd* [1903] 2 Ch 284, in the following way:

> ... if a charge has the three characteristics I am about to mention it is a floating charge:
>
> (a) if it is a charge on a class of assets of a company present and future;
>
> (b) if that class is one which, in the ordinary course of business of the company, would be changing from time to time; and
>
> (c) if you find that by the charge it is contemplated that, until some future step is taken by or on behalf of those interested in the charge, the company may carry on its business in the ordinary way as far as concerns the particular class of asset I am dealing with.

In the case of *Re Spectrum Plus Ltd* [2005] 2 BCLC 269, the House of Lords considered this dictum once again and provided fresh insight into its significance. Lord Scott proffered an analysis of the history of the case law surrounding this issue. As part of this analysis, he pointed out two key things:

(a) that Romer LJ's dictum was never intended to be definitive, nor would a charge always have to demonstrate all three characteristics to be classed a floating charge;

(b) that the first two characteristics were not, in any event, distinctive of a floating charge, albeit they may be quite typical. It was the third characteristic which distinguished a floating charge from a fixed.

As regards this second point, Lord Scott expressed a view that 'if a security has Romer LJ's third characteristic . . . it qualifies as a floating charge, and cannot be a fixed charge, whatever may be its other characteristics'. For this reason, he held that:

> ... the essential characteristic of a floating charge, the characteristic which distinguishes it from a fixed charge, is that the asset subject to the charge is not finally appropriated as a security for the payment of the debt until the occurrence of some future event.

At first sight, a floating charge would seem to give no security at all to the lender since the company can continue to deal with the assets which are charged. However, a floating charge 'fixes' on the charged assets owned by the company at the time when the charge 'crystallises'. A floating charge crystallises when:

(a) The winding up of the company commences. (In the case of a winding up by the court this is usually when the winding-up petition is presented (s129(2) Insolvency Act 1986 (IA 1986)); in the case of voluntary winding up it is when the winding-up resolution is passed (s86 IA 1986)).

(b) A receiver is appointed by the court.

(c) An administrator or receiver is appointed by the lender under a power given by the debenture.

(d) Any other event occurs which the debenture specifies will cause crystallisation.

12.8.5 Advantages and disadvantages of floating charges

From a lender's point of view, a floating charge suffers from a number of disadvantages when compared with a fixed charge. In particular:

(a) its value as a security is uncertain until crystallisation;

(b) it is postponed to **preferential creditors** on the liquidation of the borrowing company;

(c) it is postponed to later fixed charges in most cases;

(d) a percentage of monies realised under the floating charge must be set aside for the benefit of unsecured creditors in a liquidation (the so-called 'prescribed part');

(e) it may be invalid as a security if the company goes into liquidation or administration within one or two years after its creation, due to provisions in the IA 1986.

(You are recommended to consult **Chapter 28** where security is explained in the context of the insolvency of a company.)

Historically, the great advantage of a floating charge over the whole of the assets and undertaking of a company was that it allowed the chargee the ability to take control of the company in certain circumstances by appointing an administrative receiver, who would then realise the charged assets of the company on the chargee's behalf. This possibility was removed in all but a few well-defined circumstances by the changes which the Enterprise Act 2002 made to the IA 1986. However, it may now, instead, be possible for a floating charge-holder to appoint an administrator in such circumstances, which gives an alternative value to a floating charge. (See **Chapter 28** for further discussion.)

12.9 Registration of charges

12.9.1 Introduction

Most security granted by companies must be registered at Companies House. In this way, they are said to be 'perfected'; that is, they are effective against third parties. The current relevant provisions are contained within Pt 25 CA 2006.

12.9.2 Registration with Registrar of Companies

Section 859A requires registration with the Registrar of Companies of nearly all types of charge and mortgage created by a UK-registered company. As such, registration is required of all floating charges and other charges over a company's land, goodwill, book debts and most other types of property.

Certain types of charge are excluded from registration by the effect of s859A(6), for example security interests over shares in another company owned by the borrowing company (as they are excluded from registration by the Financial Collateral Arrangements (No 2) Regulations 2003); nor is any security interest registrable which relies upon possession of the property in question; that is, a pledge or lien (although these are extremely rare in a corporate finance context).

12.9.3 Method of registration

Registration of security must be made by delivering to the Registrar:

(a) prescribed particulars of the charge on form MR01 (ss859A(2) and 859D);

(b) a certified copy of the original instrument creating the charge (s859A(3)); and

(c) a fee of £24 or £15 (depending upon the method of registration adopted).

Registration must occur within the period of 21 days beginning with the day after the date of creation of the charge (s859A(4)). In turn, s859E sets out how this rule is to be applied in various circumstances, but the main trigger is usually the date the relevant charge document becomes effective.

The ability to register is afforded to the relevant company or any person interested in the charge (s859A(2)). It is very much in the interests of the lender to make sure that the charge is registered, so often they will process this.

12.9.4 Register of charges at Companies House

The Registrar keeps a register of the charges created by each company (s859I), on which are placed both the registered particulars and the certified copy of the charge document. As this document is open to inspection by the public, the system allows for certain sensitive information to be redacted from it prior to its registration (s859G).

12.9.5 Certificate of registration

Once a charge has been registered, the Registrar gives a certificate of registration to the person who registered the charge (s859I(3)). The certificate is conclusive evidence that the necessary documents were delivered in time (s859I(6)). The certificate will bear a unique 12-digit reference code which will match the one on the Companies House register.

12.9.6 Extension of time limit for registration (s859G)

If the charge is not registered within 21 days, the court may extend the time limit provided that it is satisfied that the failure to register was:

> . . . accidental, or due to inadvertence or to some other sufficient cause, or is not of a nature to prejudice the position of creditors or shareholders of the company, or that on other grounds it is just and equitable to grant relief . . .

The court may impose terms and will, in practice, always impose a condition that the registration is not to prejudice rights acquired by other persons before registration finally takes place.

12.9.7 Effect of non-registration

Section 859H(3) provides that failure to register a registrable charge shall result in the relevant security being void against a liquidator, an administrator and any creditor of the company. The importance of this provision is that if the company goes into liquidation before the loan has been repaid, the unregistered chargee loses its security. This is so even if a later secured creditor had actual notice of the charge when they took their security (*Re Monolithic Building Co* [1915] 1 Ch 643).

The practical problem is that although the debt is not extinguished by non-registration of the charge, the chargee will only rank as an ordinary creditor in a liquidation of the company. This means that the chargee will have to wait until those with valid, registered fixed and floating charges (and preferential creditors) have been paid out of the company's assets. The chargee ranks with all the other ordinary creditors and, if there are insufficient assets to pay all the ordinary creditors, may only receive a fraction (or none) of the money due to it.

Furthermore, s859H(3) is stated by s859H(4) to be:

> . . . without prejudice to any contract or obligation for repayment of the money secured . . . and when a charge becomes void under this section, the money secured by it immediately becomes payable.

The chargee can, therefore, demand payment immediately if the charge is not registered, even if the instrument creating the charge provided for repayment at a later date.

12.9.8 Company's charges information

Section 859P requires the company to keep copies of all registrable charges at its **registered office**, where they must be open to inspection free of charge by members and creditors and open to inspection by anybody else on payment of the prescribed fee.

12.9.9 Redemption of charges

Once debt owing by a company is paid off, the need for the security lapses. In turn, it is possible (but not compulsory) to notify Companies House of this fact on form MR04 (pursuant to s859L CA 2006). Receipt of this form will require the registrar to include on the company's register either (as appropriate):

(a) a statement of satisfaction of the debt; or

(b) a statement of the fact that the property in question has been released from the charge.

12.9.10 Other types of registration: charges over land

In addition to registration under the 2006 Act, mortgages of, and charges on, land owned by a company may have to be registered at HM Land Registry or at the Land Charges Department (depending on whether the land is registered or unregistered, respectively). Time limits and/or priority periods for these need to be observed.

12.10 Searches of the register

Any prospective lender to a company should always make a charges search at Companies House against the company. This will provide information as to the security granted to date by that company. (The rules on priority of charges–see the next section–mean that such knowledge is important to lenders.) If any security is also proposed against real property owned by the company, a relevant search at the Land Registry or against the Land Charges Register should also be conducted.

12.11 Priority of charges

12.11.1 Fixed charges

As between fixed charges, priority is given to the first in time.

EXAMPLE

A Ltd borrows £25,000 from Big Bank plc and grants it a fixed charge over an asset then worth £30,000.

A Ltd subsequently borrows £20,000 from Small Bank plc and grants it a second fixed charge over the same asset.

A Ltd goes into insolvent liquidation. At the time it does so:

- it owes Big Bank plc £21,000;
- it owes Small Bank plc £19,000;
- the charged asset is now worth £33,000.

Upon realisation of the asset:

- Big Bank will receive the full amount of its debt;
- Small Bank will receive the balance of £12,000 and will stand as an unsecured creditor in respect of the balance of its debt.

A company which creates a floating charge retains the right to deal with the assets which are subject to the charge. One consequence is that unless it contractually agrees not to do so, the company is free to deal with the assets by charging them further, in particular by granting fixed charges over certain assets to support further borrowing. A floating charge, even though properly registered, is normally postponed to a later fixed charge, such that the fixed charge-holder has a first entitlement to the proceeds of the asset in question. In turn, this means that the value of the floating charge will be eroded.

The floating charge will usually only have priority over later fixed charges if:

(a) the instrument creating the charge contractually prohibits the creation of later fixed charges ranking in priority to or *pari passu* (ie equal) with the floating charge (such a provision is usually in the form of a 'negative pledge'); *and*

(b) the later fixed chargee has *notice of this prohibition* at the time when they take the charge.

12.11.2 Floating charges

As between several floating charges, the *first in time* will have priority provided that it is properly registered. However, a later floating charge over a particular type of asset will probably take priority over an earlier floating charge which generally relates to the whole of a company's property (*English and Scottish Mercantile Investment Co v Brunton* [1892] 2 QB 700).

12.12 Remedies of debenture holders

If the company fails to pay interest or the principal money (ie the debt itself) the lender may sue as a creditor for those amounts or petition for winding up of the company. In addition, the debenture may contain an express power of sale and/or a power to appoint a receiver in respect of the charged asset(s). The debenture will state the circumstances in which these powers are to arise. It may, for example, give such powers to the lender when interest is in arrears for a specified period, when the company breaks any term of the debenture, when any other creditor of the company appoints a receiver and when the company suffers execution by a judgment creditor.

Section 101 LPA 1925, in any event, gives the lender implied power to sell and/or to appoint a receiver if the debenture is made by deed and interest is two months in arrears or principal money has not been paid three months after it becomes due. In drafting a debenture, express powers should be given since they can be made wider than the implied powers; if the debenture is not executed as a deed, express powers are essential.

Further, the holder of a qualifying floating charge (see Sch B1, para 14 IA 1986) has the right to appoint an administrator over a company. An administrator must perform their functions in the interests of the creditors as a whole but, in doing so, will recognise the status and rights of any secured creditor. (See **Chapter 28** for further discussion of administration.)

KEY POINT SUMMARY

- A lender to a company will want to ensure that the company in question will be contractually bound to repay its borrowing, together with any interest thereon, and may want any security to back up this obligation.
- A lender who requires security has effectively three main possibilities:
  - a mortgage;
  - a fixed charge;
  - a floating charge.
- A lender will usually look to charge a variety of assets with an appropriate combination of these security devices.
- A lender may also seek a qualifying floating charge which will grant it the ability to put the company into administration should the need arise.
- A lender may also seek contractual comfort in the form of a guarantee, either from directors or from a parent company, as appropriate.
- It is possible for more than one charge to exist simultaneously over an asset; however, this will trigger the effect of the rules of priority to determine which charge-holder is first to receive any proceeds of realisation of the asset.
- Some of the steps which any lender should take when lending to a company are to:
  - search at Companies' House to confirm what charges, if any, have previously been registered against the company;
  - search at the Land Registry or Land Charges Department (as appropriate), if a charge is to be taken over land;
  - ensure that all contractual commitments of the company are properly authorised by the directors and that all supporting documentation is properly executed by the company;
  - ensure that any charge is registered within 21 days at Companies House (and subsequently at the Land Registry if registered land has been charged).

PART D
Corporate Governance and Compliance

CHAPTER 13
The Articles of Association of a Private Limited Company

FUNCTIONING LEGAL KNOWLEDGE

This chapter considers the following functioning legal knowledge included in the SRA's SQE 1 assessment specification:

Procedures and documentation required to incorporate a company/form a partnership/LLP and other steps required under companies and partnerships legislation to enable the entity to commence operating:

- constitutional documents

Corporate governance and compliance:

- rights, duties and powers of directors and shareholders of companies
- company decision-making and meetings: procedural, disclosure and approval requirements

AUTHORITIES UNDERPINNING PRACTICE

The key authorities that underpin this area of practice are listed below. Note that for legislation you are linked to legislation.gov.uk.

Although much of the legislation on this government website is available in its amended form, the incorporation of new amendments into the text of legislation can be delayed. You should refer to legal databases to ensure you are referencing the most up-to-date legislation.

- Companies Act 2006
  https://www.legislation.gov.uk/ukpga/2006/46
- Companies (Model Articles) Regulations 2008
  https://www.legislation.gov.uk/uksi/2008/3229

13.1 Introduction

After consulting this chapter, you will have been introduced to:

(a) the likely basis for articles of association of a private company;
(b) some of the major matters which the articles of a private company are likely to address;
(c) the method by which articles of association can be altered during a company's lifetime;
(d) any legal restrictions on alteration to the articles.

As has already been explained at **3.10**, articles of association are, by statutory implication, a contract between the shareholders and the shareholders and the company. In many ways, articles of a company should be looked on as all other contracts–there are likely to be as many variations as there are similarities. Therefore, it is important never to assume the contents of a company's constitution and any lawyer needs to be satisfied that the articles have been accurately complied with.

However, whereas most contracts can only be altered with the consent of all parties to them, a company's articles can always be altered by special resolution of the shareholders (s21 Companies

Act 2006 (CA 2006)). The extent to which the majority can reformulate this relationship against the wishes of the minority is considered later in this chapter.

13.2 The availability of 'standard' articles

All companies are required to have articles of association and these articles define and regulate the relationships within the company. 'Standard' articles are made available through regulation and a company can either adopt these articles wholesale or have articles specifically drafted for it (often based on those standard articles).

For many years Table A was the standard set of 'default' articles available for adoption by both private and public companies. As part of the changes to company law effected by the CA 2006, a new set of articles for use by private companies was introduced as the standard 'default' articles for private companies. The so-called Model Articles have been effective since 1 October 2009. However, the Model Articles are not compulsory for companies nor do they automatically replace the articles of companies incorporated prior to their introduction.

To put all this into context:

(a) many companies which were formed prior to the availability of the Model Articles may have Table A articles or articles based on Table A.

(b) companies formed since 1 October 2009 are likely to have the Model Articles as their articles or articles which are a variation thereon.

The focus of this chapter will be the Model Articles for private companies.

13.3 Provisions concerning shares and membership

13.3.1 Share capital

A company needs to reserve for itself the power to create and allot shares. Accordingly, the Model Articles contain such a power to allot shares of differing rights (art 22). Article 21, in addition, specifically requires all shares to be fully **paid-up** on issue, which reflects the rarity of partly paid shares in private companies.

13.3.2 Issue of shares

A general delegation of power from the company to its board of directors is contained in art 3. Power delegated to the directors will include the right to issue shares. However, this right may not be exercised unless authorisation to do so is given to the directors either by ordinary resolution or in the articles (s551 CA 2006).

The Model Articles do not give directors automatic authority to issue shares. However, the effect of s550 CA 2006 is that directors of private companies with only one class of shares are able to allot further shares of the same class without the need for authority from the shareholders, so the absence of such a provision may have little consequence. In any event, an ordinary resolution can be sought from shareholders should the need arise.

An issue of shares may trigger the statutory pre-emption rules set out in s561 CA 2006, unless the articles make alternative provision. (The Model Articles do not make any such provision.) A company should consider whether such an exclusion would be appropriate, bearing in mind that this possibility is only available to private companies (s567 CA 2006). Several approaches are possible, on the basis that the effect of s561 may be excluded generally or only in respect of anticipated allotments of a particular description.

Pre-emption rights can always be excluded on an 'as needs' basis in any event, by special resolution, so the absence of a s567 exclusion in a company's articles is not necessarily material.

13.3.3 Transfer of shares

In the case of many private companies, it may be appropriate that shareholders should not be free to transfer their shares to anyone they choose. Such a restriction prevents unwanted external influence in the future. Article 26(5) of the Model Articles accordingly grants the board absolute discretion to refuse the registration of any transfer.

Notice that a majority vote of the directors is needed to *refuse* to register the transfer. If, for example, directors' votes on such a resolution are equally divided, the transferee will become entitled to be registered.

The power to refuse to register a transfer does not prevent an existing shareholder from selling shares or giving them away; it simply prevents the transferee from becoming the legal owner of the shares. If registration is refused, then the existing shareholder holds the shares on trust for the transferee, who becomes the equitable owner of the shares. However, this is an undesirable situation for the transferee to be in. Therefore, every effort should be made in advance to ascertain that there will be no such problems.

The provisions of the Model Articles are relatively unsophisticated and a company may wish for a transfer provision which is more specific in its operation. The details of such clauses vary considerably. Some examples are:

(a) complete freedom to transfer, so long as to a family member or another shareholder, otherwise the directors may refuse to register the transfer;

(b) complete freedom to transfer, subject to specifically defined exceptions, such as transferees who are not based in the UK or corporate transferees.

As an alternative or additionally, pre-emption rights may be granted to existing shareholders on transfer. The CA 2006 does not impose any pre-emption rights where a shareholder wishes to transfer shares so, if thought desirable, they must appear in the articles. (These should not be confused with the statutory pre-emption rights which arise on the issue of new shares.)

In its simplest form, a pre-emption right on transfer will provide that if a shareholder wishes to transfer their shares, they must first offer them to some or all of the existing shareholders pro rata the size of their shareholdings. (See **10.4** for further discussion.)

13.4 Shareholder meetings

13.4.1 Relationship with statute

The CA 2006 contains a number of provisions which, subject to anything contrary in the articles, determine how shareholder meetings are called. The Model Articles do not displace these provisions so the Act is determinative if these are the chosen articles of a company.

What follows is an explanation of those provisions which commonly need specific consideration. (**Chapter 18** contains more detailed coverage of shareholder meetings.)

13.4.2 Notice of general meetings

No specific provision is included in the Model Articles, as s307(1) CA 2006 is relied upon. The notice period stipulated is a minimum and s307(3) provides that companies may wish to include longer notice periods for general meetings in their articles; however, in most circumstances this is unlikely to be an attractive option.

13.4.3 Consent to short notice

No specific provision is included in the Model Articles, as the conditions set out in s307(4)–(6) CA 2006 for relevant consent are relied upon. It is possible to impose a higher percentage threshold than 90%, but this is unlikely to be of any material benefit to the company or its shareholders.

13.4.4 Quorum of shareholders' meeting

Article 38 of the Model Articles stipulates that a quorum is necessary for valid business to be transacted at a general meeting, but relies upon the provisions of s318 CA 2006 to determine the number, which is:

(a) two members present or their proxies or representatives (in the case of corporate shareholders); or

(b) if the company has only a single member, this figure is reduced to one.

Section 318 is subject to contrary provision in the articles, so companies can include alternative quorum requirements to suit the requirements of their shareholders.

13.4.5 Voting on a poll

Article 44 of the Model Articles regulates the demand for a poll, which may be demanded:

(a) in advance of the relevant meeting;

(b) at the meeting itself prior to the matter being put to the vote on a show of hands;

(c) immediately after the vote on a show of hands.

The following persons may demand a poll:

(a) the chairman of the meeting;

(b) the directors;

(c) two or more shareholders having the right to vote at the meeting;

(d) one or more shareholders holding at least one-tenth of the total voting rights.

13.4.6 Proxy notices

A shareholder may send a proxy in their stead to attend a meeting. Articles 45 and 46 govern the form and delivery of a proxy notice. It is important to fulfil the requirements of both these articles to avoid the appointment being invalidated.

13.5 Provisions concerning directors

13.5.1 Appointment of directors

The appointment of directors is a constitutional matter for a company. The position under the Model Articles is that a director may be permanently appointed to the office of director either by ordinary resolution or by a decision of the directors (art 17).

As regards any executive role which a director may be expected to perform, art 19(1) leaves this entirely for determination by the directors. Article 19(2) also allows directors' remuneration to be determined by the directors.

13.5.2 Retirement by rotation

Retirement by rotation is a corporate governance device. If directors come up for reappointment by ordinary resolution on an annual basis, shareholders are given influence and control over poor or unpopular management. If such provisions are absent, this can make investment in that company unattractive. However, such issues are only really germane to public, listed companies. For closely held, private companies, retirement by rotation is likely to be an administrative nuisance, which explains why the Model Articles contain no such mechanism (although, by contrast, the Model Articles for public companies do provide for retirement by rotation).

13.5.3 Removal of directors

The members of the company have power to remove a director from office by ordinary resolution (see s168 CA 2006). It may be considered appropriate to include in the articles a *Bushell v Faith* clause (see **15.3.4.4**) which will grant a director *who is also a shareholder* weighted voting rights on any resolution for their removal. These will effectively give the director the power to defeat such a resolution. (No such clause exists in the Model Articles.)

Whilst a *Bushell v Faith* clause is acceptable, any attempt to deprive shareholders of their rights under s168 is not, so any attempt to provide shareholders with 'replacement' methods of removal in the articles must be treated with caution. However, it may be possible (and thought desirable) to include alternative (and additional) methods of removal in the articles, such as the ability to remove a director by special resolution. It would also appear to be acceptable to allow the board to decide on the removal of a director. The mechanism commonly employed is to state that a director must resign if requested by all other directors to do so.

13.5.4 Directors' decision-making

Articles 7–16 of the Model Articles govern board decisions. Article 7 provides for two methods of decision-making by the directors:

(a) by majority decision at a board meeting;

(b) by the method provided for in art 8.

Discussion of both these methods follows.

Any director can call a board meeting by giving appropriate notice to every other director (art 9(1)). The notice must contain details of when and where the meeting is to take place. Notice need not be in writing, which presumably allows notice by email, text or other electronic method which the directors may find suitable.

Article 10 allows for the fact that directors need not be in the same place to hold a board meeting, so long as they can communicate to each other any relevant information or opinions. This is supported by a requirement in art 9(2)(c) that the notice of the meeting must indicate how it is proposed that the directors should communicate with each other if they are not to be in the same place during the meeting.

Alternatively, art 8 allows directors to make decisions unanimously outside the forum of the board meeting if they all indicate to each other *by any means* that they share a common view on a matter (art 8(1)). One possible method of doing so is by a written resolution of all directors (art 8(2)). Other possibilities might be email exchange or simply informal discussions outside a specific board meeting.

It is suggested that possible dangers lurk with such practices, namely evidential problems with recording such decisions. Also, the absence of a properly recorded discussion and decision in a board meeting may make it harder for the board to defend its position at a future date, especially in terms of demonstrating fulfilment of legal duties.

13.5.5 Quorum of directors' meeting

Article 11(2) permits the board to determine the necessary quorum but:

(a) if no such determination is made, the default requirement is two directors;

(b) the quorum cannot be set at less than two.

It may seem unusual to stipulate a minimum quorum of two directors when a private company need only have one director. However, art 7(2) of the Model Articles contains a carve-out in respect of companies with only one director, such that none of the provisions regarding directors' meetings applies and the sole director may take decisions in whatever way is thought suitable.

13.5.6 Chairman's casting vote

As a way of avoiding deadlock–that is, equality of votes on a resolution–the chairman of the board of directors may be provided with a casting vote. As such, the Model Articles contain a casting vote provision (art 13). (Note that this option is not possible at *shareholder* meetings.)

The inclusion of such a provision needs careful consideration to ensure that one director is not given disproportionate power at board level.

13.5.7 Restrictions on voting

See **14.6.6** for discussion of this issue.

13.6 Distributions to shareholders

It is usual for a company's articles to confirm the circumstances in which dividends will be paid out and the method of payment (eg arts 30–34 Model Articles). Often companies will also make provision to capitalise profits, which will enable them to allot fully paid shares to shareholders, as an alternative to a cash dividend (eg art 35 Model Articles). (See **Chapter 8** for further consideration of dividends.)

13.7 Single-member companies

Much of the previous discussion assumes that companies will have at least two directors and/or shareholders. It is possible to create a private company with only one director and one shareholder. This situation will normally arise when either a sole trader is looking for the benefit of limited liability or where a company is a **wholly owned subsidiary** of another.

In such a situation, specific thought needs to be given to articles which reflect the reality of the situation, particularly in relation to meetings of both the board and shareholders, although to a certain extent the Model Articles do attempt to do this.

13.8 Alteration of articles

13.8.1 Power to alter

Section 21 CA 2006 gives a company power to alter its articles by special resolution.

The articles of a company may not be made unalterable. A clause in the articles which purports to prevent the shareholders from altering the articles is invalid. However, a contract between shareholders as to how they will vote on a resolution to alter the articles is not void (*Russell v Northern Bank Development Corporation* [1992] 1 WLR 588).

13.8.2 Registration

Once the special resolution altering the articles has been passed, the resolution and a printed copy of the amended articles must be sent to the Registrar within 15 days (ss30(1) and 26(1) CA 2006 respectively).

The company must ensure that copies of the altered articles are prepared so that the directors may consult them and in case any member exercises their statutory right to a copy of the articles (s32 CA 2006).

13.8.3 Alteration to be for the benefit of the company

There are no provisions in the 2006 Act giving shareholders power to challenge the validity of an alteration to the articles. However, the courts have held that an alteration is invalid if it is not 'bona fide in the interests of the company as a whole' (per Lord Lindley MR in *Allen v Gold Reefs of West Africa Ltd* [1900] 1 Ch 656). The test is very much easier to state than to apply to the facts of particular cases. Also, the court is very reluctant to interfere with decisions made by the majority in a company.

In *Allen v Gold Reefs of West Africa Ltd*, the articles contained a provision imposing a lien on partly paid shares. One shareholder owed money to the company and the articles were altered to impose a lien on fully paid shares as well as on partly paid shares. The court regarded the fact that one (and only one) shareholder was indebted to the company at the time of alteration as something exciting suspicion as to the bona fides of the company, but nevertheless came to the conclusion that the alteration was in the interests of the company as a whole. Clearly, it is in the interests of a company that it should have **security** for money due to it and no discrimination against particular members was expressed in the altered articles.

Shuttleworth v Cox Brothers and Co (Maidenhead) Ltd [1927] 2 KB 9 is perhaps a stronger illustration. The majority of the directors suspected that one of the board had been guilty of misconduct but they had insufficient proof of any grounds giving a right to dismiss him. They therefore altered the articles to say that any director would cease to hold office if requested to resign by the majority of the directors. The test applied by the court was whether any reasonable person could come to the conclusion that the alteration was in the interests of the company. If it was open to a reasonable person to come to that conclusion, the alteration would only be invalid on proof of actual bad faith. The court was satisfied that a reasonable person could come to the conclusion that the alteration was in the interests of the company and so, since the plaintiff could not prove actual bad faith, the alteration was held to be valid.

The courts have recognised that an alteration to the articles cannot be in the interests of the company as a whole if it discriminates against some members, however few. A good illustration of the type of case where an alteration *was* discriminatory and so void is given by the Australian case *Australian Fixed Trust Proprietary Ltd v Clyde Industries Ltd* (1959) SR (NSW) 33. In that case, the articles were altered so as to require shareholders who were unit trust managers to obtain the approval of the majority of their unit-holders before exercising the voting rights attached to their shares. This clearly discriminated against shareholders who happened to be unit trust managers and so was void.

The narrowness of the distinction between cases which are, and cases which are not, discriminatory is well illustrated by the cases of *Sidebottom v Kershaw, Leese and Co Ltd* [1920] 1 Ch 154 and *Brown v Abrasive Wheel Co* [1919] 1 Ch 290.

In *Sidebottom v Kershaw, Leese*, the articles were altered so as to give the directors power to direct a shareholder who was concerned with a competing business to transfer his shares. This was held to be a valid alteration. The company could properly come to the conclusion that it was in its interests that competitors be excluded from membership. In *Brown v Abrasive Wheel Co*, the articles were altered to give 90% of the shareholders power to require the minority shareholders to sell their shares. In fact, the majority shareholders (who owned 98% of the shares) had good commercial reasons for wanting the alteration, but nevertheless the court held that the alteration was invalid. Although it was in the interests of 98% of the present shareholders, it was not in the interests of the other 2%, so the alteration could not be treated as for the company's benefit as a whole.

13.8.4 Summary

The two basic rules which seem to have evolved from the cases are:

(a) The members may generally decide themselves whether an alteration is bona fide in the interests of the company as a whole; however, the key factor is demonstration of benefit to the company.

(b) The court will interfere with their decision where the members could not properly come to that decision because it discriminates between groups of members, for example where the majority's actions target minority shareholders.

For a good summary of the authorities, see *Arbuthnott v Bonnyman* [2015] EWCA Civ 536, [2015] BCC 574.

It should be noted that much of the usefulness of the common law has been superseded by the availability for shareholders to claim unfair prejudice. The alteration of articles to the prejudice of some part of the members may be good grounds under which to bring an action under s994 CA 2006. (Unfair prejudice is dealt with in more detail in **Chapter 19**.)

KEY POINT SUMMARY

- A company is free to adopt any articles it chooses. However, over time, the focus of articles has, to a certain extent, become generic, not least because of the influence of standard, 'ready-made' articles, first in the form of Table A and now the Model Articles.
- Matters which a company's articles are likely to address are:
  - shares and share capital;
  - shareholder rights and entitlements;
  - conduct of shareholder meetings;
  - conduct of directors' meetings;
  - appointment and removal of directors;
  - distributions to shareholders.
- Whilst articles of association can be altered by shareholder decision, the motives behind such an alteration may, in certain circumstances, allow a court to declare the alteration invalid.

CHAPTER 14
Company Directors and Secretary

FUNCTIONING LEGAL KNOWLEDGE

This chapter considers the following functioning legal knowledge included in the SRA's SQE 1 assessment specification:

Corporate governance and compliance:

- rights, duties and powers of directors and **shareholders** of companies
- company decision-making and meetings: procedural, disclosure and approval requirements
- documentary, record-keeping, statutory filing and disclosure requirements
- appointment and removal of directors

AUTHORITIES UNDERPINNING PRACTICE

The key authorities that underpin this area of practice are listed below. Note that for legislation you are linked to legislation.gov.uk.

Although much of the legislation on this government website is available in its amended form, the incorporation of new amendments into the text of legislation can be delayed. You should refer to legal databases to ensure you are referencing the most up-to-date legislation.

- Companies Act 2006
  https://www.legislation.gov.uk/ukpga/2006/46
- Companies (Model Articles) Regulations 2008
  https://www.legislation.gov.uk/uksi/2008/3229

14.1 Introduction

After consulting this chapter, you will have been introduced to the law relating to a company's officers; that is, the directors and the company secretary. The relevant law is a combination of:

(a) statute;

(b) common law; and

(c) regulations under a company's **articles of association**.

In respect of this last limb, we will consider mainly the Model Articles for Private Companies. (Further relevant discussion of the articles can be found in **Chapter 13**.)

Directors are deemed to hold the 'office' of director. In parallel with this relationship with the company, it is also possible for a director to be allocated specific executive functions. This second relationship is often one of employment.

Appointment and removal of directors is considered in **Chapter 15**.

14.2 Division of powers within a company

The power to take decisions on behalf of a company is divided between the directors and **members**. In most instances, the directors will be able to conduct the business of and manage the company without reference to the shareholders. This is because there will be a general delegation of such authority from the company to the directors through the articles of association.

Most corporate behaviour will, therefore, be at the instigation of the directors.

However, there are a small number of powers which are exercisable only by the members under various provisions of the Companies Act 2006 (CA 2006), for example the power to change the articles. Furthermore, the directors may have to seek authorisation from shareholders prior to committing the company to a transaction, for example a buy-back of **shares** or a loan to a director.

14.3 Nature of directors

Whilst the assumption is that a director will be a 'natural person', it is possible for a company to act as a director. However, for both private and public companies at least one director is required to be a 'natural person' (s155 CA 2006).

Section 87 of the Small Business, Enterprise and Employment Act 2015 will at some point amend s155 to remove the possibility of the appointment of corporate directors, although this provision has not yet been brought into force. When it does so, there will also be exceptions to the general prohibition introduced which will enable the continued use of corporate directors in certain instances. It is also understood that any such corporate director will have to be a UK-registered entity and that any directors of that company will have to be natural persons. (At the time of writing it was understood that enabling regulations would be introduced at the same time as related provisions of the Economic Crime and Corporate Transparency Act 2023 (ECCTA 2023). The reader is advised to check the latest position to confirm the existence or otherwise of such regulations and their effect.)

14.4 Maintenance of information on directors

Section 162 CA 2006 requires every company to keep at its **registered office** a register of directors. In respect of each director, the following information must be recorded:

(a) present forename(s) and surname, and any former name;

(b) a service address (which need not be a residential address);

(c) the country or state (or part of the UK) in which they are usually resident;

(d) nationality;

(e) business occupation (if any);

(f) date of birth.

Further, s165 imposes an obligation on companies to maintain a register of directors' residential addresses. In contrast to the register of directors, this register is not available for inspection by either shareholders or outsiders. In this way, a certain amount of confidentiality is maintained regarding directors' details.

Any appointment, retirement or removal of a director will necessitate a change to these two registers. (At the time of writing, it was understood that provisions within the ECCTA 2023 (s51 and Sch 2) will at some point remove the need for companies to maintain these registers. The reader is advised to check the latest position regarding the introduction of such provisions.)

14.5 Powers of directors

14.5.1 Defining directors' powers

The powers of the directors are delegated to them through the articles including, in particular, power to manage the business of the company. For example, art 3 of the Model Articles for Private Companies provides that:

> Subject to the articles, the directors are responsible for the management of the company's business, for which purpose they may exercise all the powers of the company.

However, art 4 contains a qualification to this delegation in that:

> The shareholders may, by **special resolution**, direct the directors to take, or refrain from taking, specified action.

Article 4 effectively represents a view, long supported by judicial authority, that the shareholders cannot supplant the authority of the board of directors by means only of an **ordinary resolution** (see *Automatic Self-Cleansing Filter Syndicate Co v Cunninghame* [1906] 2 Ch 34 and *Breckland Group Holdings Ltd v London & Suffolk Properties Ltd* [1988] 4 BCC 542).

14.5.2 Delegation of directors' powers

It is very common for one of the directors of a company to be appointed managing director, chief executive or chief operating officer. The functions actually performed by the managing director vary from company to company, but in practice they will usually be either the most senior **executive director** in the company's hierarchy or second in command to the chairman. Other executive roles can also be created, for example chief finance officer.

To allow persons in these roles a certain amount of latitude, it may be necessary to delegate some of the board's powers to them. In turn, the ability to do so needs to be provided for in a company's articles. For example, the Model Articles contain wide powers of delegation, allowing directors to delegate 'to such persons . . . to such an extent . . . as they think fit' (art 5).

14.6 Exercise of directors' powers

14.6.1 Introduction

Decisions of the directors must normally be taken either at a board meeting at which a quorum is present or by unanimous (written) agreement. This is, however, subject to the directors' power to delegate (eg to a managing director, committee of directors or appointed agent).

14.6.2 Calling a board meeting

Article 9 of the Model Articles provides that any director may call a board meeting or require the company secretary (if one exists) to do so at any time. No particular period of notice is required, so that a meeting will be validly held if reasonable notice is given. Notice need not be in writing but it must contain details of when and where the meeting is to be held. Also, in recognition of the use of digital technology to enable meetings to take place, if it is anticipated that directors will not all be in the same place for the meeting, details of how communication will take place should be provided.

14.6.3 What constitutes a meeting?

At face value, a meeting will require the presence of directors in the same venue. However, this can be restrictive and can result in practical difficulties for the board. It also does not allow the use of modern communication methods. A company's articles may, therefore, recognise a wider concept of what a board meeting may be. For example, art 10 of the Model Articles for Private Companies treats any director as participating in a board meeting if they can communicate to other directors any information or opinions they have on the business being discussed. Furthermore, any method of communication is acceptable and the location of any director is irrelevant as to whether or not they are participating in the meeting.

14.6.4 The requirement for a quorum

As with any formal meeting, the presence of a quorum will be necessary to render a meeting valid. Such a requirement will be stated in a company's articles, for example art 11 of the Model Articles stipulates the presence of two directors as necessary for a quorum.

14.6.5 Decisions at board meetings

Decisions at board meetings are taken by majority vote; if there is an equality of votes, the chairman may have a casting vote, if the articles so provide. The chairman is chosen by the directors from among themselves. The chairman's casting vote prevents deadlock (without it a resolution fails, if there is an equality of votes), but it also means that the director, who is the chairman, has considerably more power than the others.

Article 13 of the Model Articles allows the chairman a casting vote.

14.6.6 Prohibition on director voting on resolution in which he is interested

Directors should avoid a conflict of interest with their respective companies (s175 CA 2006). As a way of reinforcing this duty, the articles may impose a prohibition on directors voting and counting in the quorum in a conflict situation. Such a provision can be found in the Model Articles (art 14).

Article 14 can be broken down into three main elements (see **Table 14.1**):

(1) the situation in which the prohibition applies;

(2) any carve-outs or exceptions to the prohibition;

(3) a mechanism to allow the prohibition to be disapplied.

Note that the relevant director will only be excluded from the business of the meeting in respect of which the conflict arises; in all other aspects of the board meeting, the director can take full part.

The application of art 14 may not produce a definitive answer. If there is any doubt about a director's capacity to vote, it is probably preferable to err on the side of caution, especially if there are other directors who can constitute a quorum and pass the necessary resolution.

This type of article can cause problems where a company has, for example, only two directors, one or both of whom are interested in specific resolutions. Prima facie, the relevant board meeting

TABLE 14.1 Element of art 14

Prohibition	Art 14(1): a director cannot count in the quorum or vote on a decision of the directors which concerns an actual or proposed transaction with the company in which the director is interested.
Exceptions	Art 14(3)(b): the prohibition does not apply where the director's interest cannot reasonably be regarded as likely to give rise to a conflict of interest. Art 14(3)(c): the prohibition does not apply, even if there is conflict, when that director's conflict of interest arises from a 'permitted cause'. Art 14(4): there are three permitted causes, namely: (a) a guarantee given by or to a director in respect of an obligation incurred by or on behalf of the company; (b) a subscription for shares/securities of the company or the underwriting or guaranteeing of a subscription for shares/securities; (c) arrangements for providing benefits to employees or directors which do not provide special benefits to directors.
Disapplication	Art 14(3)(a): the effect of art 14(1) can be disapplied by ordinary resolution. (It is suggested that this disapplication can be as specific or a general as the company requires.)

will be inquorate and the resolution will not be able to be passed validly. The short-term solution would be to seek the disapplication of the prohibition by ordinary resolution of the shareholders. Alternatively, if it is thought that the problem will recur, this type of article could be removed by special resolution (or not adopted at all).

Independently of the articles, a director is obliged by s177 CA 2006 to make a declaration of any interest they may have in any proposed transaction with the company.

14.6.7 Directors' decision by way of unanimous agreement

The articles may allow the directors to pass valid resolutions without holding a board meeting. For example, art 8 of the Model Articles permits the use of a **written resolution** consented to by all the directors, but also treats as valid a decision where 'all eligible directors indicate to each other *by any means* that they share a common view on a matter'. This would presumably include such things as the use of text messaging or email exchange. Such informality does have practical benefits but, for evidential purposes, a written record of any such decision would still be necessary.

14.7 Directors' statutory duties under CA 2006

14.7.1 Introduction

One of the most significant changes introduced by the CA 2006 was the statutory statement of the duties owed by directors to a company. Previously, the majority of directors' duties were founded on common law rules and equitable principles. The statutory duties are based on these principles and are stated in s170(3) CA 2006 to 'have effect in place of those rules and principles as regards the duties owed to a company by a director'. However, the common law rules and equitable principles will continue to have relevance. Section 170(4) CA 2006 states that the statutory duties:

> shall be interpreted and applied in the same way as the common law rules or equitable principles, and regard shall be had to the corresponding common law rules and equitable principles in interpreting and applying the . . . duties.

As such, it would be incorrect to assume that the wealth of judicial precedent which exists is no longer significant.

What follows is a brief summary of a large and important branch of company law. Reference should be made to one of the standard company law texts for a fuller analysis of this topic.

Each of the statutory duties will be considered separately but, to summarise them, they are:

(a) to act within the company's constitution and to exercise their powers for proper purposes;
(b) to promote the success of the company;
(c) to exercise independent judgement;
(d) to exercise reasonable care, skill and diligence;
(e) to avoid conflicts of interest;
(f) not to accept benefits from third parties;
(g) to declare interests in existing and proposed transactions or arrangements.

14.7.2 Duty to act within powers

Section 171 CA 2006 requires that a director must:

(a) act in accordance with the company's constitution; and
(b) only exercise powers for the purposes for which they were conferred.

This provision is based on a common law principle illustrated in the case of *Hogg v Cramphorn Ltd* [1967] Ch 254. In that case, directors issued shares to trustees for the benefit of employees.

The purpose of the directors in issuing the shares was found to be the prevention of a **takeover** of the company. It was held that the issue could be challenged (even though the directors believed it to be in the interests of the company as a whole), since the purpose of giving directors the power to issue shares is primarily to enable them to raise capital. (Many of the cases on this type of breach of duty were concerned with the issue of shares by directors at a time when there existed less statutory regulation than today.)

14.7.3 Duty to promote the success of the company

Under s172 CA 2006, a director must act in the way in which they consider, in good faith, would be most likely to promote the success of the company for the benefit of the members as a whole. In doing so, they should have regard (amongst other matters) to:

(a) the likely long-term consequences of any decision;

(b) the interests of the employees;

(c) the need to foster relationships with suppliers, customers and others;

(d) the impact of operations on the community and the environment;

(e) the need to maintain a reputation for high standards of business conduct;

(f) the need to act fairly as between members of the company.

This requirement is designed to result in companies taking account of a wide range of stakeholders who are potentially affected by their business activities. However, a reasonable interpretation of s172 is that what has been generated is simply a clearer iteration of the previous common law position.

First, the fact is that the overriding duty under s172 remains that of acting for the benefit of the members as a whole, as under the previous regime. Directors must have regard to those factors listed but to do so is merely incidental to complying with the main single duty. Secondly, it would appear that, as before, subject to good faith, the decision as to what will promote success is to remain one for a company's directors not the courts. In other words, the test remains primarily a subjective one (*Regentcrest plc v Cohen* [2001] 2 BCLC 80).

Under the pre-statutory regime, the duty was considered to shift to the interests of a company's creditors in an insolvent situation (*West Mercia Safetywear Ltd v Dodd* [1988] BCLC 250). However, it is important to note that a duty was not owed directly to the creditors; rather, the duty was still owed to the company whose interests now included those of the creditors.

No statutory formulation of this rule is included in s172; instead, there is a clear statement in s172(3) that the duty is subject to any rule which requires directors to consider or act in the interests of the company's creditors. In this way, the pre-existing duty remains.

14.7.4 Duty to exercise independent judgement

This duty is set out in s173 CA 2006. It recognises the long-held view that directors must act autonomously in performing their functions and not willingly fetter their discretion. However, the duty will not be infringed by a director where they act in accordance with an agreement duly entered into by the company or in accordance with the company's constitution.

14.7.5 Duty to exercise reasonable care, skill and diligence

This duty, required by s174 CA 2006, is to be judged by reference to the care, skill and diligence that would be exercised by a reasonably diligent person with:

(a) the general knowledge, skill and experience that may reasonably be expected of a person carrying out the functions carried out by the director in relation to the company; and

(b) the general knowledge, skill and experience that the director has.

This test, which combines objective and subjective views, is similar to that applied in judging conduct in relation to wrongful trading under s214 of the Insolvency Act 1986 (IA 1986) which, of itself, received judicial approval as a correct summation of the previous common law position (*Re D'Jan of London Ltd* [1993] BCC 646).

A breach of duty may be evidenced by carelessness of a director, resulting in loss to the company. But the duty also imposes a basic level of diligence on directors in terms of their stewardship of a company's interests. A failure to understand what is going on in a company or a failure to monitor important aspects of the business are likely to amount to a breach of this duty.

14.7.6 Duty to avoid conflicts of interest

A director is required, by s175(1) CA 2006, to avoid a situation where they have, or can have, a direct or indirect interest that conflicts, or possibly may conflict, with the interests of the company. Section 175(2) makes specific reference to situations involving the exploitation of any property, information or opportunity, whether or not the company could itself take advantage of such situation.

It is important to note, however, that the section is of no relevance to situations involving contracts with the company itself (s175(3) CA 2006). Moreover, if the situation in question is one which cannot reasonably be regarded as likely to give rise to a conflict of interest, the duty is not infringed (s175(4)(a) CA 2006).

The previous non-statutory position was based on the idea that directors are in a fiduciary relationship with their companies. That is, they are in the same position in respect of their powers as trustees or agents with respect to the company. As a result, they should not put themselves in a position of conflict with the company nor should they profit from their fiduciary status, sometimes referred to as a 'secret profit'.

The concept of secret profit is a rather intangible one; it does not, of course, prevent directors from receiving remuneration for their services. A profit is a secret profit if it comes to the director because of their position as a director. In *Cook v Deeks* [1916] 1 AC 554, two directors of a company negotiated a construction contract with the Canadian Pacific Railroad on behalf of their company. At a late stage in the negotiations, they decided to take the contract in their own names. The Privy Council held that they were accountable to their company for the profit; it was only through their position as directors of the company (which had previously contracted with the Canadian Pacific) that they were able to make the profit. (This type of scenario would today fall under the duty in s175(1) CA 2006.)

Although the fiduciary duty is to hand over what are described as secret profits, it seems that secrecy in this context means failure to obtain permission rather than any clandestine intent. In *Regal (Hastings) Ltd v Gulliver* [1967] 2 AC 134, the plaintiff company owned a cinema and wished to buy two others in the same town with a view to selling all three together. The company could not raise sufficient money to buy the other cinemas and so another company was set up partly owned by Regal (Hastings) Ltd and partly by some of the directors of Regal (Hastings) Ltd who had money of their own to invest. The new company then purchased the other two cinemas. The purchasers who wished to acquire all three cinemas then purchased all the shares in Regal (Hastings) Ltd and in the new company, thus acquiring control of the companies. The result was that the previous directors who had subscribed for the further shares sold them on at a profit. The new board of directors then instituted proceedings on behalf of Regal (Hastings) Ltd against its former directors. It was held by the House of Lords that a secret profit had been made since the opportunity to invest in the new company only came to the defendants because they were directors of Regal (Hastings) Ltd. This profit was ordered to be paid to Regal (Hastings) Ltd even though that company had been unable to raise all the money needed for the purchase itself and even though, realistically, the consequence of the order was that the purchaser who had negotiated the purchase of the shares at a fair price got some of the purchase price repaid to their own company.

The strictness of the previous common law position has been maintained in s175(2), which specifically states that it is immaterial to a finding of conflict whether or not the company could have taken advantage of the property, information or opportunity which the director, instead, benefited from.

Any potential conflict of interest can, however, be authorised by the directors (s175(4)(b) CA 2006). (The director with the conflict is not to be counted in the quorum of the relevant meeting, nor must he vote on the matter (s175(6) CA 2006).) Clearly, this may encourage directors in a position of conflict to disclose the same to their boards.

This right is given to private companies automatically, provided that their articles do not contain more restrictive provisions. The Model Articles for private companies do not displace this right. The right is also available to public companies but only if their constitutions expressly provide for such right (s175(5)(b) CA 2006).

14.7.7 Duty not to accept benefits from third parties

A director of a company is prohibited, by s176 CA 2006, from accepting a benefit from a third party conferred by reason of their being a director or their doing (or not doing) anything as a director. There is an exception to this prohibition if the acceptance of the benefit cannot reasonably be regarded as likely to give rise to a conflict of interest. This duty is a statutory version of the previous common law duty not to make a secret profit.

14.7.8 Duty to declare interest in proposed or existing transactions or arrangements

A director is obliged to declare the nature and extent of their interest in any proposed transaction or arrangement with the company before the company enters into this arrangement (s177 CA 2006). (This deals with the apparent gap in s175 excluding such contracts from the ambit of that section.)

The declaration may be made at a board meeting or by notice in writing to all directors (s177(2) CA 2006). A general notice may also be given by a director, under s185 CA 2006, to the effect that they are connected with a particular company or specified person, and should therefore be regarded as interested in any transaction or arrangement that may, after the date of the general notice, be made with that company or person.

The obligation is, however, waived if:

(a) the director's interest cannot reasonably be regarded as likely to give rise to a conflict of interest;

(b) the other directors are already aware of the interest or, at least, ought reasonably to be aware of it;

(c) the interest arises out of the terms of the director's **service contract** with the company, which have been or are to be considered by the board.

Where the making of a declaration is effectively of neutral consequence, a director is likely to make it, rather than rely upon the above exceptions. However, where a director (possibly for reasons of an obligation of confidentiality) would prefer not to make a declaration, these exceptions and their ambit are much more significant.

Finally, in those instances where directors are simply unaware of their obligation or neglect to fulfil it, these exceptions may be relied upon as a defence in any action for breach of duty.

The s177 declaration should be contrasted with the alternative declaration to be made pursuant to s182 CA 2006 in relation to *pre-existing* arrangements entered into by the company, in which a director is interested. (This obligation is particularly relevant at the moment a director is appointed.) Whilst the method for making this declaration and the exceptions to doing so are very similar to those under s177, this is not technically a duty and so the consequences of failing to comply with s182 are different. Instead of this being a breach of duty, it is a criminal offence punishable by a fine (s183 CA 2006).

14.7.9 Breach of directors' duties

The consequences of a breach (or threatened breach) of the statutory duties are the same as if the corresponding common law rule or equitable principle applied. Hence, the duties are enforceable by a company in the same way as any other fiduciary duty owed to a company by its directors.

In this regard, it should be noted that liquidators have the right to instigate litigation in the name of the company against a director for alleged breach of duty (s212 IA 1986). This is particularly relevant in respect of any alleged breach of s172 where it is claimed that the interests of creditors have not been taken into account.

Additionally, members are able, with court approval, to commence derivative actions should the company itself choose not to pursue a director (see **Chapter 19**).

In very simple terms, directors who are proven to have breached their duties can be made to account for any benefit or profit received and/or to compensate the company for any loss resulting to it from the breach. There is, however, statutory discretion under s1157 CA 2006 for a court to relieve a director from liability either fully or partially if:

(a) the director acted honestly and reasonably; and

(b) having regard to the circumstances of the case, the director ought fairly to be excused.

(For a recent example of a case in which ss172, 174 and 1157 CA 2006 were all considered, see *Re Pro4Sport Ltd (in liq)* [2015] EWHC 2540 (Ch), [2016] BCC 390.)

It should also be noted that where a director has breached a duty or trust, or has conducted themselves in a negligent manner, this conduct may be ratified by an ordinary resolution of the members of the company (s239(2) CA 2006). However, if the director in question is also a shareholder, that director and any person connected with them (in accordance with s252 CA 2006) is prevented from consenting to the resolution (s239(3) and (4) CA 2006).

14.8 **Directors' disqualification**

Companies legislation contains a number of provisions under which directors can be **disqualified** either automatically or by court order. The most important of these are contained in the Company Directors Disqualification Act 1986 (CDDA). This Act provides for disqualification from acting as a director, liquidator, receiver or manager of a company and from being concerned with the management of a company for up to 15 years.

Disqualification can be imposed in several contexts; however, for these purposes perhaps the two most important are:

(a) persistent default in filing returns with the Registrar (s3 CDDA). Persistent default is usually proved following three instances of default within five years. Instances of default are either convictions for failure to make returns or the imposition of certain 'default orders' as indicated in s3 in respect of certain filing obligations. The maximum period of disqualification in this case is five years. (It is anticipated that the scope of s3 will be widened by s31 ECCTA 2023 to include further instances of non-compliance with companies' legislation, such as acting as a director when one's identity has not been verified or acting as a director when no notification of one's appointment has been provided to Companies House. This provision was not in force at the time of writing, so the reader is advised to confirm the up-to-date position at the time of reading.);

(b) a finding that a person is 'unfit' to be concerned in the management of a company (s6 CDDA). The order may only be made against a person who is or has been a director of a company which has become insolvent while or after they were a director. For these purposes, a company is insolvent if it goes into insolvent **liquidation**, enters administration or an administrative receiver is appointed. Where an order is made on the ground of unfitness, the disqualification period must be for a minimum of two years and a maximum of 15. A director's conduct in relation to an overseas company, as well as a UK one, will be taken into account in disqualification proceedings under this section.

Additionally, persons who are not directors but who have directed the actions of directors who become disqualified under s6 CDDA may themselves be subject to disqualification proceedings (s8ZA CDDA).

The Rating (Coronavirus) and Directors Disqualification (Dissolved Companies) Act 2021 increased the potential grounds for disqualification to include directors of companies which are dissolved whilst still solvent and the circumstances indicate that their conduct makes them unfit to manage a company.

Section 1A CDDA 1986 allows directors to give an undertaking to the Secretary of State for Business, Innovation and Skills not to be involved in the management of a company for a specified period of time. Such an undertaking acts as an alternative to disqualification proceedings under s6. This process of 'fast track' disqualification is intended to increase efficiency in dealing with errant directors.

Acting in contravention of a disqualification order or undertaking is a criminal offence (s13 CDDA). Additionally, persons who are involved in the management of a company whilst disqualified face personal liability for debts which that company incurred whilst that person was involved in its management (s15 CDDA).

More generally, s40 ECCTA 2023 has from 4th March 2024 introduced an explicit prohibition on disqualified persons being appointed as directors (s159A CA 2006). Any such appointment is automatically void. Further, any existing director who is subsequently disqualified will automatically cease to hold the office of director (s169A CA 2006).

The Secretary of State has power under s15A CDDA to apply for a compensation order against a disqualified director of an insolvent company if their conduct has caused loss to one or more creditors. A successful application will mean that that director will have to pay a specified sum for the benefit of a creditor or creditors specified in the order. In turn, such a director has the right to challenge such an order and ask either for the amount payable to be reduced or for the order to be annulled.

In addition to the prohibition imposed by disqualification, a further prohibition has been imposed by the introduction of s11A CDDA through s36 ECCTA 2023. The result will be that any person subject to relevant director disqualification sanctions imposed by regulations made pursuant to the Sanctions and Anti-Money Laundering Act 2018 will commit an offence if they act as a director or directly or indirectly take part in the promotion, formation or management of a company.

14.9 Shadow directors

A **shadow director** is defined by s251(1) CA 2006 as 'any person in accordance with whose directions or instructions the directors of a company are accustomed to act'. The definition is designed to cover persons who are not *de jure* directors but who exercise material influence over the behaviour of the actual directors. However, a person who gives advice in a professional capacity to the directors is not to be taken to be a shadow director. A similar definition is also contained in s251 IA 1986.

Under a number of provisions of the 2006 Act, shadow directors are, for most purposes, treated in the same way as directors of the company. Examples of the provisions which apply to shadow directors are:

(a) the general duties of directors;

(b) the statutory restrictions on substantial property transactions and loans;

(c) the requirement to disclose interests in contracts with the company to the board; and

(d) the provisions relating to service contracts.

In addition, and perhaps more significantly, shadow directors are deemed to be directors for the purpose of wrongful trading under ss214 and 246ZB IA 1986 (see **Chapter 28**), by which they may become personally liable to contribute to the assets of an insolvent company. Under the CDDA, shadow directors may also be disqualified from holding office or being concerned in the management of a company, as if they were directors.

14.10 The directors and protection of outsiders

14.10.1 Introduction

A company is not a natural person and so can only exercise its powers through agents. Usually contracts will be made on behalf of the company either by the directors or by managers acting on the directors' authority. If a contract is made in accordance with the articles of the company, it will be binding on the company. Where, however, a contract is made by the wrong people (eg an employee acts without delegated authority from the directors) or in the wrong way (eg a board meeting is held but it is not quorate), the whole transaction is, prima facie, void. Contracts and other transactions decided upon without proper authority (or without a proper exercise of authority) are described as 'irregular'.

In dealing with irregular contracts, the law is faced with a dilemma. If the contract is declared irregular and void, the outsider will not be able to enforce it against the company even though they may be unaware of the irregularity. On the other hand, if the company is held to be bound by irregular contracts, the directors will, in effect, be able to ignore the requirements of the company's constitution, to the possible detriment of the shareholders.

The law deals with this dilemma by providing that irregular contracts are often binding on the company; in other words, commercial certainty for outsiders is regarded as desirable. These circumstances result partly from statute and partly from the general law of agency.

14.10.2 Statutory protection

Section 40(1) CA 2006 provides:

> In favour of a person dealing with a company in good faith, the power of the directors to bind the company, or authorise others to do so, is deemed free of any limitation under the company's constitution.

The sphere of directors' actions can be limited by a company's constitution in two main ways:

(a) any restrictions on a company's objects contained within the articles, which directors have a duty to observe; and
(b) any regulations governing directors' activities contained within its articles, such as a requirement for the board to seek shareholder approval for certain transactions or for it to act in accordance with instructions provided by special resolution.

In respect of the first issue, the following should be borne in mind:

(a) Companies which are set up under the provisions of the 2006 Act will have objects which are unrestricted, unless any contrary statement appears in the articles. On the basis that few companies will want to restrict their objects, the possibility of directors committing those companies to an action outside its objects will not be an issue.
(b) The objects clauses of companies set up under the previous 1985 Act will be deemed to be absorbed into the articles (from the memorandum of association). Directors of those companies will still, therefore, have to consider the ambit of the objects clause, unless their company chooses to remove the objects clause altogether from the articles.

The effect of s40 CA 2006 is that:

(a) where an unconnected third party;
(b) acting in good faith;
(c) enters into a contract with a company;
(d) which contract has been decided on or authorised by the board of that company; then,

notwithstanding any restrictions on the board's powers under the company's constitution (and whether or not the third party is aware of any such restriction), the contract will be valid.

(However, the directors may be liable to the company for any loss caused on the basis that they have breached their duty to the company to observe its constitution.)

It should be noted that under s40(2)(a), a person dealing with the company is not under an obligation to enquire as to any limitation that the directors may be subject to.

The protection of s40 is given only to persons who act in good faith. However, good faith is presumed unless the contrary is proved (s40(2)(b)(ii)) and knowledge that the directors are acting beyond their powers is not of itself sufficient proof of bad faith (s40(2)(b)(iii)).

14.10.3 Transaction with connected party

Section 41 CA 2006 makes a limited exception to s40. This applies where the board of a company exceeds its powers in respect of a transaction with a director or a person connected with a director.

In such cases, the transaction is voidable by the company; that is, the company has the option to avoid the contract but the contract is not void per se.

Whether or not it is avoided, the director or connected person and any director who authorised the transaction is liable to account to the company for any gain they make and to indemnify the company against any loss.

Where a transaction is irregular and is made between the company, a director and one or more third parties, the court has a wide discretion which enables it to protect any innocent third party. As such, the company's right to avoid a contract under s41 is lost if:

(a) restitution becomes impossible;
(b) a third party who has acquired rights bona fide for value would be affected;
(c) the transaction is affirmed by the shareholders; or
(d) the company has been fully compensated by an indemnity against any loss or damage.

14.11 Agency

14.11.1 General position

A company can only act through agents; the authority of agents to act for a company depends on the general law of agency. The actions of an agent are binding on a principal if the agent has actual authority or authority arising from estoppel.

The agent may also be personally liable to the third party (ie to the outsider) if the principal (ie the company) is not liable for breach of warranty of authority.

14.11.2 Actual authority

The scope of the actual authority of a company's agents depends upon the constitution of the company. The board of directors, acting collectively, usually has very wide powers to act on behalf of the company. The articles will usually permit delegation of some or all of these powers to committees of directors and to a managing director (or to other directors exercising similar executive functions). If appropriate delegation of the board's powers to an individual director has taken place, then the director in question will be acting with express actual authority and their individual actions, if within the scope of their authority, will bind the company.

Of fundamental concern, therefore, is the status of the agent director. Section 161 CA 2006 provides that the acts of a director are valid notwithstanding that it is afterwards discovered that:

(a) there was a defect in their appointment;
(b) they were disqualified from holding office;
(c) they had ceased to hold office;
(d) they were not entitled to vote on the matter in question.

This section protects an outsider dealing with a company and means that it does not have to be concerned with any procedural or legal irregularities which may have occurred and which that outsider may not have been aware of or able to discover when dealing with the director.

14.11.3 Agency by estoppel

A company may be bound by the acts of a person acting on its behalf when it is estopped from denying that person's authority. The estoppel may prevent the company from denying that the alleged agent is its agent or that they have power to bind the company in a particular way.

Agency by estoppel may result either from 'holding out' (ie a representation that the agent has authority, even if no actual authority existed) or from a representation that the agent is a member of a particular class of agent which is recognised to have certain powers to bind its principals.

14.11.3.1 Apparent authority

Directors do not generally have authority to act alone, so a company is prima facie not bound by the actions of a single director unless the board has conferred upon them actual authority by formal delegation of that authority. However, directors may conduct company business in all manner of contexts, either as a board or individually. Contracting third parties need the comfort of knowing that whenever they deal with a director, the director's actions can be relied upon. Effectively, apparent authority serves this purpose and ensures that the company is still bound, irrespective of the existence or otherwise of actual authority.

The main requirement is that the company has represented to the third party that the director has authority in the particular transaction. The representation does not need to be formal or active; often it will simply be the fact that the director is allowed to conduct themselves in a particular way.

Possibly the leading case on this is *Freeman and Lockyer v Buckhurst Park Properties* [1964] 1 All ER 630, where a director was often left in overall charge of the company due to the absence overseas of the other main board member. The director in question had engaged the services of a firm of surveyors, without reference to his fellow board members. The company in due course refused to pay the surveyors' fees on the basis that the director had engaged the surveyors without actual authority to do so. The Court of Appeal held that the company was so bound, due to the apparent authority of the director.

14.11.3.2 Usual authority

A well-established rule of the law of agency is that a principal is estopped from denying that an agent of certain recognised classes has the authority normally associated with that class. In relation to companies, this rule has been applied to managing directors.

If a company describes one of its directors as a managing director, it is estopped from denying that they are a managing director (even if they have not been appointed as such) and that they have the authority of a managing director (even if their appointment includes terms restricting their authority). This type of authority can be described as 'usual authority' or may also be categorised as implied actual authority. (See *Hely-Hutchinson v Brayhead Ltd* [1967] 3 All ER 98.)

14.11.4 Liability of agent to third party

A person purporting to act as agent for a company will be personally liable to a third party for breach of warranty of authority if it turns out that they had no authority to bind the company.

14.11.5 Ratification

If a contract is made by an agent without authority so that the company is not bound by the contract, the company can ratify, and thus retrospectively validate, the contract. Ratification may be effected by the people with actual authority to bind the company (ie normally the board but in some cases the members in **general meeting** (see s239 CA 2006)). Ratification will usually be implied where the company has accepted performance of the contract.

14.12 The company secretary

14.12.1 Appointment

Section 270 CA 2006 has removed the requirement for a **private company** to have a secretary. (It remains a requirement under s271, however, for *public* companies to have a secretary.) Private companies therefore have the option of incorporating with or without an appointed secretary. In the latter instance, a secretary may be appointed at a later date.

14.12.2 **Responsibilities and powers**

The secretary is responsible for keeping the various records of the company, such as minutes of board and general meetings and the various records which must be kept at the registered office. A secretary is also an officer of the company and so is liable to a fine if the company is in breach of the provisions of the 2006 Act which require information to be filed with the Registrar of Companies.

Where a private company has no secretary, the duties of a secretary may be carried out by a director or any person authorised by the directors to carry out such duties.

Many company secretaries are given powers far in excess of those contemplated by the 2006 Act. Often the secretary is responsible for the administration of the company and performs the functions of a compliance manager as well as of a record-keeper. The courts have, therefore, recognised that an outsider is entitled to rely on a decision taken by the secretary which relates to administration even if it turns out that the decision was not authorised by the board (ie the secretary has usual authority to make such contracts). Thus, in *Panorama (Developments) Guildford Ltd v Fidelis Furnishing Fabrics Ltd* [1971] 2 QB 711, the Court of Appeal held that a company was bound to pay for the use of cars hired by the secretary purportedly on behalf of the company but in fact for his own use.

14.12.3 **Register**

Companies are required to keep a register of secretaries (where appointed) and to notify the Registrar of Companies within 14 days of any change (ss275 and 276 CA 2006 respectively). (At the time of writing, it was understood that the combined effect of s51 and Sch 2 ECCTA 2023 will at some point remove this requirement. The reader is advised to check the latest position regarding the enactment of these provisions at the time of reading.)

Any appointment of a secretary must be notified to the Registrar on form AP03; the termination of a secretary's appointment must be notified on form TM02. (The appointment and removal of secretaries is a matter for the board of directors.)

CONDUCT POINT

Matters of professional conduct

If you have a corporate client, it should be remembered that the company itself can only act through its directors. As such, you will receive instructions through the board. Often this will involve contact with individual directors. It is important to recognise (and confirm) that those directors are acting on the company's behalf in instructing you. Further, if your retainer is with the company, you should avoid providing individual advice to directors in matters which affect the company.

EXAMPLE

Harriet, a solicitor, receives instructions through the chief executive officer of ExampleCo 999 Ltd that the majority of the board want to remove a particular director, Georgia. Harriet is obviously in a position to advise the company on the process for removal of Georgia and any consequences for the company arising from such an act.

A week later, once Georgia has found out about this proposal, she contacts Harriet and asks for her advice about her position in law.

Clearly Harriet cannot advise Georgia.

KEY POINT SUMMARY

Important issues raised by this chapter regarding directors (and secretaries) are:

- Directors are office-holders. In parallel, they may be required to carry out specific executive functions.
- A company must act through its directors, hence the need for a delegation of powers to the board.
- Directors may act collectively as a board. Alternatively, certain functions may be delegated down to individual directors.
- Companies will be committed to contractual obligations through the actions of their directors. This can raise issues regarding the authority of the relevant directors.
- Directors are subject to statutory duties which they owe to the company. In turn, it is the company which is the appropriate claimant to enforce any breach.
- The law also recognises the concept of a shadow director; that is, a person who performs the functions of and exercises the influence and power of a director without ever having been appointed to the office of director.
- The company secretary is another officer of the company. The appointment of a secretary to a private company is discretionary; it is compulsory for a **public company**.

CHAPTER 15
The Appointment and Removal of Directors

FUNCTIONING LEGAL KNOWLEDGE

This chapter considers the following functioning legal knowledge included in the SRA's SQE 1 assessment specification:

Corporate governance and compliance:

- rights, duties and powers of directors and **shareholders** of companies
- appointment and removal of directors

AUTHORITIES UNDERPINNING PRACTICE

The key authorities that underpin this area of practice are listed below. Note that for legislation you are linked to legislation.gov.uk.

Although much of the legislation on this government website is available in its amended form, the incorporation of new amendments into the text of legislation can be delayed. You should refer to legal databases to ensure you are referencing the most up-to-date legislation.

- Companies Act 2006
  https://www.legislation.gov.uk/ukpga/2006/46/contents
- Companies (Model Articles) Regulations 2008
  https://www.legislation.gov.uk/uksi/2008/3229

15.1 Introduction

Note that provisions of the Economic Crime and Corporate Transparency Act 2023 (ECCTA 2023) will affect certain elements of this chapter. However, many provisions of ECCTA 2023 are yet to come into force. Readers should, therefore, confirm the status and content of those provisions at the time of consulting this chapter. 15.5 (At the time of writing, only two commencement orders had been introduced, namely, the Economic Crime and Corporate Transparency Act 2023 (Commencement No 1) Regulations 2023 and the Economic Crime and Corporate Transparency Act 2023 (Commencement No 2 and Transitional Provision) Regulations 2024.) Provisions fully in force as at 4th March 2024 are explained accordingly; a summary of changes expected to come into force after that date is given at 15.5.

After consulting this chapter, you should be in a position to describe and explain the processes governing the appointment and removal of a company's directors. As such, you will be in a position to distinguish between the regulations which govern either the appointment or removal of a director.

These regulations result from a combination of statute and a company's **articles of association**. In respect of this second limb, we will consider the Model Articles for Private Companies, by way of example.

You will also become familiar with the dual status which directors often enjoy; that of office-holder and employee.

15.2 Appointment of directors

15.2.1 Introduction

Section 154 of the Companies Act 2006 (CA 2006) provides that a **private company** must have at least one director and that a **public company** must have at least two directors. For both private and public companies, at least one director is required to be a 'natural person'; that is, not a company or corporation (s155 CA 2006).

15.2.2 First directors

The first directors of a company are the people who are named as such and whose details are provided to the Registrar as part of the process of registration (in form IN01); they automatically become directors on the company's incorporation (s16(6) CA 2006). As such, the identities of such persons need to be considered right at the outset of the process of incorporation.

15.2.3 Additional directors

From time to time, it will be necessary to appoint further directors, either because one of the existing directors has ceased to hold office or because it is decided to increase the size of the board of directors. Apart from a few statutory restrictions (dealt with later), the company is free to make whatever provision it wishes in its articles as to the appointment of directors. In particular, there is no general requirement that directors should be shareholders or that they should be chosen by the shareholders. Note, however, that any purported appointment of a person as a director when under the age of 16 is void (s157 CA 2006).

15.2.4 Provision for appointment in a company's articles

Statute makes no special provision for the method of appointing directors. It is, therefore, a matter for the articles. Companies may adopt various methods to deal with this issue. What follows is a general summary of the more common approaches.

Normally, the main power to appoint directors is given to the **members**. This provides for appointment by **ordinary resolution** (ie by a simple majority of the members).

Instead or additionally, the articles may provide for the appointment of additional directors by the board itself. For example, art 17 of the Model Articles for Private Companies allows a permanent appointment of a director to be made either by ordinary resolution of the members or by a decision of the directors.

15.2.5 Service contracts

It is common for managing and other **executive directors** to enter into **service contracts** with a company on their appointment to the board. Notwithstanding that both events will usually occur within very close proximity to each other, it is important to understand the distinction between a person:

(a) being *appointed* to the *office* of director; and

(b) entering into a service contract.

On being appointed to the office of director, the director's conduct is defined primarily by the company's articles, common law and legislation. On entering into a service contract to carry out an executive role, the director has various rights and obligations defined primarily by the terms of the contract as negotiated with the company.

An executive director is both a director and usually an employee of the company. Like other employees, they may have certain statutory rights against the company, if they are unfairly dismissed or made redundant.

The distinction is of particular importance should a director be removed from office (discussed later).

Because directors are in a fiduciary relationship with their companies, they are technically not permitted to be rewarded for being a director. However, it is arguable that this restriction does not extend to the right under a service contract to receive a *salary* and related remuneration in return for carrying out defined obligations. However, an express provision in the articles removes any doubt. Therefore, it is always necessary to consult and comply with the articles in this regard. For example, the Model Articles for Private Companies stipulate that all forms of directors' remuneration can be determined by the board (art 19).

The terms of any service contract will be negotiated between the proposed director and the existing board; it will be the board's decision to commit the company to the final, agreed version. However, members' prior approval by ordinary resolution will be required if the guaranteed term of the contract is longer than two years (s188 CA 2006). This approval only extends to the term of the contract itself and not the contract as a whole. Failure to obtain the necessary resolution will result in the explicit term of the contract being void (s189(a)) and the contract will, instead, be terminable by the company on reasonable notice (s189(b)). Shareholder approval is not valid unless a memorandum setting out details of the proposed contract is made available to shareholders in advance of seeking the resolution (s188(5)).

EXAMPLE

ExampleCo (343) Ltd is looking to enter into a service contract with Billy, a director of the company.

- If the contract was terminable at any time by the company on six months' notice, no shareholder approval would be necessary.
- If the contract was terminable at any time by the company on three years' notice, shareholder approval would be necessary.
- If the contract was for a fixed term of five years with no ability for the company to terminate in advance of its expiry, shareholder approval would be necessary.
- If the contract was for a fixed term of five years with the ability for the company to terminate at any time in advance of its expiry on 12 months' notice, no shareholder approval would be necessary.

15.3 Removal of directors

15.3.1 Introduction

An important distinction should be drawn at the outset between a director voluntarily leaving office and a director ceasing to hold office either through circumstances or because the company wishes to remove them.

15.3.2 Retirement by notice

The most straightforward way in which a director may vacate office is to retire by giving notice to the company. (See, for example, art 18(f) of the Model Articles for Private Companies.) Usually this takes the form of a letter to the board.

If a director is also performing an executive function, the company will want to ensure that the director resigns from their employment relationship with the company as well.

15.3.3 Automatic cessation of office

In certain circumstances stipulated by the articles, a director may automatically cease to hold office. See, for example, art 18 of the Model Articles, which states, inter alia, that a director ceases to hold office on becoming bankrupt or when prevented by law from being a director. In many instances, these circumstances will reflect specific legal requirements. So, for example, undischarged bankrupts commit a criminal offence if they act as a director of a company (s11(1) Company Directors Disqualification Act (CDDA) 1986). A similar situation arises should a director continue to act as such when subject to a **disqualification** order (or undertaking) (s13 CDDA). To put the matter beyond doubt, s40 ECCTA 2023 has introduced two provisions into CA 2006 which provide that as from 4th March 2024:

(a) no disqualified person can be appointed as a director; and

(b) any director who becomes disqualified automatically ceases to hold the office of a director.

However, such persons will remain liable for their actions if they continue to act as a director or act as a shadow director.

The Model Articles do not contain any express power for the directors to remove one of their kind. However, it is possible for articles of association to reserve such a power, for example a provision stating that a person will cease to be a director if that person receives notice to that effect signed by all the other directors. There is judicial authority for the fact that such a power is fiduciary and must be exercised in the best interests of the company (see *Samuel Tak Lee v Chou Wen Hsien* [1984] 1 WLR 1202).

It is always possible for directors to decide to terminate a director's service contract with the company (in accordance with its terms). In turn, a well-drafted service contract will often contain a provision that the director in question must also resign from office once the contract is terminated.

15.3.4 Removal of directors under s168 CA 2006

15.3.4.1 Power to remove by ordinary resolution

Section 168(1) CA 2006 provides for removal of directors *from office* by ordinary resolution at a **general meeting** (ie purported removal by way of a **written resolution** is not effective). The power given by the section overrides anything in the company's articles (even, eg, an article naming a 'life' director) or in an agreement with the director.

Section 168(1) provides the most effective means by which majority shareholders who object to the way in which their company is being run can keep control of the company. However, where the directors themselves are the majority shareholders, as will frequently be the case in a private company, this threat is obviously more imagined than real.

15.3.4.2 Procedure

No resolution purporting to remove a director from office is valid unless special notice has first been given to the company of an intention to remove a particular director (s168(2) CA 2006). This usually emanates from the shareholder or shareholders who wish to remove the director. In effect, this gives the company a minimum period of 28 days' 'grace' before any steps are taken by the shareholders in question to remove the director (s312(1) CA 2006). On receipt of the notice, a company is obliged to send a copy to the director whose removal is proposed (s169(1) CA 2006).

However, special notice is not sufficient to cause a meeting to be held at which the necessary resolution can be proposed or to have such a resolution included on the agenda of any forthcoming meeting (see *Pedley v Inland Waterways Association* [1977] 1 All ER 209). Unless the board is sympathetic to the proposal and calls a general meeting itself, the shareholders concerned must invoke their right under s303 CA 2006, or any special right they may have under the company's articles of association, to cause the directors to call a general meeting for the purpose of considering the director's removal.

Whether or not the director in question is a shareholder, they will be entitled to attend the relevant general meeting and speak on the resolution (s169(2) CA 2006).

EXAMPLE

Some of the shareholders of ExampleCo (343) Ltd are looking to remove Billy from the office of a director pursuant to s168 CA 2006.

As a preliminary step, they must give at least 28 days' (special) notice to the company of their intention to seek to pass such a resolution.

The directors may choose to exercise their power to call a general meeting for this purpose. If they do so and the meeting is called earlier than the 28-day time period in the shareholder notice, any resolution subsequently passed at this meeting will still be valid (s312(4)).

Instead, the directors may choose to do nothing, in which case, so long as those shareholders hold between them a minimum of 5% of the voting share capital of the company, they may request that the board calls a general meeting pursuant to s303. In turn, the board is obliged to comply with this request under s304.

For this reason, it is sensible for both a s312 special notice and a s303 requisition to be sent simultaneously to the company.

At the subsequent general meeting, a simple majority of shareholders must vote in favour of the resolution to remove Billy, in order for it to be effective.

15.3.4.3 Director's right to compensation and damages on removal

The shareholders have an absolute right to remove a director. However, this does not deprive the director of any rights to compensation or damages they may have (s168(5) CA 2006). When considering these rights, it is important to maintain a distinction between the right to a payment for loss of office and the right to claim damages where there is a service contract between the director and the company.

Should the director be removed *from office*, then the only compensation for such loss of office is a payment approved by the company by ordinary resolution under s217 CA 2006. However, removal from office will almost certainly terminate any service contract as it will be impossible for the director to fulfil their obligations (*Shindler v Northern Raincoat Co Ltd* [1960] 1 WLR 1038). Such termination could be unlawful, in which case the director may be entitled to damages (usually based upon either the director's contractual notice period or any unexpired period of a fixed term contract). It is therefore important for the shareholders to consider the financial cost of removing a director. (Payment of damages does not require shareholder approval, as the company is legally bound to pay them (s220(1) CA 2006).)

Aside from issues of compensation, depending on the basis upon which the company was supposed to be owned and managed, the removal of a director who is also a shareholder may amount to unfairly prejudicial conduct under s994 CA 2006. (See **Chapter 19** for further discussion.)

15.3.4.4 Special voting rights on resolution to remove director

In the case of *Bushell v Faith* [1970] AC 1099, the articles of the relevant company provided that:

> in the event of a resolution being proposed at any general meeting of the company for the removal from office of any director, any **shares** held by that director shall on a poll in respect of such resolution carry the right to three votes per share . . .

The director whose removal was proposed owned one-third of the shares, but with this enhancement could exercise 60% of the votes on any resolution to remove him. As such, he could not be removed. Nevertheless, the article was held to be valid. All that the CA 2006 stipulates is that an ordinary resolution may be used to remove a director. A clause of this type does not, therefore, prevent such a resolution from being proposed; although it does make it impossible to remove the director without their consent.

The inclusion of a so-called *Bushell v Faith* clause in a company's articles is a matter of negotiation for those involved in a company and it can obviously have far-reaching ramifications. (Note that the Model Articles contain no such right.)

A further consideration of such a clause is that it may be removed at any time from the articles by a **special resolution**. If the director who benefits from the clause can prevent such a resolution (by possessing more than 25% of the voting capital), then the status of the clause is secure. However, if this is not the case, the only way to make the director properly secure is to grant that director additional enhanced voting rights on any resolution to alter or remove the *Bushell v Faith* clause itself.

EXAMPLE

Exampleco (2020) Ltd has two directors, Andrew and Björn.
The company also has the following shareholders:

Andrew: 100 ordinary shares

Björn: 100 ordinary shares

Conan: 100 ordinary shares

Delores: 100 ordinary shares

Etta: 100 ordinary shares

Each of Andrew and Björn negotiate the inclusion of a *Bushell v Faith* clause in the company's articles which grants them ten votes per share on any resolution for their removal.

All of the shareholders (with the exception of Andrew) attempt to pass an ordinary resolution pursuant to s168 CA 2006 to remove Andrew as a director. The resolution will be unsuccessful, as Andrew will have 1,000 votes compared to the combined votes of the other shareholders of 400.

However, if those shareholders first propose a special resolution to amend the articles to remove the *Bushell v Faith* clause, this resolution will be successful, as Andrew only has 20% of the votes in this instance. Once the clause is deleted, the shareholders will then be in a position to move a successful s168 resolution.

Therefore, in order for Andrew (or Björn) to be properly protected, they should each have been granted similar enhanced voting rights to cover any purported removal or amendment to the *Bushell v Faith* clause.

Note: it is arguable that the special resolution to change the articles may be unlawful, depending on the context–see discussion at **13.8.3**.

15.3.4.5 Alternatives to removal under s168

The statutory power under s168 is sacrosanct. It is not, therefore, lawful to include in a company's articles any provision which purports to displace its availability to shareholders. However, it may be considered appropriate to make available to the shareholders *alternative* methods for the removal of directors, for example removal by special resolution. In turn, this would circumvent the need for special notice and, in the case of a private company, could be achieved by written resolution, albeit that an increased majority of shareholders (75%) would have to consent to the removal.

15.4 **Filing consequences of appointment or removal**

The appointment of any director (other than on incorporation of the company) will trigger an obligation on a company

(a) under s167 CA 2006 to notify the Registrar of Companies on form AP01 within 14 days of the appointment.

(b) under s162 CA 2006 to amend the company's register of directors by the entry of the new directors' details;

(c) under s165 CA 2006 to amend the company's register of directors' residential addresses by the entry of the new directors' details.

The removal or retirement of any director will trigger an obligation on a company

(a) under s167 CA 2006 to notify the Registrar of Companies on form TM01 within 14 days of the removal or retirement.
(b) under s 162 CA 2006 to amend the company's register of directors by the removal of the directors' details;
(c) under s165 CA 2006 to amend the company's register of directors' residential addresses by the removal of the directors' details.

If a director has entered into a service contract, a copy thereof must be kept for inspection at the company's **registered office** for the duration of the contract and for the 12-month period thereafter (s228 CA 2006).

15.5 Impact of the Economic Crime and Corporate Transparency Act 2023

15.5.1 Introduction

This section sets out the expected changes to the CA 2006 yet to be brought into effect by ECCTA 2023, that is, those to be introduced after 4th March 2024. Most will be concerned with new controls on the appointment of directors. It should be remembered that directors can be appointed both on the incorporation of a company and subsequently. Readers should confirm the status of the relevant provisions of ECCTA 2023 when consulting this chapter.

15.5.2 Identity verification

Any appointment of a director will trigger the need to notify Companies House of such an event (see **15.4**). ECCTA 2023 will amend the CA 2006 to require such notice to include, inter alia, a statement that the identity of any proposed director has been verified. Additionally, any director who has not had their identity verified will be prevented from acting as a director. Anybody who does act without such verification will commit an offence.

Further, a company will be required to ensure that an individual does not act as a director unless their identity has been verified. Failure to do so will be an offence by both the relevant company and every officer of the company in default.

The combined effect of these new provisions will be that the identity of any proposed director will need to be confirmed before the appointment takes place.

Existing directors will also be required to confirm their identities. The specifics of how and when this needs to be done are not yet confirmed.

It would appear that verification will only need to take place once, so pre-existing verification will suffice. Full details of the system of verification are expected to be introduced by secondary legislation and will, in turn, be implemented by Companies House. In simple terms, verification will be able to be undertaken directly by Companies House or by the provision to Companies House of a verification statement in respect of the relevant person. (Such a statement will need to be generated by an authorised corporate service provider.) It is recommended that the reader consults the Companies House website for the up-to-date position and for further information on the mechanics of the process of verification.

15.5.3 Appointment of directors on incorporation

As part of the process of incorporating a company, details of initial directors of a company need to be provided in the registration documentation (see **3.5**). In future, it is expected that registration documentation will have to include statements confirming that:

(i) the identity of any proposed director is verified; and
(ii) any proposed director is neither disqualified nor ineligible to be a director.

(See **3.16.2** for further discussion of the proposed new requirements for incorporation of a company.)

15.5.4 Notification of appointment

Currently, directors can start to act in that capacity immediately on appointment. Section 44 of ECCTA 2023 will introduce a material change which is that, until formal notification of the appointment of a director is given to Companies House, the relevant appointee must not act as a director. (This provision will only be applicable to the appointment of directors post-incorporation of a company.)

If they do so act, they will commit a criminal offence, although any acts they undertake as a director during that time will remain valid and effective. A statutory defence will, however, be available to protect the appointee if they reasonably believed that relevant notification had actually been delivered to Companies House.

15.5.5 Abolition of registers

Once s51 of ECCTA 2023 is in force, companies will no longer be required to maintain (inter alia) either registers of directors or registers of directors' residential addresses, the idea being that registers centrally held at Companies House should be sufficient. (This topic is also discussed in **Chapter 20**.)

KEY POINT SUMMARY

- Directors will usually be appointed by a method stipulated in the company's articles; normally either by the board or by ordinary resolution of shareholders.
- Directors often have dual status of office-holder and employee.
- The appointment or removal of a director will trigger appropriate changes to a company's internal registers and the requirement to notify **Companies House** of the event.
- If a director is to have a service contract, this will trigger consideration of s188 CA 2006 and whether or not the term of the contract will require shareholder approval.
- Shareholders have the right under statute to remove a director from office through the means of an ordinary resolution.

CHAPTER 16
Statutory Controls on Contracts Between Companies and Directors

FUNCTIONING LEGAL KNOWLEDGE

This chapter considers the following functioning legal knowledge included in the SRA's SQE 1 assessment specification:

Corporate governance and compliance:

- rights, duties and powers of directors and **shareholders** of companies
- company decision-making and meetings: procedural, disclosure and approval requirements
- documentary, record-keeping, statutory filing and disclosure requirements

AUTHORITIES UNDERPINNING PRACTICE

The key authorities that underpin this area of practice are listed below. Note that for legislation you are linked to legislation.gov.uk.

Although much of the legislation on this government website is available in its amended form, the incorporation of new amendments into the text of legislation can be delayed. You should refer to legal databases to ensure you are referencing the most up-to-date legislation.

- Companies Act 2006
  https://www.legislation.gov.uk/ukpga/2006/46
- Companies (Model Articles) Regulations 2008
  https://www.legislation.gov.uk/uksi/2008/3229

16.1 Introduction

Because of the high degree of control which directors are able to exercise over their companies, over time an increasing number of statutory provisions have been included in the Companies Acts for the protection of shareholders. These provisions are primarily concerned with regulating contractual arrangements between directors and their companies. After consulting this chapter, you will have been introduced to those provisions which are now to be found in the Companies Act 2006 (CA 2006).

What will be understood is that the main mechanism employed under the statute is to require shareholders' consent by **ordinary resolution**. In turn, this may also require the provision of relevant information regarding the proposal to the shareholders in advance.

Additionally, whilst the focus of this chapter is statutory controls, you should remain aware that whenever the directors commit a company to a contract, they should ensure that they are fulfilling their duties to the company, in any event. (See **14.7** for discussion of directors' duties.)

16.2 Directors' service contracts

The terms of directors' **service contracts** will usually be determined by the board. Section 188 CA 2006 requires the approval of the **members** by ordinary resolution of any provision in a director's service contract which provides for a guaranteed term exceeding two years. Technically, therefore, the shareholders are not approving the service contract as a whole; they are approving the duration of the contract. Approval may also be required where an existing contract is extended, if the aggregate term exceeds two years.

The rationale for this approach is to remove from directors total discretion as to the duration of their service contracts.

If a company agrees to a provision in contravention of s188, the provision is void to the extent of the contravention (but not the contract as a whole) and the company is deemed to be able to terminate the contract by reasonable notice at any time (s189 CA 2006).

EXAMPLE

(a) David's service contract is for a fixed period of four years and contains no provision for early termination by the company. This contract would require shareholder approval.

(b) David's service contract is for an indefinite period, terminable at any time by the company on six months' notice. This contract would not require shareholder approval.

(c) David's service contract is for an indefinite period, terminable at any time by the company on three years' notice. This contract would require shareholder approval.

Approval from the shareholders is not effective unless a memorandum setting out details of the relevant contract is provided to shareholders in advance (s188(5) CA 2006). The method of provision is determined by the mechanism sought to achieve the passing of the resolution, namely:

(a) if by **written resolution**, at the time when the resolution is sent or submitted to the members;

(b) if by **general meeting**, by being made available for inspection at the **registered office** for not less than 15 days ending with the date of the meeting and at the general meeting itself.

16.3 Substantial property transactions

16.3.1 Relevant transactions

Section 190 CA 2006 controls arrangements whereby:

(a) a director of a company (or its holding company), or a person connected with that director, is to acquire from the company a substantial non-cash asset; or

(b) a company is to acquire a substantial non-cash asset from one of its directors (or a director of its holding company) or a person connected with that director.

EXAMPLE

The situations s190 is concerned with are:

(a) Co A buys from or sells to Erik, a director of Co A, a substantial non-cash asset.

(b) Co A buys from or sells to Tierney, a person connected with a director of Co A, a substantial non-cash asset.

(c) Co A buys from or sells to Kwame, a director of the holding company of Co A, a substantial non-cash asset.

(d) Co A buys from or sells to Fred, a person connected with a director of the holding company of Co A, a substantial non-cash asset.

16.3.2 Connected persons

For the purposes of s190, a connected person includes (among others) a director's spouse, child or step-child (ss252 and 253 CA 2006). Additionally, there are complicated rules for determining the extent to which a company is connected with a director. Put simply, if a director owns at least 20% of the share capital of a company, that company is connected with the director (s254(2) CA 2006).

EXAMPLE

Company A Ltd buys a substantial non-cash asset from ExampleCo Ltd.

Ash is both a director of Company A Ltd and a 30% shareholder in ExampleCo Ltd.

As such, Company A Ltd is buying a relevant asset from a person connected with one of its directors.

16.3.3 Substantial non-cash asset

A substantial non-cash asset is defined by s191 CA 2006 as an asset which has a value which, at the time of the relevant arrangement:

(a) exceeds 10% of the company's net asset value and is more than £5,000; or

(b) exceeds £100,000.

A company's asset value will normally be determined by reference to the company's most recent statutory accounts.

EXAMPLE

EG 123 Ltd has a net asset value of £330,000. It proposes to buy an asset from a director.

(a) If the asset is worth £4,000, it will not be substantial as it is worth less than £5,000.

(b) If the asset is worth £114,000, it will be substantial as it is worth more than £100,000.

(c) If the asset is worth £20,000, it will not be substantial as its value does not exceed 10% of the company's asset value, despite being worth more than £5,000.

(d) If the asset is worth £52,000, it will be substantial as its value exceeds 10% of the company's asset value, and is worth more than £5,000.

It will usually be a straightforward matter to identify an asset which is 'non-cash', for example a plot of land. However, reference should be made to s1163(1) CA 2006 in this regard where 'non-cash asset' is defined as 'any property or interest in property, other than cash'. In addition, the acquisition of a non-cash asset can include the creation of an estate or interest in any property (s1163(2)). In turn, this could mean, for example, that taking a lease from or granting a lease to a director involves a non-cash asset.

The value to be attributed to the asset in question raises two issues. The first is that this value must be the market value of the asset, otherwise directors could manipulate the price paid to fall outside the ambit of the section.

Secondly, should the market value be adjudged by reference to any special value which the asset may have to the relevant director? In *Micro Leisure Ltd v County Properties and Developments* [2000] TLR 12, this question was answered in the affirmative. Lord Hamilton put forward the example of a ransom strip of land which, when purchased by a director, would substantially increase the development potential of the director's existing land. It is submitted, however, that situations where the objective market value and the 'director-specific' value are different will be rare.

16.3.4 Requirement for shareholders' approval

Any arrangement to which s190 does apply must be approved by the company's members by ordinary resolution in advance of the transaction being entered into or it must be entered into conditionally on the basis that such approval will subsequently be given. (This requirement does not apply, however, where the company in question is a wholly owned **subsidiary** (s190(4)(b) CA 2006).)

Additionally, if the relevant director or person connected with that director is:

(a) a director of the company's holding company; or

(b) a person connected with a director of the company's holding company;

an ordinary resolution of the members of that holding company must also be obtained or the transaction must be made on the basis that such approval will subsequently be given.

EXAMPLE

(a) B Ltd is a wholly owned subsidiary of A Ltd. Zahid is a director of both companies.

If B Ltd were to sell a substantial asset to Zahid, an ordinary resolution of A Ltd would be necessary, but not one of the shareholders of B Ltd itself (as it is 100% owned). (Although the board of B Ltd would have to resolve to sell the asset, in any event.)

(b) S Ltd is an 80% subsidiary of T Ltd. Cecil is a director of T Ltd only.

If S Ltd were to sell a substantial asset to Cecil, an ordinary resolution of both T Ltd and S Ltd would be necessary–the sale is to a director of S Ltd's holding company and S Ltd is not wholly owned. (As in the previous example, the board of S Ltd would have to resolve to sell the asset, in any event.)

16.3.5 Failure to comply

In accordance with s195(2) CA 2006, any contract made in contravention of the above requirements is voidable by the company unless:

(a) the contract is subsequently affirmed within a reasonable time by ordinary resolution of the members of the company and any holding company, as necessary (s196 CA 2006);

(b) restitution of the money paid or the relevant asset is no longer possible;

(c) the company has been indemnified by any other persons for the loss or damage suffered by it; or

(d) third party rights (acquired for value without notice) would be affected by avoidance.

In respect of any transaction which contravenes s190, pursuant to s195(3) and (4), the following persons are potentially liable to account to the company which entered into the transaction for any gain that they made and any loss which the company suffered as a result of the transaction:

(a) any director of the company or its holding company who was a party to the transaction;

(b) any person with whom the company entered into the arrangement who is connected with a director of the company or its holding company;

(c) the director of the company or holding company with whom any such person is connected; and

(d) any other director of the company who authorised the transaction.

Liability may be avoided by a director where the transaction was with a person connected with a director of a company or its holding company and the relevant director shows that they took all reasonable steps to secure the company's compliance with s190 (s195(6) CA 2006). In addition, the parties detailed at (b) and (d) above will not be liable if, at the time of the transaction, they were unaware of the circumstances constituting the contravention of s190.

16.4 Loans to directors

16.4.1 The general prohibition

The provisions relating to loans and similar indirect transactions (quasi-loans and credit transactions) are contained in ss197–214 CA 2006.

Any company may not:

(a) make a loan to a director of the company or its holding company; or

(b) guarantee or provide **security** in connection with a loan made by any person to such a director;

unless the transaction has been approved by ordinary resolution (s197(1) CA 2006).

This requirement does not apply, however, where the company in question is a wholly owned subsidiary (s197(5)(b) CA 2006).

In addition, in those instances where the relevant director is a director of the company's holding company, an ordinary resolution of that company's shareholders is required (s197(2) CA 2006).

EXAMPLE

Carrington Ltd lends money to a director–an ordinary resolution of the shareholders of Carrington is required.

Carrington Ltd guarantees a loan made by Credit Bank to a director–an ordinary resolution of the shareholders of Carrington is required.

Carrington Ltd lends money to a director of its holding company–an ordinary resolution of the shareholders of the holding company is required. Whether or not the shareholders of Carrington must also approve the loan will depend upon whether or not it is a wholly owned subsidiary.

16.4.2 The wider prohibition: public companies

Public companies and *companies associated with public companies* (which can be either public or private companies) are subject to wider controls in a number of ways. (For the meaning of 'associated', see s256 CA 2006.)

First, they must seek shareholder approval for:

(a) any loan made by the company to a person connected with a director or with a director of any holding company (s200(2)(a) CA 2006); or

(b) any guarantee or security provided by the company in connection with a loan made by any person to such a connected person (s200(2)(b) CA 2006).

Secondly, such companies must also seek shareholder approval before:

(a) entering into any arrangement with a director or with a director of any holding company which amounts to a *quasi-loan* (s198(2)(a) CA 2006);

(b) providing any guarantee or security in respect of a *quasi-loan* made by any person to either a director or a director of any holding company (s198(2)(b) CA 2006);

(c) entering into any arrangement with any person connected with a director or with a director of any holding company which amounts to a *quasi-loan* (s200(2)(a) CA 2006); or

(d) providing any guarantee or security in respect of a *quasi-loan* made by any person to a person connected with a director or with a director of any holding company (s200(2)(b) CA 2006).

Quasi-loans (as defined by s199 CA 2006) are effectively situations where a director incurs a payment obligation and the company agrees to meet that obligation on the director's behalf or agrees to reimburse the relevant amount to the director, on the understanding that the director will repay the sum in question to the company.

Thirdly, public companies and companies associated with public companies must also seek shareholder approval before:

(a) entering into any arrangement with a director or with a director of any holding company which amounts to a *credit transaction* (s201(2)(a) CA 2006);

(b) providing any guarantee or security in respect of a *credit transaction* made by any person to either a director or a director of any holding company (s201(2)(b) CA 2006);

(c) entering into any arrangement with any person connected with a director or with a director of any holding company which amounts to a *credit transaction* (s201(2)(a) CA 2006); or

(d) providing any guarantee or security in respect of a *credit transaction* made by any person to any of those persons mentioned in (c) (s201(2)(b) CA 2006).

Credit transactions (as defined by s202 CA 2006) are effectively situations where the company sells or leases an asset to the director in return for payment by the director in instalments or on the basis that payment is to be deferred.

In all circumstances specific to public companies and companies associated with public companies where shareholders' approval is required:

(a) such approval is unnecessary if the company in question is a wholly owned subsidiary (ss198(6)(b), 200(6)(b) and 201(6)(b) CA 2006);

(b) it will also be necessary to seek the approval of the shareholders of the relevant holding company if the transaction involves either a director of that holding company or a person connected to such a director (ss198(3), 200(3) and 201(3) CA 2006).

EXAMPLE

Partington plc agrees to guarantee a loan made by Credit Bank to the husband of one of its directors. In contrast to a **private company**, where shareholder approval would not be necessary for the guarantee of a loan made to a connected person, an ordinary resolution would be necessary here.

If Partington plc were either to enter into a credit transaction with or make a quasi-loan to any of the following persons:

(a) a director;

(b) a director of its holding company;

(c) a person connected with a director of its holding company;

shareholder approval would be necessary as follows:

(i) in respect of example (a), an ordinary resolution of Partington's shareholders, unless Partington was a wholly owned subsidiary;

(ii) in respect of example (b), an ordinary resolution of the shareholders of the holding company and of Partington's shareholders, unless Partington was a wholly owned subsidiary;

(iii) in respect of example (c), an ordinary resolution of the shareholders of the holding company and of Partington's shareholders, unless Partington was a wholly owned subsidiary.

16.4.3 Provision of information to shareholders

In any instance where shareholder approval is required, a memorandum setting out prescribed details of the relevant transaction must be made available to the members in advance of the resolution being passed. The method of provision is determined by the mechanism sought to achieve the passing of the resolution, namely:

(a) if by written resolution, at the time when the resolution is sent or submitted to the members;

(b) if by general meeting, by being made available for inspection at the registered office for not less than 15 days ending with the date of the meeting and at the general meeting itself.

16.4.4 Exceptions

There are a number of exceptions to the above requirements for members' approval, most notably:

(a) Any company may, without members' approval, provide a director (or a director of its holding company) with funds to meet expenditure incurred or to be incurred by that director for the purposes of the company or for the purpose of enabling that director properly to perform their duties, provided that the aggregate value of any such transactions with that director does not exceed £50,000 (s204).

(b) Companies need not seek members' approval for any loan, guarantee, security or quasi-loan if the value of that transaction, together with any other similar transactions, does not exceed £10,000 (s207(1)).

(c) Companies need not seek members' approval for any credit transaction or guarantee or security related to a credit transaction, if the value of that transaction, together with any other similar transactions, does not exceed £15,000 (s207(2)).

(d) Any company may, without members' approval, provide a director (or a director of its holding company) with funds to meet expenditure incurred or to be incurred by that director for the purposes of defending (or avoiding) criminal or civil proceedings which arise out of any alleged negligence or breach of duty or trust of that director in relation to the company (s205). (Note that there are a number of detailed conditions which must be fulfilled for the loan to fall within this exception.)

16.4.5 **Failure to comply**

The consequences of failing to obtain the necessary shareholders' approval for a loan, quasi-loan or credit transaction (or related guarantee or security) are similar to those in respect of substantial property transactions, namely:

(a) the transaction or arrangement is voidable at the company's instance (subject to issues of impossibility or third party rights acquired in good faith) (s213(2));

(b) the relevant director of the company or its holding company and any other director of the company who authorised the transaction is liable to account to the company which entered into the transaction for any gain that they made and to indemnify that company for any loss which it suffered as a result of the transaction (s213(3) and (4)). These provisions also extend to any relevant connected persons and the directors to whom they are connected.

Subsequent affirmation within a reasonable time by ordinary resolution is also possible (s214). This prevents the transaction in question being avoided subsequently by the company, but does not remove any personal liability imposed under s213.

16.5 **Payments for loss of office**

This issue is discussed at **15.3.4.3**.

16.6 **General matters**

Any transaction or contractual arrangement will require board approval so that the company is properly committed to it. If that transaction or arrangement is with a director (directly or indirectly), that raises two important issues.

1 Do the company's articles impose any restriction on the relevant director voting and counting in the quorum at the board meeting at which the transaction is to be approved? (See **14.6.6** for further discussion.)

2 Is the director is obliged to make a declaration of their interest in the matter to the company pursuant to s177 CA 2006? (See **14.7.8** for further discussion.)

Secondly, both in terms of the director in question and the board as a whole, the obligation to comply with their statutory duties generally must also be considered. (See **14.7**.) The provisions discussed in this chapter are designed to reinforce controls on directors' activities rather than being the sole control thereof.

KEY POINT SUMMARY

- Matters which directly involve directors should always be considered carefully. First, the particular transaction with the director needs to be categorised to assess if it is:
  - a substantial property transaction requiring shareholders' approval;
  - a loan or other credit arrangement requiring shareholders' approval;

- a term of duration of a service contract requiring shareholders' approval; or
- a payment for loss of office requiring shareholders' approval.

- Secondly, it is the directors who will commit the company to the contract/transaction. Shareholder approval (usually by ordinary resolution) should, therefore, be seen as a 'green light' for the directors.
- In terms of any board approval of the transaction, it must be established whether:
  - the company's articles impose any restriction on the relevant director participating in the decision-making process;
  - the director is obliged to make a declaration of his interest in the matter to the company pursuant to s177 CA 2006.
- In addition to compliance with statutory requirements, the obligation of directors to comply with their statutory duties generally must also be considered whenever a company is committed to a contract.

CHAPTER 17
Shareholders

FUNCTIONING LEGAL KNOWLEDGE

This chapter considers the following functioning legal knowledge included in the SRA's SQE 1 assessment specification:

Corporate governance and compliance:

- rights, duties and powers of directors and **shareholders** of companies
- company decision-making and meetings: procedural, disclosure and approval requirements

AUTHORITIES UNDERPINNING PRACTICE

The key authorities that underpin this area of practice are listed below. Note that for legislation you are linked to legislation.gov.uk.

Although much of the legislation on this government website is available in its amended form, the incorporation of new amendments into the text of legislation can be delayed. You should refer to legal databases to ensure you are referencing the most up-to-date legislation.

- Companies Act 2006
  https://www.legislation.gov.uk/ukpga/2006/46/contents
- Companies (Model Articles) Regulations 2008
  https://www.legislation.gov.uk/uksi/2008/3229

17.1 Introduction

After consulting this chapter, you will have looked at the following issues:

(a) registration of membership;

(b) the powers of shareholders in relation to their company;

(c) the legal protection given to shareholders;

(d) the function of a shareholders' agreement.

References to shareholders can be found throughout this manual; this chapter is intended to deal with their position in the company in general terms.

17.2 The right to membership

It has already been explained (see **Chapter 3**) that all private companies must have at least one '**member**'. Section 112 of the Companies Act 2006 (CA 2006) provides that:

> (1) The **subscribers of a company's memorandum** are deemed to have agreed to become members of the company, and on its registration become members and must be entered as such in its register of members.

(2) Every other person who agrees to become a member of a company, and whose name is entered in its register of members, is a member of the company.

This means that membership begins either:

(a) when a company is registered, in respect of the subscribers to the memorandum; or
(b) when the shareholder's name is entered in the register of members, in any other instance.

In respect of this second instance, the *right* to become a member may result from:

(a) a contract between the company and the purchaser of new **shares** from the company;
(b) an existing shareholder voluntarily transferring shares to someone else by sale or gift;
(c) the death or **bankruptcy** of an existing member, at which point the shares are automatically transmitted to the **personal representative** or **trustee in bankruptcy**.

From this, we can see that it is the ownership of shares which entitles the shareholder to become a member of a company, but a company must formally register that person as a member for their membership to take effect. This process of registration will be governed by relevant provisions in the company's **articles of association**.

However, whilst discussion of membership usually involves consideration of shareholders and their shareholdings, companies limited by guarantee may not have a share capital; as such, membership is governed instead by the guarantee which the member enters into with the company. Nothing further will be said, however, about such companies and their members.

When someone becomes a shareholder and is registered as a member, that person normally acquires some influence over the company's activities through the votes which attach to their shares, as well as ownership of a percentage of the company.

17.3 Registration of membership

17.3.1 Contents of the register

Every company must keep a register of its members and their shareholdings (s113 CA 2006). The following information must be recorded:

(a) the names and addresses of the members;
(b) the number of shares held and, where the company has more than one class of issued shares, the number of each class held by each member;
(c) the amount paid or agreed to be considered as paid on the shares of each member;
(d) the date on which each member was entered in the register;
(e) the date on which each member ceased to be a member.

Additionally, pursuant to s123 CA 2006, if the company has only one member, the register must also contain:

(a) a statement to that effect and of the date when this occurred;
(b) if the company formerly had only one member, a statement that the number has increased to two or more and the date when this occurred.

The register must normally be kept at the **registered office** of the company and, if kept elsewhere, the Registrar of Companies must be notified (s114 CA 2006). The register of members itself is not sent to the Registrar but the annual confirmation statement made by a company may contain details of the membership.

No particular form of register is required, but under s115 CA 2006 an index is required if the register is not kept in the form of an index and there are more than 50 members. (This provision is of little relevance to private companies since very few of them have more than 50 members.)

17.3.2 **Impact of the Economic Crime and Corporate Transparency Act 2023**

Section 46 of the Economic Crime and Corporate Transparency Act 2023 (ECCTA 2023) is expected to amend the CA 2006 by introducing altered requirements for the register of members. (At the time of writing, such provision was not yet in force, so the reader is, therefore, advised to confirm the up-to-date position when consulting this chapter.)

The register of members will be required to continue to include the information iterated at **17.3.1**, but with two material differences, namely:

(a) where the member is an individual, the name entered on the register must include both a forename and surname (except where the member is a peer or is known by a title, in which case, their title will be sufficient); and

(b) the address of the member need only be a service address, that is, an address at which documents may be effectively served on the member.

Further, to assist companies in keeping an up-to-date register of members, formal duties will be imposed on relevant persons in two main ways:

(a) any person who becomes a member of a company will be under a duty to provide the company within two months with both their name and a service address (unless either that information has already been provided to the company or it was included in the application for registration of the company); and

(b) any member of a company will be under a duty to provide the company with details of any change to either their name or service address within two months of such a change occurring.

Companies will also be empowered to make a formal request for such information from a member, providing one month from the date of the notice for compliance with the same.

Any member who, without reasonable excuse, either fails to comply with either of these new duties or who fails to respond appropriately to a notice for information from the company will commit a criminal offence.

17.3.3 **Trusts**

In certain instances, the legal and beneficial title to shares is split by the owner appointing a nominee to hold the *legal* title in the shares on their behalf, normally for reasons of anonymity or convenience.

Section 126 CA 2006 provides that 'no notice of any trust . . . shall be entered on the register of members . . .'. The effect of this is that the company need only deal with the nominee, as the legal owner of shares, even if it knows that they are held on trust.

The company must, therefore, pay dividends to the nominee and allow the nominee to exercise any voting powers attached to the shares. Accordingly, the beneficial owner is technically disenfranchised. (Although this situation does not, of course, affect the position as between the nominee and the true owner. The nominee must, therefore, hand over to the beneficial owner any dividend they receive and vote in accordance with the owner's wishes.)

17.4 **Member as person exercising significant control**

The acquisition of shares in a company may result in that person being treated as exercising significant control (a PSC). Alternatively, the introduction of a new member may affect the status of an existing PSC. (Further details of PSCs can be found in **Chapter 20**.)

Either way, a change to the company's PSC register may be necessary (and corresponding notification to **Companies House**). (Note, however, that provisions within ECCTA 2023 are expected to remove the need for a company to maintain its own PSC register, although at the time of writing such provisions were not in force. The reader should check the status of these provisions for the current position.)

EXAMPLE

Synthetic (Example) Ltd has three shareholders, owning shares as follows:

Isaac: 60 ordinary shares

Rosie: 30 ordinary shares

Catherine: 10 ordinary shares

Isaac and Rosie are, therefore, PSCs (each owning more than 25% of the issued share capital in the company) and their details will have been entered in the PSC register.

If Isaac sells 30 of his shares to Ronan:

(a) Isaac remains a PSC, albeit with a smaller percentage shareholding;

(b) Rosie remains a PSC;

(c) Catherine's status is unaffected; and

(d) Ronan also becomes a PSC.

In consequence, there will need to be a revision made to Isaac's entry in the register and Ronan will have to be entered into the register.

Alternatively, if Synthetic Ltd allots 50 shares to Tim:

(a) Isaac remains a PSC, albeit with a smaller percentage shareholding;

(b) Rosie ceases to be a PSC, as her percentage shareholding no longer exceeds 25%;

(c) Catherine's status is unaffected; and

(d) Tim becomes a PSC.

In consequence, there will need to be a revision made to Isaac's entry in the register and Tim will have to be entered into the register. Rosie will be noted as no longer being a PSC, but, due to the effect of s790U CA 2006, their details cannot be removed from the register for ten years.

17.5 Powers and duties of shareholders

17.5.1 Sources of shareholders' powers

In most companies, it is the directors who actually run the company (see **Chapter 14**). To ensure that shareholders have a measure of influence over the board, the law steps in to provide shareholders with specific influence over certain designated company activities, either through the 2006 Act or through the articles.

For instance, shareholders are normally granted the right to appoint directors in the articles. Additionally, the 2006 Act stipulates that certain specified transactions between a company and one of its directors will usually require the prior approval of the shareholders to be lawful (see **Chapter 16**).

More generally, whilst directors are usually permitted to exercise all the powers of a company (by delegation thereof through the articles), a residuary right of control by **special resolution** may be reserved for shareholders through the articles, for example art 4 of the Model Articles for Private Companies.

17.5.2 Powers of control

The powers of shareholders are normally exercised by passing a specified resolution at a **general meeting**. Alternatively, a **written resolution** may be used, unless the company is public. (Company meetings and resolutions are dealt with in detail in **Chapter 18**.)

As such, the size of a shareholder's holding will determine their influence over such a resolution. Most resolutions must be passed by a simple majority as **ordinary resolutions**, but a small number of decisions require a special resolution, which must be passed by at least a 75% majority. A shareholder who controls 75% of the votes is, therefore, able to exercise powers which a shareholder with a simple majority (ie over 50%) could not exercise alone. Conversely, a shareholder with more than

25% but less than 50% of the votes can block a special resolution even though they do not have enough votes to be in control of the company. (This is sometimes called negative control.)

In practical terms, any shareholding in excess of 50% is regarded as a majority shareholding which would grant the holder de facto control over the company. By contrast, a minority shareholder often has no real power (unless they are also a director and/or can persuade the majority to agree with them), but their position is protected by a number of rights, mostly statutory. (Some of these are discussed later in this chapter, others in **Chapter 19**.)

17.5.3 Duties of shareholders

Just as the powers and rights of members largely depend on the proportion of votes that they control, so the duties of members differ depending on whether or not they are in control of the company. The basic rule is that members (whether or not in control) can exercise their right to vote as they wish, so that they can take account of their own interests to the exclusion of conflicting interest of other shareholders. However, this does not mean that shareholders are *entirely* free to vote as they please; should the majority act purely out of naked self-interest, this may entitle those minority shareholders affected by such actions to bring an action in the courts. (See **Chapter 19** and **13.8.3**.)

17.6 The constitution as a contract between members and company

17.6.1 Introduction

Section 33 CA 2006 states that:

> The provisions of a company's constitution bind the company and its members to the same extent as if there were covenants on the part of the company and of each member to observe those provisions.

In turn, s17 defines the constitution as including the articles and any special resolutions of the shareholders.

The effect of this important section is that the constitution forms an agreement which contractually binds:

(a) a company to each of its members; and
(b) the members of the company to each other.

Thus, if specific provisions are not observed, an action may be taken to enforce the obligations imposed by the company's constitution.

Disputes between shareholders are considered in more detail in **Chapter 19**. In this chapter, we will simply focus on the idea that a member may have specific constitutional rights which they are seeking to enforce.

17.6.2 Membership rights

An obligation imposed by the constitution on a member or on the company for the benefit of a member is only enforceable if it relates to membership rights. The most obvious examples of membership rights which have been enforced as a result of actions based on the section include:

(a) the right to a dividend once lawfully declared (*Wood v Odessa Waterworks Co* (1889) 42 ChD 636);
(b) the right to share in surplus capital on a winding up (*Griffith v Paget* (1877) 5 ChD 894); and
(c) the right to vote at meetings (*Pender v Lushington* (1877) 6 ChD 70).

The most obvious obligation of a member which may be enforced by a company is the obligation to pay for shares issued by it.

It should be noted that a company's articles are a contract complete in themselves. The court will not normally, therefore, imply any additional terms into the articles. A good example of this rule is found in *Bratton Seymour Service Co v Oxborough* [1992] BCC 471, where the rule worked in favour of the members as the company, which was set up to manage a development of flats, claimed unsuccessfully that the members had an implied obligation to contribute to the upkeep of certain communal areas related to the flats.

17.6.3 **Other rights**

Obligations imposed by the constitution which do not relate to membership rights are not enforceable under s33. A member may, therefore, be left without any remedy even though the company has failed to observe an article which would have benefited them. This is illustrated by the case of *Eley v Positive Government Security Life Assurance Co* (1876) 1 ExD 88. When the company was formed, a provision was included in the articles naming the plaintiff as solicitor of the company. He was never, in fact, appointed to the office but did become a member of the company. It was held that he could not sue the company (under the provisions of earlier corresponding legislation) because the right to be appointed as solicitor was not a *membership right* of the plaintiff.

Similarly, in *Beattie v E and F Beattie Ltd* [1938] Ch 708, a dispute arose between a company and one of its directors concerning the repayment of sums improperly paid to the director. The director wished to refer the matter to arbitration in accordance with an article requiring arbitration of disputes with members, but was held not entitled to insist on arbitration since the dispute was between the company and the plaintiff in his capacity as *director* not in his capacity as shareholder.

17.6.4 **Implied contracts**

The terms laid down in the constitution may be impliedly incorporated into a contract made with the company. For example, in *Re New British Iron Co, ex p P Beckwith* [1898] 1 Ch 324, there was no express agreement between the directors and the company regarding their remuneration. However, the articles stated that the board was to receive an annual sum of £1,000. This was held to be a binding obligation on the company even though the directors were not claiming in their capacity as members.

17.6.5 **Shareholders' agreements**

Shareholders may wish to regulate their dealings with each other outside the articles (or as a supplement to them). For example, they may wish to stipulate that there must be unanimity between them regarding the appointment of a new director, irrespective of the mechanism for appointment of directors in the articles. Such provisions can be enshrined in a shareholders' agreement rather than the articles.

In essence, a shareholders' agreement will govern how shareholders choose to exercise the powers that they have. To put it another way, a shareholder's right to vote at a general meeting will originate from a combination of the CA 2006 and the articles; however, how shareholders will actually vote on a particular matter may be governed by the shareholders' agreement.

The important thing to note is that such an agreement will only bind those shareholders who are parties to it. The constitution binds all shareholders at any time in the life of the company because of the effect of s33 CA 2006. As such, a shareholders' agreement is more suited in the context of a company which can anticipate little or no change in its shareholders.

Some important distinctions can be drawn between articles and shareholders' agreements, namely:

(a) the articles can be changed at any time by a special resolution; an agreement can only be altered by unanimous consent of all its parties;

(b) the articles are a public document; an agreement can be entirely private. This may be attractive to professional investors who would rather the terms of their investment remained private;

(c) enforcement of rights under the articles may sometimes throw up complications. Parties to a shareholders' agreement can rely entirely on their contractual rights and the full gamut of enforcement remedies available to them;

(d) articles can be adopted in a 'standard' form, for example, the Model Articles. A shareholders' agreement can be entirely bespoke to the needs of the shareholders. The negotiation of an agreement can often provide a useful focus for shareholders to identify and provide for key aspects of their relationship with each other and with the company.

KEY POINT SUMMARY

This chapter has covered the following topics:

- The concept of membership and the importance of registration as a member in a company's register of members.
- The corresponding status of a shareholder member as a person with significant control.
- The origin of shareholders' powers and their interrelationship with directors' powers.
- The idea that duties of shareholders are virtually non-existent and shareholders are free to exercise their powers as they see fit.
- The significance of a company's constitution as a contract between the members of a company and the company itself.
- The use of a shareholders' agreement as an alternative method of regulating the relationship between members of a company.

CHAPTER 18
Company Meetings and Resolutions

FUNCTIONING LEGAL KNOWLEDGE

This chapter considers the following functioning legal knowledge included in the SRA's SQE 1 assessment specification:

Corporate governance and compliance:

- company decision-making and meetings: procedural, disclosure and approval requirements
- documentary, record-keeping, statutory filing and disclosure requirements

AUTHORITIES UNDERPINNING PRACTICE

The key authorities that underpin this area of practice are listed below. Note that for legislation you are linked to legislation.gov.uk.

Although much of the legislation on this government website is available in its amended form, the incorporation of new amendments into the text of legislation can be delayed. You should refer to legal databases to ensure you are referencing the most up-to-date legislation.

- Companies Act 2006
  https://www.legislation.gov.uk/ukpga/2006/46
- Companies (Model Articles) Regulations 2008
  https://www.legislation.gov.uk/uksi/2008/3229

18.1 Introduction

After consulting this chapter, you will have looked at:

(a) meetings of **shareholders**;

(b) the resolutions which may be passed at such meetings;

(c) the rules governing the calling and validity of such meetings;

(d) **written resolutions** of shareholders as an alternative to meetings.

It is important to recognise that all the above matters will be governed by a combination of statute and the relevant company's articles. In some instances, statute will be prescriptive; in others its effect can be displaced or modified by the articles.

A solicitor advising a company or a shareholder must be able to recognise situations where shareholder decisions are necessary and, as such, may be called upon to see that the correct procedures are adopted to achieve those decisions. Moreover, those procedures will have to be evidenced in correctly drafted documentation, such as notices of meetings or minutes of meetings. Again, this is usually produced by the advising solicitor.

We are not concerned in this chapter with directors' meetings (which are dealt with in **Chapter 14**), we are only concerned with meetings of shareholders.

18.2 Background

The position under the previous Companies Act 1985 was relatively complicated. Much of what the Companies Act 2006 (CA 2006) did was to streamline the governance of shareholders' meetings, particularly for private companies.

Historic company documentation for relatively established companies, for example minutes of meetings etc, may reflect the old system. It is important, therefore, to be able to recognise the differences which existed prior to the introduction of the 2006 Act.

The changes which the 2006 Act brought about were as follows:

(a) The number of possible shareholder resolutions was reduced from four to two. Under the 2006 Act, only two shareholders' resolutions are now recognised:
   (i) ordinary; and
   (ii) special.

(b) Under the previous regime, the type of resolution to be proposed determined the length of notice required for the meeting. The 2006 Act now requires 14 days' notice in every circumstance, except the **annual general meeting** of a **public company**, where 21 days' notice is required.

(c) Previously *all* companies were required to hold an annual general meeting. Only *public* companies must now hold annual general meetings.

18.3 Annual general meetings

Company meetings are of two types: annual general meetings and **general meetings**.

Only public companies are required to hold annual general meetings (AGMs) (s336 CA 2006). An AGM must be held in each period of six months beginning with the day following the company's accounting reference date (see **21.3**).

Normally, public companies use the AGM as an opportunity to fulfil certain statutory or regulatory requirements, for example that they lay before the company in general meeting copies of their annual accounts (s437 CA 2006).

18.4 General meetings

Any meeting which is not an AGM is a general meeting (GM). As a consequence, both public and private companies may hold GMs. A GM is held as and when necessary.

The procedure for calling GMs will be considered shortly, but first it is necessary to consider the types of resolution that shareholders may be required to pass.

18.5 Shareholder resolutions

A company in general meeting can only transact business by passing the appropriate type of resolution.

There are two types of shareholder resolution:

1 ordinary; and
2 special.

18.5.1 Ordinary resolutions

An **ordinary resolution** is one which requires a simple majority of votes in favour, if it is to be passed. A simple majority means more votes in favour than against–an equality of votes is not sufficient (s282(1) CA 2006).

An ordinary resolution is sufficient to transact any business at a general meeting, save in those cases where the 2006 Act or the company's articles require a **special resolution**.

18.5.2 Special resolutions

A special resolution requires a 75% majority–that is, at least three votes must be cast in favour of the resolution for every one cast against it (s283(1) CA 2006).

18.5.3 Which type of resolution is required?

The 2006 Act sets out a number of circumstances in which shareholders' resolutions are required, either to cause something to happen or, more commonly, to allow the company to commit itself to a course of action. A company's articles may also impose further requirements for a decision of the shareholders; however, instances of these tend to be relatively rare.

As a basic rule, special resolutions are required where the deemed prejudice to shareholders could be considerable. Therefore, a proposed change to the **articles of association** requires such a resolution to bring it into effect (s21 CA 2006).

By contrast, ordinary resolutions normally act as shareholder permission for a transaction. For example, a proposed substantial property transaction between a director and a company needs the prior consent of the shareholders by ordinary resolution (s190 CA 2006) but the directors must still decide to commit the company to the transaction. (See **16.3** for specific discussion of substantial property transactions.)

It is not the intention of this chapter to set out all possible instances of special and ordinary resolutions. Reference to the necessary resolution is made, as appropriate, in the other chapters dealing with company law issues. However, the following instances of shareholders' decisions serve as useful examples:

18.5.3.1 Special resolutions

(a) To alter the articles of association.

(b) To change the company's name (subject to any alternative mechanism in the articles).

(c) To disapply statutory pre-emption rights on an allotment of **shares**.

18.5.3.2 Ordinary resolutions

(a) To approve a substantial property transaction with a director.

(b) To approve the duration of a **service contract** of a director where the guaranteed term of the contract exceeds two years.

(c) To provide directors with authority to allot shares (where so required).

(d) To remove a director from the company compulsorily.

18.6 Calling a general meeting

18.6.1 Introduction

Once the need for shareholder consent has been identified, it is necessary to seek this either:

(a) in a general meeting of the shareholders; or

(b) by written resolution of the shareholders (if so permitted).

Written resolutions are considered at **18.10**. In this section, we will look at calling a general meeting, although it should be noted at the outset that private companies with relatively few shareholders are likely to use written resolutions in preference to holding shareholders' meetings.

As with so many aspects of company law, the rules governing general meetings are partly statutory and partly depend on the provisions of the company's own articles. Most of the statutory rules are designed to protect the shareholders whose voting rights would be worthless if they were not backed up by rights to be notified of meetings or to call meetings themselves.

18.6.2 Call by directors

Section 302 CA 2006 gives directors power to call general meetings of a company. In any event, the articles of many companies are likely to contain a provision granting directors the authority to call shareholders' meetings. Either way, general meetings of a company will normally be called by the directors, so a board meeting is the usual starting point in the process.

18.6.3 Shareholders' right to requisition meeting

18.6.3.1 Requisition to directors

Section 303(1) CA 2006 permits a specified percentage of shareholders to request the directors to call a meeting. This can be a valuable right in circumstances where the shareholders disagree with the approach of the board and want to air their views in a formal environment.

Such a request can be in paper or electronic form (s303(6)) and must state the general nature of the business the shareholders want dealing with at the proposed meeting. It can include the text of any specific resolution to be proposed to the meeting (s303(4)).

The specified percentage is sufficient **members** of the company to represent at least 5% of the **paid-up share** capital of the company as carries the right to vote at general meetings (s303(2) and (3)).

Once such a request is made of the directors, they must call a meeting within 21 days, which must be held on not more than 28 days' notice (s304(1)). Such notice must include a copy of any proposed resolution received from the requisitionists (s304(2)) and if that resolution is a special resolution, the specific requirements for special resolutions contained within s283 must be complied with in the notice otherwise directors are deemed not to have fulfilled their obligation under this section (s304(4)).

18.6.3.2 Power of shareholders to call meeting in default

If the directors of a company fail to comply properly with a s303 request, s305 CA 2006 permits the requisitionists (or any of them representing more than one half of the total voting rights of all of them) to call a meeting instead. In doing so, the meeting must be called as far as possible in the same manner as a meeting called by the directors (s305(4)).

The date of such a meeting must be no later than three months from the date on which the directors' obligation under s304 arose (s305(3)).

18.6.4 Court power to order meeting

Section 306(1) CA 2006 gives the court power to order meetings if for any reason it is impracticable either:

(a) to call a meeting of a company in any manner in which meetings of that company may be called; or

(b) to conduct a meeting in the manner prescribed either by the Act or by the company's articles.

An application to court for such an order can be made by either a director or shareholder (s306(2)).

This section is often useful to get round practical problems to do with calling meetings or to resolve issues of deadlock in 'two-man' companies, where a dissenting shareholder refuses to attend a general meeting thus rendering it inquorate and invalid. A court can order a meeting of just one shareholder to enable specified business to be conducted. (For discussion of quorum issues, see **18.8.1**.)

18.7 Notice of meetings

18.7.1 Service of notice

Section 301 CA 2006 makes it a precondition of the validity of any resolution of the shareholders that notice of the meeting and the resolution is given in accordance with the 2006 Act and the company's articles.

Subject to any provision in the articles, every member and every director of a company must receive notice of a general meeting (s310). It is common practice for the board of directors to approve the content of any such notice and agree that it should be distributed to all relevant persons.

The following explanation will look at the statutory requirements which will have universal application. It will also be important to consider the articles in every instance to ascertain any specific further requirements which must be fulfilled.

Section 308 CA 2006 permits a notice of a general meeting to be given either:

(a) in hard copy form; or
(b) in electronic form (most commonly by email or possibly by text message); or
(c) via a website; or
(d) by a combination of any or all of the above.

Schedule 5 to the 2006 Act sets out rules for any communications sent out by a company, including those in electronic form or via a website. Communication in either of these two forms requires the prior consent of a shareholder.

Additionally, in respect of website communications:

(a) Shareholders must still be notified of the presence of the information or notification on the website and that it is in respect of a general meeting, including a statement of the time, date and place of the meeting (s309).
(b) As an alternative to seeking the consent of every member in every circumstance, a company may by a provision in its articles or by a shareholder resolution provide for website communication, after which shareholders must be asked to agree to the supply of information via a website and will be deemed to do so unless they specifically object within 28 days of such a request.

In respect of closely held companies with few shareholders, the use of a website is probably academic because email or paper notification is likely to be the most appropriate method. However, the website method may have more attraction to companies with a large number of shareholders.

18.7.2 Length of notice

18.7.2.1 Full notice

The length of notice required depends on the nature of the meeting and the company. For private companies, all general meetings must be called on at least 14 days' notice (s307(1) CA 2006). For public companies, all general meetings must be held on at least 14 days' notice, except AGMs, where 21 days' notice is required (s307(2) CA 2006).

The calculation of the notice period should be treated with care. Section 360 CA 2006 clarifies the issue by excluding from the notice period both the day of giving the notice and the day of the meeting itself. As such, 14 calendar days' notice would be insufficient.

The above notice periods are minima, laid down by the 2006 Act. Each company must decide upon the notice periods it wants and state them in its articles of association. Clearly, most companies will elect to follow the 2006 Act, but companies can provide for different notice periods provided that they do not fall below the statutory minima.

Note that the articles may also include rules for deeming when a notice is received, so this needs to be factored into the calculation of the notice period as well. The golden rule is always to err on the side of caution.

EXAMPLE

If a company calls a general meeting on 1 March for 14 March, this would be inadequate notice. In order to provide 14 clear days' notice, it would be necessary to call the meeting for 16 March.

However, if the company's articles deem all notices from the company to be received after 48 hours, then the notice given should also take this into account and the meeting should be called for 18 March.

18.7.2.2 Short notice procedure

For many companies, it is often unnecessarily burdensome to wait for full notice periods to elapse. There exists, therefore, a mechanism for 'short-circuiting' the process, by allowing for shorter notice than already mentioned.

For private companies, s307(5) provides that shorter notice than that normally required may validly be given in respect of all general meetings of such a company if agreement to the same is received from:

(a) a majority in number of members;

(b) owning not less than 90% of the shares that carry an entitlement to attend and vote at the relevant meeting.

EXAMPLE

Scenario one

Random Ltd has three shareholders, Francis, Theo and Tasmin, who each own 30%, 30% and 40% of the voting share capital in the company.

In order to fulfil both criteria of s307(5), consent to short notice of a general meeting of Random Ltd can only effectively be given by all the members of the company.

Scenario two

Colston Ltd has four shareholders, Khaled, Sara, Eve and Emily, who each own 45%, 45%, 5% and 5% of the voting share capital in the company.

(a) If Khaled and Sara only consent to short notice, this is not effective consent as they do not constitute a majority in number, despite owning between them 90% of the voting share capital.

(b) If Khaled, Eve and Emily only consent to short notice, this is not effective consent–whilst they constitute a majority in number, they only own between them 55% of the voting share capital.

(c) If Khaled, Sara and either Eve or Emily consent, this is effective consent.

For *public* companies, shorter notice than that normally required may validly be given if:

(a) in the case of an AGM, all the members entitled to attend and vote at the meeting agree to short notice (ss307(7) and 337(2)); and

(b) in the case of any other general meeting, a majority in number of members owning not less than 95% of the voting shares and entitled to attend and vote at the meeting agree to short notice.

For many private companies (especially family-owned companies or companies where the only members are all directors), the possibility of short notice allows a meeting to be held at very short notice–normally by informally gathering together all the relevant shareholders and then obtaining their consent to formal notice of the general meeting, which can then be held at that time.

However, for companies with a large number of shareholders, it is not normally a practical alternative to the giving of proper notice.

18.7.3 Contents of notice

The notice of a meeting must state the date, time and place of a meeting (s311(1) CA 2006). It must also sufficiently describe the business which is to be transacted for members to be able to decide whether they wish to attend (s311(2) CA 2006).

If a special resolution is to be proposed, its wording must be set out verbatim in the notice and must be expressed to be proposed as a special resolution (s283(6) CA 2006).

It is a question of judgement in each case how much detail of the business needs to be stated. However, in drawing up a notice it is better to err on the side of inclusion rather than exclusion. A company's articles can demand fuller information than that required by s311(2) in any event. For both of these reasons, there is normally no distinction drawn between ordinary and special resolutions and full wording of either type of resolution will usually be set out in the notice.

Section 325 CA 2006 requires that any notice of a general meeting should always tell a member of their right under s324 to send a proxy (who need not be a member) to attend and speak and vote on their behalf. If any additional rights in this regard are afforded by the company's articles, these rights should also be stated.

These issues are demonstrated in the following example notice.

EXAMPLE NOTICE OF GENERAL MEETING

ExampleCo 456 Limited ('The Company')

NOTICE is hereby given that a general meeting of the Company will be held at [PLACE OF MEETING] on [DATE OF MEETING] at [TIME OF MEETING] for the purpose of considering and, if thought fit, passing the following [ordinary/special] resolution[s] of the Company:

[HERE INSERT WORDING OF PROPOSED RESOLUTION(S)]

By order of the board of directors

..Chairman

Date:

Registered office: [HERE INSERT ADDRESS OF REGISTERED OFFICE]

Note:

A member entitled to attend and vote at the meeting convened by this notice is entitled to appoint a proxy to attend and vote in their stead. A proxy need not be a member of the Company. To be valid, any proxy notice must comply with the requirements of article [X] of the Company's articles of association and be received by the Company at its registered office before the time appointed for the holding of the meeting.

[FOR EDUCATIVE PURPOSES ONLY. NOT INTENDED TO BE RELIED UPON AS A PRECEDENT IN ANY CIRCUMSTANCES.]

18.8 Proceedings at meetings

18.8.1 Quorum

A meeting will not be valid unless a quorum is present at the time when the meeting proceeds to business. Unless the articles otherwise provide or the company has only one member, two members personally present or their proxies or their representatives (in the case of a corporate shareholder) are a quorum (s318).

The appointment of a representative of a corporate shareholder is governed by s323 CA 2006 and ss324–331 contain provisions about the appointment of proxies.

18.8.2 Voting at general meetings

18.8.2.1 Show of hands

A vote on a resolution will normally be decided on a show of hands; that is, one shareholder, one vote (s284(2) CA 2006) or, if such is appointed, one proxy, one vote (s285(1)). However, the inequities of this when there are diverse shareholdings are obvious. Therefore, a vote may instead be taken on a poll; that is, one vote per share (s284(3)). (Again, if a proxy is appointed, that person will have as many votes as the shareholder who appointed them (s285(3)).)

18.8.2.2 Poll

A poll must be demanded at the relevant meeting and a company's articles will make provision for how this is done. The only stipulation the CA 2006 makes is that a provision in the articles is void if it renders ineffective a call for a poll from either at least five members or members holding more than 10% of the voting rights or any member or members with 10% of the paid-up capital with a right to vote (s321(2)).

It is quite normal for articles to provide for more extensive rights by allowing any two members (instead of five) or the chairman of the meeting to call for a poll as well.

Proxies have the same right to call for a poll as the member or members they represent (s329(1)).

The following examples demonstrate the difference between voting on a show of hands and voting on a poll.

EXAMPLE

Cotton Ltd has four shareholders, Nydia, Benjamin, Alanna and Miriam, whose respective shareholdings in the company are as follows:

Nydia: 45%

Benjamin: 40%

Alanna: 10%

Miriam: 5%.

Assume that in each of the scenarios which follows all of the shareholders in Cotton Ltd attend the meeting in question and that there are no abstentions.

Scenario one–ordinary resolution: vote on a show of hands

At least three of the four shareholders must vote in favour for the resolution to be passed.

Scenario two–ordinary resolution: vote on a poll

Any permutation of at least three shareholders voting in favour will be sufficient for the resolution to be passed.

If only two shareholders vote in favour, it must either be Nydia and Benjamin or Nydia and Alanna. (Neither Nydia and Miriam nor Benjamin and Alanna constitute a majority.)

Scenario three–special resolution: vote on a show of hands

Any permutation of at least three shareholders voting in favour will be sufficient for the resolution to be passed.

Scenario four–special resolution: vote on a poll

Irrespective of how Alanna and Miriam vote, Nydia and Benjamin must vote in favour.

18.9 Minutes and returns

Minutes must be kept of all decisions taken at general meetings and must be available for inspection by the members at the **registered office** (ss355 and 358 CA 2006).

Copies of any special resolutions passed must be sent to the Registrar of Companies within 15 days of being passed (s30 CA 2006), as must a copy of any ordinary resolution authorising directors to allot shares under s551 CA 2006 (s551(9)).

18.10 Written resolutions

18.10.1 Introduction

The use of a written resolution of the shareholders as an alternative to a formal meeting was possible under the previous Companies Act 1985. However, the consent of *all* shareholders to such a resolution was required for it to be effective.

The 2006 Act liberalised the use of written resolutions by allowing them to be passed by the same majority as is required in a general meeting. As such, for many private companies, particularly those with a small number of shareholders, written resolutions are often a preferred (and more efficient) alternative to the holding of a general meeting.

18.10.2 Validity

A **private company** may pass shareholder resolutions in writing under s288 CA 2006 without a meeting or any previous notice being given. Such a company may pass any type of resolution–ordinary or special–using this procedure, save for two exceptions:

1 the removal of a director under s168 CA 2006; or

2 the removal of an **auditor** under s510 CA 2006.

For a written resolution to be effective, a required majority of the members of the company entitled to vote on the resolution (so-called 'eligible members' as defined in s289(1) CA 2006) must consent to it as follows:

(a) For ordinary resolutions, members representing a simple majority of the *total* voting rights of the members entitled to vote on the resolution (s282(2)).

(b) For special resolutions, members representing at least 75% of the *total* voting rights of the members entitled to vote on the resolution (s283(2)).

Section 284(1)(b) stipulates that in respect of a written resolution each member has one vote for each share held.

Therefore, whilst the validity of resolutions at *general meetings* is based on a count of the votes cast by the members actually present, by contrast, the effectiveness of a written resolution is based upon all the votes which could be cast.

The date of any written resolution is determined by the time at which the required majority has signified its agreement to it (s296(4)). A member signifies their agreement when the company receives from them, either in hard copy or electronic form, an authenticated document indicating agreement to the resolution (s296(1)).

EXAMPLE

Random (Example) Ltd has three shareholders, Victor, Brad and Gillian, who each own 30%, 30% and 40% respectively of the voting share capital in the company.

In respect of a proposed *special* resolution:

(a) if the resolution is proposed at a *general meeting* and Victor and Brad only attend the meeting and vote in its favour (either on a show of hands or a poll), this will be a unanimous vote and the resolution will be passed;

(b) instead, if the resolution is proposed by way of written resolution and Victor and Brad only consent to the resolution, the resolution will not be passed as Victor and Brad only hold 60% of the voting capital in the company, not the minimum 75% required.

In respect of a proposed *ordinary* resolution:

(a) if the resolution is proposed at a general meeting and all of Victor, Brad and Gillian attend the meeting and Victor and Brad vote in its favour and Gillian votes against (either on a show of hands or a poll), in either instance the resolution will be passed by a simple majority;

(b) instead, if the resolution is proposed by way of written resolution and Victor and Brad only consent to the resolution, the resolution will again be passed as Victor and Brad hold in excess of 50% of the voting capital in the company.

Under s300 CA 2006, any provision in a private company's articles which prevents it from passing written resolutions using the statutory procedure is void.

18.10.3 Circulation of written resolutions

Section 288(3) CA 2006 stipulates that a written resolution can be proposed either by the directors or by the members.

As with the calling of general meetings, a request for a written resolution will normally be instigated by the board of a company. In this instance, s291 CA 2006 must be complied with, otherwise all officers of the company in default will commit an offence, although such default will not affect the validity of the resolution itself.

The requirements of s291 are:

(a) the resolution must go out to all eligible members;

(b) this may be done either in hard copy, in electronic form or through a website (or a combination of any or all of these methods);

(c) the resolution must be accompanied by a statement explaining how a member may consent to the resolution and the date by which the resolution must be passed. (A written resolution will lapse if not passed by either the period set out in the articles or, if there is none, by the end of the 28th day after the circulation of the resolution (s297(1)).)

Section 291 envisages either individual copies of the resolution for each member or a single copy to be submitted in turn to each member. Consent to a resolution is normally achieved by a member signing and dating a document which includes the full text of the resolution.

In instances of closely held companies, arrangements can be made for all relevant shareholders to be present to receive and agree to the written resolution simultaneously. This will provide certainty that the resolution has been received by all relevant shareholders and that it has been consented to at a particular moment in time. Posting out or emailing written resolutions to shareholders and waiting for responses thereto is much less satisfactory.

18.10.4 Requisition of written resolution by the members

In the same way that members of a company can requisition the board to call a general meeting, s292 CA 2006 provides that members representing at least 5% of the total voting rights of all members can require a written resolution to be distributed by the company at their instance. (The articles can provide for a lower percentage of members.)

If a valid request is received by a company under s292, the company will be obliged to comply with the circulation requirements set out in s293 CA 2006. (This is in similar terms to s291.)

Together with the resolution, the members may also require the circulation by the company of a statement of up to 1,000 words regarding the subject matter of the requisition (s292(3)).

18.10.5 Recording of written resolutions

Copies of all written resolutions passed must be maintained in the same way as minutes of a general meeting (s355 CA 2006).

18.11 Statutory conditions for specific resolutions

There are a number of resolutions which require specific documents to be available for inspection at the registered office in advance of the relevant general meeting and at the meeting itself for the resolution to be effective (normally for the purpose of informing shareholders), for example:

(a) authority for purchase of own shares–the relevant contract for the purchase or a memorandum thereof must be available (required by s696 CA 2006);

(b) reduction of share capital by a private company–the supporting solvency statement of the directors must be available (required by s642 CA 2006);

(c) approval of the term of duration of a director's service contract–a memorandum of the contract, including details of the relevant term, must be available (required by s188 CA 2006);

(d) approval of loans etc to directors–a memorandum setting out prescribed details of the loan etc must be available (required by s197, 198 or 201 CA 2006, depending upon the particular type of transaction);

(e) the payment of compensation for loss of office to a director–a memorandum setting out particulars of the proposed payment (including its amount) must be made available (required by s217(3) CA 2006).

If the written resolution method is chosen instead, the above requirements must be varied. The alternative requirement in each case is the supply or disclosure of specific information or documentation to all members at or before the time at which the written resolution is supplied to them.

KEY POINT SUMMARY

Some general conclusions can be reached about decision-making by shareholders.

- Whenever a shareholders' decision is required in a *private* company, there is usually a choice between achieving this decision at a general meeting or by written resolution.
- Two exceptions to the rule above are the removal of a director and the removal of an auditor, both of which must occur at a general meeting.
- The relevant procedure is likely to be governed by a combination of statute and the articles; as such, both must be considered.
- There are possibly three material factors which will influence the method adopted for reaching a decision of the shareholders: the number of shareholders in the company; which of those shareholders are known to support the proposal; and the speed at which it is desired to happen.
- Shareholders may be required to pass an ordinary resolution or a special resolution. The former is passed by a simple majority, the latter by a majority of at least 75%.
- The usual starting point for either a general meeting or a written resolution is a resolution of the board of directors either to distribute a notice of the general meeting or to circulate a copy of the written resolution.
- General meetings must be called by appropriate notice, which in most circumstances is 14 clear days, although there may be specific exceptions to this stated in a company's articles. Shareholders can consent to shorter notice. This consent must be given by shareholders who constitute a majority in number and who, between them, hold at least 90% of the nominal voting share capital. (A higher percentage of 95% is required for public companies.)
- For any meeting of the shareholders, the quorum requirement must be satisfied.
- Voting at a general meeting can be taken either by a show of hands, on the basis of one vote per shareholder, or on a poll, that is, one vote for every share held. Only the votes cast at the meeting are relevant.
- Consent to a written resolution must be given by the relevant majority of eligible members. For an ordinary resolution, a simple majority of the *total* voting rights of the members entitled

to vote on the resolution must consent to it; for a special resolution, at least three-quarters of the *total* voting rights of the members entitled to vote on the resolution must consent.

- Often a shareholder resolution will be enabling. As such, there will usually be the need for the board to approve formally a transaction or document once shareholders' permission has been obtained. For example, if shareholders' authority to a proposed allotment of shares has been necessary, the board must then formally resolve to make the allotment.
- A major exception to the above is that any decision to alter the articles is purely within the power of the shareholders. The only follow-up for the board would be to resolve to meet the registration/filing responsibilities which arise from such a decision.
- Many company decisions result in filing and/or registration obligations. These need to be identified and complied with.
- Minutes/records of decisions made by shareholders must be taken and kept.

CHAPTER 19
Disputes Within a Company and Protection of Minority Shareholder Rights

FUNCTIONING LEGAL KNOWLEDGE

This chapter considers the following functioning legal knowledge included in the SRA's SQE 1 assessment specification:

Corporate governance and compliance:

- rights, duties and powers of directors and **shareholders** of companies
- minority shareholder protection

AUTHORITIES UNDERPINNING PRACTICE

The key authorities that underpin this area of practice are listed below. Note that for legislation you are linked to legislation.gov.uk.

Although much of the legislation on this government website is available in its amended form, the incorporation of new amendments into the text of legislation can be delayed. You should refer to legal databases to ensure you are referencing the most up-to-date legislation.

- Companies Act 2006
  https://www.legislation.gov.uk/ukpga/2006/46
- Companies (Model Articles) Regulations 2008
  https://www.legislation.gov.uk/uksi/2008/3229

19.1 Introduction

After consulting this chapter, you will be familiar with the legal responses which minority shareholders can invoke if they believe either:

(a) that the interests of the company are being adversely affected by the behaviour of the directors; or

(b) that the actions of those in control of the company are affecting them prejudicially.

The essential entitlements which need to be recognised at the outset are:

1 the right to enforce a claim on behalf of the company in respect of misconduct of directors–a **derivative claim**; and

2 the right to complain that the affairs of the company are being conducted in such a way as to be both unfair and prejudicial to one's interests as a shareholder.

What follows is merely a brief summary of a substantial and complex topic. For a deeper understanding, you should consult a practitioner text on shareholder remedies.

19.2 Minority shareholders

Arguably, any shareholder with less than 50% of the voting capital in a company is a minority shareholder. However, the position is more nuanced than that as the percentage shareholdings of all other shareholders have to be taken into account, as do the combined actions of shareholders.

EXAMPLE

ExampleCo (121) Ltd has four shareholders, owning **shares** as follows:

Ned: 25 shares

Tyler: 25 shares

Austin: 25 shares

Otis: 25 shares

Based on the previous definition, all these shareholders are minority shareholders. However, it is the dynamics between them which will determine whether or not a particular shareholder is a de facto minority.

For example, if Ned and Tyler act in concert against Austin and Otis, then there is deadlock (50:50 division) so no discernible minority.

Alternatively, if Ned, Tyler and Austin act in concert against Otis's interests, then Otis is potentially a minority shareholder who the law may protect in some way.

19.3 Personal or representative action

Every **member** of a company is bound into the articles with every other member and with the company. This is the effect of s33 of the Companies Act 2006 (CA 2006). When a member sues to enforce their rights under the constitution, they are effectively bringing an action for breach of contract by the company. Any judgment they obtain will be directly enforceable by them and binding on the company.

This is perhaps the most straightforward type of action a shareholder can bring, albeit that the only rights which a shareholder can enforce are those granted on the shareholder *qua* shareholder. The rather unhelpful phrase is almost impossible to define, but is effectively a control mechanism which allows the courts to deny enforcement if the entitlement in question is not intrinsically linked to one's status within the company as a member. (See **17.6** for further discussion of this topic.)

Persistent or deliberate disenfranchisement of shareholders by those in control of a company may, in any event, be grounds for an unfair prejudice petition; see later.

19.4 Derivative action

19.4.1 History of the derivative action

A shareholder is not usually permitted to sue where a wrong is done to the company itself. This rule was known as the rule in *Foss v Harbottle* (1843) 2 Hare 461.

There were two justifications for it:

1 since a company is a legal person distinct from its members, the company is the proper claimant in an action where a wrong has been done to the company; and

2 the decision whether or not to sue can be taken either by the directors or by the members in **general meeting**, and the court is unwilling to interfere with this decision by imposing its own views on the company.

At the same time, the courts did recognise that, in some exceptional circumstances, it was appropriate to allow a shareholder to sue *on behalf of* the company, since otherwise justice could not be done. Such situations might be, for example, where the majority shareholders were using their position of power within the company to obtain a direct personal advantage or where the actions of the board had produced a result which was injurious to the interests of the company or the members as a whole.

Therefore, a number of exceptions to the rule in *Foss v Harbottle* developed on a case-by-case basis, under which a shareholder could bring an action if the company would not. This type of action was described as a 'derivative action' because the right of the member to sue *derived* from the right to sue which the company had failed to exercise.

These exceptional cases should be contrasted with cases where the personal rights of a shareholder were affected. In such cases, the shareholder did not need to bring a derivative action but could sue because of the contractual rights which they have under the articles (*Pender v Lushington* (1877) 6 ChD 70).

It was not always easy to decide whether or not a shareholder had a right of action under the exceptions to *Foss v Harbottle* or under the articles. The distinction was crucial, however, as a shareholder always has *locus standi* to enforce their own personal rights, but only a very limited right to sue on behalf of the company. Secondly, wrongs done to a company could be ratifiable by the majority and a court would bow to the wishes of the majority in such situations. However, ratification by the wrongdoers themselves could justify a derivative action (*Cook v Deeks* [1916] 1 AC 554).

19.4.2 **Impact of the CA 2006**

The CA 2006 codified derivative actions (Ch 1, Pt 11 CA 2006) and virtually all derivative actions (strictly, derivative claims) now have to be brought under the statutory provisions.

Section 260(3) states that a derivative claim must be brought in respect of a cause of action arising from an actual or proposed act or omission involving negligence, default, breach of duty or breach of trust by a director. Note that it was previously very difficult to bring a derivative action for directors' negligence (*Pavlides v Jensen* [1956] 2 All ER 518).

However, no shareholder automatically has the ability to launch a derivative claim. Section 261 imposes a 'screening process', under which such a shareholder must apply to the court for permission to pursue a claim on the company's behalf.

Effectively, this is a two-stage process, as follows:

(a) As a first step, the shareholder must demonstrate a prima facie case of their entitlement to bring a claim (s261(2)). If they fail to meet this requirement, the court must automatically dismiss the application. This is done by way of *ex parte* application.

(b) On the basis that this hurdle is cleared, the court must then decide whether or not to grant permission. In turn, the court is likely to give directions that the company be allowed to make representations to the court. Whilst not a trial of the substantive issue, nevertheless at this stage many material issues are likely to be brought before the court.

In making its decision, a court *must* refuse permission if it believes either:

(a) that a person acting in accordance with s172 CA 2006 would not seek to bring the claim. (In other words, would no director believe that there was any worth in the claim); or

(b) authorisation or ratification by the shareholders of the relevant act or omission has occurred.

Further, if the automatic grounds for refusal are not present, the following issues, set out in s263(3), must be considered by the court before it decides whether or not to grant permission to continue a claim on the company's behalf:

(a) whether or not a person acting to promote the interests of the company would or would not continue the claim;

(b) the good faith of the shareholder bringing the claim;

(c) the possibility of previous authorisation or subsequent ratification;

(d) whether the company has already decided not to pursue the claim; and

(e) whether the shareholder in question could bring a claim through alternative means (eg unfair prejudice, on which see **19.5**).

In particular, the court must take into account the views of shareholders with no personal interest, direct or indirect, in the matter.

It will be noted that any evidence of existing shareholder ratification or the possibility thereof will be a major factor in the court's decision, on the basis that if the majority of the members are reconciled to the director's actions, this is usually sufficient grounds to displace any action by a minority shareholder with a contrary view. (Note that for this reason, it is virtually impossible for a majority shareholder to bring a derivative claim.) If ratification is highly likely, a court may adjourn proceedings to allow this to take place, after which the application will likely be dismissed.

Ratification as a possibility was governed by the common law but is now governed by s239 CA 2006, which allows disinterested shareholders (ie shareholders other than the relevant director or persons connected to that director) the possibility of ratifying a director's misfeasance by **ordinary resolution**. (Under s239(7) CA 2006, however, the concept of a non-ratifiable breach is still preserved, for example an unlawful dividend cannot be 'legalised' by shareholder decision.)

If permission is granted, this will allow the shareholder to take the matter to a full trial (or at least to the next stage in the process). Any shareholder bringing a derivative action must consider three practical points:

1 If the action is successful, a remedy will be given to the company (which has been wronged) rather than to the claimant.
2 Any internal dispute in a company can deflect the attention and energies of management away from the proper business of running the company.
3 Professional costs will be incurred by all parties, including the shareholder.

On this last point, under the common law it was generally accepted that any reasonable claim brought in good faith would entitle the shareholder to an indemnity for costs from the company. This still appears to be the case, albeit that the award of an indemnity is entirely within the discretion of the court. However, if the company does end up meeting some or all of the costs of the action, this may simply erode the benefit of the action brought.

19.5 Unfair prejudice

19.5.1 Introduction

In addition to the derivative action, statute has afforded shareholders the possibility to complain about the conduct of others within a company since the introduction of s210 CA 1948. This became s459 CA 1985 which, in turn, became s994 CA 2006.

Section 994 provides that:

> A member of a company may apply to the court by petition for an order . . . on the ground (a) that the company's affairs are being or have been conducted in a manner that is unfairly prejudicial to the interests of the members generally or of some part of its members (including at least himself) or (b) that an actual or proposed act or omission of the company (including an act or omission on its behalf) is or would be so prejudicial.

Section 994 is effectively the same as the previous s459, so cases decided under the previous section are likely to be valid in interpreting its effect.

Unfair prejudice is a less than straightforward concept. What follows is a basic summary of an extensive topic. It will invariably be necessary to seek the guidance of counsel should a client be advised to seek such a remedy. Litigation in this area is notoriously lengthy and complex and there may be 'tactical' issues around whether or not an unfair prejudice petition is more appropriate than a derivative claim (assuming both are possible in the context of the shareholder's complaint).

19.5.2 Grounds

A shareholder may petition under s994 if they can show that they have suffered unfair prejudice. As will be seen from the wording of the section, the prejudice must have arisen from the way in which the affairs of the company were being conducted or from an actual or proposed act or omission by the company. Moreover, the shareholder must demonstrate that the prejudice suffered was unfair. If these things can be shown, then the court will have to consider what remedy would be appropriate. For example, perceived 'bad' management would not result in a successful petition–shortcomings in directors' abilities are one of the risks which a shareholder must accept as an investor. However, a director who exploits a company's assets for their own and their family's benefit or who withdraws excessive amounts from the company is likely to fall within s994, as the company's shareholders will be financially prejudiced by such behaviour.

19.5.3 Rights as shareholder must have been prejudiced

If the petitioner is to succeed, they must show that their rights as a shareholder have been prejudiced. In *Re Postgate and Denby* [1987] BCLC 8, it was held that such rights include all rights given under the company's memorandum and articles, statutory rights and also rights arising out of agreements and understandings between members.

The Law Commission reviewed shareholder remedies in 1997 (Law Com No 246, para 1.9). In this report, a number of guiding principles were iterated, one of which was:

> A member is taken to have agreed to the terms of the memorandum and **articles of association** when he became a member, whether or not he appreciated what they meant at the time. The law should continue to treat him as so bound unless he shows that the parties have come to some other agreement or understanding which is not reflected in the articles or memorandum. Failure to do so will create unacceptable commercial uncertainty. The corollary of this is that the best protection for a shareholder is appropriate protection in the articles themselves.

Thus, in *Re A Company (No 004377 of 1986)* [1987] 1 WLR 102, the petition failed as the articles of the company laid down exactly what was to happen if the relationship between the shareholders broke down for any reason. This included a right for a majority shareholder to buy the shares of the minority. The minority shareholder might indeed be prejudiced by such a provision but they could not claim that the prejudice was unfair as they had (by joining the company) agreed to this in advance.

19.5.4 Test for unfair prejudice

The test as to what amounts to unfair prejudice is objective. In the leading case in this area, *O'Neill v Phillips* [1999] 2 All ER 961, Lord Hoffmann explained that:

> a balance has to be struck between the breadth of the discretion given to the court and the principle of legal certainty . . . It is highly desirable that lawyers should be able to advise their clients whether or not a petition is likely to succeed.

Moreover, Lord Hoffmann was opposed to the application of a 'wholly indefinite notion of fairness'. In order to provide objectivity in the concept, his Lordship relied upon the fact that 'the manner in which the affairs of the company may be conducted is closely regulated by rules to which the shareholders have agreed' (effectively the company's constitution, but also formal and informal agreements or understandings between members).

On this basis, Lord Hoffmann came to two conclusions about unfair prejudice:

(a) A member will not ordinarily be entitled to complain of unfairness unless there has been some breach of the terms on which they agreed that the affairs of the company should be conducted.

(b) There will be cases in which equitable considerations make it unfair for those conducting the affairs of the company to rely upon their strict legal powers.

For these reasons, Mr O'Neill's claim failed. He may have had a legitimate expectation that Mr Phillips, the majority shareholder, would confer various benefits upon him (eg an increased share in profits and more shares in the company), but he had no formal grounds upon which to base a claim.

It is, however, a trap to believe that Lord Hoffmann's judgment is a fixed and finite iteration of the scope of s994. It is perhaps better to regard it as containing general governing principles.

A simpler way of looking at s994 is to say that generally, though not exclusively, s994 petitions will arise in two main contexts:

(a) Where the majority's behaviour is self-serving and/or results in harm to the financial status of the company, which has, in turn, an indirect impact on the minority shareholder. Often this may involve a breach of duty by the directors who are instrumental in such actions. In other words, compliance with relevant law and regulation is an expectation of those involved with a company, which is not being met. (Of course, this may equally be a situation in which a derivative action may be pursued. By way of a crude distinction, is the essence of the shareholder's complaint one of directors' misconduct, in which case a derivative claim may be more appropriate, or general mismanagement by the board, in which case unfair prejudice is the preferred route?)
(b) Where the company is effectively a 'quasi-partnership' and the petitioner is a director-shareholder who has been excluded from management. Here equitable considerations will be of relevance because of the basis upon which the company was set up; namely, a personal relationship between those involved based on mutual confidence, an understanding that the relevant parties will be involved in the management of the company and restrictions on the ability of those parties to dispose of their shares.

19.5.5 **Orders of the court**

If a petition under s994 is successful, the court 'may make such order as it thinks fit for giving relief in respect of the matters complained of' (s996(1)). Section 996(2) lists particular types of order which may be made but is expressly stated to be without prejudice to the general power given by s996(1).

The powers listed in s996(2) are to:

(a) regulate the conduct of the company's affairs in the future;
(b) require the company to refrain from doing or continuing an act complained of by the petitioner or to do an act which the petitioner has complained it has omitted to do;
(c) authorise civil proceedings to be brought in the name and on behalf of the company by such person or persons and on such terms as the court may direct;
(d) require the company not to alter its articles without leave of the court;
(e) provide for the purchase of the shares of any members of the company by other members or by the company itself and, in the case of a purchase by the company itself, the reduction of the company's capital accordingly.

19.5.6 **Purchase of petitioner's shares**

In practice, the most common remedy awarded to a successful petitioner is that their shares should be purchased by the wrongdoers who have caused the unfair prejudice. As it is often untenable for the petitioner to remain involved in the company, this produces a fair and pragmatic outcome.

This 'standard' outcome does, however, raise a strategic issue for the shareholder and their advisors. If a buy-out is not commercially acceptable, because the shareholder considers continued involvement with the company would be lucrative, then a derivative action may have to be considered as an alternative (should the grounds of complaint allow for such a thing).

The question of valuation of the petitioner's shares causes considerable problems when a buy-out is contemplated. The courts have held that the shares should be valued as at whatever date is fair to the petitioner. This usually means that the shares are valued at the date when the prejudice to the petitioner began. If a different date is chosen, the court will usually order that the valuer should value the shares as if the prejudice had not taken place.

Another issue for the court is whether or not any valuation of a petitioner's shares should be discounted to reflect the fact that they constitute a minority holding. Quite often the answer to this question is no and the shares are ordered to be valued on a pro rata basis; that is, a 30% shareholding equals 30% of the worth of the company. However, this is not an automatic outcome.

In *O'Neill v Phillips* [1999] 2 All ER 961, the House of Lords stressed that a *reasonable* offer from the majority to buy out the minority shareholder will usually be sufficient to defeat a future claim under s994, on the basis that the minority shareholder has already been offered exactly what a successful petition would generate in any event.

19.6 Just and equitable winding up

Companies may be wound up by a court order on a number of grounds. Winding up is the process by which a company's existence is brought to an end; it usually results from the insolvency of the company. However, one type of winding up is available as a remedy to shareholders of solvent companies; that is, winding up under s122(1)(g) of the Insolvency Act 1986 (IA 1986). This provides for winding up where 'the court is of the opinion that it is just and equitable that the company should be wound up'.

Usually (but not exclusively), this will only be considered by a court where the company constitutes a 'quasi-partnership', thus triggering the application of equitable principles. Whilst it may seem an oxymoron to describe a company as such, the essential nature of a quasi-partnership is:

(a) a company which is owned and managed by a small number of people;
(b) who usually have an equal stake in it; and
(c) who each have mutual expectations regarding involvement and participation in the affairs of the company.

Another important factor is likely to be the existence of a constitutional restriction on the ability of a shareholder to dispose of their shares to a third party.

EXAMPLE

OXP (Example) Ltd was set up by Gerry and Margaux four years ago to pursue a business venture which Gerry and Margaux devised. Both Gerry and Margaux have been the only directors since the company's creation and the only shareholders, holding 50% each of the company's share capital.

This company is likely to be regarded as a quasi-partnership.

By contrast, if RTY Ltd and FRG Ltd set up a joint venture company to pursue a mutual economic goal and their involvement and participation is fully documented in both the company's articles and a negotiated joint venture agreement, the certainty of this arrangement and its inherently 'arm's length' nature is unlikely to be regarded as a quasi-partnership, even if each party has equal management and ownership status in the joint venture company.

Winding up is a rather drastic solution to problems arising within a company and is now much less important due to the remedy for shareholders available for cases of unfair prejudice. Also, consideration must be given to whether or not winding up will provide the shareholder in question with an appropriate solution to their problem. However, it will provide an 'exit route' in that the company's assets will be sold off and the remaining proceeds, once the company's creditors have been paid off, will be returned to the shareholders.

CONDUCT POINT

Disputes within a company throw the issue of separate legal personality into sharp relief. For example, if a director is in breach of duty, the correct claimant to seek redress for the breach is the company. Each party would have to be separately represented if this became a live issue. If, however, a claim for breach of duty was not being prosecuted by a company, this may prompt a shareholder to launch a derivative claim on the company's behalf. In turn, this will prompt the need for three sets of lawyers to be involved: one to represent the shareholder; one to represent the company; and one to represent the director.

Aside from issues of the avoidance of conflicts, issues of client confidentiality can also arise. By way of summary of the relevant rules of the SRA's Standards and Regulations:

1. Details of the affairs of current and former clients must be kept confidential.
2. You must disclose to a client information in your possession which is material to their matter (unless this conflicts with your duty of confidentiality to another client).
3. You must not act for client where that client has an interest adverse to another current or former client for whom you hold information which is material to that matter.

These rules can combine to mean that acting in internal corporate disputes can become difficult or impossible for law firms in possession of relevant confidential information.

EXAMPLE

Firm Lex Scripta LLP has acted in the past for SampleCo 765 Ltd; however, it has not received any new instructions from that company for the last 18 months. (It is understood that the company is now instructing a different firm of lawyers.)

Any information which Firm Lex Scripta LLP holds about SampleCo 765 Ltd is confidential even though it no longer appears to be a client.

Firm Lex Scripta LLP is approached by Maria, a minority shareholder in SampleCo 765 Ltd, who wishes to bring a derivative claim in respect of the actions of two of the directors in that company.

Should Firm Lex Scripta LLP choose to act for Maria, this will trigger the responsibility to disclose to Maria relevant material information in its possession regarding SampleCo 765 Ltd. This will conflict with its responsibility to maintain confidentiality about information it holds about that company. To resolve this, Firm Lex Scripta LLP will then have to cease to act for Maria but not disclose the reason why.

As such, it would have been appropriate for Firm Lex Scripta LLP to decline Maria's instructions.

KEY POINT SUMMARY

- Where a minority shareholder has a cause for complaint about behaviour of others in the company, the starting point is consideration of an unfair prejudice petition.
- The likely outcome of a successful claim of unfair prejudice is that the majority shareholders be ordered to buy the shareholding of the petitioning shareholder.
- If a clear wrong has been committed by a director to the company, the appropriate claimant is the company itself.
- If, however, a company is not actively seeking to prosecute its rights, a shareholder may be better placed to launch a derivative action on the company's behalf, remembering that this entitlement is not automatic.
- In those circumstances where the relationship within the company amounts to a 'quasi-partnership' and that relationship has broken down or is operating to the exclusion of one of the parties, consideration may be given to asking a court to wind up the company; however, a value judgement must be made between this outcome and one which could be achieved under s994 CA 2006.

CHAPTER 20
Maintenance of Records by a Company

FUNCTIONING LEGAL KNOWLEDGE

This chapter considers the following functioning legal knowledge included in the SRA's SQE 1 assessment specification:

Corporate governance and compliance:

- documentary, record-keeping, statutory filing and disclosure requirements

AUTHORITIES UNDERPINNING PRACTICE

The key authorities that underpin this area of practice are listed below. Note that for legislation you are linked to legislation.gov.uk.

Although much of the legislation on this government website is available in its amended form, the incorporation of new amendments into the text of legislation can be delayed. You should refer to legal databases to ensure you are referencing the most up-to-date legislation.

- Companies Act 2006
  https://www.legislation.gov.uk/ukpga/2006/46
- Register of People with Significant Control Regulations 2016
  https://www.legislation.gov.uk/ukdsi/2016/9780111143018

20.1 Introduction

Note that provisions of the Economic Crime and Corporate Transparency Act 2023 (ECCTA 2023) will affect certain elements of this chapter. However, as at 4th March 2024, the relevant provisions of ECCTA 2023 were yet to come into force. Readers should, therefore, confirm the status and content of those provisions at the time of consulting this chapter. A summary of the expected impact of ECCTA 2023 on this chapter is given at 20.8.

After consulting this chapter, you will be familiar with the main types of registers which companies are obliged to maintain as part of their record-keeping obligations. These obligations are not discretionary; their maintenance is required by the Companies Act 2006 (CA 2006). Particular focus will be given to the register of persons with significant control, due to its complexity.

You will also be introduced to other record-keeping obligations on companies and the right for **members** to require certain documentation to be provided to them.

The requirement to generate accounts and provide financial information to members is dealt with in **Chapter 22**.

20.2 The main statutory registers

Companies are required by the CA 2006 to keep certain registers–often referred to as the company's 'books'.

There is no required format for registers and they may be kept in hard copy or electronic format (s1135 CA 2006), so the term 'books' is somewhat of a misnomer.

As far as a private limited company is concerned, the most important registers it must keep are as follows.

20.2.1 Register of members (s113 CA 2006)

This must contain each member's name, address, dates of entry on the register and cessation of membership together with details of the **shares** held.

The **subscribers to the memorandum** of association become members on the registration of the company (s112(1) CA 2006), so their details will be the first to be entered in this register. Thereafter, any person who acquires shares in a company will want to be entered in its register of members.

Conversely, should any person cease to be a member in a company, this fact will also be noted in the register as will any alteration to the number of shares held by a member.

EXAMPLE

ModelCo (44) Ltd has three **shareholders** holding shares as follows:

Jai: 50 ordinary shares

Muya: 50 ordinary shares

Nila: 50 ordinary shares

If Nila transfers all her shares to Jo and Muya transfers 25 shares to Jai, this will trigger the following changes to the register of members of the company:

(a) An increase in the shares held by Jai.

(b) A decrease in the shares held by Muya.

(c) Removal of Nila from the register.

(d) Addition of Jo to the register.

Note that s115 CA 2006 requires an index of members to be kept if a company has more than 50 members and the register is not already kept in the form of an index.

Failure to maintain a register of members is an offence by both the company and any officer in default and is punishable by a fine.

See also discussion of the register of members at **17.3**, which includes discussion of the likely changes to be introduced by ECCTA 2023.

20.2.2 Register of directors (s162 CA 2006)

This sets out in respect of each director their name, service address, country of residence, nationality and date of birth.

A separate register of directors' residential addresses must also be maintained (s165 CA 2006).

Failure to maintain either of these registers is an offence by both the company and any officer in default and is punishable by a fine.

20.2.3 Register of people with significant control (s790M CA 2006)

This is a relatively recent obligation on most companies to maintain a register of people with significant control (PSC register). The idea behind this register is to improve transparency of ownership and control of corporate entities. It will be considered further in the next section.

As with the above registers, failure to maintain this register is also an offence by both the company and any officer in default and is punishable by a fine.

20.3 The PSC register

20.3.1 Introduction

What follows is a basic summary of what is a very complicated and technical area. Full details of this new obligation can be found in Pt 21A and Sch 1A CA 2006, as supplemented by the Register of People with Significant Control Regulations 2016 (PSC Regulations 2016).

20.3.2 Persons with significant control

A PSC is usually an individual who falls into one of the following four categories:

1. A person who holds, directly or indirectly, *more than* 25% of the shares in a company.
2. A person who holds, directly or indirectly, *more than* 25% of the voting rights in a company.
3. A person who holds the right, directly or indirectly, to appoint or remove a majority of the board of directors of a company.
4. A person who has the right to exercise or actually exercises significant influence or control over a company.

(Details of the fifth category of person are beyond the scope of this manual.)

In respect of closely-held, private companies, the first and second categories are most likely to be significant.

EXAMPLE

OXP (111) Ltd has five shareholders, each of whom owns a 20% shareholding in the company. None of these shareholders need be entered in the PSC register.

OXP (333) Ltd has three shareholders, two of whom own a 40% shareholding and the third of whom owns a 20% holding. The first two shareholders must, therefore, be entered in the PSC register.

20.3.3 Entries on the register

Specific details of any person found to be a PSC will have to be entered into the company's PSC register within 14 days of the company confirming that person's necessary details (s790M(2) CA 2006).

Within 14 days after such entry in the register, the company must also notify **Companies House** of the existence of a PSC on form PSC01 (s790VA CA 2006).

In respect of categories 1 and 2 described at **20.3.2**, the size of a PSC's shareholding or voting rights will determine the statement which is entered in the company's PSC register; namely, a statement that the person holds, directly or indirectly:

(a) more than 25% but not more than 50% of the shares or voting rights in the company;

(b) more than 50% but less than 75% of the shares or voting rights in the company;

(c) 75% or more of the shares or voting rights in the company.

Other statements cover PSCs which fall into categories 3 and 4. (All relevant statements are set out in Sch 2 to the PSC Regulations 2016.)

If a company has no PSCs, it must still maintain a PSC register and note this fact in its register (reg 10 PSC Regulations 2016).

It is also possible for companies to elect, instead, that their PSC register is maintained at Companies House (s790X CA 2006); however, with this comes the corresponding responsibility to inform Companies House of any changes to enable that register to be updated (s790ZA CA 2006).

Companies are under an obligation to make enquiries of persons who might be a PSC in order to enter their details on the register (s790D CA 2006) and, once entered, they must keep the register up to date, if necessary, by making enquiries of a PSC if they think a change has occurred to that PSC (s790E CA 2006). Failure to respond to such enquiries or the provision of misleading responses to such enquiries is a criminal offence (Sch 1B, para 13 CA 2006).

As regards most closely held, private companies, it is not anticipated that this should be too onerous a task, not least because neither of these obligations applies if the company has already been informed of the relevant change and the PSC in question has themselves provided the information or it has been provided with their knowledge. (Note that there are duties upon persons who know themselves to be PSCs or RLEs to notify the company of this fact or of the fact that their status as a PSC or RLE has altered or ceased (ss790G and 790H CA 2006). Failure to fulfil such duties is a criminal offence (Sch 1B, para 14 CA 2006).)

Perhaps the major significance of this obligation for closely held private companies is that an allotment, transfer or buy-back of shares may either create or remove a PSC or alter their status.

EXAMPLE

The entire issued share capital of XYZ Ltd is 100 shares of £1 each, split equally between two individuals, Dafne and Giovani. Dafne and Giovani are, therefore, both PSCs and will be entered on the register as such.

Dafne and Giovani decide to sell their shares as follows:

(a) Dafne sells 20 shares to Valeria.

(b) Dafne sells her remaining 30 shares to Dario.

(c) Giovani sells 25 shares to Aldo.

As a result:

(a) Dafne ceases to be a shareholder, so ceases to be a PSC.

(b) Giovani remains a shareholder with a 25% holding, but ceases to be a PSC.

(c) Valeria becomes a shareholder with a 20% holding, but not a PSC.

(d) Dario becomes a shareholder with a 30% holding, and a PSC.

(e) Aldo becomes a shareholder with a 25% holding, but not a PSC.

If, at a later date, Giovani were to sell all his remaining shares to Valeria, Valeria's holding would increase from 30% to 55%. In turn, the entry in the PSC register in respect of Valeria would have to be altered to reflect the fact that Valeria's holding is now more than 50% but less than 75%.

Any change to an entry in the PSC register must be made within 14 days of confirmation of the change (s790M(6) CA 2006).

Within 14 days of this revision, Companies House must also be notified on either:

(a) form PSC04 (change of details of PSC); or

(b) form PSC 07 (ceasing to be a PSC) (s790VA CA 2006).

The details of any person who ceases to be a PSC can only be removed from the register after the expiration of ten years from the date when they ceased to be a PSC (s790U CA 2006).

20.3.4 **Relevant legal entities**

In addition to PSCs being entered on the PSC register, there is a parallel obligation for companies also to enter details of registrable Relevant Legal Entities (RLEs) within 14 days of confirmation of their status as such (s790M(5) CA 2006). Companies House must also be informed within 14 days thereafter on form PSC02 (s790VA CA 2006).

RLEs are not PSCs in their own right (because they are corporate entities), but knowledge of their existence can help discover the existence of a PSC in a chain of companies. For this reason, their details must be entered. In very simple terms, a registrable RLE is a direct corporate shareholder in a company which, if it had been an individual, would have been a PSC.

EXAMPLE

(a) Paro Ltd is 100% owned by Turners Ltd.

(b) In turn, Rupert, an individual, is a 60% shareholder in Turners Ltd.

(c) Paro Ltd's PSC register will include details of Turners Ltd as an RLE.

(d) Turners Ltd's PSC register will include details of Rupert as a PSC.

As such, in theory at least, investigation of Paro Ltd's PSC register should lead to Turners Ltd, whose PSC register will, in turn, show how Rupert fits into the picture (as a PSC of the holding company of Paro Ltd).

The above example begs the question, why is not Rupert also entered in the PSC register of Paro Ltd? To answer this question, two matters must be addressed:

1 Does Rupert have an indirect interest in Paro Ltd? And

2 If so, does that interest constitute significant control?

An interest is held indirectly if the person in question holds a majority stake in a legal entity and that entity in turn owns the shares in question (Sch 1A, para 18). Here, Rupert is a majority shareholder in Turners Ltd, which itself owns 100% of the shares in Paro Ltd. As such, Rupert does hold indirectly more than 25% of the shares in Paro Ltd. However, if a PSC qualifies as 'non-registrable' (s790C(4)) then there is no obligation for them to be entered on the register of the relevant company. The definition of 'non-registrable' is so difficult as to be impossible to paraphrase; however, the purpose behind it is to avoid duplication of entries within the same PSC register. In very simple terms, therefore, if a PSC holds an indirect interest through a registrable RLE, the existence of that registrable RLE on the PSC register will displace the need for a parallel registration of the PSC itself. As such, Rupert will not have to be entered on Paro Ltd's register.

20.3.5 **PSCs on incorporation**

The combined effect of the inclusion of the subscribers' initial shareholdings in form IN01 and s112(1) CA 2006 means that those who set up a company may effectively be either a PSC or a registrable RLE immediately on incorporation. As such, there is also an obligation to include a statement of initial significant control as part of the information provided in the application for initial registration of a company (s12A CA 2006).

EXAMPLE

Emil and Katarina decide to set up a company. They each agree to take 50 £1 ordinary shares. This information is included in the form IN01. As both Emil and Katarina will become PSCs on incorporation, the application for registration should also have included a statement of initial significant control.

Phillipa, Carl, Mortiz and Sean decide to set up a company. They each agree to take 25 £1 ordinary shares. This information is included in the form IN01. As none of Phillipa, Carl, Mortiz or Sean will be PSCs on incorporation, the application for registration need not include a statement of initial significant control.

20.4 Inspection of company books

The PSC register, the register of members and the register of directors must be kept available for inspection by members and the general public at the **registered office**. (They may also be kept at a place other than the registered office provided the Registrar is notified.)

Inspection of registers by members is free; all other persons must pay a prescribed fee. It is also possible for either members or outsiders to request a copy of the register of members on payment of a fee.

In recent years, there has been some sensitivity about the availability of directors' home addresses to the public through the right to inspect a company's registers. For this reason, the 2006 Act only requires that the register of directors include a service address, which can obviously be different from a home one. The separate register of residential addresses is not available for public inspection.

20.5 Maintenance of registers by Companies House

An alternative to record-keeping by companies themselves is for *private* companies to be able to elect to record certain information with Companies House, rather than on their own individual registers. The registers which companies may be able to dispense with are:

(a) register of members (s128A CA 2006);

(b) register of directors (s167C CA 2006);

(c) register of directors' residential addresses (s167C CA 2006);

(d) register of secretaries (although this will not be considered further, as it is unusual for private companies to appoint a secretary).

In doing so, the company in question need not maintain any of these registers itself but must provide Companies House with the information which would normally have been required for inclusion in those registers, as well as any later information which would be required to update those registers. In turn, Companies House will include that information on its central register relating to that company.

A company can be selective about which registers it wants to dispense with. Further, the election required to allow this to happen is different depending upon the register in question. (Specific forms exist for the purpose of notifying Companies House of such elections: see, for example, forms EH01, EH02 and EH05.)

If a company does not wish to maintain a register of members then:

(a) either all the subscribers must indicate this fact at the time of applying for registration of the company; or

(b) if the company has already been formed, the company must itself make the election to Companies House, but only if all the current members have consented to this election.

If a company does not wish to maintain a register of directors or a register of directors' residential addresses, then:

(a) either all the subscribers must indicate this fact at the time of applying for registration of the company; or

(b) if the company has already been formed, the company must itself make the election to Companies House, but no prior shareholder consent is required.

At the time the election is made, any registers already maintained by the company which are covered by the election are effectively put in 'stasis' and the central register at Companies House becomes the replacement repository for relevant information.

Any election can subsequently be withdrawn either:

(a) voluntarily, by a company making such a request to Companies House; or

(b) automatically, if a company ceases to be a **private company**.

Upon withdrawal of the election, the company's registers in question then become effective again and must be updated to reflect the current position as set out in the central register at the time of withdrawal of the election.

20.6 Documents to be kept by a company

Specific documents which should be kept at the registered office include:

(a) directors' **service contracts** (s228 CA 2006), which can be inspected by members free of charge. Members can also, on payment of a fee, ask to be supplied with a copy of any service contract. Any such contracts must be made available for inspection for the duration of the contract and for a 12-month period after its expiry or termination;

(b) records of shareholder resolutions of the company (passed at **general meetings** or otherwise) for a period of ten years (s355 CA 2006), which can be inspected by members free of charge;

(c) a copy of any contract pursuant to which the company has purchased or bought back shares in itself from a shareholder for ten years from the completion of the buy-back (s702 CA 2006). Such a contract can be inspected by members free of charge (see **Chapter 9** for further discussion of buy-back of shares by a company);

(d) a copy of any instrument creating or amending a charge over the company's property (s859P CA 2006). Such documentation must be open to inspection by any creditor or member of the company free of charge and by any other person, on payment of a fee (s859Q CA 2006). (See **Chapter 12** for further discussion of the granting of **security** over a company's assets.)

Companies are also obliged to record and maintain minutes of all directors' meetings for ten years (s248 CA 2006). However, the Companies Act does not require these to be maintained at the registered office for inspection.

20.7 Constitutional documents to be provided to members

Section 32 CA 2006 obliges a company, on request by any member, to provide that member with various constitutional documents. The most significant are likely to be:

(a) an up-to-date copy of the company's articles;

(b) a copy of any resolution or agreement relating to the company which affects the company's constitution;

(c) a copy of the company's certificate of incorporation;

(d) a current statement of capital.

20.8 Changes to be introduced by the Economic Crime and Corporate Transparency Act 2023

20.8.1 Expected changes

Under ECCTA 2023, the following changes are expected to be introduced; however, at the time of writing a definite timescale for their introduction had not been confirmed, so the reader is advised to confirm the up-to-date position at the time of reading.

(a) The only register to continue to be maintained by a company will be its register of members. As such, there will be no need to maintain the two registers related to director information nor the PSC register. Instead, this information will be maintained at Companies House.

(b) As a consequence of (a), the option to elect for Companies House to maintain such registers on a private company's behalf will cease.

(c) Should a secretary be appointed to the company (as explained previously, this is unusual for private companies), there will be no need to continue to maintain a register of secretaries. Again, going forward, this information will be held centrally at Companies House, if necessary.

20.8.2 PSC Information

The abolition of the need for a company to maintain a PSC register will alter its legal obligations in respect of PSC's. In very simple terms, the obligation will shift from needing to maintain its own register and to inform Companies House of any changes thereto to an obligation to inform Companies House of any information which should be included in the centrally-held PSC register for the company. In turn, the obligation of companies to investigate the existence and status of PSCs and RLEs and to make enquiries of such persons for the purpose of maintaining their own registers will shift to the purpose of providing Companies House with relevant information. As an adjunct to this, it is expected that companies will be required to notify Companies House if any such requests for information are ignored or are responded to late.

As regards the relevant information to be provided, the expectation is that a company will have to notify Companies House of:

(a) any person becoming or ceasing to be a PSC or RLE within 14 days of receiving confirmation of this fact; and

(b) changes to the required particulars of existing PSCs or RLEs within 14 days of receiving confirmation of this fact.

A company will also be required to notify Companies House:

(a) it believes that a person has become a PSC or an RLE, but that, at the time, has not had this fact confirmed; and

(b) it believes it no longer has any PSCs or RLEs.

Failure to meet these notification obligations will constitute a criminal offence by the relevant company and every officer of the company in default.

A matter discussed on the incorporation of a company was the future requirement to verify the identity of a PSC or the identity of a relevant officer of an RLE–see **3.16.2**. Persons may, of course, become PSCs or RLEs after a company's incorporation. A similar duty for those persons to verify their identity and maintain their verified status will also be introduced by ECCTA 2023.

KEY POINT SUMMARY

- Company record-keeping and registration is determined by statutory obligations set out in the Companies Act 2006.
- The main registers which a company must maintain and update as necessary are:
  - register of members;
  - register of directors;
  - register of directors' residential addresses; and
  - register of persons with significant control.
- It is possible for a company to elect instead that some or all of its statutory registers be maintained at Companies House, rather than internally.
- Companies are required to maintain copies of certain important documents, usually for inspection by their members. The most common examples are likely to be directors' service contracts and instruments creating security over a company's assets.
- Shareholders have the right to request certain specified documents from a company, the most significant being a copy of the **articles of association**.

CHAPTER 21
Changes to the Features of a Company

FUNCTIONING LEGAL KNOWLEDGE

This chapter considers the following functioning legal knowledge included in the SRA's SQE 1 assessment specification:

Corporate governance and compliance:

- company decision-making and meetings: procedural, disclosure and approval requirements
- documentary, record-keeping, statutory filing and disclosure requirements

AUTHORITIES UNDERPINNING PRACTICE

The key authorities that underpin this area of practice are listed below. Note that for legislation you are linked to legislation.gov.uk.

Although much of the legislation on this government website is available in its amended form, the incorporation of new amendments into the text of legislation can be delayed. You should refer to legal databases to ensure you are referencing the most up-to-date legislation.

- Companies Act 2006
  https://www.legislation.gov.uk/ukpga/2006/46
- Companies (Model Articles) Regulations 2008
  https://www.legislation.gov.uk/uksi/2008/3229

21.1 Introduction

Many of the features of a company are not set in stone and it may be necessary or desirable during a company's existence to change some of them. In fact, the only aspect of a company which is guaranteed not to change is its registered number.

After consulting this chapter, you will have been introduced to:

(a) the main facets of a company which may have to be altered at some point;

(b) the reasons for doing so; and

(c) the necessary method of alteration.

This chapter supplements **Chapter 3**, in that the aspects of a company which may need altering will have been determined at the time of its incorporation. So, for example, the considerations which are relevant to the choice of a company's initial registered name are equally relevant if a change to that name is proposed.

Table 21.1 later in the chapter sets out details of many of the forms which need to be submitted to **Companies House** by way of notification of any such changes.

This chapter does not consider:

- the appointment or removal of directors (dealt with in **Chapter 15**);
- changes to a company's share capital (dealt with in **Chapter 7**);
- registration of any charges granted by companies (dealt with in **Chapter 12**).

21.2 Change of name

21.2.1 Procedure

Section 77 of the Companies Act 2006 (CA 2006) allows two methods by which a company may change its name:

(a) by **special resolution**; or
(b) by any alternative method stipulated in a company's articles.

This latter method could be simpler or more onerous than a special resolution, for example:

(a) a majority or unanimous decision of the directors; or
(b) a majority or unanimous decision of the **shareholders**.

Note that the Model Articles do not contain any specific provision dealing with change of name.

In addition, the articles of companies which were set up prior to s77 coming into effect (ie companies incorporated prior to 1 October 2009) are unlikely to include any such provision, as it was not possible to do so under the Companies Act 1985.

Therefore, in default of any positive action to take advantage of an alternative approach, it may be the case that many companies will only be able to change their name by special resolution.

Readers are advised also to consult 3.6.3 where general issues regarding the choice of a company's name are discussed.

21.2.2 Notification of change of name to Companies House

Any change of name must be notified to the Registrar of Companies. The method of notification will depend upon the method by which the company's name was changed.

If a special resolution is used, both notice of the change to the name on form NM01 and a copy of the resolution must be sent to the Registrar (s78 CA 2006).

Where the change is effected by a method in the articles, the company must give notice that this is the case and notice of the change itself on form NM04 (s79 CA 2006).

A fee is also payable in either circumstance. (See Table 21.2 later in the chapter for further details of relevant fees.)

If the change is satisfactory in the opinion of the Registrar, a certificate of incorporation on change of name will be issued (s80 CA 2006), at which point the change of name is effective (s81(a) CA 2006). It is important, therefore, to recognise that the change does not take effect at the time the decision is made.

Once the name has been changed, it must be used on the company's notepaper and other documents in accordance with the disclosure requirements discussed at **3.13**.

EXAMPLE

Example (ABC) Ltd wishes to change its name to ExampleCo (Northern) Ltd.

On the basis that the only method available to the company is to effect the change by special resolution:

1 The board of directors will resolve either:
   (a) to call a **general meeting** of the shareholders; or
   (b) to circulate a **written resolution** (containing the special resolution) to all eligible **members**.
2 The wording of the resolution is likely to be:
   That the current name of the Company be changed to ExampleCo (Northern) Limited.
3 The necessary special resolution will either:
   (a) be passed at the general meeting (where the resolution will be proposed to the meeting); or

(b) a sufficient majority of shareholders will consent to the written resolution within the required time.

4 Upon passing of the resolution, the company will be obliged to notify Companies House in order to register the change.

21.2.3 Use of business name

For some companies, the registered name is somewhat of a statutory formality as they may choose to trade under a business name for the purposes of their public image. (Effectively, this will be a **trade mark** of the business. There are many examples on the High Street, for example of business names.)

To avoid companies defeating the restrictions on corporate names through the use of business names, they are regulated by Pt 41 CA 2006 (and related regulations), which impose the same restrictions on the use of business names as for corporate names.

The advantage of a business name is that any change to it is not regulated by the 2006 Act, so it can be changed at any time by board resolution. Additionally, the change does not have to be registered at Companies House (although if the business name is also a registered trade mark, a new registration would have to be made to the Trade Marks Registry).

21.3 Change of accounting reference date

21.3.1 Introduction

A company's accounting reference period is the period for which a company must produce annual accounts, as required by the CA 2006. The accounting reference period of a company is determined according to its accounting reference date (ARD).

21.3.2 Determination of ARD

A company's ARD is determined by its date of incorporation (s391 CA 2006). The situation is somewhat complicated because the date of incorporation can result in different rules being applied. However, for our purposes, the most important of these rules is that initially a company's ARD will be the last day of the month in which the anniversary of its incorporation falls.

EXAMPLE

Relevant Company Ltd was incorporated on 14 July 2020.

Its ARD would be 31 July and its first set of accounts would have to reflect the period from incorporation until the following 31 July 2021.

Thereafter, each set of accounts would represent the period from 1 August to the following 31 July.

21.3.3 Altering the accounting reference date

21.3.3.1 Reasons

A company may wish to alter its ARD for various reasons. Many companies wish to have their accounting period end at the end of the calendar or financial year. Others may be or become part of a group of companies where it makes administrative sense for each company in the group to have the same ARD and hence the same accounting period.

21.3.3.2 Method

A company may alter its ARD by giving notice to the Registrar of Companies on form AA01 pursuant to s392 CA 2006 (see **Table 21.1**).

The decision to alter a company's ARD will be taken by its board of directors. No reference to the shareholders is necessary.

Any alteration to the ARD will result in either a shortening or lengthening of the current accounting period. There are two important rules to bear in mind:

(a) If any alteration is to affect a company's initial accounting reference period, this should neither be shortened to less than six months nor lengthened to more than 18 months from the date of its incorporation.

(b) Any alteration to a subsequent accounting reference period must not lengthen it by more than 18 months.

To prevent abuse, s392(3) prevents the extension of an accounting reference period twice in any five-year period (subject to a number of well-defined exceptions).

EXAMPLE

Quartz Ltd was incorporated on 13 October 2018. Its ARD was, therefore, determined as 31 October. Its first accounts would have to have been made up to 31 October 2019. If this was unsuitable, Quartz would have had to notify Companies House of a desired change.

If the preferred date for its ARD was 30 April, Quartz must have notified the registrar of this change and applied to have its first accounting reference period end on 30 April 2019; that is, shorten the relevant period. (The alternative would result in an accounting reference period in excess of 18 months.)

Instead, if the preferred date for its ARD was 31 December, Quartz must have notified this change and applied to have its first accounting reference period end on 31 December 2019; that is, lengthen the relevant period. (The alternative would result in an accounting reference period shorter than six months.)

21.4 Change of registered office

21.4.1 Introduction

A company may operate from several sites. However, it must have a single registered address at which formal notifications, correspondence etc can be served on the company (s86 CA 2006). It need not be a place at which the company carries out any operations and could, instead, be the address of the company's accountants or lawyers. (Note that changes introduced by the Economic Crime and Corporate Transparency Act 2023 (ECCTA 2023) mean that any chosen registered office must now satisfy the definition of an 'appropriate address'–see **3.6.4**)

Any application for the incorporation of a company must include an indication of the intended **registered office** of a company in the form IN01 (s9(5)(a) CA 2006). Once the company is incorporated, this address will become its functioning registered office (s16(4) CA 2006).

21.4.2 Reasons

Reasons for a required change to a registered office will usually be entirely practical, such as moving to a new place of business. Also, if a company is acquired by another company, it makes sense for the newly acquired **subsidiary** to have a registered office identical to that of its parent.

21.4.3 Method of alteration

A company's registered office may be changed by giving relevant notice on form AD01 to the Registrar, pursuant to s87(1) CA 2006. Effectively, this is a decision for the board of directors.

The change is effective when the relevant notice is registered by the Registrar, although service of documents at the old registered office remains valid for a further 14 days after registration (s87(2) CA 2006).

It must be remembered that any alteration must be to an address within the jurisdiction of the company's incorporation.

EXAMPLE

Nomad (1275) Ltd was set up in England and Wales with a registered office in Sheffield.

The directors of this company wish to change its registered office to an address in Glasgow. This will not be possible–Scotland is a different jurisdiction.

21.5 Change to the articles of association

21.5.1 Introduction and reasons for change

In many instances, a company is likely to have been incorporated either with Model Articles or with articles based upon them. Over time, the articles may cease to remain suitable for the needs of the company and its members. If this becomes the case, they will have to be amended. It may be, for example, that the introduction of a substantial investor will necessitate a change to the articles to reflect that investor's status or the composition of the board of directors may alter, such that the provisions regarding decision-making by the directors will have to be altered.

The content of a company's articles is discussed in more detail at **Chapter 13**.

21.5.2 Method of alternation

To effect any change to the articles, the members must pass a special resolution approving the change.

In turn, the company will be obliged to send to the Registrar of Companies within 15 days of the change:

(a) an amended copy of the articles (s26(1) CA 2006); and

(b) a copy of the relevant special resolution (s30(1) CA 2006).

Failure to do either of the above will result in an offence being committed both by the company and by the directors in default.

21.6 Change to the registered email address

The introduction of this new requirement will also necessitate a method by which a company can alter its registered email address. As this is a brand-new concept, the process is not yet fully confirmed but it is assumed it will involve a resolution of the directors to effect the change, after which the relevant notification will need to be submitted to Companies House. (The reader is advised to consult the Companies House website for the up-to-date position on the method of notification required.) The change will take effect once the notice has been registered by the registrar of companies.

Any new email address chosen must be an 'appropriate email address', as defined. See further discussion at **3.6.5**.

21.7 Submission of documentation to Companies House

Provisions within the ECCTA 2023 will impose more stringent requirements regarding who will be permitted to submit documentation to Companies House on behalf of a company. (At the time of writing, these provisions were yet to be introduced. The reader is advised to confirm the latest position at the time of consulting this section.)

Oftentimes, such submissions are made by directors/officers of a company. In simple terms, any person who makes a submission to Companies House on behalf of a company will have to have had their identity verified. Further, any person subject to disqualification as a director will not be permitted to make a submission to Companies House either on their own behalf or on behalf of another.

Alternatively, submissions may also be made by lawyers, accountants and other professionals acting for a company. In future, the law will require that these persons be formally recognised as 'authorised corporate service providers' (ACSP) to be able to continue to make such submissions on behalf of a company. To become an ACSP a firm will have to be supervised by a relevant authority for the purposes of the Money Laundering Regulations and must make a formal application to the registrar of companies to be considered as such.

Details of the application process (when they are confirmed) are beyond the scope of this text, but it is worth noting that the registrar will have discretion to refuse to grant such status where it considers the applicant firm not to be a fit and proper person to carry out the functions of an ACSP.

21.8 Companies House forms and fees

Tables **21.1** and **21.2**, which follow, set out some of the more common forms and fees which a company may have to submit to Companies House in its lifetime. Some have already been referred to in this chapter. Others, such as the Confirmation Statement, the registration of a mortgage and changes to directors are relevant to other elements of the book.

Note that fees of Companies House can change. At the time of writing, it was proposed to increase certain fees from 1 May 2024. What follows reflects those proposals. However, the reader is advised to consult the Companies House website to confirm the up-to-date position.

TABLE 21.1 Main Companies House forms

Form	CA section	Purpose	Fee (see Table 21.2)
CS01	853A	Confirmation Statement	Yes
AA01	392	Change of Accounting Reference Date	No
NM01	78	Change of Name by Special Resolution	Yes
NM04	79	Change of Name by Method in Articles	Yes
AD01	87	Change of Registered Office	No
AP01	167	Appointment of Director	No
AP03	276	Appointment of Secretary	No
TM01	167	Termination of Director's Appointment	No
TM02	276	Termination of Secretary's Appointment	No
MR01	859A	Registration of Particulars of a Charge	Yes
SH01	555	Return of Allotment of Shares	No
SH03	707	Return of Buy-back	No, but attracts stamp duty
SH06	708	Notice of Cancellation of Shares (post buy-back)	No

Notes:

(a) All forms are titled according to their purpose: eg the prefix 'SH' stands for 'shares'; the prefix 'AP' stands for appointment.

(b) Every form has a statutory premise which will be referred to on the face of the form.

(c) Where a fee is payable, the form will provide details.

(d) All forms contain a checklist on the final page, which should not be overlooked when completing a form.

(e) It is usually a director or the secretary (if one is appointed) who signs a form on the company's behalf. If, however, the company is insolvent, the signatory will normally be the liquidator or administrator.

TABLE 21.2 Main Companies House fees

Paper change of name	£30.00
Digital change of name	£20.00
Digital same-day change of name	£83.00
Digital Confirmation Statement	£34.00
Paper Confirmation Statement	£62.00
Paper registration of charge	£24.00
Digital registration of charge	£15.00

KEY POINT SUMMARY

The following is a brief summary of possible changes which have been considered in this chapter.

- Company name: the name of a company can be part of its public 'persona'. As such, the need or desire to change a company's name may not be that great; however, should it be deemed necessary, it is possible either by special resolution or an alternative method stipulated in the articles should one exist.
- Accounting reference date: the date of registration of a company will determine its accounting reference date; that is, the date on which its accounting year ends. If this is not suitable, it will have to be changed to meet the promoters' needs.
- Registered office: as part of the process of registration of a company, details of the company's first registered office will have been supplied. If this address ceases to be suitable in the future, it will have to be changed.
- **Articles of association**: if a company's articles have to be amended, only shareholders can effect any such change by the passing of a special resolution approving the change. Consequent to this will be various filing requirements.

CHAPTER 22
Company Accounts

FUNCTIONING LEGAL KNOWLEDGE

This chapter considers the following functioning legal knowledge included in the SRA's SQE 1 assessment specification:

Finance:

- financial records, information and accounting requirements.

AUTHORITIES UNDERPINNING PRACTICE

The key authorities that underpin this area of practice are listed below. Note that for legislation you are linked to legislation.gov.uk.

Although much of the legislation on this government website is available in its amended form, the incorporation of new amendments into the text of legislation can be delayed. You should refer to legal databases to ensure you are referencing the most up-to-date legislation.

- Companies Act 2006
  https://www.legislation.gov.uk/ukpga/2006/46
- Small Companies and Groups (Accounts and Directors' Report) Regulations 2008
  http://www.legislation.gov.uk/uksi/2008/409
- Large and Medium-sized Companies and Groups (Accounts and Reports) Regulations 2008
  http://www.legislation.gov.uk/uksi/2008/410
- Small Companies (Micro-Entities' Accounts) Regulations 2013
  http://www.legislation.gov.uk/uksi/2013/3008

22.1 Introduction

Note that the filing obligations for small and micro-entities will be affected by provisions within the Economic Crime and Corporate Transparency Act 2023 (ECCTA 2023), which at the time of writing were not yet in force. A summary of the expected impact of these provisions is given at 22.6.4. Readers should confirm the status of the relevant provisions when consulting this chapter.

After consulting this chapter, you will have considered the statutory rules with which a company must comply in relation to its financial and accounting records. (It should be noted that many of the accounting rules which apply to companies apply equally to limited liability partnerships.)

There are three main issues to consider in respect of company accounts, namely:

- their format and content;
- their disclosure to (and approval by) **shareholders**;
- their filing at **Companies House**.

As regards the third bullet point above, a core concept of company law is that information about a company and its financial status should be made available to the public. The purpose of this policy is to enable anyone interested in the affairs of a company (whether they are current or prospective shareholders in the company or its creditors) to have access to the information they need to make an informed judgement on the company's financial affairs.

22.2 The duty to prepare and submit accounts

22.2.1 Individual accounts

As a general rule, directors are required by the Companies Act 2006 (CA 2006) to prepare a set of 'individual accounts' for each financial year of the company (s394 CA 2006). A company's financial year is determined by its accounting reference period which, in turn, is delineated by its accounting reference date. (See **21.3** for further discussion.)

Companies Act individual accounts (s395(1)(a) CA 2006) consist of a profit and loss account and a balance sheet (s396(1) CA 2006). (See **22.7** and **22.8** for discussion of both these accounts.) Any accounts prepared must give a true and fair view of the financial status of the company (s396(2) CA 2006).

(It is also possible, instead, to prepare accounts in accordance with International Accounting Standards, so-called 'IAS individual accounts' (s395(1)(b) CA 2006). These are not considered relevant in the context of this discussion.)

Individual accounts must also comply with specific regulations on format and content (s396(3) CA 2006), mainly the:

- Small Companies and Groups (Accounts and Directors' Report) Regulations 2008; or
- Large and Medium-sized Companies and Groups (Accounts and Reports) Regulations 2008; or
- Small Companies (Micro-Entities' Accounts) Regulations 2013.

For these purposes, the Small Companies and Groups (Accounts and Directors' Report) Regulations 2008 (the 2008 Regulations) are the most important, bearing in mind that they have been amended over time, including by the Small Companies (Micro-Entities' Accounts) Regulations 2013, to introduce a sub-category of small company known as the 'micro-entity'.

22.2.2 Adequate accounting records

In support of this obligation, all companies are required to maintain, on an ongoing basis, adequate accounting records which are sufficient to provide information about the financial position of the company at any time (s386 CA 2006). Failure to do so is a criminal offence by a company's officers (s387 CA 2006).

22.2.3 Group accounts

Where a company is a **parent company** it must also prepare group accounts (s399 CA 2006), which must comprise a consolidated balance sheet and a consolidated profit and loss account setting out financial details of the parent and all its **subsidiaries** (s404(1) CA 2006).

22.2.4 Notes to accounts

Whilst accounts can be considered as primarily numerical in nature, considerable information will be provided in the form of notes. The notes can, therefore, be regarded as providing background information to the 'headline' figures in the profit and loss and balance sheet. In many ways, they are as important as the figures within the accounts.

22.2.5 Directors' report

Additionally, a directors' report must accompany the accounts (s415 CA 2006). This report must contain details of all directors during the relevant financial year, the principal activities of the company throughout the year and the amount of any dividend recommended by the directors. Certain 'large' and 'medium-sized' companies (based on such criteria as turnover and number of employees) may also have to include statements explaining how the company has engaged with its employees, suppliers and customers.

22.2.6 Strategic report

Also, unless the company is 'small' (see discussion at **22.6**), the accounts must contain a strategic report (s414A) which should contain a fair review of the company's business and a description of the principal risks faced by the company (s414C(2)).

This report is designed to give shareholders the opportunity to assess how well directors have fulfilled their duty to promote the success of the company.

If the company is 'large', s414CZA requires the strategic report also to contain a statement explaining how the directors have regard to the matters set out in s172(1)(a)–(f) when performing their duty under s172.

22.2.7 Remuneration report

Quoted companies (as defined by s385 CA 2006) are required under s420 CA 2006 to produce a remuneration report which explains how directors have been rewarded during the relevant financial year. In simple terms, a quoted company is a company whose **shares** are traded on a recognised exchange, so this obligation does not apply to the majority of companies.

22.3 The requirement for audit

Subject to certain material exceptions, there is a statutory obligation for accounts to be audited (s475 CA 2006). Consequently, companies may have to appoint **auditors** annually, who are required to produce a report on the accounts. This report effectively benchmarks the contents of the accounts against certain established accounting standards.

Two main exceptions to the need for audit are either in respect of:

(a) small companies: s447 CA 2006 (see **22.6**); or

(b) dormant companies: s480 CA 2006. (A dormant company is one which has no significant accounting transactions during an accounting period: s1169 CA 2006.)

Where auditors are required, their appointment is regulated by the CA 2006. Both the board of directors and the shareholders (by **ordinary resolution**) have the power to appoint auditors in defined circumstances (s485 for private companies and s489 for public companies).

The appointment of auditors should happen annually. For public companies, therefore, the annual accounts meeting, that is, the AGM, is the most appropriate forum; for private companies, a specific **general meeting** could be called for this purpose or it could be effected by **written resolution**.

22.4 Provision of accounts to members

Annual accounts must be approved by the board and be signed off on its behalf by a director (s414(1) CA 2006). The relevant signature must feature on the balance sheet (s414(2) CA 2006).

Once this has been done, the company must send copies of the accounts to the shareholders (s423 CA 2006). For private companies, this must be no later than the deadline for submission of the accounts to Companies House, which is nine months from the end of the relevant accounting period.

For public companies, shareholders are granted greater influence. Once they have been prepared, the final accounts must be laid before the company in general meeting (s437(1) CA 2006). This meeting is called the accounts meeting (s437(3) CA 2006) and in most circumstances this will be the **annual general meeting** of the company. The relevant accounts must be sent out to shareholders no later than 21 days before the accounts meeting (s424(3) CA 2006).

Shareholders have the right to demand at any time a copy of the most recent accounts and related reports (ss431 and 432 CA 2006).

22.5 Filing of accounts

Subject to what is said later about small companies, all companies must send copies of all elements of their accounts to the Registrar of Companies as follows.

(a) In the case of private companies, this must be no later than nine months after the end of the relevant accounting period (s442(2)(a) CA 2006).

(b) For public companies, this must be no later than six months after the end of the relevant accounting period (s442(2)(b) CA 2006).

These accounts are then a matter of public record, available through Companies House.

Failure to deliver accounts on time can result in:

(a) Automatic civil penalties for the company on a scale that is linked to the length of the delay (s453 CA 2006). For private companies, these range from £150 for a delay up to a month, to £1,500 for a delay of more than six months. (Note that the penalties are higher for public companies.)

(b) Criminal penalties (by way of fine) for every relevant director (s451(1) CA 2006).

A failure to submit accounts to Companies House may also be regarded by the Registrar of Companies as an indication that a company is no longer trading. In such a case, the Registrar may initiate the strike-off procedure against a company which may result in dissolution of the same (s1000 CA 2006).

Persistent failure to file accounts may also amount to grounds for **disqualification** proceedings against the directors concerned under s3 of the Company Directors Disqualification Act 1986.

22.6 Small and medium-sized companies

22.6.1 Small companies

If a **private company** comes within the definition of a small company for a particular financial year, its duty to prepare and file accounts is modified by ss444 and 444A CA 2006.

Effectively this means that:

(a) it can generate abridged versions of its profit and loss account and balance sheet, subject to unanimous consent of the **members** of the company;

(b) the directors' report need not contain a statement regarding any recommendation of a dividend (s416(3) CA 2006);

(c) it need not prepare a strategic report (s414A CA 2006);

(d) it has the option not to file either the profit and loss account or the directors' report with Companies House (s444(1) CA 2006).

The combined effect of these provisions is that a small company can maintain a greater degree of privacy about its financial status. (There is an additional exemption for small groups of companies from the duty to produce consolidated accounts. The detail of this is not considered.)

Any balance sheet produced by a small company must contain a statement that it has been produced in accordance with the small companies regime (s414(3)(b) CA 2006).

The actual format and layout of a small company's accounts is determined by Sch 1 to the 2008 Regulations.

A private company is small if at least two of the following criteria are satisfied (s382(3) CA 2006):

(a) the company's turnover does not exceed £10.2 million;

(b) its balance sheet total does not exceed £5.1 million;

(c) the average number of employees does not exceed 50 people.

In these definitions, 'turnover' effectively means the sums earned by the company in selling goods or services before deducting expenses. The balance sheet total is, broadly speaking, the value of the company's assets without deducting any liabilities. The number of employees should be calculated as an average over the relevant financial year.

Certain companies are excluded from this regime, even if the above criteria are satisfied. Full details are provided in s384 CA 2006 but some examples are:

(a) a **public company**;

(b) a banking company;

(c) an insurance company.

The status of a small company is not permanent, nor is it safe to assume that a company will benefit from the regime simply because it fulfils the conditions for a small company in a particular financial year. Put simply, a company must either acquire small company status at the outset and then lose that status by ceasing to be a small company for two consecutive years or, if it does not start out as small, it must acquire small company status by being small for at least two consecutive years.

In addition to revised filing requirements, small companies may benefit from an exemption from audit (s477(1) CA 2006). Audit is a relatively expensive process, so the exemption can result in a cost saving for a company.

To ensure appropriate disclosure and to ensure that the exemption from audit is available to a company, the entitlement must be stated in the company's balance sheet (s475(2) CA 2006).

However, even if the board of directors decides to dispense with an audit, members holding at least 10% in **nominal value** of the company's issued share capital have the right to demand an audit (s476 CA 2006). Again, the balance sheet must contain a statement that such a request has not been made to enable the company to benefit from the exemption (s475(3)(a) CA 2006).

No small company can benefit from the audit exemption if it is public (s478(a) CA 2006).

22.6.2 **Micro-entities**

Very small companies can be classed as micro-entities for accounting purposes.

To qualify as a micro-entity, a company must meet at least two of the following conditions (s384A(4) CA 2006):

(a) annual turnover does not exceed £632,000;

(b) balance sheet total does not exceed £316,000;

(c) average number of employees must not exceed ten.

However, any company excluded from the small companies regime cannot qualify as a micro-entity.

Micro-entities must prepare a balance sheet and a profit and loss account. An auditors' report (unless the exemption from audit as a small company is claimed) must also be generated.

Any balance sheet produced by a micro-entity must contain a statement that it has been produced in accordance with the micro-entity provisions (s414(3)(a) CA 2006).

Micro-entities are exempt from the requirement to produce a directors' report (s415(1A) CA 2006).

The format of a micro-entity's accounts is different (and less detailed) to that of a small company. The actual format and layout is determined by Sch 1 to the 2008 Regulations.

The accounts of a micro-entity that comply with stipulated minimum standards will be presumed to give a true and fair view of the financial position of that company (s396(2A) CA 2006).

Micro-entities benefit from the same filing obligations as small companies, in that they are only obliged to file the balance sheet with Companies House. The filing of any further accounting information is entirely voluntary.

The micro-entity regime is entirely voluntary. It may be felt more appropriate, therefore, to prepare accounts which reflect the small companies regime, as they may provide greater information for shareholders, creditors and potential investors.

22.6.3 **Medium-sized companies**

The exemptions from reporting and filing available to small companies are available to a much lesser degree for medium-sized companies. Medium-sized companies are not exempt from the requirement to produce full accounts or from the requirement to provide accounts to their own shareholders. They must also provide complete filings of all elements of their accounts with Companies House, namely:

- balance sheet;
- profit and loss account;
- directors' report;
- strategic report;
- auditor's report on the above (unless exempt from audit).

Being a medium-sized company of itself does not produce any entitlement to an exemption from audit.

A medium-sized company is one that satisfies at least two of the following criteria (as set out in s465 CA 2006):

(a) its turnover does not exceed £36 million;
(b) its balance sheet total does not exceed £18 million;
(c) the average number of employees does not exceed 250.

These conditions should be applied in the same way as for the calculation for small companies.

A public company cannot be a medium-sized company (s467(1)(a) CA 2006).

Additionally, medium-sized company status is acquired and lost in the same way as for small companies. Any company which exceeds at least two of the above thresholds will be classed as 'large'. Large companies are subject to no exemptions or exceptions and must comply fully with all accounting and filing requirements.

22.6.4 Impact of Economic Crime and Corporate Transparency Act 2023

Provisions within ECCTA 2023 (ss. 53, 54, 57 and 58) will alter the obligations upon small companies and micro-entities discussed at **22.6.1** and **22.6.2**. The following changes are expected but were not in force at the time of writing. Readers should, therefore, consult the latest information available to confirm the up-to-date position:

(a) Small companies will have to file both a profit and loss account and a directors' report, in addition to a balance sheet, with Companies House.
(b) Micro-entities will have to file a profit and loss account, in addition to a balance sheet, with Companies House, but the option not to generate a directors' report will remain.
(c) It will no longer be possible to generate or file abridged accounts.
(d) If exemption from audit is claimed, directors must generate a statement which identifies the relevant exemption and which confirms that the company qualifies for such exemption. This statement must be contained in the company's balance sheet.

22.7 Profit and loss account

A profit and loss account is an account that shows the income received by the company over a particular period of time and the expenses incurred in producing that income. Deducting the expenses from the income provides a profit figure (or a loss, if expenses exceed income). The profit and loss account is, strictly speaking, only designed to show income profits. If a company makes a capital profit (eg if it sells land for a profit), this may be shown as an addition to the profit and loss account. It will then usually be labelled as an 'exceptional item' as opposed to the ordinary income profit.

Profit and loss accounts are almost always prepared for 12-month periods (the company may wish to produce more regularly forecasts or full accounts for its own internal purposes–usually referred to as 'management accounts'). The period covered by the accounts ends with the company's chosen accounting reference date (see **21.3**).

Companies are not required to prepare accounts which synchronise with the calendar year, although some companies do choose 31 December as their accounting reference date, in which case the accounts will be for a calendar year.

A very simple, traditional profit and loss account might look like the following:

XYZ LTD

Profit and loss account

Year ending 31 March 2021

	£	£
INCOME		
Sales		200,000
Opening stock	80,000	
Purchases	90,000	
	170,000	
Less closing stock	70,000	
		100,000
Gross profit from sales		100,000
Interest received		8,000
		108,000
EXPENDITURE		
Wages	55,000	
Miscellaneous	10,000	
		65,000
PROFIT BEFORE TAX		43,000
DEDUCT TAX		8,600
TRANSFERRED TO RESERVE		34,400

Notice the following points in relation to the above example:

(a) The account is divided into three parts. The first shows the income of the business. The second shows the expenditure incurred in earning that income and the third shows what has happened to the income, in particular the fact that the company incurs a corporation tax liability on its profits. (If any dividends were paid they would be shown as a deduction in this section.)

(b) In the income section, the opening and closing stock are shown. Unless stock is taken into account it is impossible to work out the profit. If a company has a storeroom full of goods left over from last year that it sells this year, it cannot calculate its profit unless it takes into account the fact that it paid for that stock.

(c) The figure which is labelled 'transferred to reserve' is the remaining profit after the tax has been paid; that is, profit retained in the business. This figure will also be relevant to the balance sheet–see later.

22.8 Balance sheet

A balance sheet of a company shows the assets and liabilities of the company; that is, what it owns compared to what it owes. It also demonstrates how the shareholders have funded the company by their contributions to it.

An asset is something of value or potential value. Land that a company may own is an asset; so is any money it has in the bank. Sometimes the balance sheet will also show much more intangible things such as goodwill.

The liabilities part of a balance sheet includes liabilities due to outsiders (eg money owing to suppliers) or money owed to a bank or other lenders.

The assets less liabilities of a company will generate a net asset value of the business.

In turn, this amount will balance with the total amount which shareholders have contributed to the company by way of subscription for shares and undistributed profit which remains in the company.

A simple, traditional balance sheet might look like this:

BALANCE SHEET OF XYZ LTD

As at 31 March 2021

	£	£
FIXED ASSETS		
Premises		400,000
Fixtures		10,000
		410,000
CURRENT ASSETS		
Stock (goods for sale and/or materials)	5,000	
Cash	2,000	
	7,000	
LESS CURRENT LIABILITIES		
Creditors	4,500	
NET CURRENT ASSETS		2,500
Long term liability (Bank Loan)		(10,000)
Net Asset Value		402,500
CAPITAL EMPLOYED		
Share capital	200,000	
Share premium account	160,000	
Reserves	42,500	
		402,500

Note the following points:

(a) The totals (of £402,500) balance: that is, the **net assets** of the company equal its capital. This happens because of the 'double entry' system used to record transactions in the company's books. A simple example of this is where share capital is contributed to a company. If someone buys shares for £100 at par value, this would be represented in a balance sheet by two entries. The company would have £100 in cash, a current asset; and it would have capital of £100 (a liability to the shareholder). Extrapolating this, a company's net assets will always reflect its capital, as is shown here. That is, they reflect the way in which a company has employed its capital in its business.

(b) A distinction is made between fixed assets and current assets. Fixed assets are assets likely to be held by the company for a considerable period of time; that is, they are 'static' in nature. Current assets are those likely to be used up by the company in the course of its business on an ongoing basis and whose value, therefore, will fluctuate regularly.

(c) Current liabilities (ie sums owed by the company likely to be paid within a year) are shown as a deduction from current assets. They are, accordingly, not in the same part of the account as the long-term liabilities. The money owed to the bank is included in that latter section on the assumption that it is a long-term loan. If the same amount was owed to the bank on an overdraft and, therefore, repayable on demand, it would be shown as a short-term liability.

(d) The sums shown under the heading of capital employed are all sums due to the shareholders of the company. The share capital is the liability arising from the fact that the shareholders paid the nominal value of their shares to the company at some time in the past. The share premium reflects the fact that when the shares were issued the shareholders paid more than the nominal value for them. Remember, however, that a company cannot generally return the sums invested by the shareholders until the company is wound up.

(e) The item referred to as 'reserves' is, in a way, a balancing item. If the company was wound up its assets would realise £417,000. This would be used to pay the bank and the outstanding creditors. This would then leave £402,500 for the shareholders. They would be repaid their original investment of £360,000 (shown in share capital and share premium). This would then leave £42,500. The reserve is in effect a liability owed to shareholders resulting from the fact that the company has made profits over the years which it has not chosen to distribute to them.

(g) The balance sheet is dated 'as at' 31 March. Businesses constantly acquire and dispose of assets, meet liabilities and incur new liabilities. A balance sheet is, therefore, always relevant to a particular moment in time, not to the whole of a period of time. (This is in contrast to the profit and loss account which covers income and outgoings of the business over a defined period of time).

(h) The company has a surplus of short-term assets over short-term liabilities. The resulting surplus is called net current assets. This figure is particularly important as it is a strong indication of the solvency of the company (see **Chapter 28** for further discussion of corporate insolvency).

(i) If the company were sold, a purchaser may end up paying more than the net asset value. This increased value of the business could represent the fact that it has a loyal group of customers or is a market leader in its sphere of operations (or both). The difference between the asset value and what the whole business could be sold for is classed as the goodwill of the business.

KEY POINT SUMMARY

- The duty to prepare and submit accounts for companies (and LLPs) is statutory.
- There is a presumption that company accounts should be audited. However, in many instances that presumption can be displaced by exceptions to this rule.
- The size of the relevant entity will be significant in determining the exact scope of its accounting obligations.
- The two main accounts which must be produced are the profit and loss account and the balance sheet.
- The content and format of these accounts is determined by regulation and accounting standards.
- The purpose of the profit and loss account is to compare money coming in with money going out. In turn, it will be demonstrated if the business is generating a profit or loss.
- The purpose of the balance sheet is to compare assets against liabilities. It will also demonstrate how shareholder 'funds' have been used to bring about this situation.
- Companies are obliged to file accounts annually with Companies House. Companies' published accounts are publicly available through Companies House.

PART E
Partnerships

CHAPTER 23
Partnership Management and Finance

FUNCTIONING LEGAL KNOWLEDGE

This chapter considers the following functioning legal knowledge included in the SRA's SQE 1 assessment specification:

Business and organisational characteristics (sole trader/partnership/LLP/private and unlisted public companies)

Legal personality and limited liability

Procedures and documentation required to incorporate a company/form a partnership/LLP and other steps required under companies and partnerships legislation to enable the entity to commence operating:

- constitutional documents

Finance:

- funding options: debt and equity
- types of **security**
- distribution of profits and gains
- financial records, information and accounting requirements.

Partnership decision-making and authority of partners:

- procedures and authority under the Partnership Act 1890

AUTHORITIES UNDERPINNING PRACTICE

The key authorities that underpin this area of practice are listed below. Note that for legislation you are linked to legislation.gov.uk.

Although much of the legislation on this government website is available in its amended form, the incorporation of new amendments into the text of legislation can be delayed. You should refer to legal databases to ensure you are referencing the most up-to-date legislation.

- Partnership Act 1890
  http://www.legislation.gov.uk/ukpga/Vict/53-54/39

23.1 Introduction

After consulting this chapter, you will have been introduced to:

(a) the ways a partnership can be managed;

(b) the duties and obligations which partners owe to each other; and

(c) how the finances of a partnership can be handled, both in terms of raising capital to finance the business and in the distribution of profits the business makes.

Such matters are important, as they form the basis of much of the ongoing legal relationship between the partners. **Chapter 5**, which provides an introduction to partnerships, should have been consulted before reading this chapter and the ones which follow on partnerships.

23.2 The legal relationship between the partners (s24 PA 1890)

Section 24 of the Partnership Act 1890 (PA 1890) lays down a number of rules which regulate the relationship between partners and the management of their business. These rules '. . . may be varied by the consent of all the partners, and such consent may be express or inferred from a course of conduct'. The most common way in which the rules in s24 are varied is where the partners enter into a partnership agreement (dealt with specifically in **Chapter 27**).

If partners do not wish specific provisions of s24 to apply to their business then, for certainty, contrary provisions should be incorporated in their partnership agreement. However, it is also possible that accepted and regular dealings between partners may displace the effect of s24, at least in part.

Several aspects of s24 deal with the relationship of the partners in respect of the distribution of profits and losses made by the partnership; these issues are dealt with at **23.4**.

23.2.1 Management of the business

Section 24(5) provides that:

> Every partner may take part in the management of the partnership business.

This means that each partner has an entitlement to be involved in management affairs; it does not mean, however, that each partner has to manage the firm's business. If the management structure of a particular partnership is to be different from that presumed by s24(5), express agreement should be made. For example, a large partnership may have different grades of partners, major decisions being taken only by the senior grade. Alternatively, some partners may be 'sleeping partners'; that is, partners who have contributed capital but who do not take an active part in management or decision-making.

23.2.2 Decisions of the partners

Section 24(8) states:

> Any differences arising as to ordinary matters connected with the partnership business may be decided by a majority of the partners, but no change may be made in the nature of the partnership business without the consent of all the partners.

In most circumstances, therefore, a simple majority of the partners is required to take a business decision. If there is an equality of votes, a decision has not been taken and the status quo is preserved.

Unless contrary provision already exists, a wholesale change to the nature of the partnership business must be consented to by all the partners.

23.2.3 Restrictions on majority rule

There are three main limitations imposed on the ability of the majority of the partners to bind the whole firm. First, partners are under a fiduciary duty to each other and so must exercise their powers for the benefit of the firm as a whole.

For example, in Blisset v Daniel (1853) 10 Hare 493, a power was given (by the partnership agreement) to the majority of the partners permitting them to expel a partner. The majority exercised this power with a view to obtaining cheaply the expelled partner's shares in the partnership. This was held to be an unlawful use of the power to expel, as it amounted to a breach of the duty of good faith required of a fiduciary.

Secondly, the majority may not impose their views on the minority without first consulting them (Const v Harris (1824) T & R 496). However, there is no requirement that consultation should take the form of a meeting (unless the partnership agreement so provides).

Thirdly, the following provisions of the PA 1890 limit majority rule:

(a) Section 24(8) requires unanimity for a change in the partnership business–already noted earlier. This is so that a partner who has decided to invest in one particular type of business will not be forced to invest in something else against their wishes.

(b) Section 24(7) provides that:

    No person may be introduced as a partner without the consent of all the existing partners.

    Such a rule is vital to the running of a small partnership where each partner will wish to ensure that their fellow partners cannot force them to go into partnership with someone of whom they disapprove. In a large partnership, it may be considered appropriate that s24(7) should not apply (so that, eg, the senior partners may be given power to decide who to take on as junior partners and who to promote to senior partnership), in which case the partnership agreement must exclude the requirement of unanimity in this respect.

(c) Unanimity is required by s19 for an alteration to the partnership agreement. However, the agreement of the partners to an alteration can be inferred from a course of dealings.

(d) Section 25 prevents expulsion of a partner by a majority of the partners unless all the partners have *expressly* agreed to such a power being conferred.

23.2.4 Other provisions

Other provisions of s24 which affect the relationship between the partners are as follows:

(a) Section 24(2) gives a partner a right to be indemnified by the firm in respect of payments made and personal liabilities incurred 'in the ordinary and proper conduct of the business of the firm or in or about anything necessarily done for the preservation of the business or property of the firm'.

(b) Section 24(9) gives all the partners a right to inspect and to copy the partnership accounts.

23.3 The duty of good faith

23.3.1 Equitable provisions regarding good faith

The contract of partnership is a contract *uberrimae fidei* (of the utmost good faith), so that a partner is required to disclose all relevant information in their possession to their partners. If they fail to do so, their partners may set aside transactions which they have entered into with them as a result of non-disclosure.

Similarly, a partner owes a fiduciary duty to their fellow partners; that is, they owe a duty of good faith to their partners in their dealings with them which a trustee owes to a beneficiary.

23.3.2 Statutory provisions regarding good faith

The requirement of good faith in dealings between partners is of general application, but three particular aspects of the duty are dealt with explicitly in ss28–30 PA 1890.

23.3.2.1 Duty to disclose information

Section 28 provides that:

> Partners are bound to render true accounts and full information of all things affecting the partnership to any partner or his legal representative.

Effectively, this is a reformulation of the duty of disclosure imposed by equity.

A good illustration of the working of the rule is given by *Law v Law* [1905] 1 Ch 140. One partner offered to buy the share of another at a price which seemed fair to the vendor partner, although that partner was not actively engaged in running the business. The purchaser, however, knew of facts which made the vendor's share more valuable than the vendor realised. When the vendor discovered this, it was held that he was entitled to rescind the contract of sale on the ground of non-disclosure.

23.3.2.2 Duty to account for secret profits

Section 29 states that:

> (1) Every partner must account to the firm for any benefit derived by him without the consent of the other partners from any transaction concerning the partnership, or from any use by him of the partnership property, name or business connection.
>
> (2) This section applies also to transactions undertaken after a partnership has been dissolved by the death of a partner, and before the affairs thereof have been completely wound up, either by any surviving partner or by the representative of the deceased partner.

This section imposes similar restrictions and duties on partners as apply to company directors. Any profit made in breach of the section is held on trust for the benefit of the partnership as a whole. The rule applies to, for example:

(a) transactions entered into by a partner where the opportunity came to them as a result of the partnership or their being a partner;

(b) commissions received on contracts introduced to the partnership;

(c) sales of property to the partnership by a partner; and

(d) profits derived from sales of partnership property.

A partner may, however, retain any such profit if their partners consent following full disclosure of the circumstances.

Note that the obligation continues in respect of actions by partners after any dissolution of the partnership until its winding up.

23.3.2.3 Duty to account for profits from competing business

Section 30 PA 1890 provides that:

> If a partner, without the consent of the other partners, carries on any business of the same nature as and competing with that of the firm, he must account for and pay over to the firm all profits made by him in that business.

The provisions of s30 are quite narrow. In order to succeed under this section, the partners must show that the businesses are of the same nature and that they are in fact competing for the same customers. Thus in *Aas v Benham* [1891] 2 Ch 244, a partner in a firm of shipbrokers was held not to be accountable for profits he had made from shipbuilding. However, in *Glassington v Thwaites* (1823) 1 Sim & St 124, a partner in a morning newspaper who set up an evening newspaper was held to be accountable.

It should be noted that there is a possible overlap between s30 and s29(1)–a partner may be held accountable because they are competing with their partners or because they are using 'the partnership property name or business connection'; often a partner who sets up a new business will be doing both these things.

23.3.2.4 Preventing a partner from setting up a non-competing business

A partner who sets up a *non-competing* business and who does not use the partnership property, name or business connection is not liable to their partners in any way under the Act. Many partnership agreements, therefore, provide that the partners are to devote their whole time to the partnership and specify that the partners are not to start any other businesses.

With such an agreement, the partners may be able to obtain an injunction, damages or dissolution of the partnership against the partner who sets up a new business, even though it does not compete with the firm's business. They will not, however, have any right to make that partner contribute their profits in the other business to the partnership.

23.4 Partnership finances

23.4.1 Sources of finance

A partnership will need assets and cash in order to run its business. The sources of finance for a partnership are basically the same as those available to any business. Money (or in some cases assets) may be contributed in the form of a permanent investment by the partners (capital) or it may be borrowed from either the partners or outside sources. (When a partnership comes to an end, the distinction between money invested by a partner and money lent by a partner is important, as the latter sum will be payable first.) Once the business of the partnership has started, further finance may also be provided by retention of profits.

23.4.2 Partners' capital

The permanent investment of a partner is described as 'capital'. The capital of a partner may be contributed in the form of cash and/or property (including, eg, business premises or the goodwill of an existing business). The term 'capital' refers to the actual cash or other assets contributed to the partnership by a partner and the indebtedness of the partnership as a whole to the partner resulting from this investment. A partner's capital in this sense should be contrasted with other debts which the firm owes to the partner, as repayment of the capital cannot normally be claimed from the firm until dissolution. Other indebtedness to a partner (eg a loan) may be repaid before dissolution.

23.5 The distinction between a partner and a lender

The essential nature of a partnership is that two or more people are sharing profits of a business. A person who merely lends to a partnership is not a partner. The distinction between a partner and a lender is extremely important as a partner bears unlimited liability for the debts of the partnership, whereas the lender only stands to lose the money invested if the business fails. However, if a business is successful, a partner stands to receive a share of profit, whereas a lender will receive only interest on the loan.

Many investors would like to have the best of both worlds; that is, a guaranteed return of their investment and a share of profits. However, s2(3) PA 1890 effectively restricts this type of investment. It provides that:

> The receipt by a person of a share of profits . . . is prima facie evidence that he is a partner . . . but does not of itself make him a partner . . .

The subsection then sets out some particular rules which provide that:

(a) A person does not become a partner merely because a debt or other liquidated sum is paid to them by instalments out of profits.

(b) A servant (employee) or agent does not become a partner merely because their remuneration varies with profits.

(c) A lender whose interest varies with profits is not automatically a partner if the contract is in writing and signed by all the parties.

Sharing of profits is only prima facie evidence of partnership. However, there remains a risk that anyone who receives a share of profits *may* be held to be a partner and therefore personally liable for debts.

Anyone entering into such an arrangement who does not wish to take on the risk of unlimited liability should take steps to ensure that they do not become a partner, for example by avoiding any suggestion that they have a right to take part in management and by having a written agreement setting out the terms of their involvement with the firm.

23.6 **Division of profits and sharing of losses between partners**

Section 24 PA 1890 lays down a number of rules as to division of profits. These rules may be varied by an express or implied agreement of the partners, and for the avoidance of doubt (and to avoid any unexpected outcomes) it is preferable to state in a partnership agreement how both profits *and* losses are to be shared, even if the agreement follows some of the statutory presumptions.

23.6.1 **Share of profits and losses (s24(1))**

Section 24(1) states:

> All the partners are entitled to share equally in the capital and profits of the business, and must contribute equally towards the losses whether of capital or otherwise sustained by the firm.

This rule may be broken down into three parts, which will be examined in turn. However, the basic starting point is that of equality when it comes to any profits in the firm.

In turn, this rule applies to capital as well as income profits. 'Capital profits' is the term for amounts remaining following the payment of all creditors and repayment of capital contributions to partners on the dissolution of a partnership. (In other words, the value of the partnership business as a whole exceeds both the capital contributions of the partners and its business liabilities.) Income profits will be the profits generated on an ongoing basis by the partnership business.

23.6.1.1 Sharing of capital

The first part of the rule states that 'all the partners are entitled to share equally in the capital'. On the face of it, this means that when a partner leaves the firm or when the firm is dissolved, they are entitled to take out a part of the capital corresponding with the total amount of capital divided by the number of partners.

EXAMPLE

Mark, Eliza and Zak are in partnership.

Each of Mark, Eliza and Zak contributed £20,000 to the partnership business when it started.

The capital base of the partnership is now valued at £150,000.

Ignoring liabilities, upon the dissolution of the partnership each partner would be entitled to:

(a) the return of their capital contribution of £20,000;

(b) a one-third, ie equal, share of the remainder, ie £30,000.

However, the rules in s24 are subject to contrary agreement express or implied. Where the partners have contributed unequally to the capital, there is an *implied* agreement that they are entitled to withdraw capital unequally. However, unless there is specific agreement to the contrary, any capital profits will be divided equally between the partners.

EXAMPLE

Mark, Eliza and Zak are in partnership.

Mark contributed £10,000, Eliza £20,000 and Zak £30,000 to the partnership business when it started.

The capital base of the partnership is now valued at £150,000.

Ignoring liabilities, upon the dissolution of the partnership each partner would be entitled to:

(a) the return of their individual capital contribution;

(b) a one-third share of the remainder, ie £30,000, due to the effect of s24(1).

If an unequal division of capital profits was desired, for example in the same ratio as capital was provided, the partners would need to have made this explicit in some way. The ratio in which capital profits are divided (sometimes called the 'asset surplus ratio') can be different from the income profit-sharing ratio.

23.6.1.2 Sharing of profits

The second part of the rule in s24(1) states that 'all the partners are entitled to share equally in the profits of the business'. Here we will focus on income profits.

If a partner is to receive more than an equal share of income profits because of their capital contribution or the work they do or their seniority, this must be specifically agreed and should be expressly stated in the partnership agreement or, at least, made explicit to all partners, if a partnership agreement has not been entered into.

The provision of capital in unequal shares *does not* give rise to the implication that this part of the rule has been displaced in respect of income profits.

EXAMPLE

Mark, Eliza and Zak are in partnership.

Mark contributed £10,000, Eliza £20,000 and Zak £30,000 to the partnership business when it started.

Income profits for the most recent financial year are £180,000.

Each partner would be entitled to £60,000 due to the effect of s24(1).

23.6.1.3 Sharing of losses

The third part of the rule in s24(1) states that partners 'must contribute equally towards the losses whether of capital or otherwise sustained by the firm'. This is a curious phrase because it seems to focus more on capital losses than income losses. Arguably, however, this is logical, as an income loss will simply result in partners being unable to take out any profit share and, in turn, they must presumably write off their share of the loss against next year's profits or any outstanding undrawn profits. (This will often be dealt with by partners' current accounts, which will act as a record of allocation of profits and drawings.)

More importantly are capital losses, which usually come to light on a dissolution.

EXAMPLE

Mark, Eliza and Zak are in partnership.

Mark contributed £10,000, Eliza £20,000 and Zak £30,000 to the partnership business when it started.

The partners shared income profits equally.

The capital base of the partnership is valued at £30,000 on dissolution, having met liabilities to external creditors.

On the basis that total capital contributions from partners amount to £60,000, the question is how the £30,000 deficit is to be met.

Unless there is agreement to the contrary, each partner will bear an equal share of the loss, ie £10,000.

As such:

(a) Mark will receive nothing;

(b) Eliza will receive £10,000;

(c) Zak will receive £20,000.

Alternatively, if it has been expressly agreed that capital losses shall be borne in the same ratio as capital contributions:

(a) Mark must bear a one-sixth share of the loss (£5,000) and will receive £5,000;

(b) Eliza must bear a one-third share of the loss (£10,000) and will receive £10,000;

(c) Zak must bear a one half share of the loss (£15,000) and will receive £15,000.

Note that if the partners share profits unequally (because of an express or implied agreement to do so), then s44 PA 1890 says that losses will also be shared unequally unless there is an agreement to the contrary.

23.6.2 Interest on capital

Section 24(4) provides that: 'A partner is not entitled . . . to interest on capital.' Where capital is contributed unequally, it may be considered appropriate to make provision in the partnership agreement for interest on capital to compensate the partner who has contributed more. The agreement should specify the rate of interest or the method by which the rate is to be determined.

Interest on capital is *not* a deductible expense of the business in determining its net profits; it is merely a preferential appropriation of profits. This means that once the net profit of the partnership has been ascertained, the partners' first entitlement will be to interest, and then the remaining net profit will be allocated in accordance with the agreed profit-sharing ratio. This will be dealt with through the partners' appropriation accounts.

EXAMPLE

Mark, Eliza and Zak are in partnership.

Mark contributed £10,000, Eliza £10,000 and Zak £40,000 to the partnership business when it started.

The partners share income profits equally. It has been agreed that Zak will receive 5% annual interest on his capital contribution.

The business has generated profit of £92,000.

Zak will receive £2,000 interest on his capital, leaving £90,000 to be divided equally between the three partners.

23.6.3 Interest on loans

In the absence of contrary agreement, a loan by a partner to the partnership (in contrast to a capital contribution) carries 5% interest (s24(3)). It should be noted that this rate of interest is paid only on 'actual payments or advances'. Interest is not payable under s24(3) on a share of profits which is simply left in the business.

23.6.4 Remuneration of partners

Section 24(6) provides that:

> No partner shall be entitled to remuneration for acting in the partnership business.

This presupposes that partners are rewarded solely by a share of profit.

Where such a method of reward is regarded as unsatisfactory, it will have to be expressly agreed that some (or all) of the partners be paid a salary. As with interest on capital, a salary payable to a partner is *not* a deductible expense but is merely a preferential appropriation of profit. As with interest on capital, this will be dealt with in the appropriation account.

EXAMPLE

In a partnership with three members (Dan, Ed and Fran) it might be agreed that:

(a) the profit-sharing ratio will be Dan 20%, Ed 40% and Fran 40%;

(b) interest on capital will be paid at a rate of 10% pa (Dan's capital is £10,000, Ed's £20,000 and Fran's £30,000); and

(c) Dan is to have a salary of £20,000 pa.

If profits of £100,000 are made, they will be apportioned as follows:

		£	£	£
Profit				100,000
Interest on capital:				
	Dan	1,000		
	Ed	2,000		
	Fran	3,000		
			6,000	
Salary:				
	Dan		20,000	
Share of profits:				
	Dan	14,800		
	Ed	29,600		
	Fran	29,600		
			74,000	
				100,000

In some partnerships (particularly professional partnerships), there may be relatively junior partners who are entitled to a salary to the exclusion of any other share of profits. At first sight, it is hard to see how such 'salaried partners' can be regarded as partners at all, as partnership requires that the partners are 'carrying on business in common with a view of profit' (s1(1) PA 1890). Nevertheless, in *Stekel v Ellice* [1973] 1 WLR 191, it was held that a salaried partner could be, in law, a full partner, with all the rights and duties which that entails; however, context is everything in this regard.

23.6.5 Drawings

The amount to which a partner is entitled from the profits in a firm (as salary and interest, if agreed to, and share of profits) will not be known until the profit and loss account has been drawn up after the end of the partnership's financial year. The partnership agreement will, therefore, usually provide that a partner is to have the right to take a specified amount of money on account of their expected profits during the course of the year. Sums taken on account in this way are called 'drawings'.

If, at the end of the year, the partner has taken less than they were entitled to, they can draw the balance; if they have taken more than it turns out they were entitled to, then the partnership agreement will probably require that partner to pay back the excess and/or pay interest on it. The partnership agreement may provide that each partner is to leave undrawn in the business a proportion of their entitlement to profit. This is because businesses normally need to retain funds to meet increased costs of trading and to fund any future expansion.

23.7 Partnership property

23.7.1 Introduction

A distinction must be drawn between assets in which all partners have a proprietary interest and assets which belong to individual partners, albeit that they are used by the partnership business. In particular, such a distinction is crucial when the firm is dissolved, as each partner is entitled to retain any property which is their own personal property; whereas, property which is partnership property is used first to pay creditors of the firm and then any surplus is distributed among the partners in accordance with the terms of the partnership agreement (equally, in the absence of contrary agreement).

23.7.2 Definition

Partnership property is partly defined by s20(1) PA 1890 as:

> All property and rights and interests in property originally brought into the partnership stock or acquired, whether by purchase or otherwise, on account of the firm, or for the purposes and in the course of the partnership business . . .

Section 21 deals with a slightly different situation and states:

> Unless the contrary intention appears, property bought with money belonging to the firm is deemed to have been bought on account of the firm.

23.7.3 The test

Whether property is partnership property or remains the separate property of a partner depends on the intention of the partners, express or implied. Property is not partnership property merely because it is used by the firm. There is no automatic assumption, therefore that property introduced by a partner thereby becomes partnership property.

This is illustrated by the leading case of *Miles v Clarke* [1953] 1 All ER 779. Clarke carried on a photographic business in premises of which he owned the lease. He and Miles went into partnership and for a time the business was successful. However, eventually a petition for dissolution was presented, as the partners were unable to agree. The question arose as to which assets were partnership property and which belonged to the partners individually. Harman J held that, in the absence of express agreement, he would hold property to be partnership property to the extent necessary to give business efficacy to the agreement. Therefore, the lease of the business premises belonged on dissolution to Clarke alone, each partner was entitled to his own business connections which he had brought into the firm, and only the stock-in-trade (unused films, chemicals etc) could be regarded as partnership property.

KEY POINT SUMMARY

- Partnership is a relationship between the partners. A partnership can, therefore, be seen as matrix of legal and equitable responsibilities and obligations between partners.
- The Partnership Act 1890 will operate to regulate, in part, this relationship, subject to contrary agreement.
- In particular, partners owe each other a duty of good faith which entails particular obligations, for example a duty to disclose relevant information to fellow partners.
- Partnerships will usually finance themselves both by contributions of capital by the partners and by borrowings from external (or possibly internal) sources.
- The division of profits and sharing of losses between partners is a crucial matter. The basic presumption is equality–this is reflected in the relevant provisions of the Partnership Act 1890. It is possible for partners to agree alternative approaches.
- Property used in the partnership business may belong to individual partners or to the partnership as a whole, in which case it is partnership property. The distinction is particularly important on the dissolution of a partnership.

CHAPTER 24
Liability of Partners to Outsiders

FUNCTIONING LEGAL KNOWLEDGE

This chapter considers the following functioning legal knowledge included in the SRA's SQE 1 assessment specification:

Business and organisational characteristics (sole trader/partnership/LLP/private and unlisted public companies)

Legal personality and limited liability

Partnership decision-making and authority of partners:

- procedures and authority under the Partnership Act 1890
- common provisions in partnership agreements.

AUTHORITIES UNDERPINNING PRACTICE

The key authorities that underpin this area of practice are listed below. Note that for legislation you are linked to legislation.gov.uk.

Although much of the legislation on this government website is available in its amended form, the incorporation of new amendments into the text of legislation can be delayed. You should refer to legal databases to ensure you are referencing the most up-to-date legislation.

- Partnership Act 1890
  http://www.legislation.gov.uk/ukpga/Vict/53-54/39

24.1 Introduction

In the course of carrying on a partnership's business, the partners will incur debts and other obligations in respect of third parties. After consulting this chapter, you will have been introduced to:

(a) the nature of partners' liabilities in these circumstances as well as the extent to which the actions of an individual partner can bind the partnership as a whole;

(b) whether or not it is possible for individuals who are not partners at the time the debt or obligation was incurred to be liable for the same.

24.2 Nature of liability

Partners are liable for the debts and obligations of the partnership operations without limit (s9 Partnership Act 1890 (PA 1890)). Their liability is joint in the case of contractual obligations and joint and several in the case of tortious obligations (see **24.6**).

The significance of this distinction was much reduced by s3 of the Civil Liability (Contribution) Act 1978, which allows proceedings to be brought successively against persons jointly liable despite an earlier judgment against others.

Where a partnership is unable to pay its debts out of *partnership property*, the creditor is entitled to obtain payment from the private estates of the partners. Special rules apply in such cases in an attempt to do justice both to the creditors of the firm and to the creditors of the individual partners.

It is not the intention to deal with these rules in detail. However, they may be summarised as follows:

(a) In the first instance, the partnership property is used to pay partnership creditors in priority to private creditors and the private property of each partner is used to pay their private creditors in priority to partnership creditors.

(b) If the partnership creditors cannot be paid in full from partnership property, then those creditors rank equally with the private creditors in having their claims met by the partners' private property.

(c) If the private creditors of a particular partner cannot be paid in full from private property, then those creditors may claim from partnership property only after all the partnership creditors have been satisfied.

24.3 Partnership and agency

24.3.1 Introduction

The relationship between partnership law and agency is very close; most of the rules regulating the relationship between a partnership and the outside world can be explained purely in terms of particular applications of agency principles. As partners are agents of each other, the actions of a single partner can have major consequences for the partners as a whole.

24.3.2 Types of authority of a partner

The partnership as a whole is bound by a partner acting within the scope of their authority. The authority of a partner may arise in three ways:

1. First, the authority of a partner may be specifically agreed upon by the partners. Authority of this type is called 'express actual' authority.
2. Secondly, authority may be implied either from a course of dealings between the partners (which amounts to an actual agreement) or because the authority is a natural consequence of an authority actually given to the partner. This is normally called 'implied actual' authority.
3. Thirdly, authority may arise from the fact that a person dealing with a partner is, in those circumstances, entitled to assume that the partner has authority to bind the firm. This type of authority is generally called 'apparent' or 'ostensible' authority, although terminology in agency law is far from consistent.

24.3.3 Express and implied actual authority

The scope of express and implied actual authority depends on the agreement or arrangements between the partners. The partnership agreement may specify what powers the partners individually are to have and may specify that some are to have greater powers than others.

The extent of actual authority, whether express or implied, is not, in practical terms, of great significance to a third party dealing with a partner. This is because, whether or not there is actual authority, the third party will be able to rely on apparent authority in most circumstances. The outsider need only rely on actual authority where the partner has done something which the law does not consider to be within the apparent authority of a partner.

The PA 1890 has little to say about a partner's actual authority. However, s6 recognises that a firm is bound by 'acts or instruments':

(a) entered into in the firm's name;

(b) by an authorised person (albeit that person need not be a partner);

(c) showing an intention to bind the firm.

Note, however, that a single partner cannot bind a partnership to a deed (in contrast to a contract), unless their authority to do so is itself expressly granted by deed, for instance a power of attorney. If there are a small number of partners, it may, therefore, be preferable for all partners to execute the deed personally.

24.3.4 **Apparent authority**

24.3.4.1 General principles

The scope of apparent (or ostensible) authority is sometimes said to result from a type of estoppel whereby the principal (in this case the partnership as a whole) represents, by words or conduct (in a relatively wide sense), that the agent (ie the partner who is negotiating with the outsider) has authority to bind the firm. Once such a representation is acted upon by the outsider, the partnership cannot deny the authority of the individual partner to bind the firm.

24.3.4.2 Section 5 PA 1890

The liability of a firm may result from the actual holding out of an agent (not necessarily a partner) as having a particular authority. However, in most cases the outsider seeks to rely on an apparent authority resulting from the fact that a person is known to be a partner in a firm. The outsider is then entitled to assume that the partner has the usual authority of a partner to bind their firm.

This principle is laid down in s5 PA 1890, which says:

> Every partner is an agent for the firm and his other partners for the purpose of the business of the partnership; and the acts of every partner who does any act for carrying on in the usual way the business of the kind carried on by the firm of which he is a member bind the firm and his partners, unless the partner so acting has in fact no authority to act for the firm in the particular matter, and the person with whom he is dealing either knows that he has no authority, or does not know or believe him to be a partner.

To understand the scope of the section, it is necessary to examine each of the qualifications on a partner's authority which the section recognises.

Partner can only bind the firm 'for the purposes of the business of the partnership'

The first qualification is that the partner can only bind the firm 'for the purposes of the business of the partnership'. The section does not say, therefore, that *anything* which a partner does binds the firm. The partnership agreement may be of some assistance in deciding what is the scope of the partnership business. However, it is not conclusive. In *Mercantile Credit Co Ltd v Garrod* [1962] 3 All ER 1103, Mocatta J held that the test as to whether a type of business is within the scope of the partnership depends on what is apparent to the outside world in general. Consequently, a sleeping partner in a garage business whose agreement specifically excluded dealing in cars was held liable on a contract for the sale of a car as this was within the scope of what outsiders would expect the business to include.

Partner must do act 'for carrying on in the usual way the business of the firm'

The second qualification in s5 is that the partnership is only bound if a partner does an act 'for carrying on in the usual way the business of the firm'. This restriction excludes the liability of the firm where the transaction is for the purposes of the business but is itself of an unusual type. For example, in *Niemann v Niemann* (1890) 43 ChD 198 a debt was owed to a partnership; one of the partners intended to accept payment of the debt in the form of **shares** in a company. This was held not to be binding on the other partner in the absence of a specific agreement. Similarly, *Powell v Brodhurst* [1901] 2 Ch 160 decided that a partner does not have ostensible authority to accept payment of a debt due to another partner personally rather than to the firm.

No actual authority and outsider knows this or does not know or believe that person is a partner

The third qualification to s5 is that the firm is not bound if the partner has no actual authority and the outsider either knows this or does not know or believe the person with whom they are dealing to be a partner. In such cases, the outsider cannot say that they have relied on any representation, nor can they claim that there appeared to be authority when they know this to be untrue or do not think they are dealing with an agent at all.

By way of a further example of how significant a third party's actual knowledge is, s8 PA 1890 provides that any agreed restriction placed on the powers of a partner will be effective to prevent the firm being bound, if the third party has notice of it.

A partner who makes a contract with an outsider without authority will be personally liable to the outsider for breach of warranty of authority where the partnership as a whole is not made liable on the contract, thus giving the outsider a cause of action against that partner. However, where a contract made without authority is ratified by the partnership (ie formally approved after the event), it becomes binding on the firm as well as on the outsider.

24.3.5 Examples of apparent authority

The question of what apparent authority a partner has in a particular case is determined by the application of s5 to that particular case. This is, in part, a question of fact. However, over the years the courts have decided upon examples of powers which will usually be assumed to be covered by apparent authority in the case of all partners.

The courts have also recognised certain powers which it will be assumed all partners in a trading partnership have, in the absence of some special circumstance. The powers of partners in a trading partnership are more extensive than the powers of partners in general. This is because the court recognises the need of the partners and the persons dealing with them to rely on normal trading practices.

Examples of powers assumed to be available to partners generally include:

(a) power to buy and sell goods (not just stock) used in the business;
(b) power to hire employees;
(c) power to receive payment of debts due to the partnership;
(d) power to pay debts owed by the partnership including a power to draw cheques for this purpose;
(e) power to engage a solicitor to represent the firm.

A partner in a trading partnership will be assumed to have all the above powers and also:

(a) power to grant **security** for borrowings (this does not, however, include a power to create a legal mortgage);
(b) a wider power than is given to a non-trading partner to deal with cheques and bills of exchange.

24.4 Persons held out as partners: s14 PA 1890

So far we have only considered the liability of actual partners to outsiders. A person who holds themselves out as a partner or who 'suffers himself to be represented as a partner' is liable to anyone who 'on the faith of such representation' gives credit to the firm as if they were a partner (s14 PA 1890). Whilst this rule is of general application, perhaps the commonest example of its application is where a person allows their name to be continued to be used by the partnership (eg on notepaper or the firm's website) after they have ceased to be a partner.

The wording of s14 is extensive as it applies to any person 'who by words spoken or written or by conduct represents himself or who knowingly suffers himself to be represented' as a partner. As such, it can equally apply to an 'active' representation by the person in question as well as a 'passive' one, for example by allowing their name to be given as a partner. For this reason, a departing partner should ensure that their details are removed from stationery, the website and any other partnership literature.

Section 14 only applies where credit is given to the firm. This is construed widely so that, for example, the apparent partner is liable where goods are delivered, as well as where money is lent, to the firm.

(For further discussion of this topic, see **25.5.3.4**.)

24.5 Liability of new partners

Section 17(1) PA 1890 provides that 'a person who is admitted as a partner into an existing firm does not thereby become liable to the creditors of the firm for anything done before he became a partner'. This provision ensures that an incoming partner is not liable to the existing creditors of the firm merely because they have become a partner.

It should always be remembered that partners' liabilities to the outside world are legally predetermined. However, it is possible for partners to agree between themselves how they may choose to discharge those liabilities. As such, as between the incoming partner and the existing partners, the incoming partner may agree to assume responsibility for a share of debts owed to existing creditors. This does not, however, make them directly liable to the existing creditors.

24.6 Partners' liability in tort

A partner who commits a tort is liable according to general principles of the law of tort. The liability of the firm as a whole is governed by s10 PA 1890, which states:

> Where, by any wrongful act or omission of any partner acting in the ordinary course of the business of the firm, or with the authority of his co-partners, loss or injury is caused to any person . . . the firm is liable . . . to the same extent as the partner so acting or omitting to act.

It should be noted that the firm (as opposed to the actual tortfeasor) is only liable if either the commission of the tort was authorised by the partners or it was committed 'in the ordinary course of business'. This latter phrase has been given a wide meaning to make it effective. Arguably, no firm is in the business of committing torts; however, if the tortious actions of the partner occur within the context of what a partner is normally required to do, the firm will usually be liable.

A partnership is also liable to the same extent as other employers (under common law principles of vicarious liability) for torts committed by its employees.

24.7 Suing or being sued

A partnership is not a separate legal entity. Nevertheless, the partners should usually sue or be sued in the firm's name under para 5A.3 of Practice Direction 7A to the Civil Procedure Rules. All the partners at the date when the cause of action accrued are then parties to the action. Where an action is brought against a partnership in the firm's name, the claim form may be served on any partner, or any person having control or management of the business at the principal place of business (r6.5 Civil Procedure Rules).

KEY POINT SUMMARY

This chapter has addressed the following topics:

- Partners' liability for debts and obligations of the partnership business is unlimited.
- Partners are agents of each other, with the result that any partner's actions may be binding on the firm as whole.

- Partners can act with both actual and apparent authority. Either type of authority is sufficient to bind the firm.
- Liability of partners only extends to the duration of their membership of the firm. A partner will be liable for matters which occurred whilst a partner and will not cease to be liable on leaving the partnership. In turn, partners joining a firm will not automatically assume responsibility for any liabilities or obligations in existence prior to the date of their joining.
- Tortious actions of one partner may result in liability for all partners if the tort was committed in the course of the partnership business.
- A partnership is not a legal person separate from its partners. Usually, however, a claimant has the ability to sue the firm as a whole.

CHAPTER 25
Termination of and Retirement From a Partnership

FUNCTIONING LEGAL KNOWLEDGE

This chapter considers the following functioning legal knowledge included in the SRA's SQE 1 assessment specification:

Business and organisational characteristics (sole trader/partnership/LLP/private and unlisted public companies)

Legal personality and limited liability

Partnership decision-making and authority of partners:

- procedures and authority under the Partnership Act 1890
- common provisions in partnership agreements

AUTHORITIES UNDERPINNING PRACTICE

The key authorities that underpin this area of practice are listed below. Note that for legislation you are linked to legislation.gov.uk.

Although much of the legislation on this government website is available in its amended form, the incorporation of new amendments into the text of legislation can be delayed. You should refer to legal databases to ensure you are referencing the most up-to-date legislation.

- Partnership Act 1890
  http://www.legislation.gov.uk/ukpga/Vict/53-54/39
- Insolvent Partnerships Order 1994
  https://www.legislation.gov.uk/uksi/1994/2421/contents/made

25.1 Introduction

After consulting this chapter, you will have been introduced to the legal consequences of a partner leaving the partnership. On the basis that partnership is a legal relationship between partners, the departure of any partner will be a significant event.

An individual will cease to be a partner on the happening of one of the following events:

(a) retirement (as a partner);

(b) death;

(c) **bankruptcy**; or

(d) expulsion from the partnership.

Under the Partnership Act 1890 (PA 1890) these events result in automatic dissolution unless the partnership agreement provides otherwise. If an event occurs which causes a partnership to be dissolved, the partnership relationship ceases and any partner may demand that the assets of the business are realised to pay off creditors, after which any surplus can be distributed to partners (a so-called 'general' dissolution).

Dissolution is such an extreme step that it is advisable for partners to provide expressly in their partnership agreement that dissolution is *not* to occur automatically on the occurrence of the events specified in the PA 1890.

Further, the 'retirement' of a partner is, technically speaking, not retirement at all but a dissolution of the partnership, on the basis that the partnership will no longer continue in the way it was originally constituted. However, a well-drafted partnership agreement will preserve the partnership business and allow it to continue under the guise of the new partnership formed by the remaining partners.

Finally, dissolution can be agreed upon by all the partners or can be brought about by the actions of an individual partner, either by application to court for an order for dissolution or because the partnership is 'at will'.

These matters will be considered within this chapter.

25.2 The methods of dissolving a partnership

25.2.1 Dissolution by notice

Under ss26 and 32(c) PA 1890, any partner can, at any time, give notice to their fellow partners to dissolve the partnership, if its duration is undefined. This notice takes effect from the date specified in the notice but if the notice is silent on the point, it takes effect from the date when all partners received the notice. Dissolution under ss26 and 32(c) can result in an immediate dissolution of the partnership. This could have serious consequences for the firm's business.

The effect of ss26 and 32(c) can be displaced if the partnership agreement contains provisions to the contrary. As a result, a well-drafted partnership agreement should require a minimum period of notice to be given before the partnership is dissolved. It may also stipulate dates during the year when such notice can only be given, which can provide an element of predictability. Further, a defined duration for the existence of the partnership may be stipulated.

25.2.2 Dissolution by agreement

The partnership agreement can specify circumstances which cause the partnership to be dissolved, such as the occurrence of a particular event. The agreement can also specify the manner in which the partnership will be dissolved. Irrespective of this, if all partners agree to a dissolution, then this will trigger the same.

25.2.3 Automatic dissolution

A number of events cause partnerships to dissolve automatically (subject to contrary agreement).

25.2.3.1 Bankruptcy, death or charge

The death or bankruptcy of a partner causes the partnership to be automatically dissolved, unless the partnership agreement contains provisions to the contrary (s33(1) PA 1890). In consequence of this, many partnership agreements provide that instead of causing automatic dissolution, the death of a partner shall give rise to the same consequences as a retirement (see **25.5**). A bankruptcy is often treated in the same way as an expulsion (see **26.5.3**).

If a partner allows their share of the partnership property to be charged in support of their personal debts, the other partners have an *option* to dissolve the partnership (s33(2) PA 1890).

25.2.3.2 Illegality

Partnerships formed to carry out an illegal activity or which are contrary to public policy are automatically dissolved. A change of circumstances (including a change in the law) can subsequently make illegal a partnership initially formed for a legal purpose, for example the introduction of licences into a particular business sector without which the business would be unlawful. In these circumstances, s34 PA 1890 provides that the partnership is dissolved on the happening of the event which makes the business unlawful (eg the date the change in the law takes effect). A provision to the contrary in the partnership agreement will not override s34.

25.2.3.3 By expiration

Under s32(a) and (b) PA 1890, a partnership is dissolved:

- if it was entered into for a fixed term, upon the expiration of that term;
- if it was entered into for a single purpose or undertaking, upon the completion of that purpose or undertaking.

A provision to the contrary in the partnership agreement overrides s32(a) and (b) but obviously must anticipate the situation after either expiry of the term or completion of the purpose.

If the agreement is silent and the partnership continues despite the occurrence of the events set out above, s27 provides that a partnership at will, dissolvable by notice, is brought into existence. Such a partnership is subject to the terms of the original agreement to the extent that these do not conflict with the incidents of a partnership at will.

25.2.4 Dissolution by the court

A partner may apply to the court for dissolution of the partnership provided one of the statutory grounds for dissolution by the court exists. This is only really an appropriate step when an easier method of dissolution is not available, either under the PA 1890 or under any partnership agreement.

Section 35 PA 1890 sets out grounds for dissolution by the court. Those grounds which give the partners a remedy in the event of a dispute (s35(c), (d) and (f)) are considered in more detail at **26.2**.

The full list of s35 grounds follows.

25.2.4.1 Section 35(a)

This subsection is repealed and is now covered by s16 of the Mental Capacity Act 2005, under which a court may make an order, the effect of which is to dissolve a partnership of which a partner is a **member** (s18(1)(e) Mental Capacity Act 2005), if that partner is deemed to lack capacity, as defined by s2 of the same Act.

25.2.4.2 Section 35(b)

> When a partner, other than the partner making the application to court, becomes permanently incapable of performing his part of the partnership contract.

Whether or not a partner has become *permanently* incapable is a question of fact. Since there may be difficulties in proving either that the partner is incapable or that their incapacity is permanent, and since there will be difficulties in running a partnership where a partner has a long illness, it is common to include a term in the partnership agreement allowing expulsion or insisting on retirement once a partner has been absent through illness for more than a specified time.

25.2.4.3 Section 35(c)

> When a partner, other than the partner making the application to court, has been guilty of such conduct as, in the opinion of the court, regard being had to the nature of the business, is calculated to affect prejudicially the carrying on of the business.

25.2.4.4 Section 35(d)

> When a partner, other than the partner making the application to court, wilfully or persistently commits a breach of the partnership agreement, or otherwise so conducts himself in matters relating to the partnership business that it is not reasonably practicable for the other partner or partners to carry on the business in partnership with him.

25.2.4.5 Section 35(e)

> When the business of the partnership can only be carried on at a loss.

In order for s35(e) to be invoked, the circumstances must be such as to make it a practical impossibility for the partnership to make a profit. If the partners who find themselves in this position cannot agree to bring the partnership to an end, this may be a valuable right if a delay in terminating the partnership will increase the amount of the loss, for which all the partners will be personally liable. It is important to note that a partnership is not necessarily insolvent simply because it is making a loss. It may well have valuable assets which, when sold, will discharge all liabilities and provide a surplus for the partners.

25.2.4.6 Section 35(f)

> Whenever in any case circumstances have arisen which, in the opinion of the court, render it just and equitable that the partnership be dissolved.

Usually it will have to be demonstrated that the continued operations of the partnership have become untenable, often due to a breakdown in the relationship between the partners which has led to either deadlock or management 'paralysis'. Alternatively, this ground may be evoked where the purposes of the partnership business can no longer effectively be achieved.

25.3 The legal consequences of dissolution

25.3.1 Continuing authority of partners for purposes of winding up (s38 PA 1890)

Subsequent to the dissolution of a partnership, various steps will need to be taken to wind up the affairs of the firm. Section 38 provides that, after the dissolution, the authority of each partner to bind the firm (as well as the other rights and obligations of the partners) continues despite the dissolution, but only to the extent necessary to wind up the affairs of the partnership and to complete transactions begun but unfinished at the time of the dissolution.

However, where the dissolution is by order of the court, this authority can be terminated by the appointment of a receiver (who will simply wind up the business) or of a receiver and manager (who will continue running the business but only with a view to the beneficial realisation of the assets by means of, eg, a sale of the business as a going concern). Such appointments are likely to be made where there is a possibility of dispute if the former partners try to wind up the affairs of the partnership.

25.3.2 Realisation of partnership property on dissolution

Once the firm has been dissolved, the value of the assets owned by the partnership will be ascertained, as will the extent of the debts and liabilities owed to creditors. Insofar as it is necessary, the assets will be sold to raise the funds to discharge the debts. The partners may merely sell the assets used in the business or they may decide to sell the business as a going concern.

If the partners decide to adopt the latter course of action, they may be able to sell the business for more than the aggregate market value of the assets used in the business because the sale price may take into account the 'goodwill' attaching to the business. (It should be borne in mind that the purchasers in this instance may well be some of the partners from the dissolved firm who wish to continue the business under a new guise.)

Goodwill has been defined judicially as 'the whole advantage, whatever it may be, of the reputation and connection of the firm' (*Trego v Hunt* [1896] AC 7). This 'advantage' can arise as a result of various factors. If the partners have considerable expertise in their chosen field, their customers may return repeatedly. This 'goodwill' may, however, be largely personal to the partners, with the result that it would disappear if they ceased their involvement in the business.

Conversely, if the firm is situated in a prime location (eg the main shopping street in the town), the business may be very successful because of the convenience of access for its customers. In this latter case, the goodwill may attach to the premises rather than the partners and so may be a very valuable asset of the partnership since it can be passed on to successors.

Where goodwill is sold, the purchasers will want to protect their investment against the loss of custom arising from the former owners setting up in competition in the same vicinity. Accordingly, the purchaser may wish to impose a restrictive covenant in the sale agreement to guard against this possibility. If the purchasers are some of the partners of the dissolved partnership, they too should consider imposing restrictive covenants on the outgoing partners to protect their interests.

25.3.3 Application of the partnership property on dissolution (ss39 and 44 PA 1890)

Once the assets and liabilities have been ascertained, s39 entitles each partner to have the property of the partnership applied so that the debts and liabilities of the firm are discharged first. Once these liabilities have been met, any surplus is distributed to the partners (after deducting any sums for which each partner is liable to contribute to the firm, eg contributions to make up losses or deficiencies of capital).

In order to ensure that the assets of the partnership are not distributed to the partners personally before the outside creditors are paid off, s39 goes on to give each partner the right to apply to the court to wind up the business and affairs of the firm in such a way as to ensure that the s39 order for application of assets is observed.

Section 44 provides that once the creditors of the firm have been paid, subject to any contrary agreement, the assets of the firm shall be applied in the following order:

(a) in repaying advances (ie, loans) received from partners;

(b) in repaying the amounts shown as standing to the credit of each partner on their capital account; and

(c) any balance being divided between the partners in accordance with the profit-sharing ratio.

If the partnership has made losses (including losses or deficiencies of capital), these shall be met in the following order:

(a) from profits;

(b) from capital;

(c) by the partners in the proportion in which profits are divisible.

Both parts of s44 are subject to contrary agreement. In particular, the partners may agree to share surplus assets and to contribute to capital losses in a ratio different from the one used for normal profit-sharing.

25.3.4 Notification of the dissolution

Any partner in a dissolved firm is entitled publicly to notify the fact of the dissolution and can seek the concurrence of other partners in achieving this aim (s37 PA 1890).

25.4 Financial problems on dissolution

25.4.1 Introduction

When the value of the partnership business is insufficient to pay back all monies owing, problems can arise on a dissolution. Such a shortfall can result in two main outcomes:

(a) either the outside creditors can be paid off but there is insufficient cash to pay back partners' capital contributions; or

(b) there is not even enough to pay back outside liabilities.

Each of these will be looked at in turn.

25.4.2 Insufficient funds to pay back partners' capital

This is best explained by reference to a number of examples.

EXAMPLE 1

Alun, Rhian and Eda are in partnership sharing profits equally, each having contributed £50,000 to the partnership. If only £90,000 remains (after paying off creditors), then there is a shortfall (loss) of £60,000, which according to s44(a) should be borne equally.

Technically, each partner should pay into the business £20,000 so that each can draw out their £50,000 in full. It is plainly impractical to do this, however, and each partner would simply draw out £30,000.

EXAMPLE 2

Suppose that Alun, Rhian and Eda are in partnership sharing profits equally, each having contributed £50,000, £40,000 and £10,000 respectively to the partnership.

If only £40,000 remains to satisfy partners' contributions, there is a shortfall of £60,000, which should be borne equally.

Prima facie, each partner will have to pay in £20,000 to receive back their original contributions.

In reality, however, Alun and Rhian will pay nothing and Eda will contribute £10,000. (This figure is reached by setting off Eda's capital entitlement against the £20,000 contribution.)

The resulting £50,000 (£40,000 + £10,000) will then be divided between Alun and Rhian to give them £30,000 and £20,000 respectively, which amounts to their initial capital contributions less £20,000.

EXAMPLE 3

Suppose in Example 2 that Eda could not, in fact, contribute any further money. According to *Garner v Murray* [1904] 1 Ch 57, Alun and Rhian would not have to make good this deficiency but would simply pay in £20,000 each in the usual way.

The resulting £80,000 would then be distributed between Alun and Rhian according to their ratio of contribution; that is 5:4. In this way:

(a) Alun would receive £44,444.45 (5/9 × £80,000); and

(b) Rhian would receive £35,555.55 (4/9 × £80,000).

Alternatively, the above could be carried out as a paper exercise, but then, instead of paying in any money, the £40,000 available would be distributed as follows:

(a) Alun would receive £24,444.45 (£44,444.45 – £20,000); and

(b) Rhian would receive £15,555.55 (£35,555.55 – £20,000).

25.4.3 Insufficient funds to meet liability to creditors

So far it has been assumed that liabilities to creditors and partners' loans have been fully satisfied. If the assets of a partnership prove insufficient to meet these liabilities first, the situation is much the same; any deficiency must be made up by partners according to their profit-sharing ratios (subject to any contrary agreement). Again, the problem comes when a partner is unable to contribute. Here the situation is more pressing because the overriding effect of s9 means that outside creditors are not concerned with the niceties of s44 and the partners who can pay must pay to satisfy these liabilities. If this is not done, then the outside creditors will look to enforce their entitlements by legal means.

The inability of partners to pay off their creditors is a topic in itself–such partners will face potential bankruptcy. However, since the Insolvent Partnerships Order 1994 (amending the previous Order of 1986), it has been possible for creditors to apply to have a partnership wound up as if it were an unregistered company. This procedure is essentially the same as for a registered company. However, often such an application is made in conjunction with bankruptcy petitions against the partners in question.

The law on insolvent partners/partnership is labyrinthine and less than satisfactory, so reference to a dedicated text on this issue should be made to discover more. However, the important factor to remember is that not only will the partners have creditors which arise from the operation of the partnership business, they will usually also have personal creditors. In turn, there are two pools from which these creditors may be satisfied: partnership assets (the so-called 'joint estate') and each partner's personal estate. In very basic terms, the firm's creditors will claim against the joint estate, whilst the individual creditors will claim against the personal estates. On the basis that either the firm or one or more of the partners is insolvent, these two separate pools will be insufficient to meet all liabilities. As such, the priorities between these two classes of creditors is where many of the complications lie.

25.5 Retirement of a partner

25.5.1 Circumstances when 'retirement' occurs

In the partnership context, 'retirement' simply means leaving the partnership voluntarily, irrespective of the age of the partner in question. (This is in contrast to *compulsory* retirement, which is considered at **26.5**.)

25.5.2 Retirement under the Partnership Act 1890

Partnership agreements can, and should, contain provisions dealing with retirement by partners. This is because the PA 1890 does not specifically allow for retirement (as was explained at the outset of this chapter). Under the Act, the only option available to a partner is to give notice under s26 (assuming it is applicable in the circumstances). If notice is given pursuant to s26, the partnership will be *dissolved in its entirety*; the section does not permit a partner to retire leaving the partnership business otherwise unaffected. To avoid this, suitable provisions must be included in the agreement.

One common form of wording provides that the partner wishing to retire should give written notice of a specified length (say, six months). On expiry of the notice period, the retiring partner will leave and may be entitled to some financial settlement from their former partners but, otherwise, the partnership and its business continues unaffected (although, technically speaking, this will be a new partnership).

25.5.3 The legal consequences of retirement

25.5.3.1 Debts incurred before retirement

The mere fact that a partner retires does not release them from their obligations in respect of debts incurred while they were a partner. Section 17(2) PA 1890 provides that:

> A partner who retires from a firm does not thereby cease to be liable for partnership debts or obligations incurred before his retirement.

To avoid the problems of having to meet such debts after retirement, the retiring partner should, if possible, ensure that the debts are paid before they leave. Since this may be difficult in many cases, the partner will be concerned to gain protection in other ways. The retiring partner is, therefore, likely to seek an indemnity from their former partners in respect of such debts. However, this is only likely to be granted where the sum paid to the retiring partner is discounted to reflect that partner's proportionate liability for those debts.

25.5.3.2 Debts incurred after retirement

The general rule is that only partners are liable for debts incurred by the partnership and so ceasing to be a partner prevents a retiring partner becoming liable on future debts, as retirement terminates the agency relationship. However, this general rule is subject to ss36 and 14 PA 1890. Under these sections, a former partner may become liable for debts incurred *after* they have left the partnership in certain circumstances.

25.5.3.3 Section 36

Section 36(3) provides that the estate of a partner:

> who, *not having been known to the person dealing with the firm to be a partner*... is not liable for partnership debts contracted after the date of the... retirement.

The date at which knowledge is tested for the purposes of this subsection is the date of retirement. If a creditor does not know at that date of the retiring partner's connection with the firm, the former partner will not be liable; the fact that the creditor may subsequently discover the former membership cannot make the former partner liable.

The subsection was considered in *Tower Cabinet Co Ltd v Ingram* [1949] 2 KB 397. A and B were in partnership. A retired and B continued the business under the old name. The business ordered goods from a new supplier and failed to pay. The supplier sought to enforce judgment against A. The only knowledge the supplier had of A's connection with the firm was that A's name appeared on headed notepaper which, contrary to A's express instructions, was still being used after his retirement. The court found that as the customer had no knowledge prior to A's retirement that A was a partner in the firm, A was completely protected by s36(3). (A further question arose of A's possible liability under s14(1)–see **25.5.3.4**.)

In cases where creditors *know* of the partner's connection with the firm before the former partner retires, s36(3) is of no assistance. Section 36(1), instead, provides that:

> Where a person deals with a firm after a change in its constitution, he is entitled to treat all apparent members of the old firm as still being members of the firm until he has notice of the change.

It is necessary, therefore, to consider what constitutes 'notice' for this purpose, and what makes a former partner an 'apparent' member of the continuing firm.

Notice

Section 36(2) provides that in respect of persons who had *no* dealings with the firm before the date of the dissolution or change, a notice in **the *Gazette*** (where the firm has its principal place of business in England and Wales) will be sufficient notice. Thus, to protect themselves from liability to new customers who knew of their connection with the firm, a retiring partner should ensure that a notice is published in *The Gazette*.

Notice in *The Gazette* will not be sufficient to relieve the former partner from liability in respect of customers who had dealings with the firm prior to the dissolution or change. If the retiring partner wishes to be protected from liability for future debts to those customers, those customers should be given formal notification of the retirement. In any event, the retiring partner will try to negotiate an indemnity from the existing partners in respect of any personal liability for future debts, as a further layer of protection.

Apparent membership

Where persons dealing with the firm know that a person was a partner, that partner will be liable for new debts so long as they are an apparent member of the firm (and until they give the required notice). Persons may be 'apparent members' either because a customer has had dealings with them before or because their names appear on the notepaper or on a sign on the door, or because the customer has some indirect information about their being partners.

25.5.3.4 Section 14 PA 1890

Liability for subsequent debts may also arise under s14 PA 1890. Section 14(1) provides that:

> Every one who by words spoken or written or by conduct represents himself, or who knowingly suffers himself to be represented, as a partner in a particular firm, is liable as a partner

to any one who has on the faith of any such representation given credit to the firm, whether the representation has or has not been made or communicated to the person so giving credit by or with the knowledge of the apparent partner making the representation or suffering it to be made.

Therefore, even if no liability arises under s36, the former partner may be liable to any person (whether they had previous dealings with the firm or not) who has given 'credit' to the firm on the faith of a representation that they are still a partner which is made by the former partner or which they have 'knowingly' allowed to be made.

The word 'apparent' in s14(1) has the same meaning as in s36(1) so that the decision in the *Tower Cabinet* case (see **25.5.3.3**) is equally relevant in these circumstances. In that case, it was alleged that the former partner had allowed himself to be held out as a partner. However, since the former partner had not authorised the use of the old notepaper, he had not 'knowingly' allowed himself to be held out as an 'apparent' partner and so no liability under s14 arose.

A retiring partner should ensure that their name is removed from any business signage, that any existing firm stationery indicating their status as a partner is destroyed and that the firm's website is duly altered to remove any reference to them. These steps (and any others which are contextually relevant) should minimise any successful claim that they knowingly allowed themselves to be represented as a partner.

25.6 Death of a partner

25.6.1 Avoidance of automatic dissolution

Subject to contrary agreement, death causes the automatic dissolution of a partnership. In order to avoid inconvenience to the surviving partners, it is common to provide in the partnership agreement that instead of causing an automatic dissolution of the partnership, the death of a partner will have the same effect as their retirement.

25.6.2 Liability for debts

Every partner is jointly liable for debts and obligations of the firm incurred while they are a partner. In addition, s9 PA 1890 provides that the estate of a deceased person is severally liable for such debts and obligations so far as they remain unsatisfied *but* subject to the prior payment of the deceased partner's personal debts. A partnership creditor can, therefore, proceed against the estate of a deceased partner in respect of partnership debts (even after obtaining a judgment against the other partners) provided some part of the debt is unsatisfied. However, partnership creditors are postponed to the deceased partner's own creditors.

So far as subsequent debts are concerned, s36(3) PA 1890 provides that the deceased partner's estate is not liable for partnership debts contracted after death.

25.7 Financial outcomes of death or retirement

25.7.1 Treatment in the partnership agreement

Assuming that a partnership agreement makes specific provision regarding the retirement or death of a partner, corresponding provisions should also be included to deal with the former partner's entitlement to payment for their share in the partnership, including how this will be valued (which may or may not include goodwill) and how this entitlement will be satisfied. In this way, the winding up of the business and a settlement of accounts between partners can be avoided.

However, if there is no specific provision dealing with purchase of the partner's share, it is likely that the retiring partner (or their estate) would be entitled to bring a claim that their share be properly valued and that the business of the partnership be wound up in order for that share to be realised. It may, instead, be the case that a court would require the remaining partners to buy out the share of the outgoing partner (to produce the same financial result for that partner). Either way, the position is both doubtful and unsatisfactory for all partners involved. Such an outcome should, therefore, be avoided by ensuring that the position is explicitly addressed in the partnership agreement.

25.7.2 Raising the finance

Raising a large capital sum to pay to the estate of a retiring or deceased partner may strain the resources of a partnership which is continuing after the death or retirement. This issue is normally dealt with by the partners in the partnership agreement as follows:

(a) by taking out insurance cover;

(b) by providing that on death and/or retirement, capital sums due should be paid by yearly instalments over a specified period–interest being payable on the amount outstanding;

(c) by providing for a method of calculating the amount due and the appointment of an agreed expert to carry this out;

(d) by providing that the deceased or retiring partner is to be entitled to a fixed amount in lieu of a share of profits. This avoids the need to apportion profits to the date of death or retirement.

25.8 Failure by continuing partners to settle accounts

It may be that a partner dies or a partner leaves and the remaining partners carry on the partnership business for some time before the outgoing partner's share in the business is realised or paid for. In such a situation, the continuing partners are benefiting financially from the other partner's interest in the business. To address this issue, s42(1) PA 1890 provides for the situation where any member of a firm has died or otherwise ceased to be a partner and the surviving or continuing partners carry on the business of the firm without any final settlement of accounts as between them and the outgoing partner or their estate.

The outgoing partner or their estate is entitled to claim:

(a) such share of the profits made since the dissolution as the court may find to be attributable to the use of their share of the partnership assets; or

(b) interest at the rate of 5% pa on the amount of their share of the partnership assets.

Any amount due from the surviving partners to the outgoing partner or the deceased partner's **personal representatives** in this context is a debt accruing at the date of the death or the departure of the outgoing partner (s43).

One major difficulty with the application of s42(1) is that its effect is premised on the value of the share of the outgoing partner. This may or may not be easy to determine. Further, any claim for a share of profits must be attributable to the outgoing partner's share. If such a causal nexus cannot be proven, the partner only has the option to claim interest.

Section 42 does not apply to capital profits, only income ones. Any entitlement that a former partner may have to capital profits which occur after departure will be determined by reference to the provisions of s24(1).

Section 42(1) is subject to contrary agreement and is, in any event, displaced if the continuing or surviving partners have the right to purchase the outgoing or deceased partner's share and exercise that right (s24(2)). As such, it is suggested that it is only likely to be relevant in a situation where there is no formal agreement between the partners as to how an outgoing or deceased partner's share is to be valued and paid for.

KEY POINT SUMMARY

This chapter has addressed the following topics:

- The dissolution of a partnership, that is, the dissolving of the legal bonds which connect the partners legally. In turn, this raises important issues about the winding up (or otherwise) of the partnership business and the satisfaction of partnership creditors' debts.
- The effect of retirement or death of a partner, and how this can be legislated for in a partnership agreement to allow minimum disruption to the continuance of the partnership business.
- The entitlement of a retired partner or the estate of a deceased partner to be rewarded for the value of their share of the partnership business which they have left behind and which has been taken over by the continuing partners.
- The continuing liability a retiring or deceased partner's estate may face for debts and liabilities incurred whilst a partner.
- The possibility that a retiring or deceased partner's estate may incur liability for debts and liabilities incurred by the partnership business after retirement or death.

CHAPTER 26
Partnership Disputes

FUNCTIONING LEGAL KNOWLEDGE

This chapter considers the following functioning legal knowledge included in the SRA's SQE 1 assessment specification:

Business and organisational characteristics (sole trader/partnership/LLP/private and unlisted public companies)

Partnership decision-making and authority of partners:

- procedures and authority under the Partnership Act 1890
- common provisions in partnership agreements

AUTHORITIES UNDERPINNING PRACTICE

The key authorities that underpin this area of practice are listed below. Note that for legislation you are linked to legislation.gov.uk.

Although much of the legislation on this government website is available in its amended form, the incorporation of new amendments into the text of legislation can be delayed. You should refer to legal databases to ensure you are referencing the most up-to-date legislation.

- Partnership Act 1890
  http://www.legislation.gov.uk/ukpga/Vict/53-54/39

26.1 Introduction

After consulting this chapter, you will have been introduced to the remedies available to a partner who is in dispute with their fellow partners. These remedies include:

(a) dissolution of the partnership;

(b) appointment of a receiver; or

(c) solutions available under the partnership agreement itself.

We saw at **23.2.2** that a decision of the majority of the partners on an 'ordinary matter' is binding on the minority. The wishes of the majority prevail over those of the minority who object. However, partnership law provides some machinery for protecting the partner who is aggrieved by the behaviour of their fellow partners.

26.2 Dissolution by the court

Dissolution of a partnership may occur:

(a) automatically (eg on the death or **bankruptcy** of a partner);

(b) by notice (eg any partner can give notice dissolving a partnership at will); or

(c) by court order (eg in the case of permanent incapacity of a partner).

The various circumstances in which dissolution takes place are considered in **Chapter 25**. In this section we intend to consider only those methods of dissolution by the court which provide a remedy to a partner in dispute with their co-partners.

Bear in mind that the consequence of dissolution is to provide for the winding up of the affairs of the partnership, so that the aggrieved partner can be released from the partnership and can realise their financial interest in the business.

26.2.1 Section 35(c): conduct prejudicial to the business

Section 35(c) of the Partnership Act 1890 (PA 1890) provides that a partner may apply to the court for dissolution:

> when a partner, other than the partner suing, has been guilty of such conduct as, in the opinion of the court, regard being had to the nature of the business, is calculated to prejudicially affect the carrying on of the business.

This provision may be relied upon even though the prejudicial conduct has nothing directly to do with the partnership. A conviction for dishonesty, for example, would be likely to be regarded as prejudicial conduct in the case of many professional partnerships, even though the dishonesty did not relate to the practice as such. The test is an objective one, so that it need not be shown that the guilty partner *intended* to affect the business (this is so, despite the use of the word 'calculated' in s35(c)).

26.2.2 Section 35(d): breach of partnership agreement

Section 35(d) provides that a partner may apply to the court for dissolution:

> when a partner, other than the partner suing, wilfully or persistently commits a breach of the partnership agreement, or otherwise so conducts himself in matters relating to the partnership business that it is not reasonably practicable for the other partner or partners to carry on business in partnership with him.

This paragraph contemplates that the trust and confidence between partners has broken down. If this breakdown results from persistent breaches of the partnership agreement or conduct in relation to the business, then the court can order dissolution.

Many of the cases under this paragraph have revolved around financial irregularities (eg failure to account for money received on behalf of the partnership or payment of private debts from partnership money). In *Bishop v Golstein* [2014] EWCA Civ 10, it was held by the Court of Appeal that it was not necessary to find an instance of repudiation, in the strict contractual sense, for a court to declare a dissolution of a partnership, as the court's power to order dissolution under s35(d) is discretionary; persistent or sustained breaches of the obligations of trust and confidence between partners were sufficient. Moreover, the partner not in breach may 'soldier on' in such a situation without a court regarding such action as affirming any breaches or automatically displacing s35(d).

26.2.3 Section 35(f): just and equitable dissolution

Section 35(f) provides that a partner may apply to the court for dissolution:

> whenever in any case circumstances have arisen which in the opinion of the court render it just and equitable that the partnership be dissolved.

This provision is the equivalent of s122(1)(g) of the Insolvency Act 1986, which applies to companies. The cases decided under s122(1)(g) (and its predecessors) are relevant also to s35(f) PA 1890, especially where the company which was the subject of the petition was intended to be run as if it were a partnership. Deadlock or other irreconcilable differences between partners are the most likely grounds on which a successful petition could be based. Exclusion of a partner from management (contrary to s24(5)) would also be grounds for petition, although this case would also probably be covered by s35(d).

26.3 Appointment of a receiver

A court has power to appoint a receiver to run the business of a partnership or manage its dissolution when there exists a dispute between the partners. The receiver's duty is to carry on the business of the partnership for the benefit of the partners generally, not to realise **security**, so that their position is quite different from that of a receiver appointed by a **debenture** holder over a company's assets. There is comparatively little authority as to when a receiver will be appointed, but it does seem to be an exceptional step and the court is particularly reluctant to make an appointment in the case of a professional partnership (*Floydd v Cheney* [1970] 2 WLR 314).

26.4 Arbitration

Disputes may be solved by arbitration if the partners agree to this. It is common to make provision for arbitration in the partnership agreement. The rationale is to provide a cost-effective, relatively informal and private solution to partnership disputes.

As in other types of contract, an arbitration clause cannot effectively oust the jurisdiction of the court altogether. A clause drafted with such a purpose in mind will be held to be void. If an action is commenced despite the presence of an arbitration clause, the court has a discretion to stay the proceedings to enable the arbitration to take place.

Court action can continue without there being any question of a stay when, as a matter of construction, the court decides that the dispute which has arisen is not covered by the arbitration clause in the partnership agreement or that the effect of the clause is to deprive a partner of a specific statutory entitlement.

26.5 Expulsion of a partner

26.5.1 Introduction

We have seen that it is possible for a partnership to be dissolved by the court as a way of resolving a dispute within a partnership. However, the circumstances of the dispute may be such that some partners would prefer to get rid of one or more of their co-partners without fully dissolving the partnership and bringing the business to an end.

26.5.2 Requirement for provision in partnership agreement

This is only possible if an appropriate provision is included in the partnership agreement, as s25 PA 1890 provides that:

> No majority of the partners can expel any partner unless a power to do so has been confirmed by express agreement between the partners.

The question as to whether expulsion should be provided for and, if so, by what majority, is one of the issues which must be considered when a partnership agreement is being drafted.

26.5.3 Content of expulsion clause

Where an expulsion clause is included in the agreement, it will normally state that specific activities (eg fraud) or breaches of certain terms of the partnership agreement (eg that requiring a partner not to compete with the partnership or to devote the whole of their time to the business) will justify expulsion.

Bankruptcy of a partner is a ground for the automatic dissolution of the whole partnership (s33(2) PA 1890) but, in order to avoid the consequences of dissolution, it is common for the partnership agreement to provide that a bankruptcy will not cause dissolution, rather that it will justify expulsion.

An expulsion clause will generally deal with the manner in which the expulsion is to be effected. It is normal to provide that written notice must be given to the offending partner and that it is to have immediate effect.

26.5.4 Exercise of expulsion clause

If an expulsion clause is included in the partnership agreement, then the power must be exercised strictly in accordance with the agreement and in a bona fide manner and for the benefit of the partnership as a whole (*Blisset v Daniel* (1853) 10 Hare 493). An improper motive may render the expulsion ineffective.

26.5.5 Compulsory retirement clause

In addition to an expulsion clause, a partnership agreement may contain a clause effecting compulsory retirement of a partner, usually by notice of the same from the other partners. The difference between the two clauses is that compulsory retirement does not require the partnership to demonstrate just cause, as for expulsion; however, the clause should still only be exercised bona fide, as for an expulsion clause.

Such a provision should be contrasted with a provision which sets a retirement age for any partner, at which point they are expected to leave the partnership. Such a clause is arguably discriminatory and would, therefore, fall foul of equality legislation, which explicitly protects partners, inter alia, from age discrimination (s44 Equality Act 2010). However, if it can be demonstrated that such a clause operates as a proportionate means of achieving a legitimate aim, the clause will not be discriminatory (s13(2) Equality Act 2010). The answer to such a question will be highly fact-specific and contextual. (Similar considerations apply to retirement age provisions in an LLP agreement (s45 Equality Act 2010).)

CONDUCT POINT

Advising on disputes within a partnership can trigger issues of professional conduct for the unwary solicitor.

Assume that you have acted for a partnership of four persons for the last three years on general legal matters affecting it. In that time, you have had frequent contact with all partners in the firm and have acquired considerable information regarding the operations of the partnership. You take a call from one of the partners who explains that they are sick of the behaviour of their fellow partners and want your advice regarding what to do about it. For reasons of both maintenance of confidentiality and avoidance of conflicts, you must decline to act for the partner in question and ask them to seek separate representation. Should the matter be progressed by the unhappy partner, the other partners may seek your advice about how to respond and manage the situation from the partnership perspective. There is arguably no problem with this, so long as those partners are acting in unison. However, should their views or their preferred outcomes differ, you would be obliged to ask that each partner seeks separate advice.

KEY POINT SUMMARY

Where a dispute arises between partners, the following should be taken into consideration:

- Any partner may apply to court for an order dissolving the partnership (assuming that dissolution is not available by right).
- Any partner may apply to court for an order for the appointment of a receiver to manage the partnership business, although this is an option which is rarely sought.
- Whether or not any partnership agreement in existence provides for the referral of a dispute to arbitration.
- Whether or not any partnership agreement in existence provides for the expulsion/compulsory retirement of a partner who may be the cause of the dispute (bearing in mind that the exercise of each of these clauses must be done bona fide).

CHAPTER 27
The Partnership Agreement

FUNCTIONING LEGAL KNOWLEDGE

This chapter considers the following functioning legal knowledge included in the SRA's SQE 1 assessment specification:

Procedures and documentation required to incorporate a company/form a partnership/LLP and other steps required under companies and partnerships legislation to enable the entity to commence operating:

- constitutional documents

Partnership decision-making and authority of partners:

- common provisions in partnership agreements

AUTHORITIES UNDERPINNING PRACTICE

The key authorities that underpin this area of practice are listed below. Note that for legislation you are linked to legislation.gov.uk.

Although much of the legislation on this government website is available in its amended form, the incorporation of new amendments into the text of legislation can be delayed. You should refer to legal databases to ensure you are referencing the most up-to-date legislation.

- Partnership Act 1890
  http://www.legislation.gov.uk/ukpga/Vict/53-54/39

27.1 Introduction

After consulting this chapter, you will have been introduced to some of the provisions which should be considered for inclusion in a partnership agreement.

In addition to some of the possible contents of a partnership agreement, consideration will also be given to whether a formal, written agreement is necessary at all.

Much of the contents of a partnership agreement will address issues already considered in **Chapters 5** and **23–6**. That previous commentary should be borne in mind when reading this chapter.

Note that this chapter does not purport to be comprehensive in its coverage of all possible provisions of a partnership agreement.

27.2 Is a written partnership agreement necessary?

A written agreement is not required for the formation of a partnership. This contrasts with the position of a company where **articles of association** must not only be in writing but must also be registered with the Registrar of Companies.

Many provisions of the Partnership Act 1890 (PA 1890) apply to regulate the relationship of the partners, except to the extent that there is contrary agreement. As such, this is another potential reason why a partnership agreement may be considered otiose. However, it is unlikely that the implied terms of the PA 1890 will entirely coincide with the wishes of persons setting up a partnership. Moreover, their consequences may not always be desirable.

Further, a written agreement can provide clarity about the relationship between partners and can assist in any future disputes which may arise.

If properly advised, therefore, prospective partners are likely to decide that the agreement between them as to how their ongoing relationship is to be regulated should be reduced to writing. Such an agreement is often called a partnership agreement or a partnership deed.

A partnership agreement is entirely confidential–there is no requirement for its contents to be released to anybody other than the partners.

The contents of a partnership agreement will, of course, depend upon the circumstances and the intentions of the partners, but set out next are some of the more important matters which need to be considered.

27.3 Possible clauses of a partnership agreement

27.3.1 The parties

The parties to the agreement will be the partners at the time the agreement is entered into.

27.3.2 The commencement date and term of the partnership

Although the date the partnership agreement was entered into can determine the commencement of the partnership, partnership agreements often include a term stating the date on which the partnership commenced, which may predate the execution of the agreement.

As regards the duration of a partnership, if left up to the Act, the continuance of the partnership will be subject to notice to dissolve being given at any time by any partner, either pursuant to either s26 or s32(c). The case of *Moss v Elphick* [1910] 1 KB 846 indicates that any express provision between the partners which addresses the issue of duration will displace this possibility.

Additionally, it will be important to consider two particular possibilities:

1 the retirement of an individual partner, which does not result in a total dissolution of the affairs of the partnership; and

2 the situations in which the partnership and its operations will cease and the mechanisms to bring this about.

See **27.3.13** for further discussion of this.

It should also be recognised that a partnership may be entered into for a specified duration or to fulfil a specified purpose.

27.3.3 The nature of the partnership's business

Issues of *ultra vires* do not apply in a partnership context; partners are natural persons with unlimited capacity. The business to be undertaken should, however, be specified so that a partner who objects to what is being done by way of new types of business can insist on the agreement being followed. (Also, material deviation away from this understanding may ultimately be grounds for an application to court for an order for dissolution pursuant to s35 PA 1890.)

Unless the partnership agreement provides to the contrary, the business which the partnership undertakes can only be altered with the unanimous agreement of the partners (s24(8) PA 1890). A decision may have to be made, therefore, to maintain this or provide for an alternative, such as a majority decision of the partners being sufficient.

27.3.4 The partnership name

The name of the partnership should be specified, bearing in mind that both the content and disclosure of business names are regulated by Pt 41 of the Companies Act 2006 and the Company, Limited Liability Partnership and Business Names (Sensitive Words and Expressions) Regulations 2014.

27.3.5 Profit-sharing

If the partnership agreement is silent on the point, the partners will share the profits of the partnership equally. Even if this is in accord with the partners' wishes, it is best to state specifically the way in which the partnership's profits will be shared. However, in many partnerships this simple position may not be what the partners require. The share of profits between the partners may be unequal to reflect differing levels of contributions of capital or differing levels of involvement in the partnership's business.

Some partnerships may choose to build a mechanism into their partnership agreements for regular reviews of the profit-sharing ratios to take into account the relative achievements of the partners.

If the partners have agreed among themselves that some or all of them should receive 'interest' on capital or a 'salary', these arrangements should also be set out in the partnership agreement. However, in most circumstances such payments will simply be a defined, predetermined element of a partner's profit share.

It is usual to provide for partners' advance drawing of profit throughout the year to enable them to access a source of funds to meet their everyday living expenses. Such a provision will also usually require any over-drawing of profit for an accounting year to be repaid, possibly subject to interest.

27.3.6 The capital of the partnership

A clause should be included dealing with the financial relationships between the partners. This should state:

(a) what investment each partner is to make in the business;

(b) how each partner will satisfy their obligation to contribute capital (eg whether in cash or assets);

(c) whether or not a capital contribution is not to be made in full on admission to the partnership or to be met over a defined time period.

Although it may be difficult to specify the circumstances, there may be value in giving thought to the circumstances in which further capital might have to be introduced throughout the duration of the partnership.

The reverse of these provisions is what should happen to the capital when the partnership is dissolved or a partner retires. What are the arrangements for a partner to withdraw capital and how are any capital profits (or losses) to be dealt with when a partner leaves? Examples of how capital may be dealt with are given at **25.4**.

27.3.7 Generation of accounts

Unlike companies, partnerships are under no obligation to generate accounts; however, it would be unfeasible for any business not to generate appropriate financial information on an annual basis (or more regularly). As a consequence, a clause requiring the generation of a profit and loss account and balance sheet for each financial period will usually be included. In turn, it will be necessary for partners to agree upon a 'year end' date for such financial periods.

27.3.8 The property of the partnership

The partnership agreement should include a provision specifying which property is to be regarded as partnership property and which is to remain the property of individual partners. This clarity is particularly important when the partnership is dissolved–only partnership property can be included in the final accounts between partners.

27.3.9 The management of the partnership

Small partnerships of two or three people will usually be run by the partners and each partner will have an equal say in management. In a large partnership, a more complex management structure may be considered desirable and the structure should be specified. In the absence of contrary agreement, all partners have an equal say in management.

Linked to this issue is the mechanism by which partners make decisions. This may be relatively formal; that is, in the forum of a partners' meeting or could simply be by any method which indicates agreement. Further, it may be that a simple majority (50%+) is necessary in all circumstances to validate a decision or the agreement may specify certain decisions which should be reserved for a 'super-majority'; that is 75% or, even, unanimity in certain circumstances.

27.3.10 The effect of prolonged absence

It may be appropriate to include in a partnership agreement a clause dealing with the consequences for a partner who is absent from the business for a prolonged period. This may be through illness, maternity leave or compassionate leave. The nature of the provisions will be determined by the necessity for the partners to balance the needs of the business with supporting their fellow partner. However, these provisions often mirror corresponding provisions found in employment contracts (so that a partner may be permitted to be away from the partnership's business for, for example, six months due to illness before they can be expelled or the partnership agreement may provide maternity leave provisions similar to the statutory provisions which employees enjoy).

27.3.11 Restrictions on partners

Terms may be included dealing with the partners' obligations to the firm, for example to provide that the partners are to give their whole time to the business of the firm or to provide that they are only to take up other businesses with the approval of their partners.

Consideration should also be given to the inclusion of a clause preventing competition with the firm during the lifetime of the partnership (even if the partners are not full time), although such competition would, in any case, normally be a breach of the partners' duty of good faith.

More significantly, it is often desirable to include a restrictive covenant to prevent competition with the firm by a partner after they have left the firm. Such a term must be reasonable (in scope and duration), otherwise it may be declared void as being a term in unreasonable restraint of trade.

The partners may also decide to place specific restrictions on the activities of particular partners in relation to the running of the business. For example, a partnership agreement could prevent any individual partner from:

(a) charging or selling any of the partnership's assets (even in furtherance of partnership business);

(b) committing the partnership to contracts in excess of a specified value;

(c) employing a new member of staff or dismissing an existing member of staff;

(d) releasing a debtor of the firm from their debt or compromising the same.

27.3.12 Partnership disputes

It is sensible to anticipate that problems may arise within the partnership and so provide for how disputes should be resolved. Commonly, clauses dealing with disputes require the partners to refer the dispute (whatever the subject matter of the dispute may be) to an independent arbitrator. This approach may lead to the resolution of the dispute and thus avoid court proceedings or the forced dissolution of the partnership.

27.3.13 Dissolution, death and retirement of partners

It may be appropriate to set out the circumstances in which:

(a) the partnership will be dissolved and the business wound up; or

(b) a partner can 'retire' (which, technically speaking, will be a dissolution which is not followed by a winding up of the business); or

(c) a partner can be expelled from the partnership (remembering that without the express reservation of this power, no partner can be expelled by majority decision–s25 PA 1890).

As many events involving partners can result in dissolution of the partnership (eg death and **bankruptcy**), there is usually value in including a clause which recognises this fact and provides for the partnership business to be continued by the remaining partners without triggering the need for a formal winding up (sometimes known as a technical dissolution).

Any outgoing partner will be concerned to secure the value attributable to their partnership share which is being left behind for the benefit of the remaining partners.

This raises two important issues:

(a) how should that share be properly valued; and

(b) in what way should the partnership pay for that share?

It should be remembered that the outlay of a capital sum in one go may be undesirable for the remaining partners, so any payment may be made in instalments.

27.3.14 Admission of new partners

The agreement should specify how new partners are to be admitted to the partnership. In the absence of agreement to the contrary, new partners may only be admitted with the unanimous consent of the existing partners (s24(7) PA 1890).

Any new partner will be expected to commit to the partnership agreement in its entirety. This is usually achieved by the new partner executing a 'deed of adherence', which is effectively a covenant by the partner to comply with and be bound by all the terms of the partnership agreement.

KEY POINT SUMMARY

- A partnership agreement is unnecessary for the *creation* of a partnership; that is entirely a matter of law.
- A partnership agreement is unnecessary for the *operation* of a partnership; however, it is advisable as the default provisions within the Partnership Act 1890 may be unsatisfactory.
- In simple terms, the possible clauses of a partnership agreement can be divided into the following categories:
  - the existence and purpose of the partnership;
  - financial matters, eg funding from partners, allocation of profits/losses;
  - management arrangements;
  - changes to partners and their effect, eg retirement, death, admission of further partners;
  - partner disputes and their resolution;
  - the termination of the partnership.

PART F
Insolvency

CHAPTER 28
Company Insolvency Proceedings and Claw-Back

FUNCTIONING LEGAL KNOWLEDGE

This chapter considers the following functioning legal knowledge included in the SRA's SQE 1 assessment specification:

Insolvency (corporate and personal):

- options and procedures
- claw-back of assets for creditors
- order of priority for distribution to creditors

AUTHORITIES UNDERPINNING PRACTICE

The key authorities that underpin this area of practice are listed below. Note that for legislation you are linked to legislation.gov.uk.

Although much of the legislation on this government website is available in its amended form, the incorporation of new amendments into the text of legislation can be delayed. You should refer to legal databases to ensure you are referencing the most up-to-date legislation.

- Insolvency Act 1986
  http://www.legislation.gov.uk/ukpga/1986/45/contents
- Insolvency (England and Wales) Rules 2016
  http://www.legislation.gov.uk/uksi/2016/1024/contents/made
- Insolvent Partnerships Order 1994
  https://www.legislation.gov.uk/uksi/1994/2421/contents/made
- Enterprise Act 2002
  http://www.legislation.gov.uk/ukpga/2002/40/contents
- Companies Act 2006
  http://www.legislation.gov.uk/ukpga/2006/46/contents

28.1 Introduction

In this chapter we shall deal with the procedures available when a company is insolvent or facing financial difficulties. We shall also look at the way insolvency practitioners can collect in and, in certain circumstances, 'claw back' assets for distribution to creditors of insolvent companies, and the order in which such assets, or their proceeds, should be distributed.

Note that, whilst the text refers to 'company' or 'companies', these procedures are also applicable to limited liability partnerships (LLPs). For partnerships that are not LLPs, see **28.12**.

28.2 Moratorium

28.2.1 Introduction

This procedure provides a company that is facing financial difficulties with a moratorium. This is a period of time during which creditors cannot enforce claims against it, during which the directors can develop a plan to turn around the company's situation. The aim of the moratorium is the recovery of a viable company–as opposed to the realisation of its assets for creditors (see **28.5**)–with lower costs and fewer formalities than other procedures.

28.2.2 Obtaining a moratorium

The directors of a company–provided it is not subject to an outstanding winding-up petition (see **28.5**) and is not an overseas company–may obtain a moratorium by filing at court relevant documents. These are:

(a) From the directors:
- a notice that they wish to obtain a moratorium; and
- a statement that, in their view, the company is likely, or likely to become, unable to pay its debts.

(b) From a proposed 'monitor', statements that:
- they are a qualified person and consent to act as the monitor of the moratorium;
- the company is an eligible company; and
- in their view, it is likely a moratorium would result in the rescue of the company as a going concern.

The moratorium comes into force at the time which the documents are filed with the court.

Where a company is subject to an outstanding winding-up petition (see **28.5**) or is an overseas company, a moratorium requires directors to make an application to the court, accompanied by the above relevant documents. The court may then order a moratorium or make any other order it thinks appropriate. In the case of a company subject to a winding-up petition, it may only order a moratorium if it is satisfied that it would achieve a better result for the company's creditors as a whole than would be likely if the company were wound up (without first being subject to a moratorium). In these cases, the moratorium comes into force at the time at which the court makes the order.

28.2.3 Effects of moratorium

The directors of the company will continue to deal with the day-to-day running of the company, whilst looking to develop a plan to turn around the company. At the same time, the company's finances and operations will be overseen by the monitor, a licensed insolvency practitioner. The main effects of the moratorium are that:

(a) the company has a payment holiday for most debts incurred pre-moratorium that have fallen due before the moratorium or that fall due during the moratorium;

(b) no steps may be taken to commence any other insolvency procedures, unless by the directors; and

(c) floating charge-holders may not give any notice which would cause the charge to crystallise or restrict any disposal of property by the company.

In addition, none of the following can be undertaken except with court permission:

- a landlord exercising a right of forfeiture;
- steps to enforce **security** over the company's property;
- steps to repossess hire-purchase goods.

However, during the moratorium, the company remains liable to pay amounts in respect of:

- the monitor's remuneration and expenses;
- goods or services supplied during the moratorium;
- rent in respect of the moratorium period;
- wages or salaries;
- redundancy payments;
- debts or other liabilities under a contract involving financial services.

This final form of liability is of particular importance because it would include any liability under a loan agreement. The practical effect of this is that it is likely a company will need the support of any major lender if it plans to obtain a moratorium. The latter would have the option to accelerate and demand its debts be paid if it did not support a moratorium. (Although, as to the effect of this in a subsequent administration or **liquidation**, see **28.9.6**.)

28.2.4 **Period of moratorium**

28.2.4.1 Initial period

The initial period of a moratorium is 20 business days, beginning with the business day after the day on which the moratorium comes into force (see **28.2.2**).

28.2.4.2 Extension without creditor consent

The directors may, without creditor consent, extend the moratorium by a further 20 business days. To do so, they must file a notice with the court, accompanied by a statement that the company has paid its moratorium debts and is, or is likely to become, unable to pay its pre-moratorium debts. The monitor must also provide a statement that it is likely that the moratorium will result in the rescue of the company as a going concern.

28.2.4.3 Extension with creditor consent

The directors may, with creditor consent, extend the moratorium by a number of days agreed with the creditors. The procedure and documentation required is the same as that in **28.2.4.2**, with the addition of a directors' statement that creditor consent has been obtained and of the revised end date. With creditors' consent, a moratorium may be extended more than once.

28.2.4.4 Alternative means of extending the moratorium

There are also provisions that allow the directors to apply to the court for an extension of the moratorium at any time after the first 15 business days of the initial period, and for an extension whilst a proposal for a creditors' voluntary arrangement (see **28.4**) is pending.

28.2.5 **Termination of moratorium**

The moratorium will come to an end automatically on the expiry of the moratorium term. In addition, it will terminate if:

- the company enters another insolvency procedure;
- a restructuring plan or scheme of arrangement is sanctioned;
- the court orders its termination.

The monitor is required to terminate the moratorium if they believe any of the following:

- its objective of rescuing the company as a going concern has been achieved;
- it is no longer likely to result in the rescue of the company;

- the company is unable to pay any moratorium debts or pre-moratorium debts for which it does not have a payment holiday;
- as a result of failure by the directors to provide requested information, the monitor is unable to carry out their functions.

28.3 Administration orders

28.3.1 Introduction

28.3.2 Persons entitled to appoint an administrator

A person may be appointed as an administrator of a company by:

(a) the holder of a floating charge;

(b) the company or its directors; or

(c) an order of the court.

An administrator must be a qualified insolvency practitioner and, once appointed, will be an officer of the court.

28.3.3 Objectives of administrator

An administrator must perform their functions with the objective of:

(a) rescuing the company as a going concern; or

(b) achieving a better result for the company's creditors as a whole than would be likely if the company were wound up (without first being in administration); or

(c) realising property to make a distribution to one or more secured or **preferential creditors**.

These objectives are a hierarchy. The administrator is required to perform their functions to achieve objective (a) unless either it is not reasonably practicable to do so, or the objective in (b) would achieve a better result for the company's creditors as a whole. The administrator may seek to achieve objective (c) only if they think it is not reasonably practicable to achieve either (a) or (b), and they do not unnecessarily harm the interests of creditors of the company as a whole.

Thus, subject to objective (c), the administrator must perform their functions in the interests of the company's creditors as a whole. They must also perform their functions as quickly and efficiently as is reasonably practicable.

28.3.4 Appointment of administrator by floating charge-holder

28.3.4.1 Power to appoint

The holder of a qualifying floating charge over the company's property may appoint an administrator. The charge must be enforceable at the time of the appointment. The holder must first:

- give at least two business days' written notice to the holder of any prior qualifying floating charge; or
- obtain written consent to the appointment from such person.

The floating charge-holder may not appoint an administrator if a provisional liquidator has been appointed.

28.3.4.2 Notice of appointment

The appointing charge-holder must file with the court a notice of appointment. This must include a statutory declaration by or on behalf of the person who makes the appointment including statements that:

(a) the person is the holder of a qualifying floating charge in respect of the company's property;
(b) each floating charge relied on in making the appointment is (or was) enforceable on the date of the appointment; and
(c) the appointment is in accordance with Sch B1 to the Insolvency Act 1986 (IA 1986).

The statutory declaration must be made within a prescribed period.

The notice of appointment must identify the administrator and be accompanied by a statement from the latter:

(a) that they consent to the appointment;
(b) that in their opinion the purpose of administration is reasonably likely to be achieved; and
(c) giving any other information and opinions as may be prescribed.

The administrator may, in making their statement, rely on information supplied by the company's directors (unless they have reason to doubt its accuracy).

28.3.4.3 Time at which appointment takes effect

The appointment of an administrator by a holder of a qualifying floating charge takes effect when the notice provisions set out in **28.3.4.2** have been satisfied.

28.3.5 **Appointment of administrator by company or directors**

28.3.5.1 Power to appoint

A company or its directors may appoint an administrator of that company, unless:

(a) there is a pending winding up petition; or
(b) there is a pending administration application; or
(c) an administrative receiver is in office.

In addition, no administrator may be appointed by the company or its directors during a period of 12 months beginning with the date:

(a) on which a prior appointment of an administrator by the company or its directors ceases to have effect; or
(b) when a moratorium (see **28.2**) ends with no voluntary arrangement in force; or
(c) on which a voluntary arrangement made during a moratorium ends prematurely.

28.3.5.2 Notice of intention to appoint

Directors or companies must give at least five business days' notice to any person holding a qualifying floating charge. This notice must identify the proposed administrator and be in the prescribed form. A copy of this notice must also be filed with the court and be accompanied by a statutory declaration including statements that:

(a) the company is or is likely to become unable to pay its debts; and
(b) the company is not in liquidation.

The charge-holders to whom notice has been given may either agree to the proposed appointment or appoint an alternative administrator, although a moratorium (as described in **28.3.7.1**) will take effect immediately the company or directors file the notice of intention at court. (This moratorium can only be lifted with the leave of the court.)

If charge-holders do not respond to the notice of intention to appoint, the company's or directors' appointee will take office after the notice period has expired and a notice of appointment is filed at court.

28.3.5.3 Notice of appointment

The administrator takes office when a notice of appointment is filed with the court. An appointment may not be made after a period of ten business days beginning with the date on which the notice of intention to appoint is filed.

The notice of appointment must include a statutory declaration stating that the application meets all the necessary requirements set out in para 29 of Sch B1 IA 1986. It must also identify the administrator and be accompanied by a statement from the latter:

(a) that they consent to the appointment;

(b) that in their opinion the purpose of administration is reasonably likely to be achieved; and

(c) giving any other information and opinions as may be prescribed.

The administrator may, in making their statement, rely on information supplied by the company's directors (unless they have reason to doubt its accuracy).

28.3.6 **Appointment of administrator by court**

28.3.6.1 Application for administration order

The following may apply to court for an administration order in respect of a company:

(a) the company;

(b) one or more directors of the company;

(c) one or more creditors of the company;

(d) the designated officer for a magistrates' court (where a fine has been imposed on a company); or

(e) a combination of (a) to (d).

This route would be followed in the event of one or more of the restrictions described in **28.3.5.1** applying. This court route also thus provides a means seeking a company administration for creditors without qualifying floating charges, eg unsecured creditors.

28.3.6.2 Notice of application

An applicant must, as soon as is reasonably practicable after making the application, notify any person entitled to appoint an administrator by virtue of holding a qualifying floating charge.

28.3.6.3 Effect of application

Whilst an application is pending, a moratorium (as described in **28.3.7.1**) takes effect. This moratorium can only be lifted with the leave of the court.

28.3.6.4 Powers of court

On hearing an administration application the court may:

(a) make an administration order;

(b) dismiss the application;

(c) adjourn the hearing;

(d) make an interim order;

(e) treat the application as a winding-up order; or

(f) make any other order it thinks appropriate.

The court make only make an administration order if it is satisfied that:

(a) the company is or is likely to become unable to pay its debts; and
(b) the order is reasonably likely to achieve the purpose of administration (see **28.3.3**).

28.3.6.5 Time at which appointment takes effect

Where the court makes an administration order, the appointment takes effect at the time appointed by the order or, if no time is appointed, at the time the order is made.

28.3.7 **Effect of administration**

28.3.7.1 Moratorium

Once a company is in administration, creditors may not, without the consent of the administrator or the permission of the court:

(a) take steps to enforce security over the company's property;
(b) repossess goods in the company's possession under a hire-purchase agreement;
(c) commence or continue any legal process against the company or its property; or
(d) exercise a right of forfeiture in respect of premises let by the company.

In addition, no resolution may be passed for the winding up of the company and no winding-up order made. Finally, any administrative or other receiver will be required to vacate office.

The object of these rules is to preserve the assets of the company to improve the ability of the administrator of rescuing the company as a going concern.

28.3.7.2 Effect on winding up

A petition for the winding up of a company will be dismissed on the making of an administration order. While a company is in administration following an appointment by the holder of a qualifying floating charge, a winding-up petition will be suspended.

28.3.8 **The administration process**

28.3.8.1 Announcement of appointment

The administrator must send notice of their appointment to the company and publish a notice of their appointment in the prescribed manner as soon as reasonably practicable. Notice must also be sent to the Registrar of Companies within seven days of appointment, and to the company's creditors.

28.3.8.2 Statement of affairs

The administrator must require a statement of affairs to be prepared. This will usually be required from the directors of the company, but the administrator may also require others involved in the company's business to provide or contribute to the statement. The statement must be provided within 11 days of the date of receipt of notice of the requirement.

28.3.8.3 Powers of administrator

The appointed administrator will run the company and its business with a view to achieving the purpose of administration. The administrator is given power to do anything necessary or expedient for the management of the affairs, business and property of the company. This includes powers to:

- sell assets;
- borrow money;
- insure;
- bring and defend proceedings;

- appoint agents;
- dispose of charged property as if it were not subject to the charge; and
- dispose of hire-purchase goods as if the rights of the owner were vested in the company.

In cases of difficulty, the administrator may apply to the court for directions. The management powers of the administrator override those of the company and its directors; they may not exercise any management powers without the administrator's consent.

In addition, an administrator may not make a substantial disposal of some or all of the company's business and assets to connected persons within eight weeks of the commencement of the administration without either:

(a) creditor approval (see **28.3.8.5**) either as part of their proposals (see **28.3.8.4**) or by a separate decision-making process; or

(b) the connected person obtaining an independently evaluated report on the reasonableness of the disposal and submitting it to the administrator.

This measure was introduced following creditor criticism of the increasing use of 'pre-pack' sales of businesses by administrators. A 'pre-pack' sale is where a sale of some or all of a company's business or assets is negotiated in advance of the formal appointment of an administrator, with the intention that it is completed very shortly after appointment.

28.3.8.4 Proposals

The administrator must prepare proposals for achieving the administration's purpose. These must be sent to the Registrar of Companies, all creditors (so far as they are aware of their claims and addresses) and all **members** (so far as they are aware of their addresses). The proposals must be sent as soon as reasonably practicable but in any event within eight weeks from the commencement of administration.

28.3.8.5 Creditors' decisions

The creditors may approve the proposals either without modification or with modifications to which the administrator consents. Unless 10% or more in value or number of creditors, or ten or more creditors, object, then the administrator can use whatever qualifying decision procedure they think fit, for example using email, electronic voting or 'virtual meetings'. An administrator may also proceed by way of 'deemed consent': if an administrator communicates a proposal to creditors and fewer than 10% in value of creditors object, the proposal will be deemed approved.

28.3.8.6 Distributions

An administrator may make distributions to secured creditors and preferential creditors without court permission, and distributions to unsecured creditors with court permission. Distributions of 'prescribed part' (see **28.9.5.2**) payments to unsecured creditors may be made without court permission. The administrator may also make payments if they think that they are likely to assist in achieving the purpose of the administration.

28.3.8.7 Fulfilling the purpose of administration

The government's Insolvency Service has stated that 'for administration to be successful it needs to have clear exit routes tied to its purpose'. Therefore, legislation provides that:

(a) The administrator's proposal may include a proposal for a company voluntary arrangement (CVA) under the IA 1986 or a scheme of arrangement under the Companies Act 2006. A company rescue is most likely to involve one of these procedures.

(b) If the company cannot be rescued, then the administrator will aim to achieve a better realisation of the company's assets than would be achieved on an immediate liquidation.

(c) Where there are no funds available for the unsecured creditors, the administrator will realise the company's assets and make payments to preferential creditors and fixed and floating charge-holders and will arrange for the dissolution of the company simply by sending a notice to the Registrar of Companies.

(d) If there are funds available for the unsecured creditors, the company will be put into voluntary liquidation, again simply by sending a notice to the Registrar of Companies.

Where the administrator thinks the purpose of administration cannot be achieved, the administrator is required to apply to court.

28.3.8.8 Ending administration

The appointment of an administrator will automatically end 12 months after the date it commenced. However, this may be extended for up to a further 12 months with the consent of the creditors or for a specified period by court order.

28.4 Voluntary arrangements

28.4.1 Proposals and nominee's report

A company's directors or a liquidator or an administrator can make proposals for a voluntary arrangement to the company and its creditors. The proposals must nominate a qualified insolvency practitioner to implement them. Where the nominee is not the liquidator or administrator themselves, the party making the proposal must submit details of the proposals and of the company's creditors, debts, liabilities and assets to the nominee. The nominee must then, within 28 days, submit a report to the court stating whether meetings of shareholders and creditors should be called to consider the proposals.

28.4.2 Content of proposals

The proposals may be as simple or as complex as the situation of the company demands. In practical terms, the creditors are usually being offered something definite as an alternative to what they might obtain if the company was, for example, to be wound up. Proposals could include one or more of the following.

28.4.2.1 Moratorium on repayment of debt

Creditors are asked not to enforce debts for a specified period. The company may be unable to pay debts at present due to cash-flow problems but may expect to be able to pay them in the near future.

28.4.2.2 Composition of debt

Creditors are offered a percentage of their debt in settlement. For example, they might be offered '65 pence in the pound'; that is, 65 pence for every pound which the company owes them.

28.4.2.3 Debt for equity swap

Major creditors may be offered the chance to swap their debt for **shares** in the company. The removal of the debt is intended to ease company cash-flow problems. The shares will usually feature preferential rights to enable repayment through dividends as soon as profits are available. Such a proposal may be combined with a reorganisation of the company's affairs.

28.4.3 Meetings of members and creditors

Where the nominee recommends that meetings should be held, they may call the meetings unless the court orders otherwise. Notice must be given to every creditor of whose claim and address the person calling the meeting is aware.

The meetings of members and creditors then consider the scheme, which they may reject, approve or approve with modifications. At the members' meeting, a simple majority is required based on voting rights attached to shares. At the creditors' meeting, the net effect is that the resolution is only validly passed if approved by:

(a) at least three-quarters (by debt value) of the unsecured creditors; and
(b) a simple majority (by value) of the unsecured creditors who are not connected with the company.

In relation to (a) only, secured creditors may count in the vote but only to the extent of the value of their claim they estimate will *not* be recovered under their security.

The result of the meetings must be reported to the court. The court can reject the scheme on grounds of unfair prejudice or material irregularity.

28.4.4 Implementation of approved scheme by supervisor

Where both meetings approve a scheme, the scheme becomes binding on all persons who had notice of the **shareholders**' or creditors' meeting and were entitled to vote at that meeting, together with any creditors who would have been entitled to vote had they been given notice of the meeting. However, unless the supervisor agrees, the scheme cannot affect a secured creditor's right to enforce their security or a preferred creditor's preference.

Once approved, the supervisor implements the scheme. The supervisor will be the same person as the nominee unless the court or meetings decide otherwise.

28.4.5 Relationship with moratorium and administration

The proposal that a voluntary scheme should be implemented does not create a moratorium so that, unless and until the scheme is approved, any creditor can seek payment of their own debt (by court action, petition for winding up, repossession or any other lawful means available to them). Even when the scheme is approved, it does not prevent secured creditors enforcing their security. A voluntary arrangement may, therefore, be more likely to succeed if a company is first the subject of the moratorium or administration procedures.

28.5 Receivership

28.5.1 Introduction

A receiver is a person who is appointed by or on behalf of a creditor to realise security, such as a charge or series of charges. Their principal duty is owed to the party who appoints them; that is, the charge-holder. Whilst receivers may also be appointed by the court, in practice nearly all appointments have been made by charge-holders.

From 1986, receivers fell into two broad categories: receivers appointed under charges over specific assets and administrative receivers, as defined by s29(2).

28.5.2 Receivers

A receiver appointed under charges over specific assets derives their powers from the charge under which they were appointed and from certain sections of the Law of Property Act 1925. The latter provides powers to manage, receive income from and sell the property over which the receiver has been appointed. Sometimes this type of receiver will be referred to as a 'receiver and manager', 'fixed charge receiver' or 'LPA receiver'. Their role is to deal with the property over which they are appointed to realise funds for the party who appointed them. A receiver need not necessarily be a qualified insolvency practitioner.

28.5.3 Administrative receivers

These were, prior to the Enterprise Act 2002, appointed by the holders of floating charges. Now they are only appointed in a number of limited and comparatively specialised circumstances. Holders of floating charges now have a power under the IA 1986 to appoint an administrator (see **28.3.4**).

28.6 Liquidation or winding up

28.6.1 Types of winding up

There are two types of winding up: compulsory liquidation and voluntary liquidation. Compulsory liquidation is initiated by petition to the court. Voluntary liquidation is initiated by a decision of the members of the company. Both types of winding up are designed to bring the existence of the company to an end and to distribute its assets to those entitled to them.

28.6.2 Compulsory winding up

28.6.2.1 Grounds

Compulsory liquidation begins with a petition to the court (Chancery Division or, in some cases, County Court–see **28.2.4**). A petition can be presented on a number of grounds. By far the most common ground is that the company is unable to pay its debts (defined in s123). A company is treated as being unable to pay its debts if:

(a) a demand for payment, in the prescribed form (a 'statutory demand'), for more than £750 (this figure may be changed from time to time by regulations) has been left at the company's **registered office** and the company has neglected to pay the debt, or to secure or compound for it (ie agree to a reasonable compromise) to the reasonable satisfaction of the creditor for three weeks; or

(b) execution or other process issued on a judgment, decree or court order is returned unsatisfied; or

(c) it is proved that the company is actually unable to pay taking into account contingent and prospective liabilities; or

(d) it is proved that the value of the company's assets is less than the amount of its liabilities taking into account contingent and prospective liabilities.

Apart from inability to pay debts, there are other grounds on which a company may be wound up. These are, however, seldom resorted to and are not considered in this manual, save that the 'just and equitable' ground is considered briefly in **Chapter 9**.

28.6.2.2 Locus standi

A petition for compulsory winding up may be presented by the company itself, any creditor or creditors (including contingent or prospective creditors), any contributory or contributories (the term 'contributory' includes the members of the company and certain former members) and, in very limited circumstances, by the Department for Business, Energy and Industrial Strategy. In practice, creditors present the overwhelming majority of petitions.

28.6.2.3 Court's discretion to refuse order

Even where a creditor has proved grounds for winding up, the court has a discretion to refuse to make an order winding up the company. An order will normally be refused where:

(a) the petitioning creditor (together with any supporting creditors) is owed £750 or less. This is by analogy with the rule whereby a statutory demand for more than £750 can be used as proof of inability to pay debts;

(b) the majority by value of the creditors oppose the winding up of the company.

28.6.3 **Voluntary winding up**

28.6.3.1 Commencement

A company can be wound up voluntarily if a **special resolution** to wind up is passed. The winding up commences from the date of the special resolution. A notice of the resolution must appear in **The Gazette** within 14 days of its being passed.

28.6.3.2 Types of voluntary winding up

There are two types of voluntary liquidation: a members' voluntary winding up and a creditors' voluntary winding up.

Members' voluntary winding up

This form of liquidation is utilised if the company is solvent. Within the five weeks immediately preceding the date of the resolution (or on that date but before the resolution is actually passed), the directors (or the majority of them if more than two) make a statutory declaration setting out the company's assets and liabilities, and stating that they have made a full inquiry into the company's affairs and are of the opinion that the company will be able to pay its debts in full within 12 months of the commencement of the winding up. The declaration must be delivered to the Registrar within 15 days after the day the resolution was passed.

Creditors' voluntary winding up

If no such 'declaration of solvency' is filed, the winding up is a creditors' winding up.

Conversion from members' to creditors' voluntary winding up

During the course of a members' voluntary winding up, it may become clear that the company will be unable to pay its debts within 12 months of commencement of the winding up. If this happens, the liquidator must report the fact to the creditors and convert the liquidation into a creditors' voluntary winding up.

28.7 **Liquidators**

For all forms of liquidation, any liquidator appointed must be a qualified insolvency practitioner.

28.7.1 **Compulsory liquidation**

When a winding-up order is made, the official receiver of the court becomes the liquidator of the company and continues in office until someone else is appointed. The official receiver may seek nominations for a liquidator from creditors and contributories. They must either do this or give notice that they intend not to do so within 12 weeks of the winding-up order. Should they give such notice, they may still be required to seek nominations if requested by one-quarter (by value) of the creditors.

Where nominations are sought by the official receiver, this is done by sending a notice to creditors and contributories. When proposals are received, the official receiver must then seek a decision on these using a suitable decision procedure or the deemed consent procedure.

28.7.2 **Creditors' voluntary winding up**

In a creditors' winding up, the directors of the company must deliver to the creditors a notice seeking their decision at a physical meeting or a virtual meeting. The decision date cannot be earlier than three business days after the notice is given, but must not be later than 14 days after the resolution to wind up the company.

28.7.3 Members' voluntary winding up

The liquidator is appointed by the members in **general meeting**.

28.7.4 Functions of liquidators

The function of the liquidator of a company is to collect in the assets of the company and to pay their value to those creditors who are entitled according to the statutory order for payment (see **28.9**). If there is anything left after all creditors have been paid their debts and interest, the surplus goes to the members. If there are two or more classes of shares, some members may have priority over others in claiming the surplus.

Legislation grants liquidators extensive powers to assist them in performing their functions. These include powers to:

(a) pay any class of creditors in full;

(b) enter into a compromise or arrangement with creditors (this can be made binding without the agreement of all the creditors in certain cases provided that the voluntary arrangements procedure (**28.4**) is used);

(c) compromise claims to which the company is entitled (the liquidator can only exercise the above power with the sanction of an extraordinary resolution in the case of members' winding up, of the court, a committee of creditors or creditors' meeting in the case of creditors' winding up, and of the court or committee in the case of compulsory winding up);

(d) bring or defend legal proceedings;

(e) carry on the company's business for the purpose of beneficial winding up (sanction is required in the case of compulsory winding up only);

(f) sell the company's property;

(g) execute documents (including deeds);

(h) borrow on the security of the company's assets;

(i) act through agents;

(j) do 'all such other things as may be necessary for winding up the company's affairs and distributing its assets'.

28.7.5 Proceedings against the company

At any time between presentation of the petition and the making of the order, the company, or any creditor or contributory, can apply to have any action pending against the company stayed.

Once an order for compulsory winding up has been made, no action can be started or proceeded without the leave of the court.

Any execution, attachment, sequestration or distress started after the commencement of a compulsory liquidation is void. However, if the attachment or execution was begun before presentation of the petition, it can only be avoided by the liquidator if it was completed after commencement of the liquidation. This last provision also applies to voluntary liquidations, the operative date being the date the resolution to wind up the company was passed.

With regard to voluntary liquidations, the liquidator, any creditor or any member may apply to the court to have actions stayed. Such a stay is not granted automatically; although, if the action is begun after the date of passing the resolution to wind up an insolvent company, it will normally be granted.

28.8 Collection and distribution of assets in liquidation

28.8.1 Property of the company

28.8.1.1 Power to sell or charge

The liquidator has power to sell or mortgage the property and to satisfy the claims of the various people entitled in the company's liquidation (see **28.7.4**).

28.8.1.2 Power to disclaim

An important power of the liquidator in relation to the company's property is a power to disclaim any of the company's property that consists of unprofitable contracts, or other property that is unsaleable or not readily saleable.

28.8.2 Assets in the hands of the company

28.8.2.1 Assets held on trust

The creditors of an insolvent company are entitled to payment from its assets. They are not entitled to any assets of which the company is the legal owner but which it holds on trust for a third party. This has been held to apply in certain cases where a company holds cash for its customers.

28.8.2.2 Assets subject to retention of title

Many suppliers of goods supply goods under contracts that contain retention of title clauses. These may often be referred to as 'RoT' or *Romalpa* clauses, the latter following from the name of a leading case. A standard RoT clause will commonly provide that the supplier will retain legal title to goods supplied until the purchaser pays for them. Therefore, if the purchaser becomes insolvent, the supplier can look to repossess those goods rather than claiming the outstanding monies as an unsecured creditor. (For the powers of an administrator to dispose of goods despite a retention of title clause, see **28.3.8.3**.)

28.9 Entitlement to assets

28.9.1 Introduction

The principal duty of the liquidator of a company is to collect in and distribute the assets to those creditors entitled and to meet the costs of the procedure. (Note also the ability of a liquidator (and, in some cases, administrators) to 'claw back' assets–see **28.13**.)

In a large majority of cases, there will be insufficient funds available to pay all the creditors in full. The question therefore arises as to how, to whom and in what order the company's assets (or monies realised from the sale of such assets) are to be paid.

In the majority of liquidations of any size, there is a high likelihood that there will be charged assets. Given that the standard form of floating charge will seek to cover all assets of a company, present and future, it will often be the case that the majority of assets available to a liquidator will fall into the class of charged assets. In such a case, the only free assets potentially available would be any amounts recovered through actions taken by the liquidator (see **Chapter 25**).

Creditors are generally required to 'prove' their entitlement to debts in a liquidation. However, creditors with 'small' debts (£1,000 or less) do not need to make a formal application to the liquidator to prove their debt as the latter should be able to establish its validity based on the accounts and financial records of the company.

With these points in mind, the best approach to understanding relevant entitlements is to look at those parties who have an interest in the assets of an insolvent company and, in each case, examine their legal entitlement.

28.9.2 Creditors with fixed charges

Creditors with fixed charges are entitled to payment out of the charged assets before those assets are used for any other purpose. As between creditors with fixed charges over the same assets, their priority to assets is governed by registration under the Companies Act 2006.

A fixed charge takes priority over any floating charge, even if the latter is created and registered first, unless the floating charge prohibited the creation of later fixed charges ranking in priority to it and the fixed chargee had notice of this prohibition when they took the charge.

If the security of a fixed charge is inadequate (ie the value of the charged assets is less than the amount of the debt), the chargee may claim the balance of its debt as an ordinary creditor (or under any valid floating charge in its favour). If the debt is oversecured (ie the value of the charged assets is more than the amount of the debt), the chargee will be paid in full and the balance will be available for other creditors.

The costs of realising fixed charge assets should be paid out of the amounts realised from the sale of such assets.

28.9.3 Costs of winding up

The expenses of a winding up should be paid out of the assets of the company available for the payment of general creditors. Insofar as these are insufficient, the expenses will be paid out of assets subject to any floating charge created by the company. (The latter can include any amounts recovered through actions taken by the liquidator.) Therefore, the expenses of a winding up are given priority over the claims of floating charge-holders in respect of floating charge assets. Note, however that is a prescribed part of these assets set aside for unsecured creditors (see **28.9.5.2**).

In terms of the costs of any legal proceedings which a liquidator seeks to take to recover property, priority is not automatic: the liquidator must first obtain approval from the relevant floating charge-holder. If this is not forthcoming, the liquidator may seek approval from the court. Approval is not required if the litigation expenses are unlikely to exceed £5,000.

28.9.4 Preferential creditors

After payment of costs and expenses, the next category of creditor is the preferred creditor. The principal preferential debts are as follows.

(a) A maximum £800 per employee for wages owed for the four months before the relevant date (usually the date of the winding-up resolution or order (as applicable)). Any amount owed above £800 will be non-preferential. Certain categories of holiday pay are preferential.

(b) HMRC is then a secondary preferential creditor for taxes collected and held by a business on HMRC's behalf, principally: PAYE income tax, *employee* National Insurance contributions and VAT. HMRC is an unsecured creditor for taxes directly owed by companies, such as corporation tax and *employer* National Insurance contributions.

Preferential creditors (to the extent of their preference) are entitled to payment in full before ordinary creditors or holders of floating charges receive any payment. If the assets are insufficient to pay a class of preferred creditors in full, each member of that class will be paid an amount in proportion to their preferred debt.

28.9.5 Creditors with floating charges

Creditors with floating charges will be paid out of charged assets, following repayment of amounts owed to fixed charge-holders, costs and expenses relating to any *receiver* appointed to realise those charged assets, and preferential claims in any such receivership. (This assumes a receiver had been appointed prior to a subsequent liquidation.) In addition, as seen in **28.9.4**, where there are insufficient free assets to pay preferential claims in a liquidation, charged assets can be applied to pay preferential claims.

In relation to assets secured by floating charges, a liquidator, administrator or receiver is to make a prescribed part of the company's net property available for the satisfaction of unsecured debts. This is calculated as follows:

(a) where the company's net property does not exceed £10,000 in value, 50% of that property;

(b) subject to the limit stated below, where the company's net property exceeds £10,000 in value the sum of:

- 50% of the first £10,000 in value; and
- 20% of that part of the company's net property which exceeds £10,000 in value.

The maximum value of the prescribed part of the company's net property that can be made available to unsecured creditors is: £800,000 for floating charges created on or after 6 April 2020; or £600,000 for floating charges created before that date.

It should be noted that the status of the proceeds of any claims brought by an administrator or liquidator (see **Chapter 25**) do not form part of the company's net property available for satisfaction of debts owed to holders of floating charges.

The prescribed part is not to be distributed to the holder of a floating charge unless it exceeds the amount required to satisfy all unsecured debts. There is an exception to this rule where the relevant office-holder believes that the cost of making a distribution to unsecured creditors would be disproportionate to the benefits.

(Remember, following **28.9.2**, that the costs of realising a fixed charge asset should be paid from the proceeds of such assets. Therefore, there will be an apportionment of costs between fixed and floating charge assets in those cases where both types of charge have been taken.)

28.9.6 Effect of a moratorium on payment of debts

If a company enters into administration or liquidation within 12 weeks of the end of a moratorium (see **28.2**), then certain debts are given a specific priority ranking. These are:

(a) moratorium debts: debts incurred by the company during the moratorium period

(b) priority pre-moratorium debts:

- the monitor's remuneration or expenses;
- goods or services supplied during the moratorium;
- rent for a period during the moratorium;
- wages or salary relating to a period before or during the moratorium;
- any liability to make a redundancy payment;
- any liability under a loan or other instrument involving financial services that is not 'relevant accelerated debt'.

'Relevant accelerated debt' is any pre-moratorium debt that fell due between the date on which the monitor made their statement as to the potential rescue of the company as a going concern (see **28.2.2**) and the last of day of the moratorium as a result of the lender exercising acceleration or early termination rights under their loan agreement. This form of debt would continue to be paid according to the standard order of priority, which means that lenders will, in the context of a moratorium, have to consider the effect of any acceleration or early termination of their loan agreements with a company.

The position of moratorium and priority pre-moratorium debts can be seen at **28.9.10**.

28.9.7 Unsecured creditors

These creditors, sometimes referred to as ordinary creditors, rank behind preferred and secured creditors save to the extent of the provision made for them in the form of the prescribed amount (see **28.9.5**). They rank equally as between themselves in proportion to their respective debt. They would be paid out of free assets or any funds available from charged assets following payment of all prior claims (ie fixed charge-holders, preferential creditors and floating charge-holders). Note the potential effect on an unsecured creditor of a retention of title clause under a supply contract (see **28.8.2.2**).

28.9.8 Interest on debts

Once all creditors have been paid in full, any surplus is first used to pay interest on debts from the date of liquidation. This interest is paid to all creditors equally, regardless of whether their debts ranked equally for payment.

28.9.9 Shareholders

Any surplus after payment of debts and interest goes to the members according to the rights attached to their shares. As with unsecured creditors, they would be paid out of free assets or any funds available from charged assets following payment of all prior claims (ie fixed charge-holders, preferential creditors and floating charge-holders).

28.9.10 Order of priorities in insolvency distributions

Figure 28.1 shows the order of priorities for floating charge realisations in insolvency distributions.

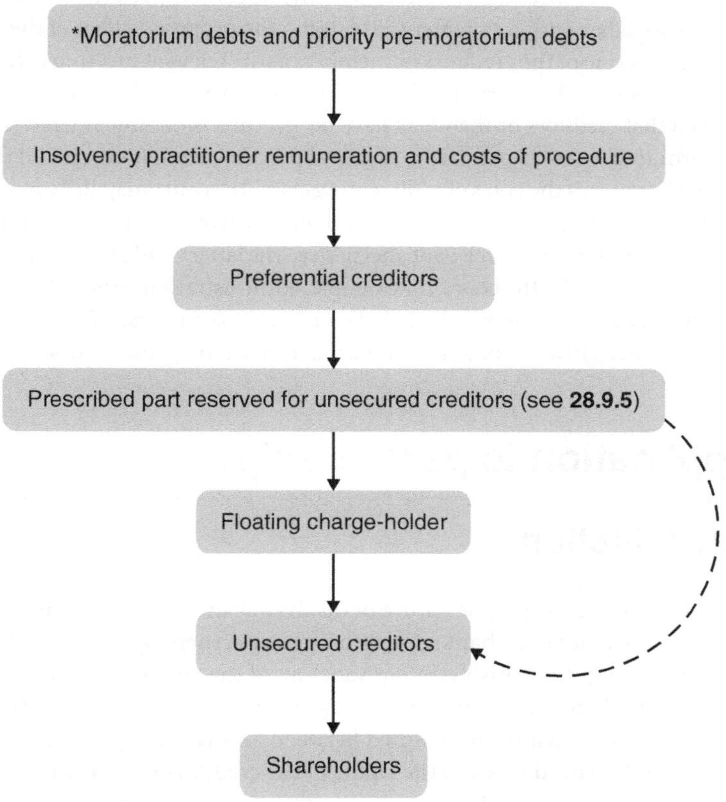

FIGURE 28.1 Floating charge realisations

28.10 Dissolution

Once winding up is complete, the company may be dissolved. This is achieved in the following ways:

(a) In compulsory liquidation the liquidator gives notice to the Registrar of Companies that they have completed the winding up. The company is then automatically dissolved three months later.

(b) In voluntary winding up, the liquidator delivers a final report to members and creditors and files certain returns with the Registrar of Companies. The company is then automatically dissolved after three months.

(c) The Registrar may dissolve a company by striking it off the register in certain circumstances where the company has ceased to trade.

28.11 Restructuring plan

The procedures set out earlier are available under the IA 1986. The Companies Act 2006 also provides a procedure for companies in financial difficulties. The focus for this is a compromise or arrangement with the company's creditors or members (or, in each case, any class of them), the purpose of which is to eliminate, reduce or prevent, or mitigate the effect of actual, or likely, financial difficulties.

The procedure may be commenced by application to court by:

(a) the company;

(b) any creditor or member;

(c) a liquidator; or

(d) an administrator.

The court may then order a meeting of creditors or members (or a relevant class of either), who will receive a notice together with a statement explaining the proposed effect of the compromise or arrangement. If 75% in value of the creditors or members at the relevant meeting vote in favour of the compromise or arrangement, the court may then sanction the proposal. It should be noted that where the court is satisfied that creditors or members have no 'genuine economic interest' in the company, they will not be permitted to participate in the approval process. In addition, should the relevant 75% approval not be met because of the votes of a 'dissenting class', the court may still sanction the plan if it is of the view that none of the members of that dissenting class would be any worse off under the plan than they would be in the event of the relevant alternative. The latter would be the most likely outcome if the plan was not sanctioned by the court: for example, administration or liquidation. This ability to stop a dissenting class of creditors or members preventing a viable proposal if they would be no worse off under the relevant alternative, is sometimes referred to as a 'cross-class cram-down'.

28.12 Application to partnerships

28.12.1 Introduction

Care must be taken to define the precise nature of insolvency in relation to a partnership. It is possible for an individual partner to be bankrupt without the partnership being insolvent. Equally, it is possible for a partnership to be insolvent without any of the partners being bankrupt. Finally, a situation could exist where a partnership was insolvent *and* some or all of its partners could be bankrupt. A distinction must be maintained between an insolvent partnership and bankrupt partners since applicable procedures and the rights of the creditors of each will vary according to which you are dealing with. The provisions of the IA 1986 relating to **bankruptcy** (see **Chapter 24**) will apply to individual bankrupt partners. In the case of an insolvent partnership, specific provisions of the IA 1986 which apply to companies can also be applied to a partnership.

28.12.2 **Insolvent partnerships**

28.12.2.1 Winding up as an unregistered company

An insolvent partnership may be wound up as an unregistered company under the IA 1986. A petition may be brought by a partner or a creditor. If it is thought that debts will not be met from the assets of the firm, bankruptcy petitions against individual partners may be brought in conjunction with the petition to wind up the partnership.

28.12.2.2 Priority of creditors on a winding up of a partnership

Priorities operate as in the case of an insolvent company, with preferred and secured creditors having priority over ordinary creditors. However, the situation becomes more complex where a partnership is being wound up and bankruptcy petitions are being brought against individual partners. In this situation, there are effectively two sets of creditors, those of the partnership and those of the individual partners. In such a situation:

(a) partnership creditors must first seek to satisfy their claims from the partnership property;
(b) creditors of individual partners must first look to the personal assets of those individuals;
(c) should there be insufficient partnership assets, partnership creditors may seek to satisfy their claims from the personal assets of the individual partners. In such a situation, their claims are apportioned amongst the individual partners and *rank equally* with those of the creditors of those individual partners;
(d) should creditors of individual partners find that those partners have insufficient assets to meet their claims, they may look to the partnership property. However, they can only do so *after* all the claims of partnership creditors have been met.

28.12.2.3 Disqualification

A court may, following a petition of the Secretary of State for Business, Innovation and Skills, find that a partner's conduct was such as to make them unfit to be concerned in the management of a company. If this is the case, the partner can be disqualified for a period of between two and 15 years from being involved in the management *of a company*. Such disqualification does *not* prevent them becoming involved in another partnership.

28.12.2.4 Administration and voluntary arrangements

Partnerships may also be the subject of administration or enter into a voluntary arrangement with their creditors.

28.13 **'Claw-back' of assets**

There are a number of rules that enable insolvency practitioners to make claims to 'claw back' assets that are not held by the insolvent company itself, to increase the assets available for distribution. The ability to take action under some of these rules is limited only to a liquidator, or a liquidator or administrator. Where a right to an action exists on the various grounds described in **28.13.1–28.13.3**, this right, together with the proceeds of such action, may be assigned by the relevant office-holder.

28.13.1 **Wrongful trading**

28.13.1.1 Grounds for claim

A director of a company may be ordered by the court to make such contribution to the assets of an insolvent company as the court thinks proper if they are found to be guilty of wrongful trading.

A liquidator or administrator may apply to the court for such an order. The court may make an order where:

(a) a company goes into insolvent liquidation or insolvent administration;

(b) a person knew or ought to have concluded (at some time before the commencement of winding up or the company entering administration) that there was no reasonable prospect that the company would avoid insolvent liquidation or administration; and

(c) that person was a director of the company at that time.

28.13.2 Defence

A defence is available to a director who shows that they took *every* step they ought to have taken with a view to minimising the potential loss to the company's creditors. In judging on this defence, the court applies a combined objective and subjective test, examining the knowledge and actions of the director as being those of a reasonably diligent person having both:

(a) the general knowledge, skill and experience that may reasonably be expected of a person carrying out the same functions as are carried out by the director in relation to the company; and

(b) the general knowledge, skill and experience that that director has.

The steps that a director must take to avoid liability for wrongful trading will vary depending on the circumstances of the case.

28.13.3 Fraudulent trading

Liquidators and administrators may apply to the court where it appears that any of the business of an insolvent company has been carried on with the intention to defraud the creditors of the company, or creditors of any other person, or for any fraudulent purpose. The court has the power to declare that any persons who were knowingly parties to such carrying of business are liable to contribute to the company's assets such amount as the court thinks proper.

28.13.4 Transactions at an undervalue and preferences

Liquidators and administrators may apply to the court for the following transactions to be set aside. (There are separate rules applicable to similar transactions in the context of personal bankruptcy–see 23.5.6.2 and 23.5.6.3.)

28.13.4.1 Transactions at an undervalue

This is where a company makes a gift to any person and receives either no consideration or consideration worth significantly less than the consideration provided by the company. However, a transaction cannot be set aside if it was entered into in good faith for the purpose of carrying on the company's business and at a time when there were reasonable grounds for believing that the transaction would benefit the company.

28.13.4.2 Preferences

This is where a company does anything or suffers anything to be done which puts a creditor, or a surety or guarantor of the company's debt, into a better position on an insolvent liquidation than they would have been in if that thing had not been done. For example:

- payment in full of a debt to a creditor who would have received partial payment on a liquidation; or
- giving security to a creditor.

For a preference to be set aside, the company must have been influenced by a desire to put the preferred party into a better position on liquidation than they would otherwise have been. This desire is presumed–although rebuttable–where the preference was given to a connected person, which includes any director of the company. Where payment is made or security given to a creditor threatening proceedings or otherwise insisting on payment, they will usually be able to show that there was no desire to put them in a better position on liquidation. This will be on the grounds that the company was merely responding to genuine commercial pressure.

28.13.4.3 'Relevant time' requirement for transactions at an undervalue and preferences

Undervalue transactions and preferences can only be set aside if entered into at a 'relevant time'. This requires both of the following to be satisfied:

(a) for a transaction at an undervalue, the transaction takes place within two years before commencement of winding up or application for administration or, for a preference, within six months before that date (unless the preference was made to a connected person, where the period is two years); and

(b) in the case of either an undervalue or preference, the company is insolvent at the time of the transaction or becomes insolvent as a result of the transaction. Where a transaction at an undervalue has been entered into with a connected person, insolvency is presumed unless it can be disproved.

28.13.4.4 Court can make order as it sees fit

Where it is shown that a transaction can be set aside as a transaction at an undervalue or preference, the court can make such order as it sees fit for restoring the position to what it would have been if the transaction had not been entered into. This could include, for example, ordering the person who entered into the transaction or who received the preference to return property or its value to the company. The position of a bona fide purchaser for value is, however, protected.

28.13.5 **Floating charges**

Under s245, a floating charge is invalid if it was made:

(a) within 12 months before the onset of insolvency; and

(b) at the time, when the company was unable to pay its debts or became unable to do so as a result of the charge.

Where the company created a floating charge in favour of a connected person, the charge is invalid if it was made within *two* years before the onset of insolvency, and even if the company was (and remained) solvent when the charge was created.

A floating charge created within the parameters described above is, however, valid to the extent of:

(a) consideration for the charge consisting of money paid or goods and services supplied to the company at or after the creation of the charge; and

(b) consideration consisting of discharge or reduction of any debt of the company at or after the creation of the charge; and

(c) interest on (a) and (b).

EXAMPLE

Montrel Ltd has a fully extended, unsecured overdraft of £20,000 with its bank. In September 2023, the bank agrees to extend the overdraft to £35,000 providing Montrel Ltd grants the bank a floating charge to secure all sums due to it. Montrel does so, as it requires £15,000 to pay wages and tax. Two months later, Montrel, having drawn down the £15,000 but not repaid any money to the bank, goes into liquidation.

The floating charge was given to the bank within 12 months of insolvency and Montrel was unable to pay its debts at the time. As a result, it is invalid. This would mean the bank would rank as an unsecured creditor in Montrel's liquidation for the sum of £35,000. However, under the exceptions detailed earlier, the charge will be valid to the extent of the consideration for the charge paid at or after its creation, namely the £15,000. Thus, the bank will, in Montrel's liquidation, rank as:

(a) a secured creditor (under the floating charge) for £15,000; and

(b) an unsecured creditor for £20,000.

Section 245 is designed to prevent a company benefiting a creditor by giving a charge for existing debt. The exceptions are designed to ensure that a company may still give security in order to obtain money or supplies when facing financial difficulties. This should not, in principle, cause any harm to existing creditors.

28.13.6 Transactions defrauding creditors

Where a company enters into a transaction at an undervalue with the specific purpose of putting assets beyond the reach of a person, that 'victim'–as well as a liquidator or administrator–may apply to have the transaction set aside. There is no time bar on this type of transaction at an undervalue but the court will have to be satisfied that the company had the relevant intent.

KEY POINT SUMMARY

- A range of insolvency procedures are available to which a company (or LLP) in financial difficulties may become subject.
- A moratorium may be sought by the directors of a company. This provides an initial period of 20 days where they, monitored by an insolvency practitioner, can develop a turnaround plan to rescue the company, safe from any enforcement action by creditors.
- Administration, which should have a specific statutory purpose, may be commenced by any of the company itself, its directors or a floating charge-holder, or by application to court.
- An administrator is given powers over the company and its assets to achieve the specified purpose of the administration. At the same time, there is a moratorium preventing any other action being taken against the company without court approval.
- A voluntary arrangement allows a company in financial difficulties to enter into an agreed arrangement with its creditors, supervised by an insolvency practitioner.
- Liquidation–or winding up–may be commenced by a creditor, usually by issuing a statutory demand for an unpaid debt which, if unmet, would establish grounds for a compulsory winding-up order being made by the court. Liquidation may also be voluntary–commenced by a resolution of a company's shareholders. If the company is insolvent, this will be a creditors' voluntary liquidation; if it is solvent, it will be a members' voluntary liquidation.
- A liquidator has powers to collect in and distribute the assets of a company to those entitled to them under a statutory order of priorities.
- In addition to procedures under the Insolvency Act 1986, the Companies Act 2006 provides a process for approval of a compromise or restructuring plan for a company in financial difficulties which, if approved by a requisite proportion of creditors or members, will bind all relevant parties.
- Both liquidators and administrators have various powers to 'claw back' for creditors assets that are not in the hands of an insolvent company: grounds include wrongful trading; transactions at an undervalue; preferences; and invalid floating charges.

CHAPTER 29
Bankruptcy

FUNCTIONING LEGAL KNOWLEDGE

This chapter considers the following functioning legal knowledge included in the SRA's SQE 1 assessment specification:

Insolvency (corporate and personal):

- options and procedures
- claw-back of assets for creditors
- order of priority for distribution to creditors

AUTHORITIES UNDERPINNING PRACTICE

The key authorities that underpin this area of practice are listed below. Note that for legislation you are linked to legislation.gov.uk.

Although much of the legislation on this government website is available in its amended form, the incorporation of new amendments into the text of legislation can be delayed. You should refer to legal databases to ensure you are referencing the most up-to-date legislation.

- Insolvency Act 1986
  http://www.legislation.gov.uk/ukpga/1986/45/contents
- Insolvency (England and Wales) Rules 2016
  http://www.legislation.gov.uk/uksi/2016/1024/contents/made

29.1 Introduction

If a partner or sole trader is in a position where:

(a) their liabilities exceed their assets; or
(b) they are unable to pay their debts as they fall due,

they may:

(a) be adjudicated bankrupt (see **29.2**);
(b) have their estate administered by a qualified insolvency practitioner under a voluntary arrangement (see **29.10**);
(c) apply for a debt relief order (see **29.11**); or
(d) apply for a debt respite scheme (see **29.12**).

Some entrepreneurs attempt to avoid the risk of personal **bankruptcy** by trading through a limited company. However, directors and **shareholder** of a company may still face personal bankruptcy if they personally guarantee a loan to the company.

29.2 The bankruptcy procedure

29.2.1 Introduction

Any of the following may commence bankruptcy proceedings:

(a) the debtor personally; or
(b) a creditor (or creditors jointly) whether secured or unsecured; or
(c) a supervisor of, or a person bound by, a voluntary arrangement (see **29.10**).

To do so, the party has to prove that the debtor is unable to pay their debts.

29.2.2 Procedure for debtor to declare bankruptcy

Debtors seeking bankruptcy must:

(a) complete an online application form, setting out personal and financial information, available from https://www.gov.uk;
(b) pay two fees: £130 for adjudication of their application, and a £550 bankruptcy deposit, to cover the costs of managing the bankruptcy; and
(c) submit the form to an adjudicator employed by the Insolvency Service.

The latter will review the application within 28 days. They may request verification of, or further, information. If so, then the decision period is extended by 14 days.

The applicant will receive a communication informing them that a decision has been made, and then sign into their application. On a successful application, the adjudicator will have uploaded a bankruptcy order. If not, a document will be uploaded explaining the reason for refusal and notifying the applicant that:

(a) within 14 days they can request a review of their application; and
(b) should the decision stand, they may appeal to the court within 28 days of the review decision.

If successful, the application and bankruptcy order are passed to the official receiver, whose office will contact the applicant within two weeks regarding next steps (see 29.2.8).

29.2.3 Procedure on a creditor's petition

Creditors seeking to have a debtor declared bankrupt must present a petition to court, together with a petition deposit of £1,500. First, certain conditions must be satisfied:

(a) The debtor must normally be domiciled or personally present in England and Wales when the petition is presented.
(b) The debt(s) must be for:
- a liquidated sum;
- of at least £5,000; and
- must be unsecured.

A secured creditor can present a petition only if they relinquish their **security** or petition only for the unsecured part of the debt.

The grounds for a petition are that the debtor appears either:

(a) to be unable to pay; or
(b) to have no reasonable prospect of paying;

the debt(s) specified in the petition and that there are no outstanding applications to have a statutory demand (see below) set aside.

To prove the grounds, the petitioner must show either that:

(a) a statutory demand served on the debtor requiring them to pay, secure or compound for the debt has not been complied with within three weeks; or
(b) execution or other process issued in respect of the debt as a judgment or order of any court has been returned unsatisfied in whole or in part.

The court may dismiss the petition if it is shown that:

(a) the debtor can pay all their debts, including contingent and prospective debts;
(b) the creditor has unreasonably refused any offer made by the debtor in response to a statutory demand; or
(c) it is appropriate to dismiss the petition for any reason, including a breach of the rules;
(d) the court *must* dismiss a petition if a statutory demand has been complied with.

29.2.4 Presentation of a petition by a supervisor of, or a person bound by, a voluntary arrangement

The supervisor of, or a person bound by, a voluntary arrangement (see **29.10**) may base a petition on the following grounds:

(a) that the debtor has failed to comply with their obligations or the supervisor's reasonable requests under the scheme; or
(b) that the debtor has provided false or misleading information in connection with entry into the scheme.

29.2.5 Consequences of presenting a petition

These are that:

(a) any disposition of property or payment of money made after the presentation of a petition–if the debtor is subsequently adjudicated bankrupt–will be void, unless the court approves the transaction either before or after it takes place; and
(b) the court has power to stay any action, execution or legal process against the debtor or their assets while bankruptcy proceedings are pending.

29.2.6 Making the bankruptcy order

Once the petition has been presented, the court may exercise its discretion to make a bankruptcy order (or, in the case of a petition presented by the debtor personally, to make an interim order so that a voluntary composition with the creditors can be arranged).

29.2.7 Procedure following the making of the bankruptcy order

On the making of a bankruptcy order:

(a) an official receiver will automatically become trustee (see **29.3**) of the bankrupt's estate, unless the court appoints another person; and
(b) the bankrupt must, unless the official receiver dispenses with the requirement, prepare a statement of their affairs within 21 days.

Failure to provide a statement of affairs is a contempt of court.

At any time after the order is made and before its discharge, the official receiver can apply to the court to order a public examination of the bankrupt's affairs.

29.3 The trustee in bankruptcy

29.3.1 Introduction

The Insolvency Act 1986 (IA 1986) provides that the administration of a bankrupt estate should be carried out by a **trustee in bankruptcy**. This will initially be an official receiver of the Insolvency Service. The only exception to this is where a supervisor of a voluntary arrangement is in place, when the court may appoint the latter as the trustee.

29.3.2 Appointment by creditors

The official receiver has 12 weeks from the making of the order to decide whether to seek an appointment by the creditors of a trustee in their place. To do so, they must give notice to the creditors and seek a decision using a suitable decision procedure or the deemed consent procedure (ss246ZE and 246ZF IA 1986). Note that one-quarter (by value) of the creditors may demand that such a decision be offered to them. If no notice is given and creditors do not make a demand, the official receiver will remain the trustee.

Where the trustee seeks any decision from the bankrupt's creditors, the trustee must at the same time give notice inviting them to decide whether they wish to form a creditors' committee.

29.3.3 Function and powers of the trustee

The function of the trustee is to get in, realise and distribute the bankrupt's estate to creditors who provide proof of debt. The IA 1986 gives the trustee wide powers to administer the bankrupt's affairs, including:

(a) carrying on the bankrupt's business with a view to a beneficial winding up;
(b) bringing or defending actions relating to the bankrupt's property;
(c) making compromises or arrangements with the bankrupt's creditors;
(d) selling any part of the bankrupt's property or business;
(e) applying to the court for orders directing the bankrupt to do any act in connection with the administration of the estate;
(f) making contracts, employing agents, executing documents and doing any act necessary or expedient for the exercise of their powers;
(g) disclaim onerous property (eg unprofitable contracts); and
(h) requiring the bankrupt to do any acts in the management or carrying on of the bankrupt's business.

29.3.4 Decision-making processes

Where decisions of a bankrupt's creditors are required, these may be made by any procedure the trustee thinks fit (s379ZA IA 1986) or by way of 'deemed consent' (s379ZB IA 1986) unless 10% in value of creditors object.

There is no requirement to hold any meetings for decision-making purposes, unless requested by 10% or more in number or value of creditors, or ten creditors in number.

29.4 Effect of the bankruptcy order on the bankrupt personally

If the court makes a bankruptcy order, the debtor becomes an undischarged bankrupt and is deprived of the ownership of their property, which vests immediately in the trustee on the latter's appointment.

An undischarged bankrupt suffers certain disabilities: for example, they cannot:

(a) practise as a solicitor or barrister;
(b) act as a director; or
(c) be involved in the management of a company.

An undischarged bankrupt also faces criminal liability if they commit specific offences, including:

(a) making gifts of, or concealing, property; or
(b) obtaining credit without disclosing the bankruptcy.

29.5 Bankrupt's family home

The trustee must, within three years, in respect of the bankrupt's interest in their family home:

(a) realise the interest;
(b) apply for an order of sale or possession in respect of the premises in which the interest subsists;
(c) apply for a charging order over the premises in respect of the value of the interest; or
(d) enter into an agreement with the bankrupt regarding the interest;

failing which the interest will revert to the bankrupt. The three-year period may be extended by application to the court.

There are, however, provisions designed to protect the family home for the benefit of the bankrupt's family.

If the family home is owned in the sole name of the bankrupt, the 1986 Act charges the right of occupation of the spouse (which includes a former spouse) of the bankrupt on the interest of the trustee in bankruptcy in the matrimonial home. If an application is made to realise the bankrupt's interest in the house, the court will consider, when deciding whether to grant the application:

- the creditors' interests;
- the needs and resources of the spouse;
- the needs of the children;
- whether the spouse's conduct contributed to the bankruptcy; and
- all other relevant circumstances, save for the needs of the bankrupt.

If the matrimonial home is owned in joint names by the bankrupt and their spouse, these discretionary factors will be taken into account when the trustee applies under s14 of the Trusts of Land and Appointment of Trustees Act 1996 to realise the bankrupt's interest. (This will usually be preceded by a offer to the joint owner to buy the bankrupt's share.) If the application is made after one year has elapsed since the bankrupt's property vested in the trustee in bankruptcy, the interests of the creditors will be paramount.

If the bankrupt's minor children lived in the home at the time of presenting the petition and when the bankruptcy order was made, the bankrupt cannot be evicted without a court order. The court will consider the creditors' interests, the bankrupt's financial resources, the needs of the children and all the circumstances when deciding whether to make the eviction order. If the application is made after one year has elapsed since the bankrupt's estate vested in their trustee, the interests of the creditors will be assumed to outweigh all other considerations, unless there are exceptional circumstances.

29.6 Items not available to trustee

Certain tenancies, including secure and assured shorthold tenancies, do not automatically vest in the trustee, being excluded from a bankrupt's estate. Should there be value in them, however, the trustee may serve notice in writing on the bankrupt, such that they vest in the trustee.

There are certain items which are not available to the trustee for distribution:

(a) property held by the bankrupt in trust for another person;

(b) the tools of the bankrupt's trade, as well as clothing and bedding necessary for the basic needs of the bankrupt and their family;

(c) the personal earnings of the bankrupt to the extent they are not in excess of what is required to satisfy the reasonable domestic needs of the bankrupt and their family.

29.7 Power to claim back assets

The official receiver or a trustee in bankruptcy has power to claim assets that are no longer in the possession or ownership of the bankrupt in the circumstances set out in the following sections.

29.7.1 Transactions defrauding creditors (ss423–425)

29.7.1.1 Grounds

An action can be brought under s423 to set aside:

(a) a transaction at an undervalue entered into between one person and another;

(b) accompanied by the requisite intent: to put assets beyond the reach of a person who is making, or may at some time make, a claim against the relevant person, or of otherwise prejudicing the interests of such a person in relation to such a claim.

29.7.1.2 Time limit

The transaction that is the subject of an action under s423 can have taken place at any time before bankruptcy.

29.7.2 Undervalue transactions (s339)

29.7.2.1 Grounds on which transaction voidable

A transfer of property at an undervalue by a person who is subsequently made bankrupt may be voidable under s339 IA 1986 at the instance of the trustee in bankruptcy if:

(a) entered into within two years of the date of presentation of the successful bankruptcy petition; or

(b) entered into within two to five years of the date of the petition, but only if the transferor was insolvent at the time, or became so as a result of the transaction.

For (b), where the transferee is an 'associate' of the transferor, the transfer will be presumed, unless it can be *proved* to the contrary, to have taken place at a time when the transferor was insolvent. 'Associate' is defined as the bankrupt's spouse or former or reputed spouse and, in relation to any of them or the bankrupt: a brother, sister, uncle, aunt, nephew, niece, lineal ancestor or lineal descendant (including relatives of the half-blood, stepchildren, adopted and illegitimate children). A company controlled by the bankrupt or any associate(s), as defined, is an associate.

29.7.3 Preferences (s340)

29.7.3.1 Grounds

A trustee in bankruptcy may apply to the court to remedy a preference, where:

(a) at a time when they are insolvent;

(b) a debtor has done or suffered anything to be done which has the effect of putting a creditor, surety or guarantor into a position which, in the event of the debtor's bankruptcy, will be better than the position he would have been in had that thing not been done; and

(c) it can be proven that the debtor was 'influenced in deciding to give it by a desire' to improve the position of the creditor.

The desire to prefer the particular creditor need not be the *dominant* intention. Where the preference is given by an individual to an 'associate' (see 29.7.2.1), the 'desire' will be *presumed*, unless the contrary is proved.

Thus, a debtor who discharges in full the debts of one unsecured, ordinary creditor, when their assets are insufficient to discharge *all* their debts in full, may have given a preference.

29.7.3.2 Time limits

A preference may be challenged if it takes place:

(a) within the six-month period preceding the presentation of the bankruptcy petition; or

(b) within two years if the person preferred is an associate.

CONDUCT POINT

Integrity, maintaining trust and acting fairly

The trustee's powers described earlier enable them to deal with transactions where assets may have been transferred out of a bankrupt's estate to put them beyond the reach of creditors or to favour a particular party. When facing financial difficulties, an individual may be tempted to follow such courses of action, for example transferring assets into the name of a spouse or partner. SRA Principle 5 requires a solicitor to act with integrity, and para 1.4 of the Code of Conduct for Solicitors states that a solicitor should not be complicit in the acts of others, including a client, which misleads the court or others. Therefore, a solicitor should neither advise in favour of transactions of the types described earlier nor, at the behest of a client, facilitate such transactions. If the client suggests the latter, a solicitor should decline the instructions and, should their client not withdraw them, refuse to continue the retainer.

29.8 Distribution of the bankrupt's assets

29.8.1 Distribution procedure

Having realised as much of the bankrupt's assets as possible without needlessly protracting the administration of the estate, the trustee must notify the creditors that they intend to declare a final dividend or that no dividend will be declared. The notice must also state a final date for creditors to prove their debts, although the court has power, on application by any person, to postpone this date. Subject to any postponement, any creditor who fails to prove by the final date may be ignored in the final dividend.

29.8.2 Order of priority for payment of debts

The bankrupt's assets must be distributed strictly according to security rights and the statutory order of priority for payment of debts under s328 IA 1986:

(a) Creditors with security will be paid, after payment of related costs of realising the charged assets, from the proceeds of the mortgaged or charged property in priority to all other claims (to the extent the security is insufficient to meet the debt the secured creditor claims as an ordinary creditor).

(b) From the realisations of the remaining assets, next will be paid the bankruptcy administration costs of the official receiver, the trustee in bankruptcy and others, including professional advisors who have given assistance.

(c) After this, any preferential debts of the bankrupt will be paid in priority to other debts which are classified as 'ordinary' and 'secondary' as in a company **liquidation** (see **28.9.4**). These debts are calculated by reference to the 'relevant date' which, generally, is the date the bankruptcy order is made (unless an interim receiver is appointed following the presentation of the petition, in which case the date is that on which the receiver is first appointed).

(d) The ordinary unsecured creditors.

(e) Statutory interest will be paid if a surplus remains after all previous claims have been paid.

(f) Any debts owed to the spouse or civil partner of the bankrupt.

(g) The bankrupt would then, should there be any, receive any surplus.

Each class of creditor must be paid in full before the next class receives anything, with each class ranking equally among themselves. If the assets are insufficient to meet the debts owed to the creditors of the class, they are paid in proportion to the value of their debt.

29.9 Duration of the bankruptcy and discharge of the bankrupt

29.9.1 Discharge of the bankrupt

A bankrupt will generally be discharged automatically–that is, without any formal application or court hearing–one year after the date of the bankruptcy order.

A bankrupt will not be discharged if there is a court order suspending their discharge, for example where the bankrupt has not cooperated with the official receiver or trustee in bankruptcy.

29.9.2 Effect of discharge

Once the bankrupt has been discharged, they are normally freed from the disqualifications suffered by undischarged bankrupts and from liability to meet their bankruptcy debts.

29.9.3 Bankruptcy restrictions order (BRO)

On an application by the Secretary of State, or the official receiver acting on a direction of the Secretary of State, a court may make a BRO for a period of between two and 15 years, if it thinks it appropriate in light of dishonest or other blameworthy conduct of the bankrupt before or after the making of the bankruptcy order. The BRO imposes restrictions which will generally take effect following the discharge of the bankrupt. These will include:

(a) not being involved as an officer or in the formation, management or promotion of a company without court permission;

(b) not seeking credit in excess of £500 without first disclosing the BRO;

(c) not being able to carry on business under a different name without providing notification of the name in which they were adjudged bankrupt.

29.10 Individual voluntary arrangement

29.10.1 Introduction

The IA 1986 provides an alternative method–with the aim of avoiding the full rigour of formal bankruptcy–by which debtors in financial difficulties can propose a binding composition or scheme of arrangement to their creditors. This individual voluntary arrangement is usually referred to in practice as an IVA.

29.10.2 IVA procedure

A debtor seeking an IVA must first:

(a) prepare a formal proposal to their creditors to pay all or part of the debts due to them, which can include a proposal that payment be deferred for a period of time; and

(b) provide the insolvency practitioner (IP) who will be the 'nominee' for the IVA with a statement of their affairs: their creditors; their debts and other liabilities and their assets.

In most cases, the debtor will prepare their proposal in conjunction with the nominee.

The debtor may also make an application to the court for an interim order (see 29.10.3) pending the IVA; however, this is not compulsory.

The nominee must report within 14 days to the creditors as to whether the IVA has a reasonable prospect of being approved and implemented, and thus whether a creditors' meeting should be called. Assuming this is the case, the proposal is put to the creditors, who may accept it without modification or request modifications to be made. Following the creditors' meeting, provided 75% or more of the creditors (by value of their debt) who either attend the meeting or respond in writing accept the proposal, it will be binding on all creditors. All creditors and the court will be formally notified of the result of the meeting. In most cases, the nominee IP will be appointed as the IVA supervisor to supervise the implementation of the agreed IVA terms.

29.10.3 Interim order

29.10.3.1 Introduction

A debtor in financial difficulties who wishes to propose an IVA to creditors has an option to apply to the court for an interim order. The effect of an interim order is that, once made:

(a) no bankruptcy petition can be presented against the debtor;

(b) no rights of forfeiture over leased premises may be exercised, except with the leave of the court; and

(c) no other proceedings, execution or legal process can, without the leave of the court, be commenced or prosecuted against the debtor or their property.

The interim order is effective for 14 days beginning with the day after the order was made, with the court having power to extend the period. Note that, whilst an application for an interim order is pending, (b) and (c) above are effective.

29.10.3.2 IVA procedure following interim order

The IVA procedure following an interim order is broadly similar to that described in **29.10.2**. However, the nominee must first report to the court as to whether the voluntary arrangement has a reasonable prospect of being approved and implemented, and whether a meeting of creditors should be called to consider the proposed IVA. Should the nominee fail to deliver the report to the court before the interim order expires, the debtor can apply to have the order renewed or extended, and also to have the nominee replaced. If the nominee decides that a meeting of creditors should not be called and the court agrees, the interim order may be discharged.

Assuming the nominee recommends a creditor's meeting be called, then the process continues as described in **29.10.2**. Once the proposal has been accepted, any interim order in force ceases to have effect and any bankruptcy petition that was stayed by the interim order is deemed to have been dismissed (subject to a court order to the contrary).

29.10.4 Challenging the decision of the creditors' meeting

29.10.4.1 Parties who may challenge

The decision of the creditors' meeting may, at any time during the 28 days commencing with the day the report is made to the court, be challenged by:

(a) the debtor;

(b) any person who was entitled to vote at the meeting;

(c) the nominee (or their replacement); and

(d) if the debtor is an undischarged bankrupt, their trustee or the official receiver.

29.10.4.2 Grounds

The grounds of challenge are limited to the following:

(a) that the voluntary arrangement accepted by the meeting unfairly prejudices the interests of a creditor; and/or

(b) that there was a material irregularity at, or in relation to, the meeting.

29.10.4.3 Effect of challenge

If the court confirms the challenge, the approval of the meeting may be revoked or suspended. Alternatively, the court may order a further meeting to be held to consider any revised proposal or, in the case of a 'material irregularity', order that the meeting be held again to reconsider the proposal.

Having ordered a further meeting to be held, the court can extend or renew the interim order. However, if the court is satisfied that no revised proposal will be submitted by the debtor, the order to hold a further meeting will be revoked and the approval given at the original meeting will be revoked or suspended.

29.11 Debt relief orders

A debt relief order (DRO) is an alternative means of dealing with personal debt available to individuals in specified circumstances. The eligibility criteria are that the individual:

- is unable to pay their debts;
- owe less than £50,000 in total;
- has £75 or less left over monthly after paying tax, National Insurance and normal household expenses;
- does not own their own home;
- has savings and specified assets that, together, are worth less than £2,000;
- is neither the subject of bankruptcy or an IVA, nor has had a DRO in the previous six years; and
- has lived, had a property or worked in England and Wales in the previous three years.

An application must be made through an approved intermediary (a professional debt advisor authorised by a body designated by the Secretary of State as having power to do so). If successful, the official receiver notifies the debtor and the latter's creditors of the DRO. During the period of the DRO, normally a year, there is a moratorium on most creditors taking action to enforce debts, and the debtor does not have to make payment of such debts. There are exceptions to this, including rent arrears and payments to bailiffs. The debtor also should continue to pay normal household expenses, including rent, council tax and utilities.

At the end of the DRO period, the debtor is freed from all debts that were the subject of the order. Being the subject of a DRO will have an effect on an individual's credit rating as to their future ability to obtain credit.

29.12 Debt Respite Scheme

The Debt Respite Scheme provides short term legal protections from creditor action to individuals in financial difficulties. There is a standard form of 'breathing space' which provides protection for up to 60 days. This includes: pausing most enforcement actions; contact from creditors; and freezing interest and charges on debts. A mental health crisis breathing space provides similar protection for the period during which the individual is receiving crisis treatment, plus a further 30 days. In both cases, applications to the scheme must be made through a regulated debt advisor. An application in respect of the mental health crisis scheme requires supporting evidence from a mental health professional. There are eligibility criteria set out in the Regulations, including details of qualifying debts.

KEY POINT SUMMARY

- An individual, sole trader or partnership whose liabilities exceed their assets, or cannot meet their debts as they fall due, may be adjudicated bankrupt.
- Bankruptcy proceedings may be commenced by the debtor personally, a creditor or a supervisor of a voluntary scheme.
- Following a bankruptcy order being made, a trustee in bankruptcy will realise the bankrupt's assets and distribute the resulting funds to the bankrupt's creditors. The trustee in bankruptcy has powers to claw-back assets in various circumstances.
- A bankrupt will usually be discharged one year after the date of their bankruptcy order.
- An alternative to bankruptcy is an individual voluntary arrangement proposed by a debtor, in conjunction with a 'nominee' insolvency practitioner, and requiring agreement by 75% in value of their creditors.
- A final option available to deal with personal debts of up to £50,000 is a debt relief order which provides a moratorium of one year on most creditors taking action to enforce debts.

PART G
Tax

CHAPTER 30
Income Tax

FUNCTIONING LEGAL KNOWLEDGE

This chapter considers the following functioning legal knowledge included in the SRA's SQE 1 assessment specification:

Income tax:

- chargeable persons/entities (employees, sole traders, partners, **shareholders**, lenders and **debenture** holders)
- basis of charge (types of income/main reliefs and exemptions)
- the charge to tax: calculation and collection
- the scope of anti-avoidance provisions

AUTHORITIES UNDERPINNING PRACTICE

The key authorities that underpin this area of practice are listed below. Note that for legislation you are linked to legislation.gov.uk.

Although much of the legislation on this government website is available in its amended form, the incorporation of new amendments into the text of legislation can be delayed. You should refer to legal databases to ensure you are referencing the most up-to-date legislation.

- Income Tax (Earnings and Pensions) Act 2003
  https://www.legislation.gov.uk/ukpga/2003/1/contents
- Income Tax (Trading and Other Income) Act 2005
  https://www.legislation.gov.uk/ukpga/2005/5/contents
- Income Tax Act 2007
  https://www.legislation.gov.uk/ukpga/2007/3/contents
- Finance Act 2024
  https://www.legislation.gov.uk/ukpga/2023/1/contents/enacted

30.1 Taxation: conduct and ethics considerations

Chapters 30–4 are directed towards the SQE Assessment Specification objective of 'taxation of a business and its stakeholders'. The latter includes directors, employees, shareholders, partners, suppliers and customers. Taxation is governed by statute and overseen and implemented by HM Revenue and Customs (HMRC).

A solicitor may be instructed by a business client or a stakeholder to:

- provide general tax planning advice;
- advise on the tax aspects of a specific transaction or scheme; or
- facilitate a transaction which has tax implications.

In addition, a solicitor will have their own tax affairs to manage, whether as an employee or partner.

The areas of instruction above–which could be in the context of any or all of the taxes in the following chapters–may all involve some element of tax planning. That is, using current tax legislation to structure finances, payments or transactions to make them 'tax efficient' and minimise the tax payable by an individual or business. This might result in avoiding tax that might otherwise be paid. Such tax avoidance should be contrasted with tax evasion: the latter refers to illegal courses of action to reduce or not pay tax.

Schemes or arrangements to avoid tax, whilst complying with the technical letter of the law, may, however, be open to challenge by HMRC. The government and HMRC have implemented a number of anti-avoidance measures to prevent schemes which enable favourable tax outcomes which were not anticipated when the relevant rules were created. These schemes are often referred to as 'abusive tax avoidance schemes', in that they are viewed as abusing the intent of the tax legislation. That is, they may technically comply with the law, but they are not aligned to the policy or spirit of the law. In short, such schemes are contrary to the intention of the law. As such, they may be challenged by HMRC and set aside. A solicitor who advises on, enables or participates in abusive tax schemes or arrangements risks breaching the Principles and Code of Conduct, and facing disciplinary action. Enabling tax arrangements which are successfully challenged by HMRC may also result in financial penalties.

The following are some of the main conduct and ethical considerations raised in the context of taxation and the anti-avoidance regime. As with all conduct issues, should there be any concern, you should refer to your compliance officer for legal practice (COLP) or contact the SRA for guidance.

Principle 1 requires solicitors to act in a way that upholds the constitutional principle of the rule of law and the proper administration of justice. This principle creates obligations not only to clients but also to third parties, such as HMRC, with whom a solicitor may have dealings. There is thus an expectation that a solicitor should, if advising on tax issues, play an important role in assisting taxpayers to comply with their legal obligations.

Principle 2 requires solicitors to act in a way that upholds public trust and confidence in the profession and the legal services provided. Actions aimed at abusive tax avoidance, whether for client or personal benefit, would undermine this trust.

Principle 5 requires a solicitor to act with integrity. This covers all professional actions and dealings, and would extend to those with HMRC. A solicitor is therefore expected to deal with HMRC on an open and honest basis, and should not seek to rely on, for example, the latter's lack of knowledge of a client's tax position.

Principle 7 requires a solicitor to act in the best interests of each client. This should not, however, extend to advising a client to pursue a scheme which is contrary to the intention of the law. Should a client propose a scheme which might result in outcomes unintended by the legislation, a solicitor should be clear as to the legal implications, and the potential costs and penalties that could be incurred should it be successfully challenged by HMRC.

Actions seeking to obtain a tax advantage unintended by the legislation may also be contrary to the following paragraphs of the Code of Conduct for Solicitors:

(a) 1.2: an abuse of position by taking unfair advantage of others;

(b) 1.4: misleading others either by your own acts or omissions or allowing or being complicit in the acts or omissions of others, including your client.

30.2 **Income tax**

30.2.1 **Basic liability**

Individual taxpayers must pay tax annually on their total taxable income: the total income received less any relevant allowances, deductions and reliefs. Liability is assessed based on the tax year, which runs from 6 April to the following 5 April.

EXAMPLE

Income earned in September 2024 will be relevant to a taxpayer's liability for the tax year 2024/25, that is, 6 April 2024–5 April 2025.

30.2.2 Sources of income

The most common sources of income are:

(a) from employment as wages or salary;
(b) from a trade or profession;
(c) interest on deposits or savings;
(d) dividend payments on shareholdings;
(e) rental income.

All sources of income earned in a relevant tax year are aggregated in calculating income tax liability for that year.

Taxpayers are required to provide a tax return to HMRC with details of all income and expenditure in a relevant tax year, and hence their total taxable income. A paper tax return must be provided by 31 October or an online return by 31 January following the tax year in question.

30.2.3 Income tax rates

30.2.3.1 England and Northern Ireland

The government sets income tax rates for specific tax years in its budgets. For 2024/25, income tax rates are:

Basic: 20% (payable on the first £37,700 of taxable income).

Higher: 40% (payable on taxable income from £37,701 to £125,140).

Additional: 45% (payable on taxable income above £125,140).

30.2.3.2 Wales

The Welsh government—the Senedd—has a power to set rates of income tax in Wales. When the power was granted, the central UK government, for Welsh taxpayers, reduced by 10% the above Basic, Higher and Additional rates. Welsh taxpayers therefore pay income tax at a rate, or rates, which are the sum of the reduced 'rest of the UK' rate and the Welsh rate. The current Welsh rate of income tax is 10%, which means that Welsh taxpayers are taxed at the same effective rate as English and Northern Irish taxpayers. It is possible that, in future years, rates could differ for Welsh taxpayers.

The Senedd's power to determine income tax rates does not extend to any income on dividends (see 33.7.2.2) or savings. In addition, it does not determine the personal allowance (see 30.2.3.3).

Tax payable by Welsh taxpayers is subject to the same systems, administered by HMRC, of tax returns and PAYE, and collection. Whether you will be a Welsh taxpayer in any tax year is determined by either:

- your residency in Wales being for the majority of the year in question; or
- the location of your main home.

30.2.3.3 Personal allowance

Most individuals receive a personal allowance that must be exceeded before income tax is payable. For 2024/25, this is £12,570. It is reduced by £1 for every £2 earned above £100,000, until it reaches zero, for those earning over £100,000. The allowance will reach zero for those whose income is £125,140 or more, ie, additional rate taxpayers.

EXAMPLE

Chris: Tax year 2024/25	£
Income	92,000
Less Personal allowance	12,570
Taxable income	79,430
Tax payable:	
£37,700 @ 20%	7,540
£41,730 (£79,430–£37,700) @ 40%	16,692
Total income tax:	24,232

30.3 Taxable profits from an unincorporated business

30.3.1 Introduction

The owner(s) of an unincorporated business are taxed on the profits made by their business: this forms part of their individual taxable income. Thus, profits earned by the business are treated as income earned by the relevant sole trader or partners. (This should be compared to the profits of a company which are treated as the income of the company, a separate legal person.)

Taxable profits are income receipts generated from trading activities *less* deductible expenditure incurred by the business plus any other sums deductible under tax legislation (eg capital allowances–see **30.3.3.3** and **Chapter 33**).

EXAMPLE

	£	£
Income receipts		375,000
Less		
Deductible expenditure	220,000	
Capital allowances	15,000	
		235,000
Taxable profits		140,000

Where total deductions exceed income, this creates a loss for tax purposes (see **30.5**).

EXAMPLE

	£
Income receipts	128,000
Deductible expenditure	163,000
Loss	(35,000)

30.3.2 Income receipts

Income receipts are usually recurrent, or capable of recurrence, and are distinguished from capital receipts which do not attract income tax. Income receipts would commonly result from, for example, sales of stock and provision of services, including professional services. Sales of fixed assets would tend to generate capital receipts.

EXAMPLE

Bathroom fittings shop: sales of fittings will create income receipts, whilst a sale of delivery vehicle or the shop itself would create a capital receipt.

Car dealership: sales of vehicles (stock) will create an income receipt.

30.3.3 Deductible expenditure

30.3.3.1 Nature of deductible expenditure

To be deductible for income tax purposes, expenditure must be:

- of an income rather than a capital nature; and
- wholly and exclusively laid out or expended for the purposes of the business.

Common examples of deductible expenditure are:

(a) salaries paid to employees (see further in **30.7**);
(b) rent for leasehold premises;
(c) utilities (electricity, gas, telecommunications etc);
(d) rates/council tax;
(e) purchases of stock for re-sale;
(f) advertising costs;
(g) business stationery.

30.3.3.2 Nature of non-deductible expenditure

Specific types of non-deductible expenditure are set out in relevant tax legislation. These include most business entertainment expenses and provisions for bad debts. If a business expense is excessively large and so also partly represents a gift, it will not be deductible as it is not wholly for the purposes of the business. Similarly, expenditure on something partly connected with the business and partly unconnected (eg there is an element of personal enjoyment) will not be deductible as it is not exclusively for the purposes of the business.

30.3.3.3 Capital allowances

Where a business buys certain types of capital assets, capital allowances may also be available to deduct from income receipts. The cost of the capital asset is not deductible as it is not expenditure of an income nature. However, a designated percentage of the purchase price–effectively deemed depreciation–may be deductible annually from income receipts. (See **Chapter 33** for further details and examples.)

30.3.4 Accounting bases

Almost all businesses produce annual final accounts. These show its profits–calculated according to normal accountancy practice–and how they are allocated to the proprietor(s).

For tax purposes, accounts have to be agreed with HMRC and must give a true and fair view of profits. These accounts do not have to be fully audited. However, certain fundamentals such as creditors, debtors, work-in-progress and stock must feature in them. In addition, in calculating profits, a business must be consistent in allocating receipts and expenses to one accounting period or to a later period. It should not manipulate receipts and expenses to avoid tax.

30.4 The basis of assessment

30.4.1 Tax year basis

For the tax year 2024/25 onwards, liability to tax is assessed on a tax year basis. Most businesses work on a 12-month accounting period which will end on a date, usually a month end, which may or not correspond with the tax year. However, regardless of its accounting period, the annual liability to tax of a business will be on the basis of the profits or losses made in the tax year that runs from 6 April to 5 April.

EXAMPLE

Jasvinder Khan (a sole trader):

Accounting period: 1 January to 31 December

Accounting period *ending* 31 December 2025: taxable profits are £48,000

Accounting period *ending* 31 December 2026: taxable profits are £40,000

Applying the tax year basis of calculation, for the tax year 2025/26, Jasvinder's taxable profits will be calculated as follows:

£36,000 (9/12* of taxable profits for accounting period ending December 2025)

£10,000 (3/12 of taxable profits for accounting period ending December 2026)

£46,000 Total taxable profits for tax year 2025/26

Thus, where an accounting period ends on a date other than the end of the tax year (5 April)**, profits as calculated in each of the two sets of accounts will be apportioned pro rata into the relevant tax year.

(*Note that, for HMRC purposes, apportionment is calculated using days, that is, the relevant fraction being a number of days/365; the above example has used months for ease of illustration. **HMRC will treat an accounting period ending on any date between 31 March and 4 April (inclusive) as effectively ending on 5 April.)

The change to the tax year basis of assessment means that, on the commencement or cessation of a business, the business will be assessed to tax on the profits or losses for that tax year. That is, if a business commences trading on 1 January 2025, it will be assessed on the basis of 1 January 2025 to 5 April 2025. If a business ceases on 15 November 2025, it will be assessed on the basis of 6 April 2025 to 15 November 2025. This product of the tax year basis of assessment compares to the previous system (see **30.4.2**), which involved a series of comparatively complex rules for the opening and closing years of a business.

30.4.2 Current year basis: tax years to 2022/23

The tax year basis–see **30.4.1**–has superseded the 'current year basis' of assessing tax. Under this system, HMRC calculated the tax of an unincorporated business on the basis of profits or losses made in the accounting period *ending* in the tax year in question. Therefore, using the example above, the profits made in the accounting period of the business that ended on 31 December 2022 would have been used as the basis for calculating its tax for the tax year 2022/23.

30.4.3 Transition: tax year 2023/24

To enable the change from the current year to tax year basis of calculation, the tax year 2023/24 is a transition year. The basis period for calculation of a business' tax will be on the current year basis, that is, profits for the accounting period ending in 2023/24 *plus*, if relevant, those for any period to the end of that tax year, ie, 5 April 2024.

EXAMPLE

Accounting period ends 30 June.

For tax year 2023/24, tax calculated on profits as follows:

(a) current year basis: profits for year ending 30 June 2023; plus

(b) transition period: profits for period 1 July 2023 to 5 April 2024.

For the tax year 2024/25, tax will be calculated on profits for period 6 April 2024 to 5 April 2025.

The example shows that, for 2023/24, the business would have to pay tax on profits of 21 months. To reduce the impact of this, these 'transition profits' will be spread evenly over a period of five years from 2023/24, unless the business elects to accelerate the charge, and pay the total liability.

30.4.4 Payment of tax

The dates for payment of tax are:

- 31 January in the tax year of assessment;
- 31 July following the tax year of assessment; and
- 31 January following the tax year of assessment.

The first two instalments are estimated (in effect, payments on account based on the previous year's tax liability). The third will be either a balancing payment or rebate, depending on whether tax had been over- or under-estimated, calculated once full details of actual profits have been received by HMRC.

EXAMPLES

Jones & Co (a partnership):

Relevant tax year 2024/25: 6 April 2024 to 5 April 2025

Tax is payable on 31 January 2025 and 31 July 2025 (estimated according to previous tax year's profits, ie, those for 2023/24), with any adjustment for 2024/25 due on 31 January 2026, together with an estimated payment on account to be made in respect of the next tax year (2025/26).

30.5 Losses under the income tax system

If a trader makes a trading loss (ie deductible expenses exceed income profits) during an accounting period, the tax assessment will be a 'nil' liability. In addition, tax relief will be available in respect of the loss.

30.5.1 Set-off against same year and preceding year income

A taxpayer may elect to deduct the loss from any other taxable income in the year of assessment in which the loss was made. Where, as is usual, the loss-making period is partly in one tax year and partly in another, HMRC will, in practice, allow the whole of the loss to be set off against the income of the tax year in which that period ends.

If a loss is not fully relieved because (a) the other income of the year of the loss was insufficient or (b) the taxpayer did not elect to take the relief, a similar election may be made in respect of the immediately preceding tax year, provided the taxpayer is still carrying on the same trade on a commercial basis.

In both cases, the loss may be set off against *any* of the taxpayer's income from whatever source. Any claim must be made in writing within 12 months of 31 January immediately following the year of assessment in which the loss arose.

Special rules apply to prevent relief being given where the trade is not being carried on with a view to profit.

Trading losses can, in limited circumstances, be set against the taxpayer's capital gains in the tax year when the loss arises or the preceding tax year. The relief only applies to such losses as have not been used up following a claim to set off against income as described earlier.

30.5.2 **Carry-forward against subsequent trade profits**

A loss may be set against profits from the *same* trade (but not from any other source) in future years, without time limit, to the extent that it has not been completely relieved against the same or preceding year's income. Relief is given by a deduction from the profits of the next tax year in which there are profits, and then the year after that, and so on until the loss is completely relieved.

EXAMPLE

Profits and losses of a trade made during tax years:

2020/21	£50,000	profit
2021/22	£200,000	loss
2022/23	£60,000	profit
2023/24	£70,000	profit

In addition to their trade, the taxpayer had part-time employment producing an income of £20,000 per annum throughout the period. If claims for relief had been made, the income tax position would have been as follows (personal allowances or other reliefs have been ignored for the purpose of the example):

	2020/21	**2021/22**	**2022/23**	**2023/24**
Trading income	50,000	nil	60,000	70,000
Employment income	20,000	20,000	20,000	20,000
	------	-------	-------	------
	70,000	20,000	80,000	90,000
Losses available		200,000	110,000	50,000
Loss relief	70,000	20,000	60,000	50,000
	------	-------	-------	------
Final income	nil	nil	20,000	40,000

Notes:

(a) The loss in the tax year 2021/22 was available to be set off against other profits being taxed in that year, or against the previous year's profits. As there were unrelieved losses once this was done, the balance was carried forward and relief sought against later profits from the same trade.

(b) Full relief was not obtained until 2023/24 even though the loss was made in 2021/22.

(c) The relief in 2022/23 was only £60,000 because losses cannot be carried forward and set off against income from other sources.

30.5.3 Carry back of losses on termination of trade

Losses from the final 12 months of a trade can be deducted from income from the same trade in the three years of assessment before the discontinuance, taking later years before earlier years. Standard set-off (see **30.5.1**) is available for the year of discontinuance.

30.5.4 Losses in early years of trade

Losses made during the first four years of a trade can be set off against the income of the three tax years before the loss, taking earlier years before later years. Losses can be deducted from all income of an individual in those years, from whatever source. This allows a sole trader who starts a trade to set losses off against income received before the business started, increasing the ability for start-up businesses to set off losses in their early years.

30.5.5 General and anti-avoidance

Where loss relief is obtained, the saving for the taxpayer is the amount of tax on the amount of the relief: a basic rate taxpayer would save £200 in tax on relieved losses of £1,000. Legislation giving relief prevents double relief being claimed in respect of the same sum. That is, for example, if losses are set off against income of the same year, then only the unrelieved balance, if any, may be carried forward against future trade profits. Where relief is given by setting a loss off against income that has already been taxed (ie carry back), the relief is provided by a tax repayment by HMRC.

30.5.6 Conduct and ethics: maintaining trust and acting fairly

As noted in **30.1**, a solicitor advising on tax matters should be considerate of their role and duties in advising on an arrangement or schemes through which their client may evade or avoid tax. This is not limited to the situation where a solicitor may propose such an arrangement or scheme. Any involvement may result in breaches of the Principles and Codes of Conduct. Thus, if a client proposes a potentially abusive tax scheme, advising in favour of, or facilitating, any aspect of the scheme could result in disciplinary action and possible criminal action. The SRA therefore advises that where a solicitor believes that they may be at risk as a consequence of any client's instructions, they should advise the client that they cannot comply with those instructions and, unless the instructions are changed, should terminate their retainer.

30.6 Income tax liability of partnerships

30.6.1 General

A partnership is not a separate legal person: it is a group of individuals. Each partner is taxed on their share of the total partnership profits or losses taking into account their personal reliefs and other sources of income. Thus, for *assessment* and *collection* of tax, each partner is treated as a notional sole trader.

30.6.2 Payments to partners: business expense or profit-share?

Normal income tax principles are used to calculate the total partnership profits by ascertaining taxable receipts and deductible expenses. However, for a partnership any payment made by the business *to a partner* is examined to determine whether it is a deductible expense or an allocation of taxable profit. The latter *cannot* reduce the taxable profit of the partnership.

The following items merit special attention.

30.6.2.1 Salary

The tax treatment of a 'salary' payable to a 'partner' depends on whether HMRC regards the recipient as a true partner sharing in the profits in a particular, agreed way or whether the recipient is merely an employee in receipt of a salary who is described as a 'partner'. HMRC will consider both the facts and the terms of any partnership agreement: the latter, on their own, are not conclusive. Where a salary is held to be an allocation of profit, it is not deductible from the firm's taxable profits. Where it is a true salary, it is deductible in calculating partnership profits and will be assessed, in the hands of the recipient, in calculating their income tax, with tax being deducted at source under the Pay As You Earn (PAYE) procedure.

30.6.2.2 Interest

Interest payable to a partner will not be a deductible expense if it is payable on a partner's contribution of capital to the firm. Such a payment is regarded as part of the agreed method of allocating profits. However, if a partner makes a loan to the partnership, interest payable on the loan will normally be a deductible expense.

30.6.2.3 Rent

Where a partnership pays rent to a partner for the use of assets owned by the partner, the rent will be a deductible expense unless it is excessive.

30.6.3 Mechanics of assessment: current year basis

The partnership is required to submit a set of accounts and a tax return in respect of total partnership profits for the accounting year ending in the tax year of assessment. Once these are agreed with HMRC, the final profit figure will be apportioned amongst the partners according to the profit-sharing ratio in force during the accounting period in question.

Each partner must then include their share of partnership profits in their tax return and is liable for the tax on that share but not that of any other partner. Partners are thus assessed to tax on an individual basis rather than being jointly liable as with all other partnership liabilities.

Note that this basis of assessment will be revised for the tax year 2024/25 onwards–see **30.4.1**.

30.6.4 Losses of a partnership

When a partnership makes a loss, each partner can choose what type of relief to claim in respect of their share of the loss.

30.6.5 National Insurance and partners

National Insurance can be a financial burden for businesses. As well as a National Insurance liability arising on an employee's earnings, the employer is also obliged to make a further payment in respect of that employee.

Partners, being self-employed, are liable to make Class 2 and Class 4 National Insurance contributions at a rate lower than the rate applicable to employees and they are entitled to deduct one half of their contributions when calculating their income tax liability. Further, as a partner cannot be employed by the partnership, no employer's contribution need be made. Note that a partnership will make such payments in respect of its employees.

30.7 Taxation of directors and employees

One of the largest ongoing expenses of most businesses–whether sole trader, partnership or company–is salary and wage costs. These are the ways in which most people receive a regular income. Employees can also be rewarded in ways other than pure salary, such as health insurance or company cars. This section considers the tax treatment of remuneration and reward from the perspectives of both employer and employee.

30.7.1 Employers: deductibility of employee remuneration

An employer will wish to ensure that remuneration or reward paid to employees will constitute a pre-tax deduction and reduce its taxable profits. As seen in **30.2.3**, to be deductible any expense must be:

(a) of an income nature as opposed to a capital outlay; and

(b) incurred wholly and exclusively for the purpose of the trade or profession.

Therefore, in general, payment of salaries, wages, pension contributions and even lump sum payments in compensation for loss of office will be deductible.

The following specific aspects of this general proposition should be noted.

30.7.1.1 'Wholly'

'Wholly' relates to quantum, so that excessive payments cannot be deducted. If a payment is held to be excessive, only such proportion of the payment as is reasonable in the light of the employee's work can be deducted.

30.7.1.2 Pensions

Contributions into pension funds are deductible as business expenses provided they are made into an approved retirement benefit scheme that complies with conditions set out in legislation.

30.7.1.3 Compensation for loss of office

Lump sum payments for loss of office are taxable as income in the hands of the recipient and as an income-deductible expense for the paying company. Redundancy payments are also deductible and are treated as having been paid on the last day on which the business was carried on if made after the discontinuance of the trade, profession or vocation.

30.7.1.4 Additional benefits

Many employers provide additional benefits such as company cars, healthcare, and so on. The cost of providing such benefits will be deductible only to the extent that they are wholly and exclusively for the purposes of the trade.

30.7.2 Social security contributions

Employers are obliged to make National Insurance contributions (NICs) in respect of each employee who has wages above a weekly threshold, as well as deducting the NICs of the employee before paying over the net wages. Both employee and employer NICs rates (referred to respectively as 'primary' and 'secondary') are set for each tax year, and vary according to earnings thresholds and employee categories. The employer secondary NICs are deductible in computing the tax liability of the employer.

30.7.3 Employees: taxation of income

Income tax is deducted at source from an employee's wages and accounted for by their employer to HMRC under the PAYE scheme. (Contrast this with 'self-employed' income, where recipients must account for tax themselves, normally some time after receipt–see **30.4** for more details.)

Employees pay tax on 'employment income', which is a charge to tax on, inter alia, 'general earnings'. 'Earnings' mean, in relation to an employment:

(a) any salary, wages or fee;

(b) any gratuity or incidental benefit of any kind obtained by the employee if it is money or money's worth;

(c) anything which constitutes an emolument of the employment.

Employment income is taxed in the tax year in which it is received, irrespective of whether or not it is actually earned in that year.

The term 'employment' is defined to include: a contract of service; 'offices' and 'office-holders'. Neither of these definitions is absolute, so it is worthwhile considering case law for guidance in these areas.

30.7.3.1 Office and office-holder

'Office' must involve a degree of continuance (not necessarily continuity) and of independent existence: it must connote a post to which a person can be appointed, which they can vacate and to which a successor can be appointed.

Office-holders have been held to include directors of UK companies, NHS consultants, bishops, judges and **personal representatives**. Remember that a director may hold the office of director and simultaneously be an employee, by performing an executive function.

30.7.3.2 Contract of service

A contract of service is generally viewed as coterminous with the expression 'employment'. That is, entering into a contract to undertake a given post or role in return for regular payments from an employer, who also pays NICs (see **30.7.2**) for the post-holder. This should be contrasted with a 'contract for services', where a business enters into a contract for specific services to be provided by a self-employed individual, who will regularly enter into a series of such contracts or operate a number of such contracts at any one time.

30.7.4 **Taxable receipts by employees**

Salary, wages or a bonus from an employer are assessable to tax. Rewards for employees, and particularly directors, may also comprise more than just salary. Common examples are company cars and subsidised healthcare insurance. These additional rewards will amount to benefits of money or money's worth and, therefore, will be taxable along with other earnings.

30.7.4.1 Benefits generally

Benefits from employment generally fall into two categories: either they amount to cash or its equivalent or they amount to the use of something at the employer's expense. An example of the former might be the payment of premiums on private health insurance; an example of the latter would be the use of a company car.

The general rule is that the cost to the employer of providing the benefit will be treated as earnings of the employee. However, a number of specified benefits are subject to their own rules.

30.7.4.2 Living accommodation

An employee who occupies premises by reason of their employment is taxed on:

- the greater of either the actual rent paid by their employer or the deemed 'annual value' of the accommodation; *less*
- the rent actually paid by the employee.

'Annual value' means the market rent that could be obtained for the premises on the assumption that the landlord will bear the costs of repair and insurance.

EXAMPLE

Scenario one

Jed, an employer, buys a £60,000 property to provide accommodation for his employee, Felicity. Felicity pays an annual rent of £4,000 to Jed. The deemed market rent of the property is £10,000 pa. Felicity, therefore, receives a taxable benefit of £6,000–the difference between the deemed market rent and the actual rent paid by the employee.

Scenario two

Rachel rents a property for £8,000 pa to provide accommodation for their employee, Tyler. Tyler pays an annual rent of £4,000 to Rachel. The deemed market rent of the property is £6,000 pa. Tyler, therefore, receives a taxable benefit of £4,000–the difference between the actual rent paid by Rachel (as it is higher than the deemed rent) and the actual rent paid by Tyler, the employee.

Where it costs an employer more than £75,000 to provide accommodation for an employee, an employee's liability is calculated on a different basis. Here, an employee is treated as receiving a percentage (based on an official rate of interest—currently 2.25%, for the tax year 2024/25) of the amount in excess of £75,000 which the employer has spent on providing the accommodation (so-called 'additional yearly rent'), *plus* any deemed receipt which the employee would normally be taxed upon under the rule described earlier.

EXAMPLE

An employer, Jon, buys a property for £100,000 to provide accommodation for his employee, Martha.

Martha is treated as receiving additional yearly rent of 2.25% of £25,000 (the amount over £75,000 paid by Jon for the property) = £562.50.

The deemed market rent of the property is £10,000 pa and Martha pays an annual rent of £6,000 to Jon.

Martha's total taxable liability for the property is, therefore:

(£562.50 + £10,000) – £6,000 = £4,562.50.

30.7.4.3 Expenses

Any allowance for expenses payable to an employee will be a taxable benefit, subject to whatever percentage of that allowance is spent on expenses incurred wholly, exclusively and necessarily in the performance of the duties of employment, in which case such expenses are deductible. For example, if a director has an expense allowance of £1,000 per month and regularly incurs deductible expenses of £800 per month, only the difference will be taxable.

The test for deductibility is stringent, particularly as expenditure has to be shown as necessarily incurred. It is always open to HMRC to argue that such necessity did not exist. In many instances, an employee will, instead, incur the expense first and be reimbursed by their employer. This does not normally produce a taxable receipt for the employee, so long as the expense fulfils the test for deductibility. As a sizeable proportion of an employee's expenses claims tends to refer to travelling costs, it is worth noting two specific aspects of the system:

1 the test for deductibility of travel expenses is less demanding, the rule being that these expenses must be necessarily incurred in the performance of an employee's duties;

2 in relation to mileage allowance, for the tax year 2024/25, any allowance of 45 pence per mile up to the first 10,000 miles and 25 pence thereafter is exempt from taxation.

30.7.4.4 Motor vehicles

An employee who is provided with a company car is deemed to receive an annual sum to represent the cash equivalent of the vehicle. This benefit in kind (BIK) rate for 2024/25 is between 2% and 37% of the official list price of the vehicle provided, depending on its carbon dioxide emissions and when it was first registered. For the majority of diesel cars, there is an additional 4% supplement added to the BIK figure.

30.7.4.5 Beneficial loan arrangements

Loans from an employer can be attractive if the rate of interest is lower than that in the marketplace. An employee will have the value of this difference attributed as earnings and thus taxed. The actual interest payable by the employee will be compared to an official rate of interest, which reflects the market rates in force.

EXAMPLE

Martha is lent £20,000 by her employer. She pays interest to her employer of 1.25% pa, thus £250. If the official HMRC rate was 2.25%, thus £450 pa, Martha would be deemed to receive a taxable benefit worth £200.

One exception to the above is that, if the aggregate amount owing to the employer by the employee does not exceed £5,000, the benefit will not be taxed.

Should the whole or part of a loan be written off or released by the employer, the amount released or written off will be treated as earnings.

30.7.5 **Terminal payments**

30.7.5.1 General principles

Sums paid at the end of an employment in accordance with the terms of the employment contract will be taxable since they will represent deferred or advance remuneration. Thus, if an employee is to be paid £10,000 a year for ten years but under the contract is to receive a lump sum of £50,000 on either the commencement or termination of the term, the sum is fully taxable.

It is more common for an employee's contract to be terminated and for the employee either to work out their notice or to be denied this right (sometimes being referred to as 'being put on gardening leave') and receive a payment in lieu of notice; that is, a sum to reflect the money that would otherwise have been earned. Note that some employment contracts specifically provide the option for an employer to make a payment in lieu rather than give notice. In all these cases, the payments will be taxable as income in the usual way.

30.7.5.2 Ex gratia payments

Where a voluntary payment is made by an employer to an employee which is not made for the work undertaken or a provision of services under the contract of employment, these 'ex gratia' payments are exempt for income tax purposes, save to the extent they exceed £30,000.

A terminal payment paid to a director near retirement age needs careful consideration, as such a payment may instead be treated by HMRC as a payment out of an unapproved pension scheme, in which case it will not attract the £30,000 exemption and will be taxed in full.

30.7.5.3 Redundancy payments

Statutory and non-statutory redundancy payments, not arising from the operation of the employment contract, will usually only be subject to tax to the extent that they exceed £30,000. However, only genuine redundancy payments are caught. So, an attempt to class a payment of less than £30,000 to a director as a redundancy payment to take advantage of the exemption will be closely scrutinised by HMRC.

30.7.6 **Restrictive covenant payments**

If an employee receives a payment in consideration of entering into a restrictive covenant, this will be subject to income tax.

30.7.7 Social security contributions

Employees must make NICs in respect of their salaries. These contributions, deducted by the employer from the employee's salary, are not deductible when calculating the employee's tax liability.

30.8 The proprietors and officers of a business

This section consolidates some important distinctions when considering income tax and the proprietors of a business.

Sole traders cannot earn a salary from their businesses. The profits they make are taxed as a receipt for income tax purposes.

Profit-sharing partners in a partnership will also pay income tax on their share of the partnership profits. They *may* also be paid a salary and will also pay income tax on this.

However, 'salaried partners'–that is, partners who have no stake in the business in question–are not entitled to any profit share and are remunerated solely by salary (and for whom the title 'partner' is, therefore, somewhat of a misnomer) will be taxed as employees.

The position of a company and its directors is different. As the company is a legal personality separate from its owners and managers, directors who work full time in the company are treated as its employees and taxed on the salaries they receive. As such, a company pays tax on its profits and directors pay tax on their salaries. With a partnership, there is only the single liability of the partner to tax.

The significance of these distinctions becomes clear in the context of deductibility. 'Salaries' payable to true partners will not be deductible. Salaries payable by a company to its directors (as employees) will be deductible from the company's overall taxable profits. There is an opportunity to manipulate a company's profits by paying directors substantial sums, such that the company incurs little or no liability to corporation tax–although note the discussion at **30.7.1.1** about excessive salary payments. In many closely held private companies this can be a common method of extraction of profit from the business. However, it should be borne in mind that increased salaries will also result in increased National Insurance payments from both the company and its directors, and attention should also be given to the differing standard and dividend income tax rates. By contrast, in a listed public limited company such manipulation of profit will be prevented by corporate governance rules and will usually be of limited impact due to the substantial profits earned by such companies.

30.9 IR35 companies

Because of the financial and practical burden of the PAYE scheme and National Insurance, employers began to favour an alternative method of rewarding certain staff. Instead of being taken on as employees, the persons in question would create a single shareholder/director company and the 'employer' would then contract with that company for it to provide the services of the shareholder/director (effectively the 'employee'). Payments made to the company by the 'employer' would not be treated as an emolument of the 'employee' but a receipt of the company, thus escaping the PAYE/National Insurance burden on the 'employer'. However, those payments would still amount to a deductible business expense for the paying 'employer'. The 'employee', as a shareholder of their company, could then extract the profits from the company by way of dividend, again avoiding any PAYE/National Insurance obligation, and the corporation tax liability incurred by the company may have been less than the income tax liability on any salary paid direct.

HMRC now has in place rules to deal with such 'IR35 companies' arrangements. (IR35 refers to the relevant press release which first announced the anti-avoidance measures.)

The basic effect of the rules is that in cases where there is, in effect, an employer–employee relationship, payments made into the intermediate company will be treated as deemed employment income of the proprietor of the company and, therefore, subject to PAYE and National Insurance liability in the usual way. This will be the case even if the company pays out no monies to the proprietor or if it pays them out in the form of dividends (in which case there will be set-off between the liability incurred on the deemed payment and the liability on the dividend payment).

KEY POINT SUMMARY

- Income tax is paid by individuals on their total taxable income during a tax year which runs from 6 April to 5 April.
- Businesses will have an accounting period which may not correspond with the tax year. Notwithstanding this, their tax liability will be calculated on the basis of profits or losses attributable to the tax year of assessment.
- Income tax for an individual's business is calculated by reference to income receipts *less* deductible expenses and any other reliefs or allowances available under tax legislation. This will result in a taxable profits (or loss) figure.
- Losses incurred by a business may be capable of being set off against other taxable income of the same year, or the preceding year. They may also be set against profits from the same trade in future years.
- Partners are taxed on their share of the total partnership profits or losses, taking into account any other personal income and their personal reliefs and allowances.
- Directors and employees will pay income tax on their income, together with any taxable benefits received as part of their employment.
- Income tax is payable at rates set annually, payable according to specific taxable income thresholds. Currently, there is a basic rate of 20%, a higher rate of 40% and an additional rate of 45%. There is also a personal allowance of £12,570 which can be earned before tax is payable; however, this may be reduced by £1 for every £2 earned over £100,000.

CHAPTER 31
Capital Gains Tax

FUNCTIONING LEGAL KNOWLEDGE

This chapter considers the following functioning legal knowledge included in the SRA's SQE 1 assessment specification:

Capital gains tax:

- chargeable persons/entities (sole traders, partners and **shareholders**)
- basis of charge (calculation of gains/allowable deductions/main reliefs and exemptions)
- the charge to tax: calculation and collection
- the scope of anti-avoidance provisions

AUTHORITIES UNDERPINNING PRACTICE

The key authorities that underpin this area of practice are listed below. Note that for legislation you are linked to legislation.gov.uk.

Although much of the legislation on this government website is available in its amended form, the incorporation of new amendments into the text of legislation can be delayed. You should refer to legal databases to ensure you are referencing the most up-to-date legislation.

- Taxation of Chargeable Gains Act 1992
  http://www.legislation.gov.uk/ukpga/1992/12/contents

31.1 Introduction

The proceeds of sale on the disposal of a capital asset may be subject to capital gains tax (CGT). A capital asset may be an entire business, a part of that business or an asset used in a business, for example land or machinery. This chapter explains how and when CGT becomes payable on the disposal of such assets and the scope of provisions that aim to prevent individuals avoiding liability. It is recommended that **30.1** on taxation and ethical elements is read with this chapter.

31.2 Capital gains tax

31.2.1 When CGT is payable

The Taxation of Chargeable Gains Act (TCGA) 1992 states that CGT is payable when:

(a) a taxable person;

(b) makes a disposal of chargeable assets;

(c) giving rise to a chargeable gain;

(d) unless an exemption or relief applies.

A 'taxable person' is anyone who is resident or ordinarily resident in the UK (including the **personal representatives** of a deceased person).

A 'disposal' is not exhaustively defined in the Act but includes a sale, gift or part disposal.

'Assets' are widely defined as including 'all forms of property' and virtually all assets are 'chargeable assets', subject to a few exceptions (eg motor cars and pounds sterling).

31.2.2 How CGT is charged and calculated

CGT is charged on chargeable gains made during a tax year (as with income tax, see **Chapter 30**). A chargeable gain will occur where, on the disposal of chargeable assets, the 'consideration for disposal' exceeds the 'allowable expenditure' permitted by the Act.

The 'consideration for disposal' is the sale price of the asset.

'Allowable expenditure' comprises:

(a) the initial expenditure (ie the original purchase price or market value if the asset was acquired by way of gift);

(b) incidental costs incurred in acquiring the asset;

(c) any subsequent expenditure (eg money spent on enhancing the value of the asset); and

(d) incidental costs of disposal.

EXAMPLE

Natalia bought a 15% shareholding in TH Ltd five years ago for £75,000. Legal fees for the purchase were £3,000.

Natalia sells her entire shareholding for £135,000. Legal fees for the sale were £5,000.

Natalia's capital gain is:

Consideration for disposal £135,000

Less allowable expenditure:

Initial expenditure:

Purchase price £75,000

Legal fees £3,000

Deduct subsequent expenditure:

N/a

Deduct incidental costs of disposal:

Legal fees £5,000

Total allowable expenditure £83,000

Capital gain £52,000

(Note: the calculation of tax on this gain is shown in the example at **31.2.5.1**.)

31.2.3 Annual exemption

Every individual has an annual exemption from CGT. For the 2024/25 tax year, the first £3,000 of capital gains is exempt from tax.

31.2.4 Rates of tax

For individuals, taxable chargeable gains are treated as the top slice of a taxpayer's taxable income. They are added on to the taxpayer's taxable income and gains falling:

- within the income tax basic rate band of £37,700 are taxed at 10%;
- above the basic rate band of £37,700 are taxed at 20%.

These rates apply to gains on all assets save for residential property (other than a main residence) where the respective rates are 18% and 24%.

Gains that straddle the income tax basic rate band are apportioned: the element within the basic rate band will be taxed at 10% and the remainder at 20%.

EXAMPLE

In the following examples, the chargeable gain shown is the amount *after* application of the annual exemption (see **31.2.3**).

Taxpayer A:

No taxable income

Chargeable gain: £25,000

The whole gain falls within the basic rate band and will be taxed at 10%.

Gain: £25,000	
Basic rate: £0–37,700	Higher rate band: £37,701–150,000

Taxpayer B:

Taxable income: £55,000

Chargeable gain: £25,000

The whole gain falls within the higher rate band and will be taxed at 20%.

Taxable income: £55,000	Gain: £25,000
Basic rate: £0–37,700	Higher rate band: £37,701–150,000

Taxpayer C:

Taxable income: £30,000

Chargeable gain: £25,000

£7,700 of the gain falls within the basic rate band and will be taxed at 10%; the remainder of the gain will be taxed at 20%.

Taxable income: £30,000	Gain: £25,000
Basic rate: £0–37,500	Higher rate band: £37,501–150,000

31.2.5 **CGT calculations**

31.2.5.1 Simple calculation

This is a simple CGT calculation, continuing the example given at **31.2.2**.

EXAMPLE

Chargeable gain on the sale of 15% shareholding in TH Ltd: £52,000.

Taxable income in year of sale: £43,000 (therefore above basic rate, making all of the chargeable gain payable at the higher rate of CGT).

Chargeable gain less annual exemption £52,000–£3,000 = £49,000

CGT liability £49,000 × 20% = £9,800

31.2.5.2 Calculation of chargeable gain where partial disposal

If there is a partial disposal of an asset, the taxpayer may deduct as allowable expenditure only the proportion that the part of the asset disposed of bears to the whole asset.

EXAMPLE

Mel sells part of a plot of land for £50,000.
The remaining land is worth £100,000.
Total allowable expenditure on the whole plot is £30,000.
Mel's allowable expenditure is:

£50,000 ÷ (£50,000 + £100,000) = 0.33

0.33 × £30,000 = £10,000

Chargeable gain is: £50,000 – £10,000 = £40,000

31.2.5.3 Calculation where loss created by allowable expenditure

Where the 'allowable expenditure' for a particular asset exceeds the sale price or market value, the loss arising is set off against other gains made during the current tax year. The gains in the current year must be reduced to nil. Only the balance of the loss, once all other gains have been eliminated, can be carried forward. Such losses can be carried forward indefinitely but must be set off against future gains as they arise. In contrast to the year in which the loss initially arises, carried forward losses need only be set against the gains of future years to the extent necessary to bring that year's gains down to the amount of the current annual exemption (see **31.2.4**).

EXAMPLE

Year 1

1	Disposal of asset	£60,000
2	Allowable expenditure on disposed asset	(£85,000)
3	Loss on disposal	(£25,000)
4	Further capital gain in 2024/25	£10,000
5	£10,000 of loss at 3 set off against further gain to reduce to nil	(£10,000)
6	Balance of loss to carry forward against future gains	(£15,000)

Year 2 (assume personal allowance for 2024/25 remains the same)

1	Loss carried forward	(£15,000)
2	Disposal of asset	£47,000
3	Allowable expenditure on disposed asset	(£30,000)
4.	Gain on disposal	£17,000
5	Use £14,000 of loss carried forward at 1 to reduce gain	(£14,000)
6	Remaining gain on disposal	£3,000
7	Apply annual exemption	(£3,000)
8	Net gain	£0
9	Balance of loss to carry forward to set off against future gains	(£1,000)

31.2.6 Disposals other than at arm's length

A disposal 'other than at arm's length' is where there is a gift element to the disposal. In such cases, the relevant consideration for CGT purposes will be the market value of the asset at the time of disposal.

Any transfer between connected persons is deemed to be 'other than at arm's length'. The main categories of connected persons are defined by s286 TCGA 1992 as:

(a) a spouse, direct relatives and relatives of the spouse of the disposer;
(b) companies under common control;
(c) partners in a business and spouses of partners;
(d) trustees and settlors (and any persons connected with the settlor).

This rule is of particular relevance to sales at an undervalue. If such a sale is an arm's length commercial transaction, the relevant consideration for CGT purposes will be the actual price paid. However, an undervalue transaction between connected persons will result in the market value of the asset being substituted.

EXAMPLE

Jack is selling a plot of land to Sarah. The market value is £120,000 but Jack needs to raise money quickly and Sarah is the only interested party. Jack therefore sells the land for £100,000.

If Jack and Sarah are not connected persons, Jack will be treated as receiving £100,000 for CGT purposes.

If Jack and Sarah are connected persons, Jack will be treated as receiving £120,000 for CGT purposes.

31.3 Exemptions and reliefs

31.3.1 Private residence relief

There is an exemption from paying CGT on the sale of a taxpayer's only or main residence, provided it has been lived in as their main home for all the time it has been owned. This relief is sometimes referred to as 'main residence relief'. If a taxpayer has more than one home, they may nominate one property as their main residence by notifying HMRC. Married couples and civil partners may only have one main residence between them.

31.3.2 Relief by deferring payment of tax

It is possible, in certain circumstances, to postpone or defer the payment of CGT. The methods by which this may be achieved are set out in the following sections.

31.3.2.1 Hold-over relief

This applies to disposals by way of a gift or there is a sale at an undervalue. The donor and donee can elect to 'hold over' any gain arising. When hold-over relief is claimed, the entire gain in question must be held over: it cannot be reduced by the donor's annual exemption.

With a gift, the result of hold-over is that the donee is treated as acquiring the asset at the donor's original acquisition value. When the donee makes a subsequent chargeable disposal of the asset, the CGT liability will be:

- any gain made whilst the asset was in the donee's possession; *plus*
- the gain which was held over.

EXAMPLE

Aria gifts an asset to Charlie when it is worth £20,000.

Aria's base cost for the asset was £8,000.

Ignoring any other allowable expenditure, the gain on the disposal is £12,000.

If Aria and Charlie elect to hold over the gain, Charlie takes over the asset with a base cost of £8,000.

If Charlie disposes of the asset five years later when it is worth £30,000, ignoring any other allowable expenditure, Charlie's taxable gain is: sale price of £30,000 *less* original base cost of £8,000 = £22,000.

With a sale at an undervalue, the whole of the actual chargeable gain cannot be held over. Instead, the gain is reduced by the amount actually received by the seller in excess of the original cost of the asset sold.

EXAMPLE

Sameen bought an asset for £10,000.

Sameen sells it to Toby (not at arm's length–see **31.2.6**) for £20,000 when it is worth £25,000.

Sameen is deemed to receive £25,000, and so, the whole chargeable gain is £15,000.

If Sameen and Toby elect to hold over, the chargeable gain must be reduced by the amount actually received by Sameen in excess of the base cost, that is:

£15,000 – £10,000 = £5,000, the amount of gain that can be held over.

Toby will thus take the asset with a base cost of £20,000 (the current market value of £25,000 less the £5,000 held over gain).

Sameen will be taxed on £10,000 worth of the gain.

Hold-over relief is available in circumstances including:

(a) transfers between spouses; and

(b) where a sole trader, business partner or person holding at least 5% of voting rights in a company ('a personal company'), gifts or sells at undervalue, business assets used in their business or personal company.

Note that business assets include **shares** in an unquoted company or in the transferor's personal company.

31.3.2.2 Business asset roll-over relief

Where an individual or a company sells certain types of assets (even at full value), they may be able to elect to 'roll over' the gain arising into replacement assets. The effect will be to reduce the acquisition cost of the new assets by the amount of the 'rolled over' gain. On any subsequent disposal of the replacement asset, the CGT liability will be:

- the rolled-over gain; *plus*
- any actual gain on that asset.

The effect is thus to defer the payment of capital gains tax.

The conditions for this relief are:

(a) The original and the replacement asset must both fall within limited categories. The most common are land, buildings and fixed plant or machinery.

(b) Both the original and the replacement asset must be used as business assets throughout their periods of ownership.

(c) The replacement asset must be purchased within the 12-month period before, or the three-year period after, the disposal of the original asset.

(d) To roll over the whole gain realised on the original asset, the full proceeds of sale must be used to purchase the replacement. If a lesser sum is used, the amount by which the sale proceeds of the original asset exceed the cost of the replacement asset will become chargeable to tax immediately. This may result in the whole gain becoming chargeable, even though the relief is theoretically available.

EXAMPLE

O Ltd is considering selling its trading premises and buying new ones. The proceeds from the sale are likely to be £155,000. It is considering three potential sites: one at £175,000 (Site A); one at £145,000 (Site B); and one at £130,000 (Site C).

Assuming the gain on any sale of the original premises would be £20,000, the following would result:

Site A: Total gain rolled over, as whole of proceeds of sale used; base cost of new premises for future CGT calculations = £155,000 (£175,000 – £20,000).

Site B: Tax chargeable immediately on £10,000 of gain. Remainder rolled over (£10,000); base cost of new premises for future CGT calculations = £135,000 (£145,000 – £10,000).

Site C: No amount of gain rolled over–difference in value between original and replacement asset is greater than amount of gain; base cost of new premises for future CGT calculations = £130,000.

31.3.2.3 EIS deferral of chargeable gains

The Enterprise Investment Scheme (EIS) allows gains realised on the disposal of any asset to be deferred if they are invested in shares in a private limited company.

Any gain realised upon the disposal of *any* asset by an individual can benefit from the relief. However, the investment must take a specified form:

(a) an allotment of fully paid ordinary shares, with no rights of redemption or preference for three years;

(b) in a company whose shares are unquoted; and which

(c) only carries on regular trading activities, for example is not an investment, property development, farming, or forestry company or the like, mainly in the UK;

(d) does not have a gross asset value (including any **subsidiaries**) of more than £15 million before the investment;

(e) has fewer than 250 full-time employees at the time of investment; and

(f) is not controlled by another company and which does not have any subsidiaries other than ones which also fulfil the requirements in (b) to (d).

The investment must take place no more than 12 months before or three years after the original disposal.

Any attempt to use the system solely to achieve a tax benefit or failure to use the funds realised in the trading activities of the company will result in the relief being withdrawn, and an immediate tax liability on the gain deferred. Similarly, it is not possible to sell shares in a company and then reinvest in that same company. Note also that a solicitor should have regard to their professional responsibilities in advising on or facilitating any scheme intended to avoid tax–see the Ethics, Professional Conduct and Client Care chapter earlier in the manual.

The investor will not be liable for tax on the deferred gain until such time as the shares are sold; there is no required minimum period of ownership.

It is not necessary to invest all of the proceeds of the original disposal to claim the deferral; an investment of an amount equivalent to the gain will be sufficient to defer the full value of it. Once the shares are sold, any increase in their actual value will be subject to CGT (unless any further exemption applies).

EXAMPLE

Sumiya disposes of an asset in January 2019 and realises a gain ('the original gain') of £40,000. In June 2020, they invest in EIS-qualifying shares worth £85,000. These shares are sold in May 2024, realising a gain of £35,000. Issues to note are:

(a) The investment takes place within three years of the original gain, so is within the time limits.

(b) The amount of the EIS investment exceeds the original gain, so the total original gain is deferred.

(c) The sale in 2024 will result in both the original (£40,000) and subsequent (£35,000) gains becoming chargeable to tax.

31.3.3 **Business Asset Disposal Relief (formerly Entrepreneurs' Relief)**

31.3.3.1 Scope and effect

This relief reduces the taxpayer's CGT liability by taxing qualifying gains at 10%. Qualifying gains are the aggregate of gains and losses relating to relevant assets.

An individual may claim for relief more than once. The cumulative lifetime limit on qualifying gains for disposals on or after 11 March 2020 is £1 million.

31.3.3.2 Availability of relief

The relief is available in respect of gains made on disposals of:

(a) all or part of a business carried on by an individual, alone or in partnership (including professions and vocations but not property letting businesses, save for furnished holiday lettings); or

(b) following the cessation of a business, assets used in that business and disposed of within three years of cessation; or

(c) shares in a trading company (or a holding company of a trading group) where the individual disposing of the shares was an officer or employee of that company (or a company in the same group) and owns 5% or more of its ordinary share capital which enables the exercise of at least 5% of the voting rights in that company.

31.3.3.3 Operation of relief

EXAMPLE

Konrad realises a capital gain of £100,000 on qualifying assets.

Konrad pays higher rate income tax, therefore normally would pay CGT at a rate of 20% on the gain = £20,000.

If relief applies, the effective rate of CGT is reduced to 10% = £10,000.

If a taxpayer realises more than one capital gain in a particular tax year, only one of which attracts business asset disposal relief:

- different rates of tax must be applied to the different gains; and
- the gain that attracts relief must first be aggregated with any income in the tax year.

This may push other gains out of the basic rate band, although these may be reduced by the annual exemption.

EXAMPLE

Vincent has taxable income of £10,000.
He has also realised in the same tax year:

(a) Gain A: £20,000, eligible for entrepreneurs' relief; and

(b) Gain B: £30,000, not eligible.

Gain A will attract CGT at a rate of 10%.
Gain B will form the top slice of Vincent's taxable receipts, calculated as follows:

Taxable income £10,000 + gains eligible for entrepreneurs' relief £20,000 (Gain A) = £30,000

Balance of Vincent's basic rate band = £7,700
Ignoring the annual exemption, Gain B will taxed as follows:

£7,700 x 10% = £770

£22,300 x 20% = £4,460

If Gain A had been, for example, £28,000, then all of Gain B would have attracted CGT at 20% (£10,000 + £28,000 exceeds the basic rate threshold).

31.3.3.4 'Associated disposal' of business assets

Where an individual qualifies for entrepreneurs' relief on a disposal of shares, relief is also available for any 'associated disposal' of an asset used in the company's (or group's) business.

EXAMPLE

A director of Q Ltd owns the premises from which the company carries on its business. She sells the premises at the same time as she sells her shares in Q Ltd. The sale of the premises may count as an 'associated disposal' and qualify for entrepreneurs' relief.

A similar rule applies to an 'associated disposal' by a partner who is entitled to relief on disposal of their interest in the assets of the partnership.

The relief on an associated disposal is restricted where the asset in question was not wholly in business use throughout the period of ownership.

The 'associated disposal' must be connected with a material withdrawal from the business: the person claiming the relief must be reducing their participation in the business by at least 5%.

31.4 **Death of taxpayer**

No CGT tax is payable when a person dies. The personal representatives of the deceased under the will or intestacy are deemed to acquire the deceased's assets at market value at the time of death. As such, there is neither a gain nor loss. Moreover, all legatees of the estate are deemed to acquire any assets at the base cost of the personal representatives. However, should an asset appreciate in value whilst in the hands of the personal representatives and be disposed of by them to third parties (as opposed to being distributed to legatees), this will result in a gain in the hands of the personal representatives.

31.5 **CGT in the business context**

Liability to CGT can arise in a variety of situations. The purpose of **31.6–31.8** is to look at the common business scenarios where such liability is likely to arise and to consider the applicability of reliefs and exemptions in such situations.

31.6 Disposals of partnership property

31.6.1 General

When a firm disposes of one of its assets, normal CGT principles apply in determining any gains made. There are difficulties involved in applying these principles to a partnership. HMRC treats each partner as owning a fractional share of each of the chargeable assets of the partnership (including goodwill) and not, for this purpose, as owning an interest in the business as a whole. When the firm disposes of an asset to an outsider, each partner is treated as making a disposal of their fractional share in the asset.

What follows is concerned with the disposal by a firm of its assets. CGT issues can also arise when partners leave and join partnerships. These are beyond the scope of this manual.

31.6.2 Assessment

The assessment and collection of CGT is treated differently from the assessment and collection of income tax. The precedent partner delivers a return to HMRC giving full details of disposals. The assessment is made on the individual partners. Each partner's share in the gain is calculated in accordance with their share in the asset disposed of.

To calculate the CGT liability of the individual partners on a disposal of assets it is, therefore, necessary to know the proportions in which assets are owned. This is often referred to as the partners' 'asset surplus ratio'.

31.6.3 Asset surplus ratio

The partnership deed may specify the proportions in which asset surpluses are to be shared. If it does, it is conclusive. If there is no express provision in the partnership deed, the asset surplus-sharing ratio is deemed to be the partnership profit-sharing ratio.

An asset surplus-sharing ratio may differ from the profit-sharing ratio where, for example, a partner has made a substantial capital contribution to the firm while contributing comparatively little to earning income profits.

When a partnership acquires an asset, each partner's share in the acquisition value is determined by their share in the asset surplus *at that time*. Similarly, in a disposal, each partner's share in the proceeds of disposal is determined by their share in the asset surpluses *at that time.*

EXAMPLE

Eric and Shannon are in partnership. They share profits equally and have made no special agreement as to sharing asset surpluses. They acquire an asset for £20,000. The acquisition value for each partner is:

Eric ½ £10,000

Shannon ½ £10,000

They sell the assets for £36,000. The share in the proceeds of the disposal of each partner is:

Eric ½ £18,000

Shannon ½ £18,000

The chargeable gain of each partner is:

Eric £18,000 – £10,000 = £8,000

Shannon £18,000 – £10,000 = £8,000

Each partner is personally liable for their own chargeable gain and will be assessed for tax at the rates appropriate to their level of income.

31.6.4 Reliefs

If there is a gain realised on the disposal, the exemptions and reliefs already referred to may be available:

- if there is a gift element in a disposal, hold-over relief (see **31.3.2.1**) is available to postpone the payment of tax;
- a disposal of partnership property in circumstances where the partners intend to reinvest the sale proceeds can attract roll-over relief (see **31.3.2.1**).

31.7 Disposals of shares

31.7.1 Disposals by individuals

A capital profit on the sale of shares by an individual will in most cases attract a liability to CGT and the general principles and reliefs already referred to will apply, with the exception of roll-over (replacement asset) relief (see **31.3.2.2**).

31.7.2 Disposals by companies

A disposal by a company of shares it owns in another company should be considered in terms of capital gains. The following should be noted:

(a) Any gain realised by a company will be classified as a chargeable gain and form part of its profits for corporation tax purposes (see **Chapter 33**).

(b) Companies can claim indexation allowance – if relevant (see **33.2.3.1**) – for the full period of ownership.

(c) A disposal of shares which formed part of a substantial shareholding in a company will be exempt from tax if certain conditions are met. A substantial shareholding must comprise at least 10% of the ordinary share capital of a company. Both the selling company and the company in which it owns shares must be trading companies, and have been for a two-year period prior to disposal. In addition, the shareholding in question must have been owned for a period of at least 12 months in the two-year period prior to the sale.

31.7.3 Reliefs

It is not uncommon for shareholders/directors or partners to own assets that are used by their respective companies or partnerships. The disposal of such assets may result in a CGT liability for the person concerned.

However, many of the reliefs mentioned previously will be available: roll-over (replacement asset) relief; hold-over relief; and business asset disposal relief (see **31.3.3**).

31.7.4 Wasting assets and business assets

Should an asset have a predictable, useful life of less than 50 years, it is deemed a wasting asset and, as such, CGT-exempt on disposal. Many such assets do not, in fact, appreciate in value and are more likely to be sold at a loss, in which case no allowable loss will be created. This exemption does not, however, apply to wasting assets that have been used in a business, and on which capital allowances (see **33.6**) have, or could have, been claimed. Any gain or loss on the disposal of such an asset, taking into account any capital allowances, will have to be included in the individual's tax return.

31.8 **Tax advice and investment advice**

As seen earlier, CGT is payable on disposals of chargeable assets, which may include disposals of shares. There are also reliefs available on such disposals (see **31.3.2.1** and 31.33) and on reinvestments in shares (see **31.3.2.3**). Arranging deals in investments and investment advice are regulated activities under the Financial Services and Markets Act 2000 (FSMA) and, unless authorised by the Financial Conduct Authority, may constitute offences.

CONDUCT POINT

When advising on CGT, solicitors should therefore be careful to limit their advice to the tax implications of the various courses of action and reliefs available to the client. Any additional advice to the client as to the specific merits of selling their shares and reinvesting in other shares, and arranging either of these forms of transaction, would need to be reviewed as to the risks of their being contrary to FSMA. For a fuller discussion of the regulation of these activities, see **8.12.1–8.12.3**).

KEY POINT SUMMARY

- Capital gains tax is payable by individuals on gains arising from the disposal of chargeable assets.
- Most assets, including property, shares and shares in a business, are chargeable assets.
- A person's main residence is exempt from CGT.
- For individuals, the rate of CGT is determined by adding chargeable gains to their taxable income, such that the gains are treated as the top slice of the total figure. Gains within the basic rate income tax band will be subject to CGT at 10%. To the extent that gains exceed the basic rate threshold, they will be taxed at 20%.
- There is an annual exemption for chargeable gains of up to £3,000.
- There are reliefs available where, if conditions are met, CGT can be deferred until a subsequent disposal of the asset.
- These reliefs are hold-over relief, roll-over relief and relief under the Enterprise Initiative Scheme.
- CGT liability may also be reduced to 10% by business asset disposal relief where gains on specified business assets are invested in a private limited company.
- CGT liability for partners where a partnership disposes of an asset is determined by the asset-surplus sharing ratio applicable to the partnership.
- There are specific rules to consider where individuals and businesses dispose of shares and other business interests.

CHAPTER 32
Inheritance Tax

FUNCTIONING LEGAL KNOWLEDGE

This chapter considers the following functioning legal knowledge included in the SRA's SQE 1 assessment specification:

Inheritance tax:

- basis of charge
- relevant exemptions and business reliefs (including business property relief)

AUTHORITIES UNDERPINNING PRACTICE

The key authorities that underpin this area of practice are listed below. Note that for legislation you are linked to legislation.gov.uk.

Although much of the legislation on this government website is available in its amended form, the incorporation of new amendments into the text of legislation can be delayed. You should refer to legal databases to ensure you are referencing the most up-to-date legislation.

- Inheritance Act 1984
  http://www.legislation.gov.uk/ukpga/1984/51/contents

32.1 Introduction

A transfer by a person of a business, a stake in a business or certain property used by a business, may give rise in certain circumstances to a charge to inheritance tax (IHT). This chapter explains how and when IHT becomes payable, and in the context of business property, the availability of business property relief to reduce the charge to IHT. It is recommended that **30.1** on taxation and ethical elements is read with this chapter.

32.1.1 The charge to IHT

IHT is payable under the Inheritance Tax Act 1984 (IHTA 1984) on a *chargeable transfer*: 'any *transfer of value* which is made to an individual but is not … an exempt transfer'. (For exemptions, see **32.1.3.2** and **32.1.3.5**.)

A transfer of value is: 'a *disposition* made by a person … as a result of which the value of his estate immediately after the transfer sis less than it would be but for the disposition …'.

IHT is payable on the *value transferred*: the amount by which the value of the transferor's estate is reduced as a result of the disposition.

Transfers of value may occur for IHT purposes in two forms:

1 Lifetime: gifts or sales with a gift element made by the transferor to another individual during their lifetime.

2 On death: where property transfers from the transferor's estate following their death.

Note that lifetime gifts and sales at an undervalue can also attract CGT (see **Chapter 31**), therefore consider both capital taxes in such a context. On the death of a taxpayer, only IHT need be considered.

32.1.2 Transfers subject to IHT

Three types of transfer may give rise to IHT (subject to any exemptions or reliefs):

(a) a transfer on death which will attract IHT at the full rate of 40%;

(b) a potentially exempt transfer (PET) which is a lifetime gift made by an individual to another individual (as opposed to a company): this will become fully exempt if the transferor lives for seven years after the transfer but may become chargeable to tax should the transferor die within that period (see **32.1.4**); and

(c) a chargeable transfer made before death which is immediately taxable at half the full rate, that is, 20% and will cause the transferee to be liable to tax at the full rate should the transferee die within seven years.

There are very few instances of chargeable transfers, the most likely being the transfer of property into a discretionary trust.

The most common subject matter of transfers are cash, real property and shares.

32.1.3 Factors in calculating IHT

32.1.3.1 IHT rates

There are two rates of inheritance tax: 40% (the 'full rate') and 20%, depending on the type of transfer (see **32.1.2**).

32.1.3.2 Annual exemption for gifts

There is an annual exemption from IHT for lifetime gifts. This is currently £3,000 of gifts per year. Any annual exemption unused wholly or partially can be carried over for one year but no longer. In addition, small gifts to individuals up to £250 per recipient are exempt, provided you have not used another exemption on the same person.

32.1.3.3 Taper relief for PETs and chargeable transfers

On death, the full IHT rate of 40% applies to transfers made on death or within three years of death. Thus, a PET or chargeable transfer (see **32.1.2**) may become subject to the full rate of IHT. For a PET or a chargeable transfer that occurs within four to seven years of the death of a taxpayer, the following sliding scale applies to reduce any tax payable:

Period of years before death when PET made	% of full rate payable	Effective rate of IHT
6–7	20	8
5–6	40	16
4–5	60	24
3–4	80	32

32.1.3.4 Nil rate band

Each taxpayer has, for IHT purposes:

(a) a nil rate band for the current tax year of £325,000; plus

(b) an additional main residence nil rate band (RNRB), which for 2024/25 is £175,000, where an individual leaves a home to their children or other direct descendants.

The RNRB is subject to a taper, which reduces it by £1 for every £2 that the net value of an estate exceeds £2 million.

The nil rate band is applied, in calculating IHT, on a 'first in time' basis–see the examples given later. Any of either nil rate band unused by a spouse or civil partner may be transferred to the surviving spouse or partner.

32.1.3.5 Spouse or civil partner exemption

Any lifetime transfers made and elements of a transferor's estate bequeathed, to their spouse or registered civil partner are exempt from IHT.

32.1.3.6 Cumulation

IHT is a cumulative tax, based on a seven-year cumulation period. This means that to calculate IHT chargeable on an individual transfer, including that of the estate on death, that transfer must be cumulated with all transfers made in the seven-year period *before that specific transfer*, to calculate the precise tax liability.

32.1.4 **Calculating IHT**

The factors set out in **32.1.3** are demonstrated in the following examples.

EXAMPLES

Example one

Keith dies in May 2024. His will provides:

- marital home to spouse;
- remaining estate, valued at £375,000, to his children.

He has made no lifetime transfers.

IHT IMPACT

Transfer of the marital home: exempt for IHT purposes because of the *spouse exemption* (see **32.1.3.5**).

Remaining estate is £50,000 in excess of the *nil-rate band* (**32.1.3.4**): IHT payable at the *full rate* of 40% gives tax charge of £20,000 (£50,000 × 40/100).

Example two

Sofia dies in July 2024. She made lifetime transfers to her daughter:

March 2016: PET of £50,000

June 2019: PET of £76,000

February 2022: PET of £100,000

On death, she leaves her main residence and only asset, worth £400,000, to her daughter.

IHT IMPACT

2016 PET is more than seven years before death, so is a 'successful' PET, and falls out of Sofia's estate for the purpose of the IHT calculation.

2019 and 2022 PETs are both within seven years of death, and are thus 'failed' PETs and chargeable.

Annual exemption of £3,000 applies to each of these PETs.

Total for IHT is therefore the cumulation of:

chargeable PETs ((£76,000 – £3,000) + (£100,000 – £3,000) = £170,000); plus death estate (£400,000)

= £570,000.

This exceeds the *nil-rate band* of £325,000.

Applying this on a *first in time* basis, the PETs are fully within the band, leaving £155,000 to set against the death estate.

This leaves £245,000 (£400,000 – £155,000).

Applying the additional *main residence nil rate band* of £175,000, this reduces the total for IHT to £70,000 (£245,000 – £175,000).

This would result in a tax charge of £28,000 (£70,000 × 40/100).

Example three

Mika, a widow, dies in June 2024. She created discretionary trusts for her son:

May 2016: £250,000

April 2021: £225,000.

She left £150,000 of cash–she had no other assets–to her son on her death.

IHT IMPACT

May 2016 trust was a *lifetime chargeable transfer* within the nil-rate band and no charge arose.

April 2021 trust, on the face of it, was also under the nil-rate band. However, it had to be *cumulated* (see **32.1.3.6**) with the May 2016 trust, because the latter was made within five years of the 2021 trust. This meant that the cumulative total exceeded the nil rate band: £250,000 + £225,000 = £475,000.

Applying the nil-rate band of £325,000, this left £150,000 to be taxed at 20% (see **32.1.2(c)**), thus IHT liability of £30,000 (£150,000 × 20/100) in 2020.

Looking at IHT on death in 2024, the April 2021 trust was set up between three and four years before Mika's death. It is therefore chargeable at the full IHT rate of 40%, subject to *taper relief* (see **32.1.3.3**).

Full IHT charge at 40% on the cumulated value above the nil-rate band of £150,000 = £60,000 (£150,000 × 40/100).

Applying taper relief of 80% reduces the charge to £48,000 (£60,000 × 80/100).

Tax is further reduced by the £30,000 already paid in 2020, leaving a tax charge of £18,000 (£48,000 – £30,000).

IHT is then payable on death estate of £150,000 at full rate of 40%–because the nil rate band has been fully used already–thus a further £60,000 (£150,000 × 40/100), creating a total IHT liability of £78,000 (£60,000 + £18,000).

32.2 **Value transferred**

For IHT, the value of items transferred is the price they might reasonably be expected to fetch if sold in the open market at the time of the gift.

In a business context:

- Quoted stocks and shares are usually valued by reference to the price at which they were being traded on the relevant day.
- The market value of unquoted shares (normally those in private companies) will take into account the company's profitability; dividend record, retained earnings and assets value.

A further concept of relevance to valuation is 'related property'. Some assets can be more valuable when combined with others of the same type (eg a collection). In a business context, shares that form part of a majority holding will be more valuable than shares which form part of a minority shareholding. The IHTA 1984 defines a variety of items as related property, include any property owned by the transferor's spouse at the time of transfer. If the transfer is made of related property, the property actually transferred and the property to which it is related is valued as a single asset. Tax is then calculated on the proportion of the total value transferred.

32.3 Business property relief

32.3.1 General

Business property relief is available on transfers of 'relevant business property' where the transferor owned the property for at least two years before the transfer. It reduces the value of relevant property transferred by either 100% or 50%, thus reducing the IHT payable.

32.3.2 'Relevant business property'

100% relief may be available on:

- a business or an interest in a business (including the interest of a sole proprietor or a partner in a business);
- a shareholding in an unquoted company or company quoted on the Alternative Investment Market.

50% relief may be available on:

- a shareholding in a quoted company which alone or with other shares owned by the transferor or with related property (see **32.2**) gave the transferor control immediately before the transfer (control means being able to exercise more than 50% of the votes in **general meeting**–temporary control will suffice);
- land or buildings, or machinery or plant, used immediately before the transfer wholly or mainly for the purposes of a company controlled by the transferor or of a partnership of which they were a **member**;
- land or buildings, or machinery or plant, used immediately before the transfer wholly or mainly for the purposes of a business carried on by the transferor and which was settled property in which the transferor had an interest in possession.

'Business' includes a profession or a vocation.

The relief is not available if the business:

- consists of dealing in securities, stocks, shares or land or buildings (save for the active management of land) or of holding investments;
- is carried on otherwise than for gain.

32.3.3 Minimum two-year period of ownership

For business property relief, the transferor must have owned the property throughout the two years before the transfer.

If property replaces other relevant business property (other than in the case of minority shareholdings), relief is available provided the aggregate period of the ownership of the original and replacement property exceeds two years in the five years before the time of transfer.

If a transferee of relevant business property makes a transfer of the same property before they have owned the property for two years, relief can still be claimed provided:

(a) the relief was available on the original transfer; and

(b) one of the transfers was a transfer on death.

On the death of a spouse, the surviving spouse can aggregate the deceased spouse's period of ownership with their own to satisfy the two-year period of ownership requirement.

32.3.4 Amount of relief

If the previous conditions are met, business property relief at the appropriate percentage is available on the full net value of the property at the time of transfer. 'Net value' means the value after any liabilities have been deducted. The relief will reduce the value of the property for the purpose of IHT.

32.3.5 Anti-avoidance

To prevent taxpayers placing private assets in a business and then trying to obtain business property relief on them, relief is not available on 'excepted assets'. These are assets that are neither:

(a) used wholly or mainly for the purposes of the business concerned throughout the whole of the previous two years; nor
(b) required at the time of the transfer for future use.

32.3.6 Business property relief and lifetime transfers

Where a transfer is made before death (whether a chargeable or potentially exempt transfer–see **32.1.2**) and the transferor dies within seven years, the original or replacement property must remain as relevant business property of the transferee from the date of the transfer to the date of the death of the transferor. If the transferee dies before the transferor within the seven-year period, relief is only available on the death of the transferee if the same condition is satisfied.

If only a proportion of the original or replacement property is owned by the transferee at the date of death, relief is available on the proportion of the property owned at that date.

As to replacement property, it should, however, be noted that:

(a) the whole of the consideration must have been applied on acquiring the replacement property;
(b) replacement property must be acquired within three years after the disposal of the original property; and
(c) the provision applies only to the first replacement and not to subsequent ones.

32.4 Payment of IHT

It is not the intention here to deal with the complex rules for determining who is liable to account for IHT to the Inland Revenue on death or to consider the rules on the burden or incidence of IHT.

IHT must be paid as follows:

- Lifetime chargeable transfer: six months after the end of the month in which the transfer is made or, if the transfer is made after 5 April and before 1 October, at the end of April in the next year.
- Transfers on death: six months after the end of the month in which the death occurred.

If tax is paid late, interest will be charged.

Inheritance tax on certain types of property can be paid in ten annual instalments. The instalment option is available in respect of:

(a) land of any description;
(b) shares or securities in a company giving the transferor control of the company immediately before death;
(c) unquoted shares or securities which do not give the transferor control (provided paying the tax in one lump sum will not cause any hardship);
(d) unquoted shares or securities not giving the transferor control in the company, provided at least 20% of the tax paid by the person paying the tax on the shares is either tax on those shares or on those shares and other instalment options;
(e) unquoted shares which did not give the transferor control and the value of which exceeds £20,000, provided they are at least 10% of all the shares of the company or are ordinary shares and at least 10% of the ordinary shares in the company; and
(f) business or interest in a business including a profession or vocation.

Shares quoted on the Alternative Investment Market are still 'unquoted' for these purposes. Control means voting control on all questions affecting the company. The relief is available whether the transfer is on death or *inter vivos* but, in the latter case, the relief is only available if the *transferee* pays the IHT. The instalment option must be claimed by a written notice to HMRC and the outstanding instalments must be paid off if the assets are sold within the ten-year period.

If the instalment option is available, the first instalment is generally due six months after the end of the month in which the gift has been made. No interest is charged on the tax provided the instalments are paid on time. Although the instalment option does not reduce the amount of tax, the relief is nonetheless beneficial.

The primary liability for IHT on lifetime chargeable transfers falls on the transferor. However, it is also possible for the transferee(s) to meet this liability. If the tax is paid by the transferor, the loss to the transferor will be the value of the gift plus any inheritance tax on it. This will mean that the inheritance tax calculation will be based on the gross loss to the donor. In those circumstances, it will be necessary to 'gross-up' the net gift before the calculation of the tax can be made. If the transferee(s) pay the IHT, no such considerations come into play. This will result in a smaller IHT bill.

The IHT liability arising on death will be met primarily by the **personal representatives** of the deceased out of the death estate. The liability of the personal representatives is limited to the amount they receive in their capacity as personal representatives.

32.5 Partnerships

The IHT legislation contains few provisions dealing specifically with partnerships. According to the general principle of IHT, any transfer of a partnership asset, or of an interest in a partnership, will be a transfer of value by the individual partners if the transfer is by way of gift or there is an element of gift in the disposition.

The transfer will be exempt if it is made between spouses. It will also be exempt if it was not intended to, and was not made in a transaction intended to, confer any gratuitous benefit and either it was an arm's length transaction between unconnected persons or was such as might be expected to be made between unconnected persons.

As a result of this provision, many *inter vivos* transfers which might appear to be transfers of value will escape IHT. For example, when a new partner is admitted and is given a share in the assets without making a payment, there would be a transfer of value were it not for this provision. This is considered in **Chapter 23**.

On death, a deceased partner's interest in the partnership will be part of their estate. Business property relief (see 21.8.6) will normally be available.

32.6 Shareholdings

The gift of shares may give rise to IHT (and capital gains tax) since inheritance tax is chargeable on the 'loss to the donor's estate'. This normally means the market value of the asset given away, but in some cases the loss is considerably more than market value. For example, if a controlling shareholder gives away enough shares to lose control of the company, the loss to their estate will be very much more than the value of the shares given away.

The most important (but not only) 'reliefs' that are relevant when shares in a company are given away are 'business property relief' and the instalment option (considered in **32.4**).

These reliefs exist because the government recognises that too high a tax burden on the disposal of shares in a company could lead to the break-up of a company as being the only way of raising funds to pay the tax. It should not be forgotten that the general exemptions (eg the spouse exemption and the annual exemption) will be available in respect of business property as well as the business property relief.

32.7 Planning for IHT

32.7.1 General

It should be clear that there can be a considerable financial benefit in disposing of assets during a lifetime, to take advantage of the facts that:

- IHT lifetime rates are lower than the death rates; and
- tax can be avoided altogether if the donor survives seven years after a potentially exempt transfer.

Even if the donor does not survive seven years, taper relief availability means it can be advantageous to make gifts, including business assets, over a period of time rather than all at once. Couples may also reduce the burden of IHT by making use of the spouse exemption to ensure that both husband and wife can take maximum advantage of their individual nil-rate bands.

32.7.2 Investment advice and arranging deals in investments

In terms of tax planning on IHT, solicitors should therefore be careful to limit their advice to the tax implications of the various courses of action and reliefs available to the client. Any additional advice to a client as to the specific merits of transferring shares and reinvesting in other shares as replacement property, and arranging either of these forms of transaction, would need to be reviewed as to the risks of their being contrary to the Financial Services and Markets Act 2000. That is because arranging deals in investments and advising on investments are regulated activities under that Act, and it may constitute an offence to carry them out when not regulated to do so. For a fuller discussion of the regulation of these activities, see **7.12.1–7.12.3**).

KEY POINT SUMMARY

- Inheritance tax (IHT) is payable on chargeable transfers of property. Relevant transfers are lifetime gifts (or sales with an element of gift) and transfers on death.
- IHT is payable at a rate of 40% on transfers on death as part of a testator's estate and at 20% on lifetime transfers.
- There is an annual exemption of £3,000 in respect of lifetime gifts, and small gifts of up to £250 per recipient are also generally exempt.
- Certain lifetime transfers are known as 'potentially exempt transfers' (PETs) on which no tax will be payable provided the donor survives for at least seven years following the transfer.
- On death, all PETs and transfers made on death (the death estate) are cumulated to calculate the IHT payable.
- There is tapering relief available: transfers made in the period from three to seven years before death will be chargeable at a reducing percentage of the full IHT rate of 40%.
- Transfers between spouses and civil partners are exempt from IHT.
- In addition, there is a nil rate band of £325,000 on transfers that will be exempt from IHT. There is also a main residence nil rate band of £175,000 where a testator leaves their main residence to children or other direct descendants.
- Where transfers are made of business property, there is available, subject to meeting qualifying criteria, business property relief. Depending on the form of property, relief may be available to reduce the IHT payable on the relevant transfers by either 100% or 50%.
- The potentially large tax charges that may result from the application of IHT rules mean that there can be benefits in planning disposals of assets to minimise the tax payable.

CHAPTER 33
Corporation Tax and Distributions

FUNCTIONING LEGAL KNOWLEDGE

This chapter considers the following functioning legal knowledge included in the SRA's SQE 1 assessment specification:

Corporation tax:

- basis of charge
- calculation, payment and collection of tax
- tax treatment of company distributions or deemed distributions to **shareholders**
- outline of anti-avoidance legislation

AUTHORITIES UNDERPINNING PRACTICE

The key authorities that underpin this area of practice are listed below. Note that for legislation you are linked to legislation.gov.uk.

Although much of the legislation on this government website is available in its amended form, the incorporation of new amendments into the text of legislation can be delayed. You should refer to legal databases to ensure you are referencing the most up-to-date legislation.

- Corporation Tax Act 2009
  https://www.legislation.gov.uk/ukpga/2009/4/contents
- Corporation Tax Act 2010
  https://www.legislation.gov.uk/ukpga/2010/4/contents
- Taxation of Chargeable Gains Act 1992
  https://www.legislation.gov.uk/ukpga/1992/12/contents/enacted
- Capital Allowances Act 2001
  https://www.legislation.gov.uk/ukpga/2001/2/contents
- Income Tax Act 2007
  https://www.legislation.gov.uk/ukpga/2007/3/contents
- Finance Act 2024
  https://www.legislation.gov.uk/ukpga/2024/3/contents/enacted

33.1 Introduction

This chapter deals with:

- the corporation tax system, which determines the tax liability of companies; and
- the tax liabilities that arise from investments in companies, whether by way of **shares** or **debentures**.

The principal corporation tax statutes are the Corporation Tax Act 2009 (CTA 2009) and the Corporation Tax Act 2010 (CTA 2010). It is recommended that **30.1** on taxation and ethical elements is read with this chapter.

33.2 Calculation of profits

33.2.1 Profits

Companies pay corporation tax on their profits. These comprise income and chargeable gains. The profits on which tax is payable are calculated as follows:

1 Add together:
   (a) income (see **33.2.2**), taking into account any reliefs available to reduce income; plus
   (b) any amount in respect of chargeable gains (see **33.2.3**), taking into account any reliefs available to reduce chargeable gains.

   This produces the 'total profits' of the company.

2 Deduct any reliefs available to be relieved against total profits (eg s189 CTA 2010, which allows a company to deduct certain qualifying charitable donations from total profits). This produces the 'taxable total profits' on which corporation tax is chargeable at the relevant rate.

33.2.2 Income

The principal income on which most companies are charged corporation tax is trade profits. CTA 2009 contains specific rules applying to the calculation of trade profits, defining receipts and expenses, and allowing or restricting specific deductions.

To be deductible for tax purposes:

- expenses must be incurred wholly and exclusively for the purposes of the trade; and
- losses must be connected with or arise out of the trade.

Other forms of income on which corporation tax is charged include income from property and from loans.

Unlike individuals, companies are not entitled to any personal allowance in calculating income.

33.2.3 Chargeable gains

Chargeable gains realised by companies are calculated according to general capital gains tax principles – see **Chapter 31**. For companies, key points to note are:

(a) Companies have no annual exemption.
(b) Most individual reliefs are not available to companies, although companies can claim roll-over relief on the replacement of business assets.
(c) Companies may, however, receive an indexation allowance which is not available to individuals and partnerships.

33.2.3.1 Indexation allowance

For assets acquired before 1 January 2018, companies may claim an 'indexation allowance' which effectively removes inflationary gains on an asset from the charge to tax. The allowance is calculated by multiplying the initial purchase price and any subsequent allowable expenditure by HMRC 'inflation factor' figures for the relevant months of expenditure. The resultant figures are then subtracted from the profit made on the sale of the asset to give the chargeable gain.

For assets acquired from 1 January 2018, there is no indexation allowance available.

33.2.4 Capital allowances

Companies can claim capital allowances (see **33.6**) at the same rates as individuals and these should be considered when calculating income (see **33.2.2**) for corporation tax. Capital allowances are treated as trading expenses of the accounting period in which they are claimed, and balancing charges are treated as trading receipts of that period.

33.3 Assessment and payment

33.3.1 Assessment

Corporation tax is calculated by reference to profits (see **33.2**) made in each accounting period of the company. An accounting period is normally 12 months ending with the company's accounting reference date (**21.3**). If the accounts are made up for a period of less than 12 months, then the accounting period is also less than 12 months; if for a longer period, special rules apply and the profits are divided on a time basis between two or more accounting periods, none of which may individually be longer than 12 months.

33.3.2 Payment

Corporation tax is currently payable nine months after the end of the company's accounting period. However, large companies–those with annual profits of not less than £1.5 million–are obliged to account for corporation tax on an instalment basis.

Such instalments are payable, in a 12-month accounting period:

- six months and 13 days from the first day of the accounting period;
- three months after the first instalment;
- three months after the second instalment; and
- three months and 14 days from the last day of the accounting period.

EXAMPLE

Wolfe Industrials plc–a large company–has an accounting reference date of 31 December. In relation to its accounting year ending on 31 December 2024, its corporation tax payments will be payable in July and October 2024 and January and April 2025.

HMRC operates a 'pay and file' system. Companies must estimate their profits and assess their own tax liability, then submit a return together with accounts to substantiate it. Companies have up to 12 months from the end of each of their accounting periods to submit this return but must always satisfy their tax liabilities on the dates set out above. Where under- or over-payments of tax are made, interest (at rates set by statutory instrument) will be payable.

33.3.3 Rates of tax

33.3.3.1 Rates for financial year 2024/25

Tax rates are fixed for financial years, which run from 1 April to the following 31 March. For the financial year 2024 to 2025 (FY 25) the main rate of corporation tax is 25%. This applies to companies with profits over £250,000. Companies with profits of £50,000 or less will be taxed at the 'small profits rate' of 19%.

Companies with profits between £50,000 and £250,000 will pay the main rate but with marginal relief applied to provide a gradual increase in their overall effective corporation tax rate. HMRC provides a calculation tool for marginal relief; however, the effect of marginal relief is equivalent to a company paying the small profits rate on its first £50,000 of profits, then an effective rate of 26.5% on its profits above that threshold. Using this effective rate in the following example illustrates the effect of marginal relief.

EXAMPLE

Company profits for FY25 = £120,000

£50,000 @ small profits rate of 19% = £9,500

£70,000 @ effective marginal rate of 26.5% = £18,550

Total corporation tax = £28,050, which is lower than if the total profits had been taxed at the main rate of 25%, ie, £30,000.

33.3.3.2 Applicable rates of tax

Whilst tax rates are fixed for financial years, companies pay tax on the profits of their own accounting periods. Thus, unless a company's accounting period ends on 31 March, its profits will be apportioned on a time basis between two financial years if different rates apply.

EXAMPLE

A company's profits for its accounting period that ended on 31 December 2023 were £1,600,000.

The single rate of corporation tax for FY23 (1 April 2022–31 March 2023) was 19% and for FY 24 (1 April 2023–31 March 2024) the main rate was 25%.

Corporation tax for the accounting period ended 31 December 2023 was therefore:

90/365 x 1,600,000 x 19% = £74,958

plus

275/365 x 1,600,000 x 25% = £301,369

which totals

£376,327

33.4 Loss relief

33.4.1 Introduction

Trading losses of companies are relieved in a number of ways; many similar to those applied in the context of income tax (see **Chapter 30**).

33.4.2 Relief for trade losses against total profits of same or previous accounting periods

A company may set off a loss made during an accounting period against any profits–income or chargeable gains–of the same accounting period. The claim for relief must be made within two years of the end of the accounting period in which the loss was made. If the loss is not entirely relieved by setting it off against profits of the same accounting period, the company may also make a claim for the unrelieved losses to be set against any profits of previous accounting periods, so far as they fall wholly or partly within the 12-month period ending immediately before the loss-making period began. A loss cannot be carried back under this provision to a period when the company was not carrying on the relevant trade.

33.4.3 Carry forward of trade loss relief

Where losses are not relieved by being set off as described above in **33.4.2**, a company may carry forward a trading loss and use it to reduce its total profits in future accounting periods. The company must submit a claim to HMRC for this relief, and the trade in question must not have become 'small or negligible' in the loss-making period. The relief given will be for that part of the trading loss for which no relief has been claimed under s37 (see **33.4.2**) or surrendered as group relief (see **33.4.6**).

If the trade in question has become small or negligible in the loss-making period, then the losses can only be carried forward against the same trade, assuming a profit is made in that trade in a later period. In this case, no claim needs to be made: it will happen automatically provided the company's tax return is completed appropriately.

There is a restriction on carrying forward trade losses: the overall amount that can be relieved is an allowance of up to £5 million plus 50% of remaining total profits after deduction of the allowance.

EXAMPLE

To illustrate the application of losses, assume a company has accounting periods commencing 1 April in each of the years below, and its profits and losses are as follows:

	Trade I £	Trade II £	Chargeable gains £
2021	100,000	50,000	20,000
2022	(300,000) loss	50,000	30,000
2023	100,000	50,000	10,000

The £300,000 loss made in Trade I in 2022 can be used to relieve fully the Trade II profits and chargeable gains for that year. This leaves losses of £220,000. These can be carried back against the total profits (income and chargeable gains) for 2021 of £170,000. This leaves unrelieved losses of £50,000.

The company can then make a claim under for these unrelieved losses to be carried forward against the total profits for 2023.

33.4.4 Tactical considerations

In deciding which method of relief to use, the company will wish to ensure, so far as possible, that the maximum tax saving is achieved. For example, with the single rate of tax having been 19% for a number of years up to and including FY23, companies subject to the new 25% main rate of tax for FY24 could benefit from carrying forward losses. However, the cash-flow problem of having to pay tax at a time when cash reserves may be low often means it is preferable not to carry forward losses but rather use them as soon as possible.

The possibility of carrying forward losses is lost in certain cases where there are substantial changes in both the ownership of the company and in the nature of its trade. This is an anti-avoidance provision designed to prevent the purchase of a company simply to take advantage of its tax losses.

33.4.5 Capital losses

If a company makes a capital loss (calculated in the same way as a chargeable gain), it may be:

(a) set off against chargeable gains of the same accounting period; and, if unrelieved

(b) carried forward and set off against chargeable gains of later accounting periods.

Although trading losses may be set off against chargeable gains (see **33.4.2**), there are no provisions allowing capital losses to be set off against income profits. Indexation allowances (see **33.2.3.1**) may operate to reduce losses. Where this occurs, note that the indexation allowance can only be used to the extent that it extinguishes any gain. It cannot create or increase losses.

EXAMPLE

If Digby disposes of an asset for £60,000 and the base cost for that asset is £45,000, Digby is left with a gain of £15,000. If the base cost also attracted an indexation allowance of £20,000, this could be used to wipe out the gain, but could not create a loss of £5,000.

33.4.6 Group relief

Where a company is a member of a group it may surrender losses and other defined amounts (eg excess capital allowances or qualifying charitable donations) to another company in the same group. The latter then deducts the loss from its total profits as if it were its own loss. Companies are in the same group for tax purposes if one is the 75% **subsidiary** of the other or both are 75% subsidiaries of a third company.

33.5 Close companies

33.5.1 Definition

A close company is a company controlled by:

(a) five or fewer participators; or

(b) any number of participators who are also directors.

'Participators' are:

(a) shareholders;

(b) loan creditors; and

(c) certain others entitled to participate in the distributed income of the company.

'Control' includes, inter alia:

(a) ownership of a majority of the share capital; or

(b) a majority of the votes; or

(c) a right to a majority of the dividends.

In assessing control, the rights of 'associates' must be added to the rights of a participator. Associates include, among others, the participator's spouse, parents, remoter forebears, children, remoter issue, brothers and sisters.

This definition is only a very brief summary but it is sufficient to show that nearly all private companies are close companies.

33.5.2 Taxation considerations

Close companies are subject to specific tax rules designed to prevent the use of the company as a vehicle for tax avoidance. (See the Ethics, Professional Conduct and Client Care chapter earlier in the manual for conduct and ethical considerations in the context of tax anti-avoidance provisions.)

If a loan is made to a participator or their associate then, under s455 CTA 2010, the company must pay a levy equal to 33.75% of the loan within nine months of the end of the accounting period in which the loan was made. Thus, for every £1,000 lent an additional £337.50 must be paid to HMRC. The levy will be repaid to the company whenever the loan is repaid, waived or written off.

If the borrower pays back the debt in full, no taxation issues arise for the borrower (except, perhaps, for the fact that any interest which has been forgone or which has been paid at less than the official rate may result in an income tax liability for the debtor based on that sum). However, if some or all of the loan is written off or waived by the company, income tax will be payable. The amount of the loan written off or waived will be included in the borrower's total income.

Note that the above rules do not apply if the amount of the loan does not exceed £15,000, either itself or when added to other outstanding loans and advances; the borrower works full time for the close company; and owns less than a 5% shareholding in the company, ie, does not have material interest in the company.

If a close company provides living accommodation or other 'benefits in kind' for a participator or their associates who are neither directors nor higher paid employees of the company (see **30.7.3.1**), then the company will be treated as making a distribution (see **33.7**).

Companies are not normally liable to inheritance tax (IHT) if they make gifts. However, if a close company makes a gift (or other transfer of value), IHT will be charged as if each shareholder in the company (except those with very small interests) had made a transfer of value proportionate to their shareholding. The transferor company is primarily liable for any IHT payable but if it does not pay within the appropriate time frame, the shareholders can become liable personally.

33.6 Capital allowances

33.6.1 General

Most businesses will need to invest in fixed assets for use in the business. Most of these will be expected to last for an appreciable time and be used to generate income for the business. Nearly all of these assets will depreciate in value over time due to wear and tear from their use in the business: they are often referred to as 'wasting assets'. This depreciation may not always be deductible from the business's trading profits.

HMRC operates a capital allowances system, under the Capital Allowances Act 2001, to encourage businesses to invest in fixed assets, and to take account of depreciation. Under this, businesses may claim relief on many types of fixed asset, in the form of deductions that can be made from income receipts when calculating taxable profits. These capital allowances are thus treated as trading expenses incurred in the accounting period in which they are claimed.

The allowances can be claimed by companies, partnerships, sole traders and self-employed persons.

33.6.2 The capital allowances system

33.6.2.1 Assets on which capital allowances may be claimed

Capital allowances are available on assets bought and kept for use in a business: generally known as 'plant and machinery'. The Capital Allowances Act 2001 does not define either 'plant' or 'machinery'; however, HMRC provides guidance on the items on which capital allowances may be claimed. The principal items will be equipment owned and used in the business: tools; machinery; office equipment; computers; vehicles; plant; and factory equipment.

The Act also provides that allowances may be available in respect of:

(a) agricultural forestry buildings;

(b) scientific research;

(c) patents and 'know-how';

(d) mines, oil wells, mineral rights, cemeteries, crematoria and dredging;

(e) hotels; and

(f) certain research and development activities and facilities.

In most cases, capital allowances cannot be claimed in respect of the purchase of or investment in land, buildings and property.

Capital allowances *may not* be claimed on items that a business buys and sells as part of its trade. These are normally treated as purchases and sales of stock or goods, and taken into account in calculating trading profits.

33.6.2.2 The allowances

Annual Investment Allowance (AIA) for small and medium-sized businesses

Small and medium-sized businesses (around 99% of businesses in the UK) are entitled to an AIA on purchases of most plant and machinery, excluding cars. Businesses can set off 100% of the total purchase price of qualifying assets against income receipts when calculating tax, up to an annual maximum. The maximum annual amount that can be claimed is £1 million.

If a qualifying business spends more than the AIA in any one period on plant and machinery, the balance above the AIA will qualify for standard writing down capital allowances (see the next section).

EXAMPLE

Machinery was purchased for £1,260,000 on 1 April 2024. The first £1,000,000 will qualify for the AIA, whilst the remaining £260,000 will qualify for standard writing down allowances.

There may be situations–for example, where it has low profits–where a business does not want to claim the full AIA. Here, it has the options of:

- claiming the full cost using its AIA in a later year;
- setting off part of the cost using its AIA and claiming part as writing down allowances; or
- claiming writing down allowances against the full cost.

Writing down allowances

Where a business purchases plant and machinery in excess of the AIA in any chargeable period, the value of assets above the AIA will qualify for a 'writing down allowance' of up to 18% of the 'qualifying expenditure' in the year of purchase and subsequent years. Allowances are set against profits to reduce the tax liability of the business.

'Qualifying expenditure' means the original cost of the asset *less* any allowances already given.

EXAMPLE

Machinery was purchased for £70,000 on 1 June 2020 and the writing down allowance of 18% claimed. This provided an allowance of £12,600 in the first year of ownership. In the three subsequent years, the allowance available was:

	Written down value		Allowance
Year 2	£70,000–£12,600 (1st Year WDA)	= £57,400	£10,332
Year 3	£70,000–£22,932 (£12,600 + £10,332)	= £47,068	£8,473
Year 4	£70,000–£31,405 (£12,600 + £10,332 + £8,473)	= £38,595	£6,948

*The AIA for that chargeable period having been fully used.

This example shows that the allowances available are calculated by reference to the relevant percentage of the *unrelieved expenditure* (ie the purchase price less the allowances already taken). Thus, the annual writing down allowance is a percentage of an ever-reducing balance so that it can take many years for the entire expenditure to be set against profits, subject to any balancing charge (see the following section) becoming payable.

Should rates change, and a business's chargeable period span two rates, a hybrid rate will operate, calculating allowances by apportioning the chargeable period at the rate in effect for each portion.

Balancing charge or allowance

When an asset is sold by a business at a price that differs from the written down value, there will be:

- a *balancing charge* if the asset is sold for *more* than the written down value; or
- a *balancing allowance* if the asset is sold for *less* than the written down value.

EXAMPLES

Compare the following examples:

Written down value	Sale price	Balancing charge
£22,055	£24,000	£1,945
Written down value	Sale price	Balancing allowance
£22,055	£18,000	£4,055

A *balancing charge* is *added to profits* for the purpose of calculating tax.

A balancing allowance provides further relief, being deductible from profits.

The effect of both is to ensure that, taking all the years together, the total relief given is equal to the amount of the actual depreciation.

Note that a balancing charge can never be more than the total amount of allowance given–any actual profit made on the sale of the asset being liable to capital gains tax, if taxable at all.

33.6.2.3 'Pooling' for the purpose of writing down allowances

Most businesses will own numerous items of plant or machinery. When calculating writing down allowances, they are given by reference to a 'pool' of expenditure: all of the assets in the pool will be treated as if they were one asset.

The amount of the writing down allowance on the 'pool' of expenditure will be up to 18% of the total of expenditure on machinery and plant *less* all allowances so far claimed. Where one item in the pool is sold, its sale price is deducted from the written down value of the pool (this deduction being known as a 'balancing adjustment'), so that smaller allowances will be available in later years. A 'balancing charge' will only apply where pooled items are sold for more than the written down value of the whole pool.

Where the AIA has been claimed in respect of the full cost of an asset, it will be included in the business's pool of assets at zero value. Should only part of the cost of an asset have been claimed by way of AIA, then the remainder of the cost of the asset will be added to the pool.

Where there have been changes in applicable writing down allowance rates, special rules, including a hybrid rate (see **33.6.2.2**), apply to calculate the overall allowances available to businesses that have pools of assets and whose chargeable periods span the relevant date on which the rate changed.

Writing down allowances are available both in the accounting period in which the asset was purchased and in all subsequent accounting periods during which the asset is owned.

While the system does not lend itself to simplification (especially from the corporation tax perspective), the basic use of a writing down allowance for a company, partnership or sole trader is that of a deductible trading expense. If such allowances exceed income receipts, the loss incurred attracts loss relief in the usual way.

33.6.2.4 Special allowances and rules

First year allowances

Certain energy and water efficient, or low emission, pieces of plant and machinery–for example, electric cars and zero-emission goods vehicles–qualify for these allowances, allowing a business to deduct their full cost from profits before tax. These allowances may be claimed in addition to the AIA in force for the relevant period.

Long-life assets

Long-life assets are those with a useful economic life of more than 25 years. Plant and machinery falling within this category attracts a writing down allowance of 6% (before April 2019, the rate was 8%). In addition, certain integral features of premises may also attract this allowance, as may cars with CO2 omissions over a certain threshold.

The long-life asset regime only applies where expenditure on such assets in a chargeable period exceeds £100,000 a year, hence the rules are only likely to affect larger businesses. Because these rules result in allowances being claimed at a slower rate than normal, businesses could be tempted to sell off assets prematurely at less than their written down value to bring an immediate balancing allowance into effect. The legislation contains provisions to defeat such activity by deeming the sale to have been at the relevant written down value.

Short-life assets

A short-life asset (SLA) is one that the owner expects to keep for no more than eight years after the end of the accounting period in which it was bought, or is likely to have worn out or broken within such period. A business must elect to treat an asset in this way and inform HMRC of this decision within two years of the end of the tax year of purchase. Having done so, the business may treat this and similar SLAs as a separate 'pool' of assets (see **33.6.2.3**) to which it can then apply the 18% capital allowance rate for a maximum of five accounting periods. This election and separation of assets is designed to enable businesses to obtain allowances for the actual net cost of the assets during their lifespan in the business if they are scrapped or sold before the end of the eight-year period.

If the business sells the asset during this period, then a balancing charge or allowance will apply (see **33.6.2.2**). Should it still own the asset at the end of this period, it must transfer its residual value back into its main 'pool' (see **33.6.2.3**), where it will be treated in the standard way.

Assets which qualify as SLAs are also likely to qualify for the AIA (see **33.6.2.2**). Therefore, the SLA rules will principally benefit those businesses investing amounts in plant and machinery in excess of the relevant AIA limit for the year of purchase, given that the latter provides a 100% allowance.

Leased assets

There are special rules on the availability of capital allowances to the lessor when plant and machinery is bought to be leased. There are also special rules for the lessees of equipment. With a 'pure' leasing contract, where the title in the assets leased always remains with the lessor, the lessor will be able to claim writing down allowances. This should be contrasted with lease-purchase or hire-purchase arrangements, where the lessee or hirer becomes the ultimate owner of the assets, normally upon payment of a final capital sum. In these cases, the lessee will be able to claim writing down allowances.

Motor cars

Cars bought and used in a business do not qualify for AIA. Businesses can, however, claim writing down allowances depending on carbon emission levels, when the car was bought and whether it was new or second-hand when bought. The detail of the specific allowances available is beyond the scope of this manual: it can be found at https://www.gov.uk/capital-allowances/business-cars.

Cars provided to employees for business purposes but also used for private purposes are treated as being used only for business purposes. Individuals or partners in a partnership, however, who use cars partly for private purposes are required to reduce their claims by the proportion of private use made of the car.

33.6.3 Investment stimulus measures

The government introduced measures in the Spring 2023 Budget designed to stimulate and support business investment. For qualifying expenditures incurred from 1 April 2023 up to 31 March 2026, companies can deduct from their profits before tax:

(a) 100% of the cost of specified main rate writing down allowance plant and machinery–this has been termed 'Full-expensing'; and

(b) in the year of purchase, 50% of the cost of special rate assets which normally qualify for the 6% writing down allowance–this is an extension of the first-year allowance scheme introduced as a stimulus measure during the coronavirus pandemic.

Where expenditure does not qualify for either of the allowances, the AIA (see **33.6.2.2**) will still be available.

There are specific rules regarding the disposal of assets the subject of these allowances.

33.7 Taxation of distributions and debenture interest

33.7.1 Introduction

Those involved with companies can receive a return from their investment in a variety of ways. This section deals with the taxation of distributions by way of dividend and of debenture interest: both are income returns on investments made in companies and, therefore, subject to income tax.

EXAMPLE

Titus is a director of a private limited company. He is also a shareholder of the company and holds debentures issued by the company in respect of a loan he has made to the company. Three possible income tax events could arise in this situation, namely:

(a) Titus is paid a salary or fee as a director (covered in **Chapter 31**).

(b) Titus is paid a dividend in respect of his shareholding.

(c) Titus is entitled to annual interest in respect of the debentures he holds.

33.7.2 Taxation of distributions by way of dividend

33.7.2.1 Definition of distribution

A shareholder is liable to income tax on any 'distribution' received in respect of shares. The following types of receipt are the most important:

(a) any dividend paid by the company including a capital dividend;

(b) any other distribution out of assets of the company in respect of shares;

(c) any interest on securities (eg debentures) where the interest varies with the profits of the company;

(d) in some circumstances, the issue of bonus shares following a reduction of share capital or the repayment of share capital after a bonus issue.

It should be noted that an issue of bonus shares (ie shares treated as paid up out of the profits of the company) is not a distribution for tax purposes unless share capital has previously been reduced. However, if the shareholders are given a choice between receiving a cash dividend (which is, of course, a distribution) or bonus shares, those who choose to take the bonus shares are taxed on the amount of cash dividend forgone in almost the same way as if it were a distribution.

33.7.2.2 Tax consequences for the company of the payment of a dividend

The payment of a dividend or other distribution is neither an expense of a company's business nor a charge on its income. It does not, therefore, reduce a company's liability to corporation tax.

33.7.2.3 Taxation of a recipient of a dividend

Corporate recipient

Where a UK company receives a dividend or other distribution from another, the general rule is that this does not create a corporation tax liability for the recipient.

Individual recipient

An individual shareholder is liable to pay tax on dividend income at specified rates. For 2024/25, these are:

- 8.75% on dividend income within the basic income tax band (up to £37,700);
- 33.75% on dividend income within the higher income tax band (in excess of £37,701 and up to £150,000);
- 39.35% on dividend income within the additional rate income tax band (over £150,000).

For the tax year 2024/25, individuals are entitled to a tax-free dividend allowance of £500. Thus, no tax is paid on the first £500 of dividend income, irrespective of total income. When calculating income tax, dividend income is treated as the top slice of an individual's income. Should dividend income fall across two income tax bands, it should be apportioned and the appropriate tax rate applied to each portion.

EXAMPLES

Chris receives a salary of £22,000 and dividends of £7,000, thus a total income of £29,000. Chris's personal allowance of £12,570 (see **30.2.3**) means that only £9,430 of salary remains to be taxed at the basic income tax rate (see **30.2.3**) of 20%. The first £500 of dividend income is covered by the dividend allowance, leaving £6,500 to be taxed at the basic dividend rate of 8.75%. Thus, Chris's tax liability will be:

£1,886 (£9,430 @ 20%) + £568 (£6,500 @ 8.75%) = £2,454 (figures rounded down)

Anton receives a salary of £43,000 and dividends of £9,000. The first £12,570 of salary is covered by Anton's personal allowance, leaving £30,430 to be taxed at the basic income tax rate of 20%. The dividend allowance covers the first £500 of the dividends, leaving £8,500 to be taxed. The threshold for higher rate tax being £37,700, the taxable dividends fall across this threshold: £7,270 in the basic rate band and £1,230 in the higher rate band. Thus, Anton's tax liability will be:

£6,086 (£30,430 @ 20%) + £636 (£7,270 @ 8.75%) + £415 (£1,230 @ 33.75%)
= £7,137 (figures rounded down)

33.7.3 **Debenture interest**

33.7.3.1 Tax consequences for the paying company

When a company issues debentures or another type of debt instrument to raise funds, and pays interest to the debenture holder, that interest will be a business expense deductible in computing profits.

33.7.3.2 Deduction of tax

A company paying 'yearly' interest to individuals–where the relevant loan is expected to last for more than one year–is required to deduct at source basic rate income tax of 20%.

The company must account to HMRC for the sum deducted. Therefore, a company borrowing £1,000 at 10% interest from an individual would annually, assuming tax rates remain the same, pay £80 interest to the lender and £20 to HMRC.

33.7.3.3 Taxation of the recipient

The gross amount of interest received by a debenture holder is taxable. Due to the borrowing company usually deducting 20% tax from the payment, the amount received is a net amount. To calculate tax payable it is therefore necessary to calculate the gross amount of interest. This is done by multiplying the net amount actually received by 100/80 (eg £80 × 100/80 = £100). If the tax rate changes, so will the fraction–the '80' represents 100 minus the rate of tax. Should tax not have been deducted at source, this calculation is unnecessary.

The gross amount of interest is investment income in the hands of the recipient and is liable to higher or additional rates tax if the recipient's income is large enough.

EXAMPLE

Piama has taxable income of £29,000 in the tax year 2024/25. She therefore has £8,700 of the basic rate band still unused. She received £10,000 gross interest on a loan to a company.

(a) Piama's net receipt was £8,000 plus credit for £2,000 tax deducted at source by the paying company.

(b) Tax to pay (on gross sum):

£0 to 8,700 × 20% = £1,740
£8,701 to 10,000 × 40% = £520
= £2,260

(c) Tax deducted satisfies £2,000 of the above liability–balance to pay of £260.

KEY POINT SUMMARY

- Companies pay corporation tax on their profits. These are calculated by combining trade income, less any available reliefs, and chargeable gains, less any available reliefs. This provides a 'total profits' figure which might also be subject to specified reliefs. The final profit figure will be subject to corporation tax at a rate set for each financial year. A financial year runs from 1 April to 31 March.
- The main corporation tax rate for the current financial year 2024/25 is 25% for companies with more than £250,000 taxable profits. Companies with profits under £50,000 pay at a small profits rate of 19%, with marginal relief being applied to companies with profits between these thresholds, so their effective tax rate will gradually increase towards the main rate as their profits increase.
- Tax is calculated by reference to profits for a company's annual accounting period, which may not align with the financial year. If differing rates of corporation tax apply for an accounting period which straddles financial years, profits are apportioned on a time basis.
- Corporation tax is payable nine months after the end of the accounting period for which it has been calculated. Large companies may pay on an instalment basis.
- There are provisions which allow companies to set off income losses against profits of the same or previous accounting periods, and also to carry forward losses. Capital losses may be set off against chargeable gains of the same or, if unrelieved, future accounting periods.
- There are specific tax rules, designed to prevent tax avoidance, for close companies, controlled by five or fewer participators, or any number of participators who are also directors. These include rules on loans, and provision of benefits in kind, to participators or associates.

- Capital allowances allow all businesses–sole traders, partnerships and companies–to claim relief for investing in specified assets purchased for the purpose of the business. These allowances include writing down allowances which take account of the depreciating value of assets.
- Writing down allowances allow a business to set off against its profits annually a specified percentage of the expenditure on particular fixed assets. The asset's value is then also written down, that is, reduced, in the company's books. Where a number of fixed assets are purchased over time, writing down allowances are calculated according to a pool of expenditure.
- When assets are subsequently sold by businesses for a higher or lower amount than their written down value, a balancing charge or allowance will result, which will respectively be added or deducted from profits for that year.
- The Annual Investment Allowance allows businesses to set off 100% of the total purchase price of qualifying assets against income receipts when calculating tax, up to an annual maximum: currently £1,000,000.
- Shareholders are liable to income tax on any distribution received in respect of shares. The most common form of distribution will be dividends paid by a company. Income tax rates on dividends are currently based on tax bands: a basic rate of 8.75%, a higher rate of 33.75% and an additional rate of 39.35%. There is an individual dividend allowance which means that no income tax is payable on the first £500 of any dividends received.
- Where a company holds shares in another, the general rule is that dividends received are not subject to corporation tax.

CHAPTER 34
Value Added Tax

FUNCTIONING LEGAL KNOWLEDGE

This chapter considers the following functioning legal knowledge included in the SRA's SQE 1 assessment specification:

Value added tax:

- key principles relating to scope, supply, input and output tax
- registration requirements and issue of VAT invoices
- returns/payment of VAT and record-keeping

AUTHORITIES UNDERPINNING PRACTICE

The key authorities that underpin this area of practice are listed below. Note that for legislation you are linked to legislation.gov.uk.

Although much of the legislation on this government website is available in its amended form, the incorporation of new amendments into the text of legislation can be delayed. You should refer to legal databases to ensure you are referencing the most up-to-date legislation.

- Value Added Tax Act 1994
  https://www.legislation.gov.uk/ukpga/2003/1/contents
- Finance Act [for relevant tax year]
  https://www.legislation.gov.uk/ukpga/2023/1/contents/enacted

34.1 Introduction

A supplier of goods and services made in the UK is liable to pay value added tax (VAT) to HM Revenue and Customs (HMRC) if they make taxable supplies exceeding £90,000 in any one-year period.

In this situation, the supplier must:

(a) register with HMRC; and

(b) account for VAT on *all* taxable supplies made.

The total payable to HMRC may be reduced by VAT paid on taxable supplies made *to the supplier.*

The actual cost of the tax will be borne by the supplier's customers (unless they can recover VAT) who are charged VAT on goods and services purchased. It is recommended that **30.1** on taxation and ethical elements is read with this chapter.

34.2 Registration

34.2.1 Turnover limits for registration

A person must register for VAT if:

(a) at any month end, taxable supplies made during the past year exceed £90,000; or

(b) at any time, there are reasonable grounds to believe that taxable supplies to be made in the next 30 days alone will exceed £90,000.

If, at any month end, a person's taxable supplies in the past 12 months or less exceed £90,000 but HMRC is satisfied that they will not exceed £88,000 in the next 12 months, the person will not have to register. These registration and deregistration (see **34.2.5**) thresholds took effect from 1 April 2024.

A person whose taxable supplies do not exceed the limit can choose to register for VAT on a voluntary basis.

34.2.2 'Person' for VAT purposes

VAT requires registration by a 'person', which includes an individual, a body corporate or a partnership. A person can only have one VAT registration (irrespective of the number of businesses run) and is therefore liable for VAT on taxable supplies made by *all* their businesses. There are exceptions to this rule, one being that a company organised into several divisions may seek registration for each division.

34.2.3 Registration documentation

HMRC VAT registration is completed online, using form VAT 1. Partnerships must also submit details of all the partners on a VAT 2 form.

34.2.4 Effect of registration

Once registered, a person is liable to account for VAT to HMRC on all taxable supplies of goods and services made in the UK.

34.2.5 De-registration

A person may apply to be de-registered for VAT if they cease to make taxable supplies or if they can satisfy HMRC that taxable supplies for the next 12 months will not exceed £88,000.

34.3 Taxable supplies and the charge to VAT

34.3.1 Taxable supplies

VAT is charged on taxable supplies of goods and services made in the UK:

(a) in the course of furtherance of business; and

(b) not classified as exempt from VAT.

Exempt supplies include most sales of land and buildings, insurance, doctors' services and certain types of education services.

34.3.2 Rates of VAT on taxable supplies

Taxable supplies are charged at one of three rates:

1 Standard: 20%.

2 Reduced: 5%.

This applies to a limited range of goods and services, such as energy supplies, and may also vary according to circumstances or who a customer is.

3 Zero:

Zero-rated supplies do not actually give rise to a VAT charge. They may, however, allow a person to recover input tax paid on supplies *received by the supplier* (see **34.4.4**). Zero-rated supplies include:

(a) food (except restaurant food and certain specified standard-rated items such as alcoholic and soft drinks, confectionary and ice cream);

(b) children's clothing and shoes;

(c) books and newspapers; and

(d) sales of new houses.

34.4 Accounting for VAT

34.4.1 Charging VAT to customers

A person should start charging VAT to their customers and keep relevant records as soon as they realise that they are liable to register for VAT with HMRC.

34.4.2 Invoice to customers

Suppliers must send customers a tax invoice setting out the:

(a) supplier's VAT registration number–provided by HMRC;

(b) date of supply;

(c) goods or services supplied;

(d) total amount payable;

(e) amount of VAT chargeable at the relevant rate.

The VAT charged to customers will meet the supplier's liability to HMRC.

34.4.3 VAT return

VAT is based on an online *self-assessment* and payment system. A registered person must submit a VAT return every three months (although monthly or annual returns may be agreed with HMRC). The return must be submitted and VAT paid within a month from the end of the three-month period to which it relates. A return must be submitted even if the registered person has no VAT to pay or reclaim.

Businesses with an estimated VAT taxable turnover of up to £1,350,000 may join HMRC's Annual Accounting Scheme under which the business:

(a) makes either three (quarterly) or nine (monthly) advance payments to HMRC of the VAT it expects to owe at the year end; and

(b) submits a single annual VAT return within two months of the end of the business's accounting period, together with any outstanding VAT payable.

If a business overpays VAT, it will be repaid by HMRC. This regular payment scheme is intended to assist businesses in managing cash flow. However, if a business regularly reclaims VAT, the scheme would not be suitable because there is only a single refund each year.

34.4.4 **Amount of VAT payable**

34.4.4.1 Calculating net VAT due

A taxable person is liable for VAT at the standard rate of 20% on all supplies of goods and services made in the relevant three-month period. This is often referred to as *output tax.*

Output tax may be reduced by *input* tax: VAT paid by the taxable person on supplies *made to* them which are attributable to supplies *made by* them.

Output and input VAT is based on invoices *issued* and *received*, even if payment has not been received or made.

EXAMPLE 1

Cost of supplies	**VAT on supplies**	**Standard rate**	**VAT on supplies**	**Net VAT**
received	received (input tax)	supplies made	made (output tax)	payable
1,000	200	1,600	320	120

If a person makes zero-rated supplies, there is no output tax charge. From a customer's perspective, it is as if it is an exempt supply. However, the taxable person can recover any input tax attributable to zero-rated supplies made by them. This is the benefit derived from zero-rated supplies compared with exempt supplies.

Thus, where a person makes predominantly zero-rated supplies, recoverable input tax may exceed output tax. If so, HMRC will repay any excess.

EXAMPLE 2

Cost of supplies	**VAT on supplies**	**Zero-rate**	**VAT on supplies**	**Net VAT**
received	received (input tax) supplies made	made (output tax)	recovered	
1,000	200	1,600	0	200

34.4.4.2 HMRC optional flat rate scheme

HMRC allows some businesses to calculate net VAT due simply by applying a flat rate percentage to their tax-inclusive turnover (the total turnover generated, including all reduced, zero-rate and exempt income). The flat rate percentage depends on the trade sector of the business. For example, the following flat rates currently apply in these sectors: legal services–14.5%; food retailing–4%; and general building services–9.5%. There is a higher 16.5% rate for what are classed as 'limited cost' businesses where goods purchased cost less than either 2% of turnover or £1,000 (if costs are higher than 2%). This is likely to apply to labour-intensive businesses where the relative input cost of goods is low, for example consultants, hairdressers, independent contractors etc. The scheme also offers a 1% discount to businesses in their first year of VAT registration.

The scheme is limited to businesses with both a VAT-exclusive estimated annual taxable turnover of up to £150,000 and a VAT-inclusive estimated annual total business income of up to £191,500.

The scheme's aim is to ease the administrative burden on small businesses. Those who opt to use the scheme can, in most cases, work out the net VAT due by simply recording their tax-inclusive turnover and applying the appropriate flat rate percentage for their trade sector. Businesses will still need to issue tax invoices to their VAT-registered customers, but will not have to record all the details of the invoices issued or purchase invoices received to calculate their VAT. However, businesses in the scheme may not generally set off input VAT on purchases against VAT on supplies made (see **34.4.4.1**). This is because the flat rate percentages contain an allowance for VAT on purchases. Businesses may be part of both the flat rate and Annual Accounting (see **34.4.3**) schemes.

34.4.4.3 Optional Cash Accounting Scheme

HMRC also offers businesses a Cash Accounting Scheme: the same annual turnover limit as for the Annual Accounting Scheme applies: up to £1,350,000 (see **34.4.3**). Rather than paying VAT on invoices issued and received, the Cash Accounting Scheme allows businesses to pay VAT on sales only when payment is received, and reclaim VAT on purchases only when payment to suppliers is made. This can, depending on circumstances, provide businesses with a cash-flow advantage.

34.4.5 **Calculation of tax on VAT-inclusive price: the VAT fraction**

A VAT-inclusive price for goods or services combines the price of the supply *and* the VAT payable. To calculate the VAT element of that price, multiply the figure by 1/6. This *VAT fraction* provides the equivalent of 20% on the VAT-exclusive price.

EXAMPLE

VAT-inclusive price of goods supplied: £2,856.

VAT payable = 1/6 of £2,856 = £476.

VAT-exclusive price of the goods = £2,856 – £476 = £2,380.

(NB: 20% of £2,380 = £476.)

KEY POINT SUMMARY

- VAT is charged on supplies of goods and services made in the UK.
- A person making supplies in excess of £90,000 in any one-year period is required to register with HMRC, and account for VAT on all supplies made. The taxable person will charge the relevant amount of VAT to their customers.
- VAT payable to HMRC on supplies made–*output tax*–may be reduced by VAT paid on purchases–*input tax*–by the taxable person.
- There is a standard VAT rate of 20%, with a reduced rate of 5% on a limited range of goods and services. Certain supplies are zero-rated, which do not give rise to a VAT charge but may allow a person to recover input tax on purchases of zero-rated items.
- A taxable person must keep VAT records and include their VAT registration number on all invoices. VAT returns must be made every three months to HMRC, although monthly or annual returns may be agreed.
- There are various schemes available via HMRC which allow varied approaches to calculating, accounting for and payment of VAT. These can, depending on the nature of the business, provide cash-flow benefits.

APPENDIX
Companies and Tax Forms, Guides and Useful Websites

Here is a list of web links to the companies and tax forms, guides and useful websites mentioned in this manual.

Guides and Useful Websites

- SRA Standards and Regulations
  https://www.sra.org.uk/solicitors/standards-regulations/
- Companies House
  https://www.gov.uk/government/organisations/companies-house
- Stock Exchange
  https://www.londonstockexchange.com/
- SRA Financial Services (Scope) Rules 2001
  https://www.sra.org.uk/solicitors/standards-regulations/financial-services-scope-rules/
- Conduct of Business Rules 2001
  https://www.sra.org.uk/globalassets/documents/solicitors/handbook/appendices/FS_CONDUCT_FOR_PREVIEW_20.pdf
- Financial Conduct Authority
  https://www.fca.org.uk/
- CREST
  www.euroclear.com
- SRA's Code of Conduct
  https://www.sra.org.uk/solicitors/standards-regulations/code-conduct-solicitors/
- Enterprise Investment Scheme
  https://www.gov.uk/guidance/venture-capital-schemes-apply-for-the-enterprise-investment-scheme

Companies Forms

- Form IN01
  https://assets.publishing.service.gov.uk/government/uploads/system/uploads/attachment_data/file/946155/IN01-V8.0.pdf
- Form RR01
  https://assets.publishing.service.gov.uk/government/uploads/system/uploads/attachment_data/file/943776/RR01-V7.0.pdf
- Form RR02
  https://assets.publishing.service.gov.uk/government/uploads/system/uploads/attachment_data/file/297516/RR02_application_by_public_company_for_reregistration_as_a_private_limited_company.pdf

- Form SH01

  https://assets.publishing.service.gov.uk/government/uploads/system/uploads/attachment_data/file/1087793/SH01_V7.0.pdf
- Form SH03

  https://assets.publishing.service.gov.uk/government/uploads/system/uploads/attachment_data/file/881208/SH03_return_of_purchase_of_own_shares.pdf
- Form SH06

  https://assets.publishing.service.gov.uk/government/uploads/system/uploads/attachment_data/file/533444/SH06_v6.pdf
- Form AP01

  https://assets.publishing.service.gov.uk/government/uploads/system/uploads/attachment_data/file/883900/LL_AP01_v6.pdf
- Form TM01

  https://assets.publishing.service.gov.uk/government/uploads/system/uploads/attachment_data/file/933642/TM01_V6.0.pdf
- Form AP03

  https://assets.publishing.service.gov.uk/government/uploads/system/uploads/attachment_data/file/882134/AP03_v6.pdf
- Form TM02

  https://assets.publishing.service.gov.uk/government/uploads/system/uploads/attachment_data/file/880912/TM02_V5.0.pdf
- Form PSC01

  https://assets.publishing.service.gov.uk/government/uploads/system/uploads/attachment_data/file/880906/PSC01_V3.0.pdf
- Form PSC04

  https://assets.publishing.service.gov.uk/government/uploads/system/uploads/attachment_data/file/882776/PSC04_V3.0.pdf
- Form PSC 07

  https://assets.publishing.service.gov.uk/government/uploads/system/uploads/attachment_data/file/880847/PSC07_V3.0.pdf
- Form EH01

  https://assets.publishing.service.gov.uk/government/uploads/system/uploads/attachment_data/file/882743/EH01_v1.pdf
- Form EH02

  https://assets.publishing.service.gov.uk/government/uploads/system/uploads/attachment_data/file/882745/EH02_v1.pdf
- Form EH04

  https://assets.publishing.service.gov.uk/government/uploads/system/uploads/attachment_data/file/890061/EH04_v2.0.pdf
- Form EH05

  https://assets.publishing.service.gov.uk/government/uploads/system/uploads/attachment_data/file/533362/EH05_v1.pdf
- Form NM01

  https://assets.publishing.service.gov.uk/government/uploads/system/uploads/attachment_data/file/933645/NM01_V5.0.pdf
- Form NM04

  https://assets.publishing.service.gov.uk/government/uploads/system/uploads/attachment_data/file/286894/NM04_notice_of_change_of_name_by_means_provided_for_in_the_articles.pdf
- Form AA01

  https://assets.publishing.service.gov.uk/government/uploads/system/uploads/attachment_data/file/943763/AA01_V5.0.pdf

- Form AD01
  https://assets.publishing.service.gov.uk/government/uploads/system/uploads/attachment_data/file/940880/AD01_change_of_registered_office_address.pdf
- CS01
  https://assets.publishing.service.gov.uk/government/uploads/system/uploads/attachment_data/file/880883/CS01_V2.0-2.pdf
- MR01
  https://assets.publishing.service.gov.uk/government/uploads/system/uploads/attachment_data/file/933654/MR01_v2.1__2_.pdf

Limited Liability Partnership Forms

- Form LL IN01
  https://assets.publishing.service.gov.uk/government/uploads/system/uploads/attachment_data/file/946125/LL_IN01-V7.0.pdf
- Form LL AA01
  https://assets.publishing.service.gov.uk/government/uploads/system/uploads/attachment_data/file/943608/LL_AA01-V5.0.pdf
- Form LL CS01
  https://assets.publishing.service.gov.uk/government/uploads/system/uploads/attachment_data/file/883597/LL_CS01_V2.0.pdf
- Form LL AP01
  https://assets.publishing.service.gov.uk/government/uploads/system/uploads/attachment_data/file/883900/LL_AP01_v6.pdf
- Form LL TM01
  https://assets.publishing.service.gov.uk/government/uploads/system/uploads/attachment_data/file/883909/LL_TM01_v5.0.pdf
- Form LL AD01
  https://assets.publishing.service.gov.uk/government/uploads/system/uploads/attachment_data/file/883894/LL_AD01_change_of_registered_office_address_of_a_limited_liability_partnership.pdf
- Form LL NM01
  https://assets.publishing.service.gov.uk/government/uploads/system/uploads/attachment_data/file/362298/LL_NM01_notice_of_change_of_name_of_a_limited_liability_partnership_llp.pdf
- Form LL PSC01
  https://assets.publishing.service.gov.uk/government/uploads/system/uploads/attachment_data/file/884086/LL_PSC01_V3.0.pdf
- Form LL PSC04
  https://assets.publishing.service.gov.uk/government/uploads/system/uploads/attachment_data/file/884089/LL_PSC04_V3.0.pdf
- Form LL PSC07
  https://assets.publishing.service.gov.uk/government/uploads/system/uploads/attachment_data/file/884094/LL_PSC07_V3.0.pdf
- Form LL MR01
  https://assets.publishing.service.gov.uk/government/uploads/system/uploads/attachment_data/file/878467/LL_MR01_v2.1.pdf

Taxation Forms

- VAT 1

  https://assets.publishing.service.gov.uk/government/uploads/system/uploads/attachment_data/file/946248/VAT1form-12-20.pdf
- VAT 2

  https://assets.publishing.service.gov.uk/government/uploads/system/uploads/attachment_data/file/372690/vat2.pdf

Glossary

The following are definitions of certain terms used in the text. They do not reflect relevant statutory definitions and should be used as a guide only and not as a substitute for explanations given in the text.

Annual General Meeting (AGM) A meeting of members which public companies are legally required to hold annually.

Articles of association The internal constitution of the company.

Auditor A person or firm appointed by a company (or LLP) for the purposes of carrying out a formal audit of the company's accounts and generating a report on the same.

Bankruptcy The legal status of an individual who has been adjudged unable to pay their debts and who is subject to a bankruptcy order.

Called-up share capital The share capital of a company which the company has been paid for or expects to be paid for because it has made a demand for payment on those shares (although the statutory definition is wider; see s547 Companies Act 2006).

Closely-held As regards a company, one in which there are very few shareholders.

Companies House The government department which deals with, inter alia, incorporation of companies and limited liability partnerships and the maintenance of information on those entities.

Debenture A document which signifies indebtedness of a company.

Derivative claim A claim brought on a company's behalf by a shareholder in respect of a breach of duty, trust etc by a director.

Director (executive) a person appointed to the office of a director who is also expected to perform a specific executive function (usually for remuneration).

Director (non-executive) A person appointed to the office of a director who is not expected to perform any specific executive function.

Disqualification (of director) A statutory process which results in a director being formally disqualified from holding the office of director for a specified time, usually due to their conduct in the management of a company.

Employee share scheme A scheme created by a company limited by shares which allows for employees either to invest in shares in the scheme or to be rewarded by the allocation of shares from the scheme.

General meeting A meeting of members (usually shareholders) of a company.

Liquidation The process of realising all the assets of a company (or LLP) for the purpose of meeting liabilities to creditors and paying back capital contributions to investors (if any surplus remains).

Member (company) A person who is entered as a member in a company's register of members and accordingly enjoys full membership rights in that company.

Member (LLP) A person who is an appointed as a member of a limited liability partnership.

National Insurance A tax on income (other than income tax) which is payable by the recipient of the income and by that persons employer, if an employment relationship exists.

Net assets As regards a business, the difference between the value of its assets and its liabilities.

Nominal value A monetary value attributed to a share in a company, eg £1, £5 etc, required by law but which does not reflect the market value of the share.

Ordinary resolution A decision of the members of a company which is passed by a simple majority of votes in its favour.

Paid-up share A share whose nominal value has been received in full by a company.

Parent company Usually a company which holds all or the majority of shares in another company (although the statutory definition is wider; see s1162 Companies Act 2006).

Partly-paid share A share whose nominal value has been received in part by a company.

Personal representative A person whose function is to administer the estate of a deceased person and to distribute that estate to the deceased's beneficiaries.

Preferential creditors Creditors who have been designated by the Insolvency Act 1986 as having an entitlement to be paid in priority to other creditors.

Private company Any company which does not meet the legal conditions to constitute a public company.

Public company A company which meets the requirements for a public company (as set out in the Companies Act 2006).

Redeemable shares Shares which are issued with a pre-determined redemption date, redemption being either at the instance of the company or the shareholder.

Registered office The officially registered address of a company (or LLP) to which all communications and notices may be sent.

Security An interest (either legal or equitable) over property which gives the holder of the security rights over that property, usually to take control of it and sell it in satisfaction of an unpaid liability or debt.

Service contract A contract between a company and a director which sets out specific executive functions which the director is expected to perform (usually for remuneration).

Shadow director A person who is not formally appointed to the office of director but under whose direction or instructions the directors of a company are accustomed to act.

Share An intangible right (constituting personal property) which signifies ownership of a stake in a company which has a share capital, carrying with it defined entitlements in respect of the company.

Shareholder A person who owns shares in a company which has a share capital. (Such persons will also usually be members of their companies.)

Special resolution A decision of the members of a company, which is passed by a majority of at least 75% of votes in its favour.

Subscribers to the memorandum Persons who wish to form a company and who, accordingly, subscribe their names to a memorandum of association of a company to indicate this wish and, in respect of companies with a share capital, to indicate that they are to take at least one share each in the company.

Subsidiary Usually a company the majority of whose shares are held by another company (although the statutory definition is wider; see s1159 Companies Act 2006).

Takeover An offer made to all the shareholders of a company to buy their shares, with the intention of taking control of the company.

The Gazette An official government journal in which various legal notices have to be published.

Trade mark A badge or indicator of origin used by a business in respect of its goods or services.

Trustee in bankruptcy An insolvency practitioner formally appointed to realise and distribute the estate of an individual who has been declared bankrupt.

Wholly-owned subsidiary A company whose entire issued share capital is owned by another company.

Written resolution A decision of the members of a company which is achieved through the medium of writing, displacing the need for a meeting.

Index

A

Printed and bound by CPI Group (UK) Ltd, Croydon, CR0 4YY